Comprehens
Business Stuc

Comprehensive Business Studies

FIFTH EDITION

Alan Whitcomb
BA, MEd, PhD

Comprehensive Business Studies

PEARSON EDUCATION LIMITED
Edinburgh Gate,
Harlow, Essex CM20 2JE
England and Associated Companies throughout the world.

First published 1986
Fifth edition 1999
Fifth impression 2006

© Alan Whitcomb 1986, 1989, 1992, 1994, 1999

A CIP catalogue record for this book can be obtained from the British Library.

ISBN-10: 0-582-33775-5
ISBN-13: 978-0-582-33775-6

All rights reserved; no part of this publication may be reproduced, stored in a retrieval system, or transmitted in any form or by any means, electronic, mechanical, photocopying, recording, or otherwise without either the prior written permission of the Publishers or a licence permitting restricted copying in the United Kingdom issued by the Copyright Licensing Agency Ltd, 90 Tottenham Court Road, London W1P OLP. This book may not be lent, resold, hired out or otherwise disposed of by way of trade in any form of binding or cover other than that in which it is published, without the prior consent of the Publishers.

Typeset in 10 / 12.5 pt Palatino
Printed in Malaysia, GPS

The Publisher's policy is to use paper manufactured from sustainable forests.

Contents

Preface to the Fifth Edition — xi
A message to students — xii
Acknowledgements — xiv

❶ The Business Environment — 1
1.1 Development of economic activity — 1
1.2 Scarcity and choice in a modern society — 6
1.3 Economic systems — 7
1.4 Types of production — 10
1.5 Interdependence of industry — 15
1.6 Activities — 16

❷ Organisation of Production — 22
2.1 Production levels — 22
2.2 The factors of production — 24
2.3 Methods of production — 28
2.4 Location of business — 29
2.5 Business size — 32
2.6 Technological change — 36
2.7 Activities — 39

❸ Business Organisation — 47
3.1 The role and functions of a business — 47
3.2 Management — 49
3.3 Small and large businesses — 55
3.4 Organisational structure — 57
3.5 Centralisation and decentralisation — 64
3.6 Activities — 65

❹ Types of Business — 71
4.1 Private and public enterprise — 71
4.2 Limited liability — 72
4.3 Private ownership — 73
4.4 Special business relationships — 79
4.5 Business growth — 81
4.6 Public enterprise — 84
4.7 Activities — 85

Contents

5. Recruitment, Selection and Training — 91
- 5.1 The Human Resources Department — 91
- 5.2 Short-lists and interviews — 94
- 5.3 Staff orientation and development — 97
- 5.4 Training — 98
- 5.5 The welfare of employees — 99
- 5.6 Staff records — 99
- 5.7 Resignation, dismissal, redundancy and grievance — 100
- 5.8 Activities — 101

6. Motivation of Employees — 110
- 6.1 Job satisfaction — 110
- 6.2 Wages — 111
- 6.3 Working conditions — 115
- 6.4 Activities — 118

7. Industrial Relations — 123
- 7.1 The importance of industrial relations — 123
- 7.2 Trade unions — 123
- 7.3 Collective bargaining — 125
- 7.4 Industrial disputes — 127
- 7.5 Assisting industrial peace — 128
- 7.6 Role of the government — 130
- 7.7 Pressure groups — 131
- 7.8 Activities — 133

8. The Marketing Department — 138
- 8.1 What is marketing? — 138
- 8.2 The marketing department — 139
- 8.3 Marketing mix — 140
- 8.4 Product lifecycle — 144
- 8.5 Merchandising — 146
- 8.6 Price determination — 147
- 8.7 Competition — 150
- 8.8 Public relations — 151
- 8.9 Trade associations — 152
- 8.10 Activities — 153

9. Market Research and Advertising — 159
- 9.1 Market research — 159
- 9.2 Types of market research — 160
- 9.3 Market research in action — 162
- 9.4 Functions of advertising — 166
- 9.5 Forms of advertising — 168
- 9.6 The advertising campaign — 169

9.7	Is advertising wasteful?	170
9.8	Consumer protection	172
9.9	Activities	178

10 The Home Market — 188

10.1	The chain of distribution	188
10.2	Wholesalers	189
10.3	Retailers	192
10.4	Activities	200

11 The International Market — 207

11.1	The importance of international trade	207
11.2	Balance of trade	210
11.3	Balance of payments	210
11.4	Methods of selling abroad	212
11.5	Difficulties faced by exporters	213
11.6	Aids to exporters	214
11.7	Free trade restrictions	215
11.8	Reasons for trade restrictions	216
11.9	Free trade	216
11.10	Activities	221

12 Business Documents — 225

12.1	Purpose of business documents	225
12.2	Trading documents	225
12.3	Purchasing	226
12.4	Despatch	227
12.5	Charging	227
12.6	Foreign trade documents	230
12.7	Activities	232

13 Transport — 238

13.1	The importance of transport	238
13.2	Choice of transport	238
13.3	Methods of transport	239
13.4	Containerisation	244
13.5	Transport terminology	244
13.6	Activities	245

14 Business Communication — 250

14.1	The importance of business communication	250
14.2	Internal methods of communication	251
14.3	Business meetings	253
14.4	External communications	255
14.5	Information technology	255

14.6	Postal communications	259
14.7	Telecommunications	263
14.8	Activities	268

15 Banking — 275

15.1	Central banks	275
15.2	Central banks and monetary control	276
15.3	Special financial institutions	278
15.4	The clearing banks	279
15.5	Bank accounts	279
15.6	The cheque system	281
15.7	EFTPOS	285
15.8	Bank services	286
15.9	Borrowing from a bank	291
15.10	Activities	292

16 Business Finance — 300

16.1	Sources of finance	300
16.2	Financial projections	301
16.3	Cash flow	303
16.4	Costs and revenues	305
16.5	A firm's accounts	306
16.6	Profit	307
16.7	Balance sheets	309
16.8	Activities	312

17 Company Shares — 319

17.1	Selling new shares	319
17.2	Selling second-hand shares	320
17.3	Types of company security traded	321
17.4	The return on shares	323
17.5	Factors affecting share prices	324
17.6	Activities	324

18 Insurance for business — 328

18.1	The purpose of insurance	328
18.2	Uninsurable risks	329
18.3	Principles of insurance	329
18.4	Types of insurance	331
18.5	The insurance contract	333
18.6	The insurance market	334
18.7	Activities	336

19 National Accounts — 341

19.1	The standard of living	341
19.2	National income	343
19.3	Gross national product	345

	19.4	National expenditure	347
	19.5	National debt	349
	19.6	Growth and development	350
	19.7	Activities	351

20 Taxation and inflation 355

20.1	Principles of taxation	355
20.2	Functions of taxation	355
20.3	Methods of taxation	356
20.4	Economic effects of taxation	359
20.5	Inflation	360
20.6	Activities	363

21 Population 368

21.1	Importance of population	368
21.2	Factors influencing population size	368
21.3	Optimum population size	371
21.4	Distribution of population	372
21.5	Mobility of labour	375
21.6	Activities	376

22 The Role of Governments 379

22.1	The responsibilities of governments	379
22.2	Government assistance to entrepreneurs	380
22.3	Government intervention in business	382
22.4	Social services	385
22.5	Activities	387

Index 394

Preface to Fifth Edition

This book is intended for use as a basic text by students preparing for GCSE and IGCSE Business Studies and other related examinations. The aim has been to present a wide-ranging and comprehensive textbook, produced in a readable and interesting style and which can be used in mixed ability situations. Each chapter is backed by a variety of activities that will help the student to form structured revision notes, to practise test questions at varying degrees of difficulty, and to carry out independent study.

The **Activities** at the end of each chapter give a variety of opportunities for 'differentiation'. The *Make a note of it* exercises could be tackled by all pupils, perhaps with the teacher deleting questions related to topics which particular students find too difficult. Differentiation here is achieved largely by outcome. There is also a collection of *Structured questions* at the end of each chapter. These are 'stepped', that is each sub-part becomes progressively more difficult, thus allowing all students to achieve introductory questions whilst stretching the more able person in the later sections. The weighting of these questions is indicated by the mark allocation suggested. Many of these questions are related to data which adds interest and aids learning. The final activities consist of a variety of *Research assignments*. These are intended to be tackled by the more able student as investigative learning, often giving the opportunity for research and providing evidence of independent thought.

This book has been immensely popular worldwide and the fifth edition has been updated and refined to meet the needs of this wider international market.

A Message to Students

In writing this book I have deliberately tried to keep the text as easy to read as possible whilst at the same time adequately covering the many topics you are required to learn. Each chapter can be broadly divided into two areas. The first is the reading related to the themes of the chapter. I cannot recommend too strongly the need to read around the topic currently being studied. I attribute the majority of my personal academic development to reading of appropriate material. The second important area of each chapter is the Activities section. This consists of three subsections:

- *Make a note of it*
  This section consists of a series of questions based on the themes of the chapter. The questions follow the same order as the text. Consequently, by writing the question followed by the answer you will formulate revision notes, as well as learning through the process.

- *Structured questions*
  These are a series of questions related to a particular area of learning that have been linked together in a structured way to help in examination preparation. These questions are 'stepped' with subsections becoming progressively more difficult.

- *Research assignments*
  A selection of assignments are given here requiring extended answers and personal research. These give you experience in the sort of activities necessary when carrying out course work for some syllabuses as well as helping you to prepare for a higher level of study.

Now for some tips about how you should interpret some of the terminology used in examination questions and what they require:

- *Compare*. Look for similarities and differences and perhaps reach a conclusion about which is preferable.

- *Criticise*. Give your opinion about the merit of one or another of the possible alternatives. Back your judgement with reasoning to support your choice.

- *Describe*. Give a detailed or graphic account of.

- *Discuss*. Investigate or examine. Give reasons for and against, advantages and disadvantages and examine implications.

- *Explain.* Make clear, give reasons for, account for.
- *Illustrate.* Explain the meaning of, or make clear, and explain using relevant examples. (It does *not* mean produce diagrams.)
- *Outline.* Give the main features, or the general principles of a topic, omitting minor details.
- *State.* Present in a brief but clear form.
- *Summarise.* Omit details and examples, but concentrate on giving a concise account of the chief points related to a particular topic.

Always read the essay title or examination question very carefully, making particular note of these key terms. Only then will you be sure what the question demands of you. You might find it useful to make a brief plan which organises the essay around the terms used in the question.

Finally, an old maxim: Answer the question, the whole question, and nothing but the question.

Best of luck of your examinations.

Alan Whitcomb

Acknowledgements

The author and publisher would like to thank the following for permission to reproduce copyright material.

The Advertising Standards Authority Ltd
Aiwa (UK) Ltd
Association Container Transportation
  Services Ltd
Barclays Bank plc
BBC
Boots The Chemists Ltd
British Telecom
British Trades Alphabet
Burger King (UK) Ltd
Cadbury Ltd
Canada Maritime Ltd
The Commission of the European Union
Dominique de Buys
Employment News
Executive Post
Financial Times
Ron Freeman (photographer)
The Hammerson Group Developments
Hoover Ltd
HSBC Holdings plc
Interflora (FTDA) British Unit Ltd*
Investors in People UK
JVC Manufacturing UK Ltd

Kenwood Ltd
KFC Ltd
D H Letchford
Lloyds Bank plc
Londis (Holdings) Ltd
McDonald's Restaurants Ltd
Mitchell Cotts Freight
Morphy Richards Ltd
Paul Mulcahy
National Girobank
National Westminster Bank plc
Office of the Data Protection Registrar
Pandair International Airfreight
Peterborough Development Corporation
Philips Electronics Ltd
Pictor International
The Post Office
Nik Rudge
Safeway Stores plc
J Sainsbury plc
The Stock Exchange
Tesco plc
Tony Stone Images
Wimpey Homes Holdings Ltd
Woolworths plc

*In the UK Interflora is a Registered Trademark of Interflora Incorporated. The Mercury Man device is the Registered Trademark of Florists Transworld Delivery Association.

1 The Business Environment

1.1 Development of economic activity

Direct production

All people have three basic *needs* – food, clothing and shelter. And much of the activity we engage in is aimed at satisfying those needs. Activities which result in the satisfaction of our needs are often referred to as 'economic activity', therefore, Man is sometimes called an 'economic animal'.

Early Man led a simple way of life. He would provide all of his needs himself without the aid of others. This is called *direct production*. He would hunt animals and gather plants and berries. Man was living in a *subsistence economy* – providing just sufficient to survive, but not improve his way of life.

Later Man began to farm in a very basic way, penning animals and planting seeds. This enabled him to settle in one place, build a permanent home and improve his way of life. One of the improvements was that he found he was producing more goods than he needed (*surplus*). He began to exchange his surplus goods with the surplus of others.

Barter

The exchange of one thing for another without the use of money is called *barter*, and this was the way that the earliest form of trade took place. But there are drawbacks to the barter system, as follows:

1. A *double coincidence of wants* has to occur for barter to take place. The person

who has a surplus to exchange not only has to find someone who wants his or her surplus, but the person found must also have what is wanted.
2 An *exchange rate* has to be agreed even if a double coincidence of wants has occurred. Imagine the difficulty in trying to agree how many chickens a pig is worth.
3 *Divisibility of goods* is not always convenient. Some rates of exchange will not allow exchange to take place because some goods cannot be split into smaller parts. For example, if one spear is worth half a chicken it is not possible to trade with only one spear because you cannot have half a chicken and also have it alive.
4 *Storage of wealth* is difficult with the barter system. At times there is a need to store a surplus for use at a future time when a scarcity exists. But many items used in barter (e.g. food) cannot be stored for long periods of time.

Money

The use of money solves all of the above problems of barter, but early money was not in the form of coins and notes with which we are familiar today. The difficulties of barter led early Man to the use of generally accepted items which everyone was willing to take in exchange for their goods. These items included such things as shells, dogs' teeth, beads, grain, spearheads, hides, arrowheads, fishhooks and animals, and they became substitute money.

Even today many things are used instead of money in some parts of the world, and when a country's economy collapses the people may revert to using goods instead of money. For example, in Germany during the latter part of the Second World War cigarettes, coffee and stockings were used as money.

Qualities of money

For something to be considered as money, or in the place of money, it must be:

- *durable* (hard wearing)
- *divisible* (easily divided into smaller units)
- *portable* (convenient to carry)
- *acceptable* (people must agree to its use).

The use of money allowed early Man to sell his surplus of goods in exchange for money and use the money to buy his needs from the surplus of others. Money was now acting as a *medium of exchange*, and the process of trading was much simpler.

In time metal became a popular substance used as money in any part of the world where it was common, and the use of metal eventually led to the development of the coins with which we are so familiar today. Look back at the list of the qualities of money. Can you see how metal money so conveniently meets all those qualities?

Functions of money

Money has three basic functions. It is a medium of exchange, a measure of value and a store of value.

1 *Medium of exchange* – money makes trading relatively simple and makes barter unnecessary. It enables workers to specialise in labour and accept money for

The Business Environment

wages rather than goods. Workers will accept money because they know it is acceptable to others in exchange for goods.

2 *Measure of value* – money can be used to measure or price the value of goods and services. This is especially important when the items cannot easily be compared. For example, how many hours of work by a farmer is a tractor worth?

3 *Store of values* – money can be stored for use at some later time, whereas to store goods such as food for a long time is inconvenient. This makes it possible to 'save for a rainy day', to have some wealth to draw on when a scarcity occurs. In other words, money can be earned at one time and spent at another.

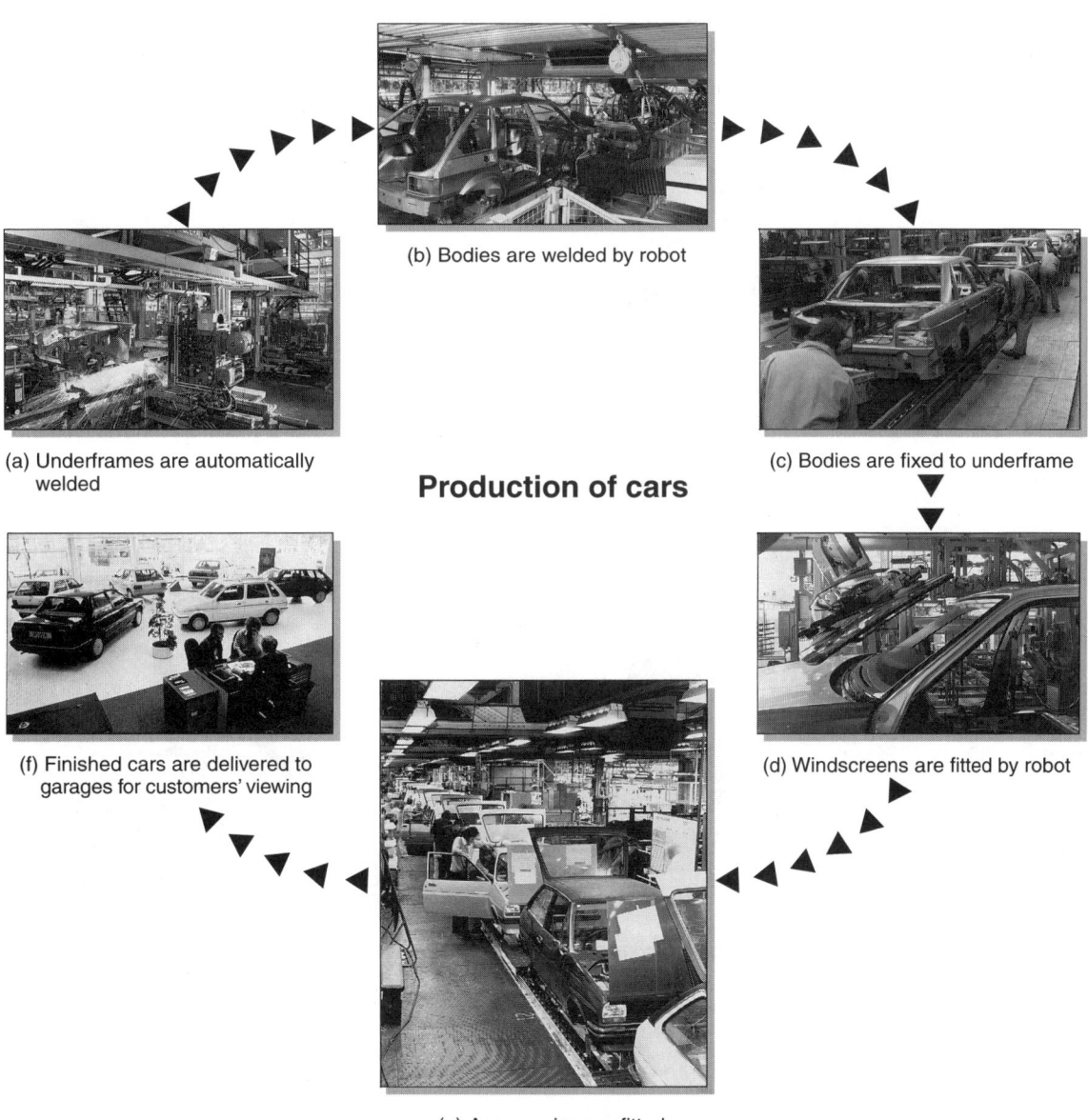

Production of cars

(a) Underframes are automatically welded
(b) Bodies are welded by robot
(c) Bodies are fixed to underframe
(d) Windscreens are fitted by robot
(e) Accessories are fitted
(f) Finished cars are delivered to garages for customers' viewing

Specialisation by process – the car factory.

Indirect production

In modern industrial society few people satisfy their needs directly. Instead they co-operate with others to indirectly produce the needs of everyone. This is often referred to as *division of labour* or *specialisation*. Work is divided among several people, allowing them each to specialise in doing what they do best, which is to the benefit of everyone. There are two main ways of looking at specialisation.

Specialisation by product

Instead of everyone trying to produce all they personally need, they each concentrate on contributing to one commodity or service, using the money that they earn to purchase the goods or services of others. In this way the total needs of an individual are met by the contributions of many others.

Specialisation by product.

The Business Environment

Specialisation by process

By organising production into several stages or processes workers become more specialised and expert in their work. For example, in a car factory each worker might specialise in a part of the assembly of many vehicles in one day as they pass along the production line. By organising production in this way, workers become more specialised and expert in their work. This enables them to produce more with the same resources.

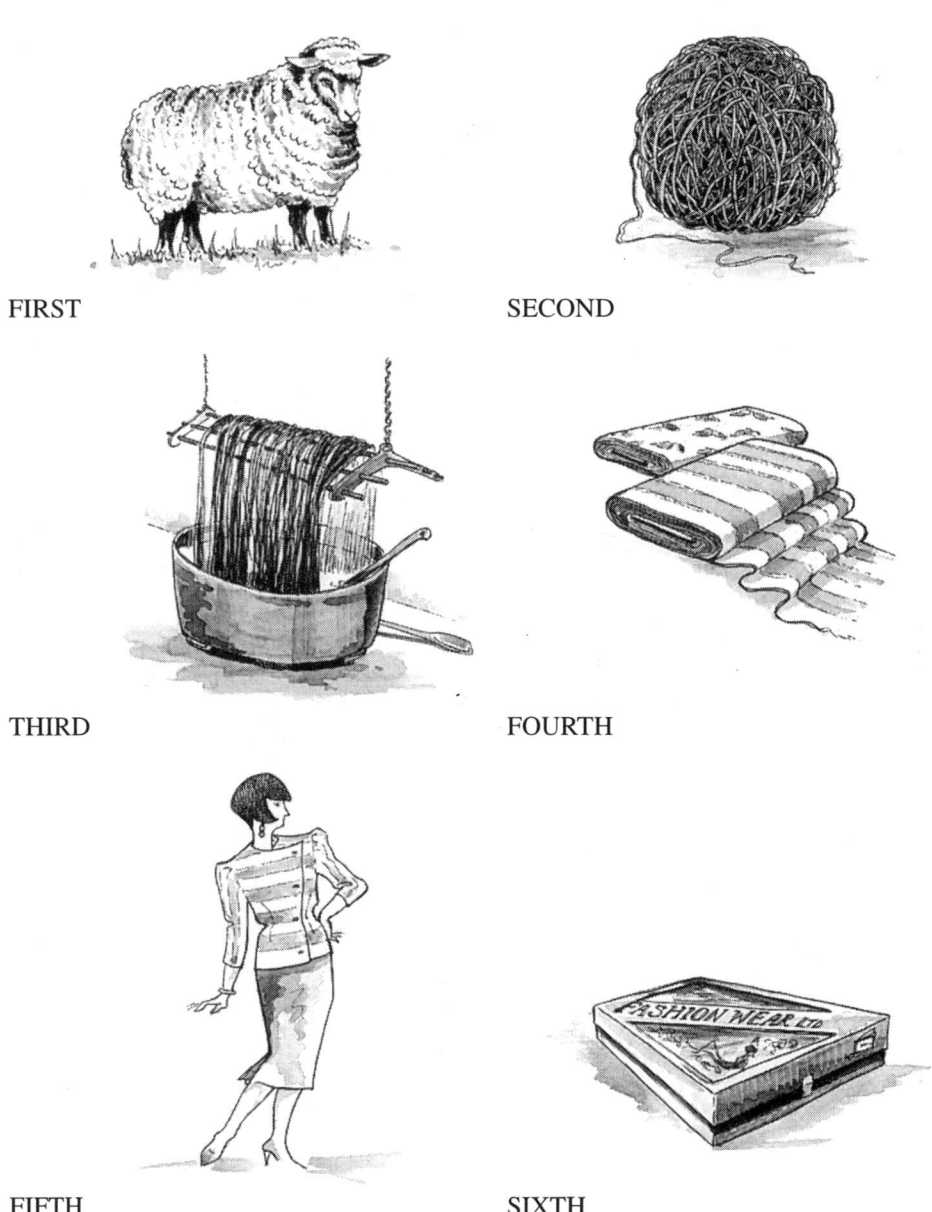

FIRST

SECOND

THIRD

FOURTH

FIFTH

SIXTH

Specialisation by process.

Advantages and disadvantages of specialisation

Advantages:
- Workers become skilled at doing a particular job.
- Jobs become simpler and easier to learn.
- Time-saving machinery and semi-skilled labour can be used.
- Costs per unit produced are less because of the simple processes and better use of labour and tools.
- Labour is potentially more mobile.

Disadvantages:
- Repeating a single task can become boring.
- Individual crafts and skills are lost by use of machines.
- Greater use of machinery can lead to unemployment of workers.
- All production may be halted by strikes, machinery breakdown or shortage of materials.
- Slow workers may be unable to keep pace with others.

1.2 Scarcity and choice in a modern society

In a world where specialisation has become highly developed with not only individuals but whole communities specialising, it is vital for exchange to take place if everyone's wants are to be satisfied. The bus driver works for wages but needs food, so the wages are exchanged to obtain his needs. This involves making choices.

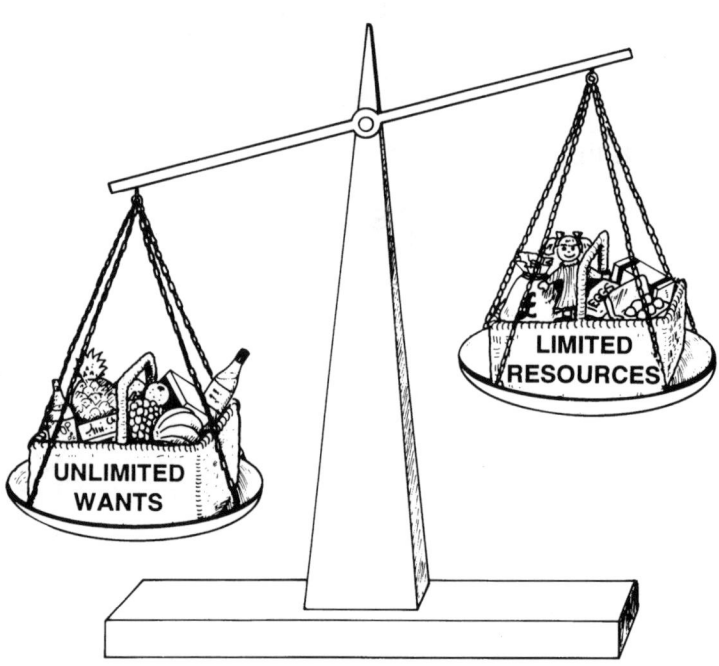

We have to balance our unlimited wants against our limited resources.

Everytime we go shopping we are involved in a basic economic activity, that of making a *choice* because of *scarce* resources. We have only limited money available, but invariably we would like to buy more than we can afford. Consequently, we have not only to make a choice, but also to form a *scale of preference*. In other words, we put what we want into an order of priority. In making choices we obviously have to give up certain things we could not have. The things we give up are known as the **opportunity cost** because we have given up the opportunity to have them.

Scarcity and choice are not problems that are restricted to individuals alone. Businesses and countries face these problems of choice also. Businesses must decide how to profitably use the capital that shareholders have provided. A country has limited resources and the people or their representatives will try to use or allocate them to the best benefit of the community.

The success with which choices are made has a considerable influence on the well-being of individuals, the prosperity of a business and the quality of life of a country's residents. This is sometimes referred to as the basic *economic problem* – how to use available resources in a community to the best benefit of the needs of society. We are fortunate today in that we have many people, organisations and agencies who are available to advise us and to help us to make wise decisions on the best way to use the scarce resources available. However, it has taken thousands of years of experience to reach this stage of human development.

1.3 Economic systems

The processes of production, exchange, scarcity and choice looked at so far in this chapter take place within a political framework. In other words, the decision of what to produce or what choices to make with the scarce resources available is influenced by the political situation within which the decision is made. No two countries are organised in the same way, but they all have to solve three basic problems:

- *What should be produced?* For example, what quantities of food, machinery or services should be produced?
- *How should production be organised?* What is the best way to combine the factors of production? Should automated or manual methods be used? What technological equipment (e.g. computers) is required? Where should production take place?
- *For whom should production take place?* Should everyone be entitled to an equal share of the production, or should some receive more than others?

Economists distinguish between four different economic systems which answer the foregoing questions. The first of these described here is the subsistence economy.

Subsistence economy

A subsistence economy is one where there is little or no specialisation or trade. In such an economy people tend to live in family groups and grow most of their own food. It is called a 'subsistence economy' because people do little more than subsist – they can provide only the basic necessities to live. This was the form of economy that was a feature of the life of early Man. Today more advanced forms of economy exist, although some countries are still at subsistence level.

Countries differ to the extent to which the government interferes with the economic system. There are three basic approaches adopted by governments in dealing with the economic problem: the free economy, the controlled economy and the mixed economy.

Free economy

A free economy is based on the private ownership of the factors (means) of production and the means of distributing goods and services. Consumers express their wants through their demand for goods and services, and the private producer seeks to satisfy the demand if the profit motive is sufficient. Therefore, in a free economy the purchaser of goods decides demand and not the state. Sometimes such economies are referred to as market economies, unplanned economies, free enterprise, laissez-faire system, or capitalist system. The USA and Japan are typical examples of a free economy.

Advantages of free economy
- All members of the community are free to participate in business enterprise for the purpose of making a profit.
- Those engaged in business enterprise have to compete with many others for

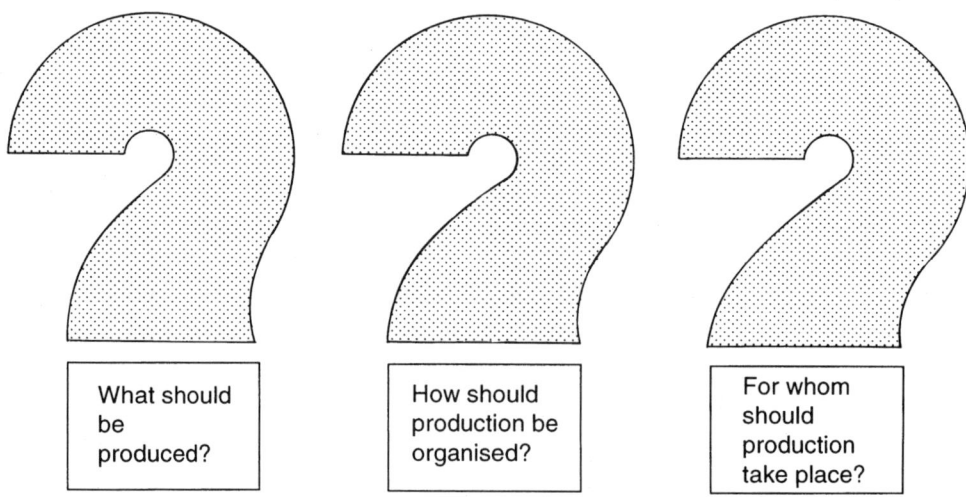

All countries have to solve three basic problems.

custom. This has the effect of maintaining efficiency, keeping prices down and improving the standard of goods and services.
- The consumers play a major part in deciding what will be produced because it is the consumer who creates the demand and the producers who try to satisfy this demand.

Disadvantages of free economy
- Advertising is a major feature of free enterprise and this can be used to create an artificially high demand for some products. In other words, demand may be created by the producer rather than the consumer.
- In a free enterprise society successful businesses may buy out smaller firms in order to obtain control of a larger share of the market. This reduces competition and increases the danger of monopolies arising.
- In response to the profit motive, companies may restrict supplies of some goods or services in order to keep prices and profits artificially high.

Controlled economy

In a controlled economy the state controls the factors of production and the means of exchange and distribution. The state estimates what quantity of goods and services the community will need over a given period, and then directs the factors of production to produce these goods and services. In other words, unlike the free economy, it is the state that decides what the community needs and consequently demand does not originate from the consumers. This type of economy is sometimes called a centralised economy, planned economy, collective economy, or a socialist system. China and Cuba are examples of controlled economies. Many controlled economies have begun to introduce elements of free enterprise into their economic structure.

Advantages of controlled economy
- The state can assess the needs of the whole community and try to provide benefit for all the population. The means of production can then be directed towards this end and wasteful competition can be eliminated.
- It is not possible for a private monopoly to emerge under this system.

Disadvantages of controlled economy
- The state has control over the factors of production and this discourages enterprise and inventiveness.
- A considerable number of non-productive government officials are required to plan and operate the economy. These officials may not necessarily have the skills needed to decide what the community needs, and decisions may be subject to many rules and regulations. This may result in delays in reaching decisions.
- Centralised production may not respond as quickly to changing conditions and trends as private enterprise.
- The absence of competition and profit motive can hinder both creativeness and efficiency.

Mixed economy

As the term implies, a mixed economy is a combination of elements taken from a free economy and some from a controlled economy. Britain is an example of this type of economic system. Some sections of British industry are owned and operated by the state but large portions of the business world remain in private hands. The contents of this book are largely set in the context of a mixed economy.

1.4 Types of production

Earlier in this chapter we examined direct and indirect production. With direct production, which is a characteristic of countries that are economically backward, individuals or small groups satisfy their wants entirely by their own efforts and unaided by others. Indirect production, which is a feature of all developed societies, involves specialisation, working for wages and using the money earned to buy the goods and services produced by other people. Indirect production can be divided into three categories, primary production, secondary production and tertiary production.

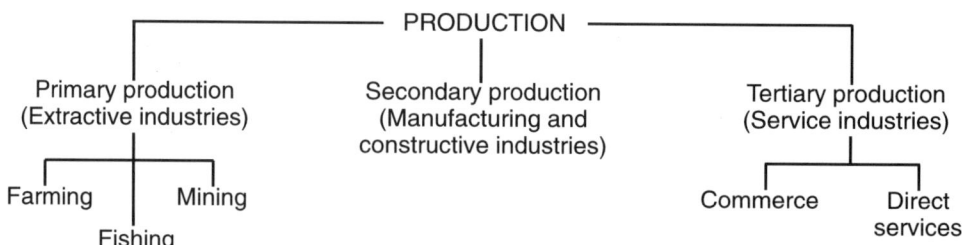

Primary production

Primary production is concerned with the extraction of basic materials provided by nature, which are either above or below the earth's surface. The extractive industries are farming, fishing and mining. Without these much subsequent production would not take place.

Farming involves production of foods in the form of fowls, animals and plants and also other produce of the land such as trees and flowers.

Fishing has always played a major part in the provision of food for Britain which is not surprising as we are a country surrounded by the sea. Deep-sea fishing is carried out in the open sea and is subject to international rules which try to ensure that each country has its own fair share of the catch. Protected fisheries are a growth industry that exists to farm fish in inland lakes and reservoirs, producing high yields from a small area.

Mining extracts raw materials such as coal, ore, oil, gas, etc. from below the earth's surface.

The Business Environment

Secondary production

Secondary production consists of the manufacturing and construction industries. They take the raw materials produced by the extractive industries and change their form into some end product.

Manufacturers may be involved in the production of a complete item, or they may make parts which will be assembled into a finished article.

Construction industries take raw materials and partly finished products and change them into buildings, roads and bridges, etc.

Tertiary production

When goods leave the producers they do not usually pass immediately to the consumer. They have to be stored, transported, insured, advertised and sold by traders. These and the many other commercial activities that make up tertiary production further the change of ownership of goods from the producer to the consumers. Tertiary production is sometimes called the service industry, but more often it is referred to as *commerce* and *direct services*.

Commerce

Commerce can be divided into two clear areas, *trade* and *services to trade*.

- *Trade* is the process of changing ownership. Traders are the businesses directly involved in the buying and selling of goods and services. Trade can either take place within a country (home trade) or between countries (foreign trade). Home trade involves the activities of wholesalers and retailers. Foreign trade involves importers (who buy goods from other countries) and exporters (who sell goods to other countries).
- *Services to trade* are the commercial activities that assist trade in its job of selling goods and services.

The activities that provide these services are:

1. *Banking* – providing short-term finance and providing facilities for easy payment transfer.

Comprehensive Business Studies

(a) Which form of production is illustrated above? Why does this form of production also depend on the others shown here?
(Copyright: *Farmers Weekly*; photo by Peter Adams)

(b) Fishing

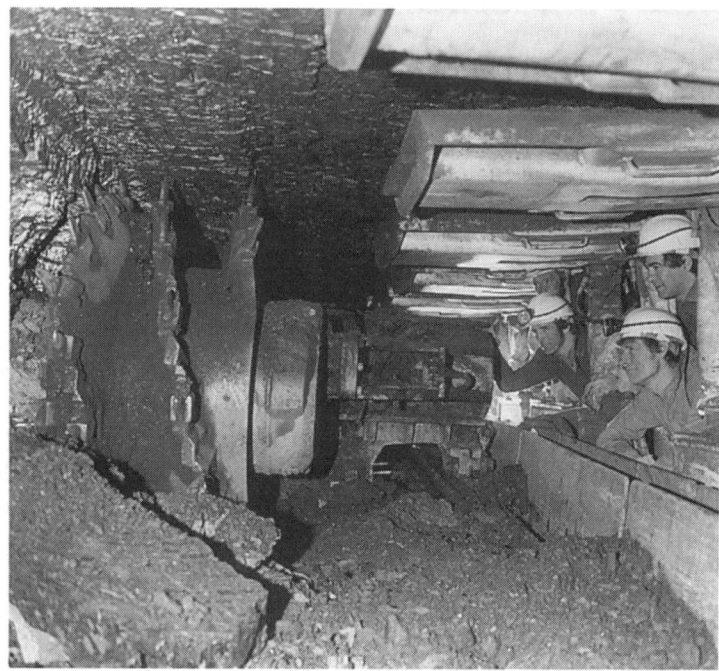

(c) Mining
(Courtesy British Coal)

2 *Finance* – various institutions (e.g. the Stock Exchange) providing long-term finance for industry, commerce and consumer credit.
3 *Insurance* – spreads the risks faced by industrial and commercial businesses.
4 *Transport* – engaged in the movement of commodities from one place to another.
5 *Communications:*
   (a) Postal – transfer of written communications through mail services.
   (b) Telecommunications – immediate distance transfer of written, verbal or data communications by electronic devices.
   (c) Advertising – provides potential customers with information about goods and services available.

All of the elements of both trade and services to trade are the subject of individual chapters in different parts of this book.

Direct services

In addition to commercial services there are groups of people who provide direct services, which are not related to trade but which people use because they

provide services which are essential to the well-being of the community. Direct service occupations include the services of doctors, nurses, teachers, actors and actresses, policemen, hairdressers, authors and many others who offer a personal service.

The chain of production

Primary, secondary and tertiary production are importantly linked. These links are said to show the **chain of production**. The link can be seen if we take a single product through the various stages involved in its development and distribution. Take milk production as an example. At the primary stage dairy cows are farmed and milked. In the secondary stage the milk is put into bottles or cartons, and tertiary production is involved in the marketing of the milk.

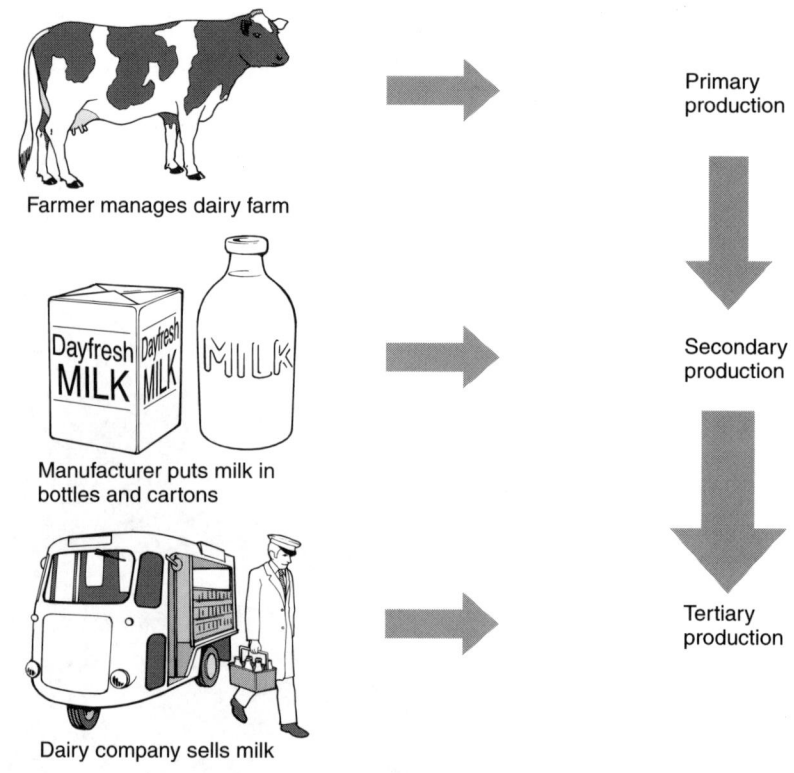

The chain of production for milk.

The Business Environment

Interdependence of industry

1.5

Let us now summarise what we have learnt from this chapter.

- *Direct production* is a characteristic of underdeveloped and primitive economies.
- *Indirect production* is a feature of all advanced economies, and this form of production is most common today.
- *Specialisation* is an essential part of indirect production and it involves people doing what they do best.
- *Commercial activities* are positioned between the producer and the consumer and these provide the means of buying and selling goods and services. They play a vital part in allowing people to specialise, earn wages and then buy their wants. They also play a major role in co-ordinating and promoting the activities of producers. We will now examine some of the ways in which this is done.

Traders support producers by carrying out the distribution of goods and bridging the time gap between production and consumption. For example, retailers and wholesalers order goods from producers and hold them until they are required. Exporters are involved in the distribution of home-produced goods overseas. This not only provides work for producers, but also raises foreign capital which is needed to pay for the imports of raw materials that the producer needs. Importers buy from other countries the raw materials and finished goods that we cannot economically produce at home, thus allowing home producers to specialise in manufacturing products for which they are best suited.

The services to trade also play a major part in combining the activities of producers and promoting their enterprise. Finance provides the money for the capital assets needed by business, and also for consumers and businesses who wish to buy on credit. Banking makes transfer of payments between buyers and sellers of goods possible and also provides a variety of other services that facilitate payment and encourage production and trade to take place. Insurance overcomes some of the risks involved in producing and trading such as the danger of loss or damage to capital assets or goods. Transport makes the physical link between producers, traders and consumers, and gets goods to the right place at the right time and in the right condition. Advertising helps producers and traders to bring their commodities to the attention of potential customers. Postal communications and telecommunications enable businessmen to communicate with each other and their customers at the various stages of production and distribution.

We can see from this section that commercial activities are essential to production, but many of the commercial activities would not be needed if it were not for producers and specialisation making exchange necessary. In other words, primary, secondary and tertiary production are interdependent.

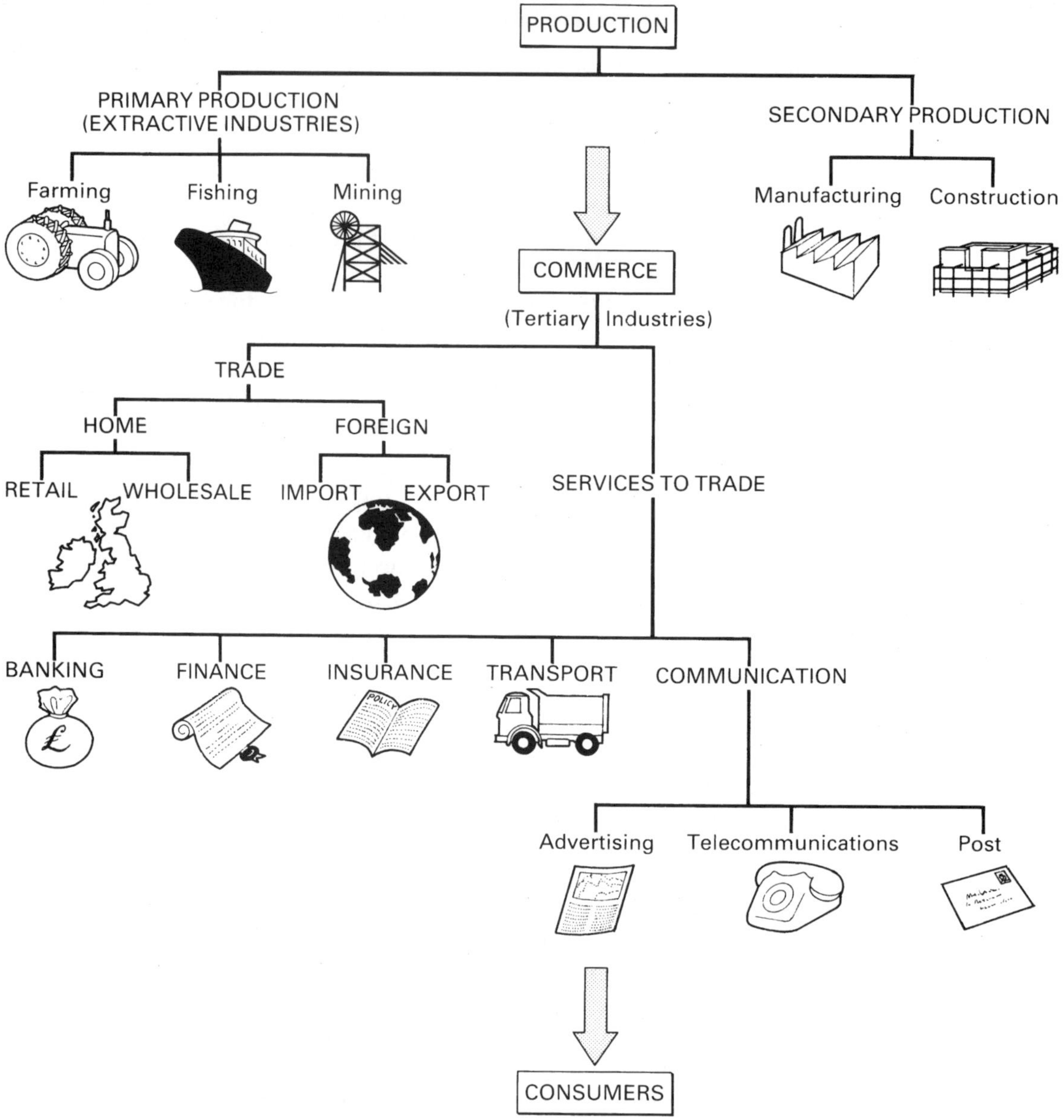

Comprehensive Business Studies

```
                    PRODUCTION
           ┌───────────┴───────────┐
  PRIMARY PRODUCTION         SECONDARY PRODUCTION
 (EXTRACTIVE INDUSTRIES)
  ┌────┬────┬────┐              ┌──────┬──────┐
Farming Fishing Mining      Manufacturing Construction

                    ↓
                COMMERCE
              (Tertiary Industries)
      ┌──────────┴──────────┐
    TRADE              SERVICES TO TRADE
  ┌───┴───┐         ┌────┬────┬────┬────┐
 HOME  FOREIGN   BANKING FINANCE INSURANCE TRANSPORT COMMUNICATION
 ┌─┴─┐  ┌─┴─┐
RETAIL WHOLESALE IMPORT EXPORT

                            COMMUNICATION
                       ┌────────┼────────┐
                  Advertising Telecommunications Post

                    ↓
                CONSUMERS
```

1.6 Activities

1. What is direct production and why does it limit the quality of life?
2. Define surplus. Why is the production of a surplus important?
3. What is barter?
4. Briefly describe the difficulties involved in trading by the barter system.

5. List six examples of substitute money.
6. What are the qualities necessary for something to be suitable for use as money?
7. What do we mean when we say that money is a medium of exchange?
8. Describe the functions of money.
9. What is indirect production?
10. Define division of labour.
11. Explain the difference between division of labour by product and division of labour by process.
12. List the advantages and disadvantages of specialisation.
13. Why is exchange so important to the success of specialisation?
14. What is the relationship between choice, scarce resources and scale of preference?
15. Why is making wise choices important to individuals, businesses and the country as a whole?
16. State the four basic problems that economic systems have to attempt to solve.
17. What is a subsistence economy and why is it not a satisfying way of life?
18. 'The free economy and the controlled economy are completely contrasting forms of economic systems.' Give a detailed explanation of this statement.
19. Give a brief description of a mixed economy.
20. Why is primary production also referred to as the extractive industries?
21. Name three examples of occupations found in primary production and three from secondary production.
22. Why is tertiary production so important to the other forms of production?
23. Briefly define tertiary production and distinguish between trade and services to trade.
24. List ten commercial occupations and briefly describe the functions of each.
25. What are direct services? Give three examples of occupations that provide a direct service.
26. Why are commercial activities as important as production?

Comprehensive Business Studies

Structured Questions

1 Refer to the diagram on page 10 and answer these related questions.

(a) Why are the extractive industries also referred to as primary production? (1)
(b) How does secondary production differ from primary production? (2)
(c) State two specific differences between home trade and foreign trade. (2)
(d) Why are advertising, telecommunications and post all recognised as forms of business communication? (3)
(e) Why is trade particularly important to producers? (4)
(f) In what ways do the services to trade support trade? (8)

2 Consider the following illustration.

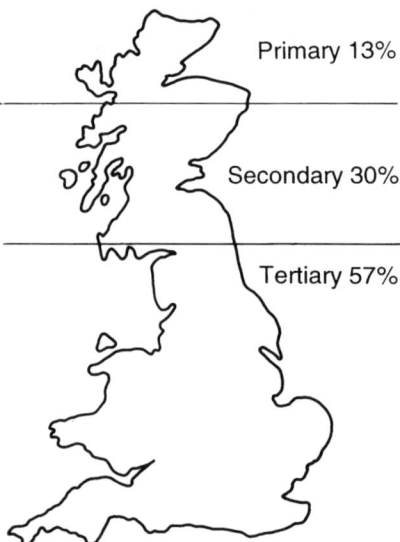

THE STRUCTURE OF UK INDUSTRY

Primary 13%
Secondary 30%
Tertiary 57%

Contribution to UK Gross Domestic Product

Our basic needs vary from one part of the world to another, and so does our ability to satisfy them. There are three stages of production in the development from natural resources to consumption.

Production in the UK can be divided into these three stages or categories: primary, secondary and tertiary. The percentage contribution each makes to UK production is shown in the illustration. The tertiary sector has been continually expanding in the UK, whereas the other two sectors have been declining.

(a) Why do the basic needs differ from one country to another? (2)
(b) In what ways does the ability of the UK to satisfy its needs differ from that of a Third World country? (2)
(c) Explain the difference between primary, secondary and tertiary production. (3)
(d) Using the data in the illustration, produce a pie chart that shows the percentage each type of production contributes to the UK economy. (3)

The Business Environment

(e) Draw a flow chart showing the development of a product through all three types of production. Include an explanation at each stage. (4)

(f) The tertiary sector has been the fastest growing element of production in the UK for many years. Give some reasons why this has been so. (6)

3 Refer to the illustration on page 3 which shows the processes involved in the production of cars.

(a) In what way is division of labour shown in this illustration? (1)
(b) Why is division of labour also referred to as specialisation? (2)
(c) Why does division of labour often result in increased production output? (3)
(d) The illustration (a) to (f) shows the processes involved in car production in logical order. Form a flow chart that shows the progression in the production of an item of furniture. (4)
(e) State three advantages and three disadvantages of division of labour. (4)
(f) Explain the difference between specialisation by product and specialisation by process. Give examples to illustrate your answer. (3)

4 The flow diagram below shows the way that a subsistence economy can develop and eventually result in a better standard of living.

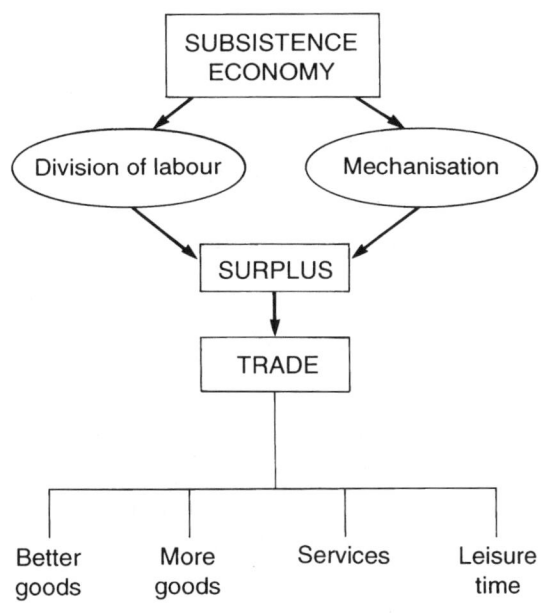

(a) What is meant by a 'subsistence economy'? (2)
(b) Why is a subsistence economy sometimes referred to as a 'trap'? (2)
(c) How can division of labour help a community to escape from the subsistence trap? (3)
(d) In what ways does division of labour help to make mechanisation possible? (3)
(e) How does the combination of division of labour and mechanisation usually result in the creation of a surplus and make it important to trade? (4)
(f) Why do the combined processes shown in this flow diagram result in 'a better standard of living'? (6)

Research Assignments

1 Make a survey of small production industries in your area (perhaps on an industrial estate). Present your survey on a simple colour-coded diagram/map to show different categories of production. See if you can identify any relationship between the size of premises and the legal identity of the firm. Comment on your findings.

2 Using library resources make a comparative study of the USA, China and the UK as illustrations of different types of economy. To what extent do you think these are changing?

3 Visit a local factory that has a production line and find out the following information about the organisation of production.

(a) What elements of the manufacturing process are done on the production line and which are not?
(b) To what extent does the factory employ 'modern technology'?
(c) How do wage rates differ between workers within the firm and why does this occur?

4 Explain to an imaginary visitor from China, the main differences between the economic system that exists in his or her country and that existing in the UK (or your home country).

5 Explain why the success of industry is influenced by the effectiveness of commerce. Use specific examples of local businesses you have investigated to illustrate your explanation.

6 What is 'division of labour'? Show how this must lead to commercial activities. Use specific examples from local businesses you have investigated to illustrate your answer.

 Organisation of Production

 2.1 Production levels

Aims of production

Production refers to the creation of goods and services, i.e. the creation of utilities. The purpose of production is to provide people with the goods which they need or want to consume. *Needs* are things that are essential to human survival. There are three primary human needs. They are:

- food
- clothing
- shelter.

Production also provides the many things that Man *wants* to consume but are not necessary for survival. These things help to make the quality of life better, for example televisions, cars, books, etc.

In what ways can what you see taking place in this photograph assist in the provision of primary human needs?

Levels of production

In Chapter 1 we said that production for the country as a whole can be divided into three main sectors: primary, secondary and tertiary. It can also be classified according to the levels of operation. These levels are dependent upon the resources available, and the extent to which the country has developed to exploit those resources. There are three basic levels of operation: *subsistence*, *domestic* and *surplus*.

Subsistence level

This level of production meets only the basic needs of the country in which it takes place. In other words, sufficient is produced only to enable the population to survive, but not enough to improve the way of life. This is the kind of problem faced by many of the under-developed communities of the world. Subsistence economy is a term usually applied where agriculture is the main source of production. In other words, people live almost entirely by what can be obtained from natural resources, and this could lead to a poor quality of life. Usually the subsistence level of production is inefficient and very dependent upon the climate and weather. Periods of drought or other bad climatic periods result in severe hardship. Fortunately the subsistence level of production is not as common today as it has been in the past, but it still exists in many under-developed countries.

Domestic level

At the level of domestic production everything is produced locally, that is in the home country. This level involves the minimum of imports from foreign countries. Both human and natural resources are employed and the whole economy is particularly dependent upon what it can produce from these resources.

Some developed countries, such as the USA, try to grow all the food they need because they have the resources to do so. The governments of developing countries encourage domestic production in order to make full use of the resources available in their country, e.g. promotion of self-sufficiency in agricultural produce.

Surplus level

Developed countries, such as the USA, Britain and Germany, have a wide variety of resources and exploit these to the full. They also have advanced technology which enables them to take full advantage of their resources.

Such countries are able to achieve a level of production which not only satisfies domestic consumption, but also produces a surplus that can be exported to other countries. This results in a better quality of life for the population because there is access to a wider variety of products and competitive prices, and an ability to earn more from production.

How a business may organise production

The way we have looked at production so far has been largely from a national point of view, i.e. a whole country. We also need to consider how production can be organised by an individual business. There are three basic methods:

1 *Job production* – where a single product is made from start to finish, to a customer's requirement, and in response to an individual order.
2 *Batch production* – where products are made in lots, with a complete lot being finished before starting the next lot.
3 *Flow production* – where products are produced continuously, e.g. mass production on an assembly line.

Which of these production methods a firm chooses will be influenced by the form of the orders it receives:

- special one-off orders (e.g. a fitted kitchen) – *job production*;
- orders from several customers, likely to be repeated – *batch production*;
- orders for production in continuous demand (e.g. bread) – *flow production*.

The foregoing factors will obviously affect the *scale of production* and will give rise to other decisions a firm must make. For example, flow production in particular will mean that the producer must decide what *levels of stocks* of raw materials will have to be held, and how much stock of finished goods will be permitted. The *number of employees* and the skills and equipment they require will also be influenced by production. And of course all firms involved in production are concerned about the *quality* of their products, and the *efficiency* of their employees and the methods used to produce their goods.

2.2 The factors of production

In Chapter 1 we learnt that there are only scarce resources to meet our unlimited wants. The scarce or limited resources which are used to produce the commodities people want to consume are collectively called the *factors of production*. They are:

- land
- labour
- capital
- entrepreneurship.

Each of the factors receives payment or reward in return for the contribution it makes to production. Land receives rent, labour wages, capital interest, and entrepreneurship (which some people argue is a fourth factor of production) is rewarded with profit, although some factors actually receive more than one return.

The factor of land

Land as a factor of production includes not only the land itself but all natural resources found in the earth and sea. Land in this sense includes:

- geographical surface area
- rivers, lakes and seas
- minerals and chemicals.

Land is fixed in supply; in other words, the supply cannot be increased, although the quality of the soil may be improved by the use of fertilisers, drainage, land reclamation, contouring and reafforestation. The search for minerals below the surface of the land and sea continues.

Production cannot take place without land. Primary, secondary and tertiary production and all economic activity involves the use of land.

The factor of labour

Labour is the factor of production which is Man's physical and mental contribution to the creation of goods and services. It is the factor that converts resources into goods and services that people want. This contribution to production is generally rewarded with wages, although sometimes profit or interest is the return received.

All production requires some labour. Even the automated factory requires workers to supervise machinery, to program computers, to operate equipment and to process paperwork. Therefore, it is important that there is an adequate supply of labour, with the appropriate skills required. In this respect, labour is often divided into three broad groups:

1. *Semi-skilled and unskilled* – jobs which involve little or no special training and usually involve working with the hands – drivers, cleaners, street sellers and some factory production line workers, watchmen, etc.
2. *Skilled* – engineers, mechanics, electricians, plumbers, trained machine operators, computer operators, clerks, junior supervisors, etc.
3. *Managerial and professional* – business executives, teachers, doctors, nurses, solicitors, architects, pharmacists, senior supervisors, etc.

These groups generally reflect differing qualities and levels of training.

Many businesses improve the quality of their labour force through education and training. This results in efficient use of the capital goods the business employs and, therefore, contributes to the growth and development of the firm. But there are many other factors which determine the supply and quality of labour.

Determinants of the labour supply

Labour supply is influenced by:

- *The size and structure of the population.* A large population will give a greater supply of labour. But a high proportion of very young or very old people will tend to reduce the supply of labour. These will be influenced by the school leaving and retirement ages.
- *The number of women at work.* This is influenced by many factors such as economic conditions in the country, wages and attitudes towards working mothers, etc.
- *Hours of work.* If there is a general trend towards a shorter working week (which is the case in developed countries), this has the effect of reducing the supply of labour.

- *Quality of labour force.* It is not enough to have sufficient numbers of people available for work. They must also have the appropriate skills that are needed. If the required skills are not available the effect will be to limit the supply of labour.

Labour quality is influenced by:

- *Quality of education.* Education plays an important part not only in producing a knowledgeable workforce, but also contributes towards making people more mobile and adaptable to change.
- *Training facilities.* A shortage of workers with particular skills can be overcome by training more of these specialists through the education system or through in-service occupational training.
- *Natural talent.* Some skills are important but are natural talents and cannot be taught, although they may be increased by training, for example acting, drawing or playing a musical instrument.
- *Health.* The standard of health of workers obviously affects their efficiency and productivity. Health is affected not only by living conditions, but also working conditions.

The factor of capital

Capital is the money and all other assets (possessions of value) which are employed in the process of production. Capital includes the buildings, machinery, equipment, stocks and many other things (producer goods) used in making the items we consume (consumer goods).

Capital in this sense takes two basic forms, fixed capital and working capital:

- *Fixed capital* – buildings, machinery and other equipment with a long life which are used many times over in the production of goods and the creation of further wealth.
- *Working capital* – stocks of raw materials, cash, bank balances and other items required for the day-to-day operation of the business and which are continually being used up.

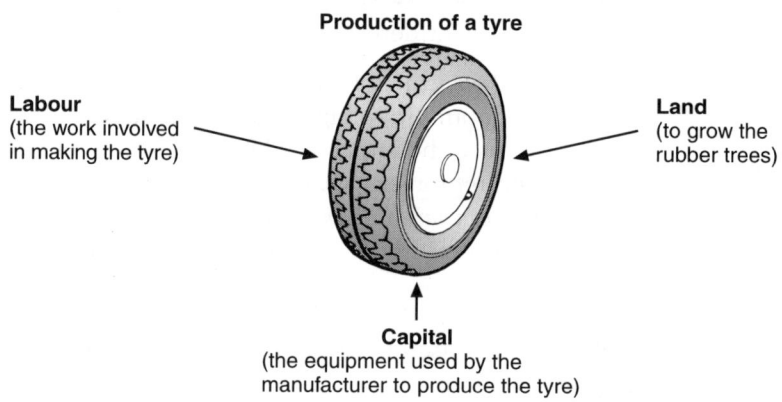

Organisation of Production

The entrepreneur

Some people argue that entrepreneurship can be considered as a fourth factor of production. Entrepreneurs are those who organise and co-ordinate the other factors of production. They are the owners of business enterprises who, by taking risks and making decisions, enable production to be carried out in anticipation of demand. This book is very much concerned with entrepreneurship.

If entrepreneurs successfully predict future demand they are rewarded by a special form of income called *profit*. If, however, their judgement is incorrect they may get no reward or may even make a loss. For example, a shopkeeper may buy stocks of a new brand of confectionery but will have no guarantee of being able to sell them. There would be far fewer businesses in existence if there were not entrepreneurs around willing to take the risks involved.

In order to participate in entrepreneurship the entrepreneur must be willing:

- to raise capital, from savings or by borrowing, necessary for investment in the business;
- to organise the various levels of labour required;
- to define and clarify business policy decisions so that all levels of personnel can understand what the firm is trying to achieve.
- to make any changes necessary in the interests of the growth and development of the business.

Can you identify the factors of production in this photograph?

2.3 Methods of production

There are three basic methods of production:

1 *Job production* (also referred to as *unit production*) refers to the process of making a single item from start to finish, usually in response to a customer's specific requirements and specifications (e.g. custom-made furniture, fitted kitchens, etc.).
2 *Batch production* involves producing groups of similar products in batches, sometimes on a production line (e.g. various flavours of soft drinks). One batch is completed before commencing the next.
3 *Flow production* (also referred to as *mass* or *flow-line production*) involves the continuous production of a large number of products on a production line. Where the product involved is in liquid or other continuous form (e.g. oil, paint, plastic, chemicals, bread), the mass production is sometimes referred to as *continuous-flow* or *process* production.

Choice of method of production

The method of production a company chooses will depend on the product, or the way in which the orders are received from customers. Where the order is for a single unique product, incorporating the customer's specification (e.g. fitted furniture, tailor-made clothing, building projects), job production will be employed. With orders for products with clear similarities (e.g. bread, cakes, biscuits, etc) from different customers, and which are likely to be repeated, the batch method will be used. Mass production will be used when very large quantities are required continuously (e.g. bottles, books, televisions, refrigerators, computers etc).

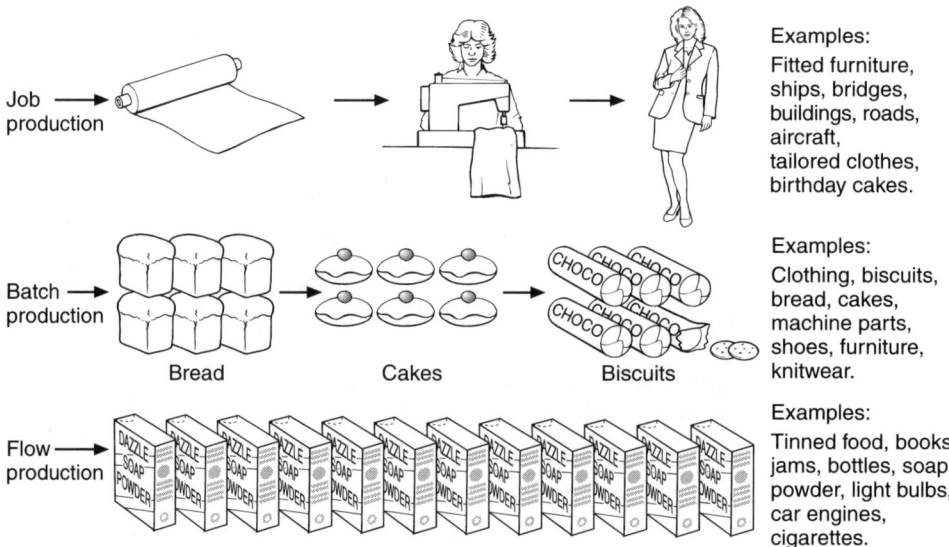

Examples of products created by the different methods of production.

Organisation of Production

Quality control

The process of ensuring that the products a company sells meets the standard the firm has set, is called *quality control*. The personnel involved in checking that such standards are being met are called *quality controllers* or *qualilty inspectors*. They may check products as they leave a production line, sometimes on a *random sampling* system. Sometimes a sample of a product will be tested to destruction to assess the life expectancy of it. *Statistical process control* is a method of quality control, whereby a machine operator checks a machine at regular intervals, to ensure that it is working correctly.

2.4 Location of business

A major decision that all firms have to take is where to site their premises. A variety of factors will influence this decision, including the size of the organisation and the expected scale of its operations, but most choices of site are a compromise between several advantages and disadvantages. The summary chart on page 30 shows the main influencing factors.

Government influence on business location

Governments can play a particularly important part in influencing where a firm sites its premises and it is worthwhile looking in greater depth at the reasons why, and how, they do so.

The main reasons the government may wish to influence the location of industry is to improve the regional balance of employment, in other words to draw production into regions of high unemployment and areas where industry has declined. Such areas are sometimes referred to as 'depressed' or 'problem regions'. These can be distinguished by the following:

- unemployment rate higher than national average;
- average income of residents is below the national average;
- large numbers of workers are leaving the area;
- workforce generally retains outdated skills;
- there is less industry than in other regions;
- factories, housing, hospitals, roads, etc., are generally outdated.

The ways in which the government can influence the location of industry include offering grants, subsidies, relief from taxes or prohibiting industrial development in other areas.

Regional development grants

Over the years the government has created areas where grants are available as incentives to businesses. Currently these are defined in the following way:

INFLUENCES ON LOCATION OF BUSINESS

INDUSTRIAL INERTIA Sometimes firms stay at a particular site even though the original reason for siting in that area (e.g. near source of raw materials) no longer applies.

RAW MATERIALS Closeness to raw materials or to the port where they enter the country may influence choice of site.

TRANSPORT ACCESS Siting near to good road, rail, sea or air links can save in distribution costs or in the movement of raw materials.

LAND Availability of sufficient suitable land, at an economically viable price, in a suitable position will attract business.

MARKET PULL Businesses are attracted to sites close to where potential customers can be found; shops near where shoppers will be, hotels near tourist areas.

LABOUR Availability of suitable labour with a good no strike record. This will be influenced by availability of social amenities such as housing and medical facilities.

GOVERNMENT INFLUENCE Some governments try to influence the location of businesses, e.g. to improve regional balance, to reduce overcrowding in cities and towns.

ENVIRONMENT Climatic conditions are important to some businesses, particularly those involved in agricultural products.

FUEL OR POWER Closeness to fuel or power are less important today than in the past, but some firms still need to locate near to sources such as water.

LINKAGE INDUSTRIES Firms will locate near other businesses on which they depend, or near to other firms in a similar line of business.

Organisation of Production

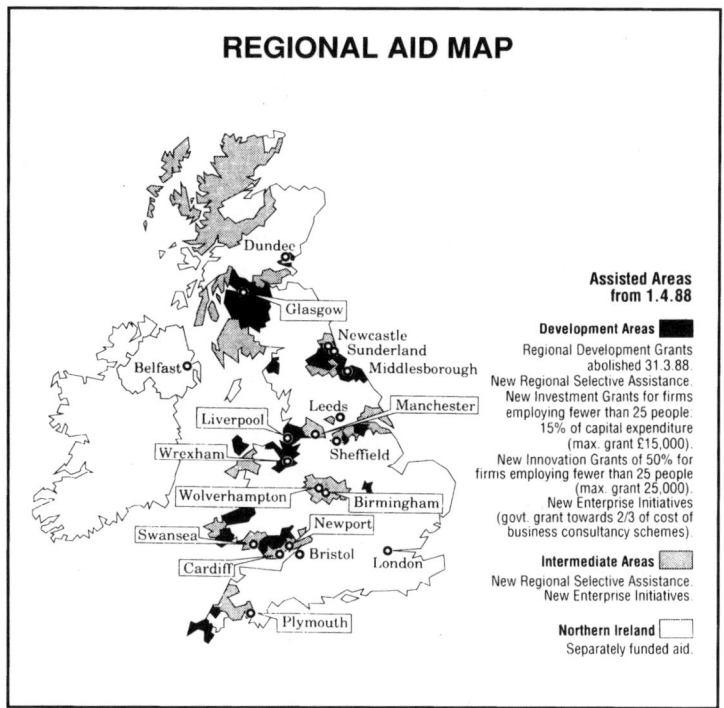

Development areas
These are areas of high unemployment and declining basic industries. Grants are available to firms to contribute to new buildings and the creation of new jobs. The grants are particularly for manufacturing industry, although some service industries also qualify.

Intermediate areas
These are areas where unemployment is high, but not as high as in development areas. Often there are indications that unemployment is increasing. The grant in an intermediate area will vary with the type of project but can include cheap rents on government-built factories and training grants for workers.

Enterprise zones
These are small geographical areas where businesses of all types are encouraged to locate or expand. Enterprise zones are particularly identified in run-down inner city areas where economic decay is particularly problematic. These areas offer incentives such as:

- rate free accommodation (ten years);
- tax advantages to firms locating in zones;
- simplified planning procedures.

In addition to the foregoing government policies, local authorities also spend considerable funds encouraging businesses to locate in their areas, and back this up with local incentive schemes.

2.5 Business size

What is large?

It is generally accepted that a large business has certain advantages over a small one (these are examined later in this chapter), but deciding whether a firm is large or small is not as simple as it appears at first sight. How do we measure the size of a firm?

The physical size of the business, e.g. how much area its premises cover or how many branches it has, can be an indicator. Another measure could be the number of people that are employed. But these tell us little about the profitability of the business, which is an important factor. However, large businesses do not always make big profits – some make very big losses.

The total value of all the assets being used by a business (the capital employed) is a good measure of the size of a business because it is through this that a firm creates its profits. But even this can be deceiving because a factory located in a busy city is generally of higher value than the same size property in a rural area.

It is generally recognised that a combination of factors needs to be taken into account in deciding whether a business is large or small. The turnover of the business is one of the most useful measures of business size because this generally indicates how 'busy' the firm is. When turnover is combined with other factors such as the value of assets owned and the number of people employed we end up with a pretty reliable measure of the size of a business.

Economies of scale

The producer has to decide how to use the factors of production to the best advantage, because the chances of making a good profit depend upon how effectively the factors are employed. The entrepreneur also has to decide on what scale to produce and what size of business to operate, because the size of the business and the scale of production can also influence profitability. These decisions have to be taken by all entrepreneurs. Obviously, the entrepreneur should aim for the scale of production which yields the greatest profit margin.

Large businesses tend to dominate certain industries because their size gives them advantages over smaller organisations. For example, by producing larger quantities they can reduce their production costs. These advantages of size are called *economies of scale*. Sometimes business growth results in disadvantages; when this occurs they are referred to as *diseconomies of scale*. You should realise that there can be advantages to a business remaining small as well as advantages to being large.

In addition to large-scale and small-scale economies of scale, there are external and internal economies of scale. *External economies of scale* refer to the benefits gained by all of a certain industry, or the whole of society. For example, a particular invention may result in benefits to all firms in an industry, or to the whole of society. Internal economies of scale refer to the benefits gained by one particular industry. Internal economies of scale can be grouped into four categories:

1 technical
2 managerial
3 marketing
4 financial.

Technical economies of scale

Greater size allows more opportunities for division of labour, the use of machinery and automation, and other methods of increasing efficiency. It also allows a company to allocate more resources to research and development, which can result in further economies through increased efficiency and effectiveness.

As a firm increases its output and employs more workers there are more opportunities to divide work into stages and, consequently, workers become more efficient in their work. Dividing the work into stages in this way also makes it easier to introduce machinery and other labour-saving equipment.

Managerial economies of scale

Larger firms are able to employ more highly skilled personnel. Such employees will be attracted to the company not only by the higher salaries offered but also by the prestige of a larger organisation and greater scope for advancement.

The employment of skilled specialists in charge of functions such as design and production results in the advantages of division of labour. Small firms often do not have sufficient work to enable them to form separate specialist departments and, therefore, managers have to undertake a variety of tasks which makes them less effective.

Marketing economies of scale

Larger firm can purchase their supplies in bigger quantities than small firms. They can also engage in mass production and they save in advertising and distribution costs. The important result of these advantages are that such firms can market their goods more cheaply than smaller competitors, and obviously consumers will be more likely to give their custom to such firms.

Most firms see public relations as an important part of their marketing strategies, because if potential customers regard the reputation of the company as 'good' they will be more likely to want to give their custom to the firm. Large businesses are in a better position to sponsor sports and public events and offer attractive prize-giving competitions, thus promoting good public relations.

Financial economies of scale

A major advantage of being a large firm is that, because they own more assets, they find it easier to borrow money and they are more able to withstand the financial pressures (e.g. of cash flow) than smaller businesses.

Banks and other lending institutions feel safer in loaning money to large companies because they feel there is less risk involved. Similarly, creditors (e.g. suppliers) feel more confident to give trade credit to larger firms than smaller ones.

Large businesses

It is generally the case that larger firms achieve bigger profits because they enjoy 'economies of scale'. That is, the cost per item falls as output increases. However, *diseconomies* of scale can also occur and these are reflected by unit costs increasing as output increases. Both of these possibilities can be examined by looking at the advantages and disadvantages of large-scale business.

Advantages of large businesses
- They find it easier to raise large amounts of capital.
- More capital is available for:
  - extensive advertising
  - research and development
  - employing specialist personnel
  - labour-saving machinery.
- Mass production allows greater possibilities of specialisation.
- They can obtain special prices and discounts.

The advantages of large businesses summarised in this list refer only to *internal* economies of scale, but there are also *external* economies of scale.

Sometimes many related businesses in a particular industry are located in one area. This will encourage the provision of skilled maintenance and other backup services such as training facilities which benefit all members of the industry. In addition, all firms engaged in a particular industry may combine together for the purposes of advertising, research or technical developments. Groups of industries will also attract good transport facilities, or special treatment from banks and other financial institutions.

Disadvantages of large businesses
- Can become too complex to manage.
- Lines of internal communication and management become unwieldy.
- Customers may find the large organisation too impersonal.
- Mass production can lead to boredom for workers and reduce quality.
- Workers find it easier to organise restrictive working practices.

The law of diminishing returns

A firm cannot continue to grow indefinitely unless some factors change. If you continue to blow up a balloon it will eventually burst because the fixed factor (the balloon) cannot contain the varying factor (the added air). The same principle applies to a growing business. If the fixed factor is factory space and the firm continues to add more workers, initially there will be more production, but eventually additional workers will result in less output per person as too many workers in a restricted space get in each other's way.

As a firm grows, it is subject to the law of diminishing returns. When a firm is growing rapidly it experiences increased returns and rising profits. But there is a point in any productive organisation when diminishing returns will begin to operate. The additional output (marginal output) achieved as a result of the addition of a unit of labour begins to fall, therefore the average output also falls. We can illustrate this by means of a table as shown below.

Units of workers	Total output	Marginal output	Average output
1	5	5	5
2	18	13	9
3	30	12	10
4	36	6	9
5	35	−1	7

Small businesses

In spite of the benefits of large-scale operations small firms continue to exist because they have their own special advantages, and in some cases (e.g. direct services such as hairdressing) do not lend themselves to large-scale operations.

Generally there is only limited management structure in small businesses and often the only management will be the owner(s) of the firm. This has its advantages in that there is less need for consultation when making decisions because the manager or owner performs all the important functions. But this person also requires a wider range of management skills than this counterpart in a large organisation.

Advantages of small businesses
- Closer communication exists between employees.
- Easier to have good working relationships.
- Employees feel a personal involvement in the business.
- There is more personal contact between employees and customers.

Disadvantages of small businesses
- Limitation on capital for expansion.
- Are not in a position to take advantage of the benefits of the economies of scale available to larger organisations.
- Cannot employ specialist workers such as accountants and information technology experts.
- Product development, market research and other important activities cannot be financed.

2.6 Technological change

The previous section of this chapter included an examination of economies of scale. One aspect of this was technical economies. What we said was that the large size of some businesses enables them to use labour-saving machinery and automation. We will now look at this in more detail.

Automation refers to the use of sophisticated machinery which is electronically or computer controlled to carry out some form of production with the minimum of human intervention.

Demand for material goods has increased dramatically throughout the world, and many of these commodities are more sophisticated that ever before. The profit available to those who can produce goods and services most economically has always required businesses to look for the most economic way to meet this demand.

The most dramatic development that has assisted this has been the relatively recent innovation and application of the silicon chip which has put computer technology within the reach of small businesses and even individuals.

Technological change: use of microchip in control panel of washing machine.
(Copyright: Hotpoint)

Computers

Computers have had an important effect on businesses. A computer is an electronic information processing machine. It can handle databases and spreadsheets as well as operate as a word processor.

A computer can accept data from a user (input), supply information to a user (output), sort, select, store and retrieve information and do calculations (process). The text or data may be in words or numbers. Computers operate on instructions (called a program) input by the operator.

A computer consists of the following main unit parts:

- *Keyboard* – an electronic keyboard used to feed information into the system.
- *Visual display unit (VDU)* – a television-like screen (monitor) used to display text prior to printing.
- *Central processing unit (CPU)* – sometimes called the computer's brain. It is the main part of the computer where the data is processed and the entire system is co-ordinated.
- *Memory system* – all computers have at least some internal memory, but this can be extended for long-term storage by recording data onto magnetic disks.
- *Disk drive* – a device that is used to feed in extended memory from disks.
- *Mouse* – some computers have a device such as this. It is a hand-held device that is used to move an icon (graphic image) across the screen. The mouse usually has two or three buttons which are used to select objects on the screen. The action is known as 'clicking'.
- *Printer* – used to print out final text (hard copy).

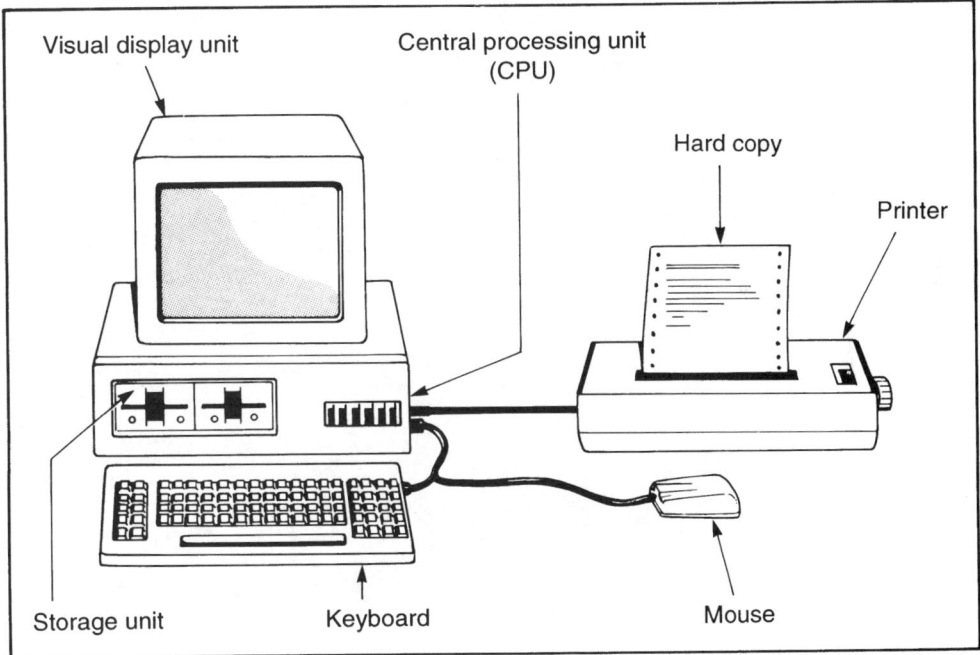

A computer system.

Computers in business

The following are just some of the ways in which computers are increasingly being used in business operations.

- *Company registers.* A company's register of shareholders is constantly changing as its shares are bought and sold, and the current holders of the shares have to be paid their share of the company's profits. The register of shareholders can be kept in the computer system and rapidly updated.
- *Stock records.* Records can be automatically updated as stocks are removed from the warehouse or from the display shelves and recorded out through the tills. The computer can automatically issue a warning when stocks fall too low, and a valuation of stock is also immediately available.
- *Accounts.* Invoices and statements of account may be issued and records of customers' accounts maintained.
- *Payroll.* The maintenance of a company's wages system can be operated by computer, including automatic deduction of income tax etc.
- *Banking.* Banks use computers for automatic cheque clearing, keeping branch records, issuing bank statements and standing order payments, and the operation of cash dispenser systems. They also use computers for immediate updating of customer accounts when deposits and withdrawals are made.
- *Word processing.* Computers can be used as word processors. Copies of letters, invoices, statements of account and other important paperwork can be keyed

Use of robots in car production.
(Photo courtesy of Ford of Britain)

Organisation of Production

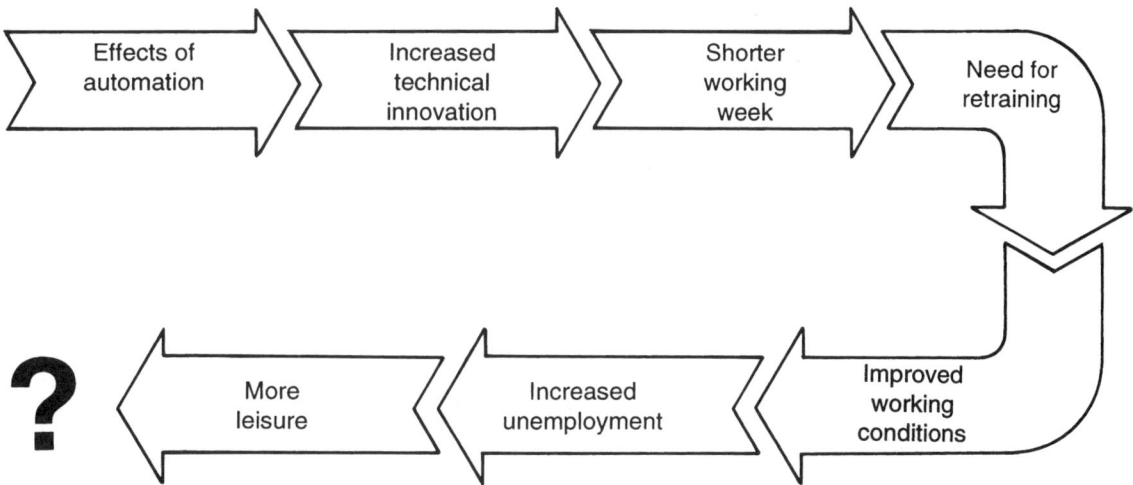

Some effects of automation. What next?

into a computer and stored for later retrieval for review on a VDU or by print-out.
- *Production line applications*. Many machines in factories are used to perform repetitive tasks and, therefore, there has been an increasing use of computers to perform these tasks, e.g. automated robotic welding.

The effects of the increased use of technology in production can be summed up as follows:

- Increased standardisation of production results in increased output and reduced costs.
- Business risk is increased because sophisticated, expensive machinery must be purchased well in advance of the sale of products.
- Often results in workforce being made unemployed.
- Leisure time can be increased by a reduced working week and a lower retirement age.
- The need for tertiary services is considerably increased.

2.7 Activities

1. What is meant by the term production?
2. Name the three primary needs.
3. In your own words explain the difference between 'needs' and 'wants'.
4. What is the aim of production?

5. Briefly describe the three levels of production.
6. Give examples of how the different levels of production can be seen in countries at different stages of development.
7. Describe separate circumstances when job, batch or flow production would be most appropriate.
8. Give a brief description of each of the four factors of production.
9. Describe some of the factors that affect the supply and quality of labour.
10. Define capital.
11. Explain the difference between fixed capital and working capital.
12. To what extent would you agree that the entrepreneur can be considered a factor of production?
13. Describe the three main methods of production.
14. Why is quality control an important aspect of production?
15. What is research and development?
16. What is 'just in time' manufacturing? Briefly describe the advantages and disadvantages of this aspect of production.
17. Give an account of what you consider are the main influences on the location of businesses.
18. What special contribution can the government make to the location of businesses? Why would the government want to contribute?
19. What factors can be reliably used to decide whether a firm is large or small?
20. What do you understand by the term 'economies of scale'? Why do 'diseconomies' also occur?
21. Briefly describe the various forms of economies of scale.
22. What are the advantages enjoyed by large firms? Why do large organisations also have disadvantages?
23. Briefly explain the difference between internal and external economies of scale.
24. In what way does the law of diminishing returns show the limits of large-scale production?
25. Why do small firms continue to exist even though large organisations have many advantages?
26. Why do you think some people are apprehensive about technological change?

Organisation of Production

27 Word processors are making considerable impact on office work. What is a word processor? Briefly describe the functions of the main parts of a word processor system.

28 In what ways are the functions of a computer wider than those of a word processor?

29 Describe four examples of the use of computers, including at least one application to office work and one related to production.

30 Define automation. What are the possible results of automation?

Structured Questions

1 Look at this photograph taken in a chocolate factory and answer the questions that follow it.

(a) In what way is secondary production illustrated here? (1)
(b) Name two factors of production that can be identified in the photograph. (2)
(c) The system of production illustrated is called 'division of labour by process'.
  • Explain what is meant by 'division of labour by process'. (2)
  • Describe one example of this process that operates within your school or college. (2)

(d) Many firms have introduced new technology into their production process, and increased the productivity of their workforce.
- Define the terms 'new technology' and 'productivity'. (2)
- State two costs and two benefits new technology can bring to a workforce. (4)

(e) One of the possible disadvantages of division of labour by process is that it can result in alienation of the workforce. What do we mean by 'alienation' and what methods might a firm use to combat it? (7)

2 The data below is used by Peterborough Development Corporation to encourage businesses to locate in its industrial areas. Answer the questions that follow the data.

British Sugar – one of Europe's largest sugar companies – moved its national headquarters from London to Peterborough in 1974.

Three hundred staff were employed as the central offices opened alongside the company's existing Peterborough factory.

Since then the number of headquarters staff has almost doubled through the emergence of Silver Spoon as a national brand leader.

A further 235 people are employed in the factory (part of a network of sugar manufacturing plants in East Anglia and the West Midlands) and this rises to about 350 during the annual autumn sugar making season.

British Sugar's Managing Director, Mr Gordon Percival, said: "From Peterborough we control the operations of all our factories and co-ordinate supply and delivery of more than one million tonnes of sugar and more than 600,000 tonnes of animal feed every year.

"We have never looked back from the days when we moved from cramped and expensive headquarters in London.

"In Peterborough the company and its workforce have prospered to the extent that sales have doubled in the last ten years to make our Silver Spoon brand the retail brand leader and largest of all grocery brands in the UK.

"In 1984, the company relaunched its range of sugars with new pack designs in an extensive advertising and promotion campaign which highlighted speciality sugars. We are continuing to invest heavily in further product development".

Mr Percival said that Peterborough, with its excellent road and rail network, housebuilding programme, leisure facilities, growth prospects and a good available workforce, was an ideal location for the company.

The company describes its locally-recruited employees as 'hard-working and dedicated professionals'.

Location of British Sugar. (Courtesy of Peterborough Development Corporation)

(a) Give one reason why British Sugar moved from London to Peterborough. (1)

(b) Why has British Sugar been able to double its headquarters staff? (1)

Organisation of Production

    (c) How could the data shown here help Peterborough Development Corporation encourage businesses other than British Sugar to move into the area? (2)

    (d) Give two reasons why both British Sugar and its workforce have prospered at Peterborough? (2)

    (e) Why would British Sugar be likely to need larger premises than a producer of computer software? (2)

    (f) What advantages might there be of siting the central offices alongside the company's factory? What disadvantages could there be? (3)

    (g) In siting its business in Peterborough British Sugar would consider the provision of local facilities such as housing, schools and transport. Why would it consider these important? (3)

    (h) Take the area in which you live and design an advertisement that aims to attract businesses to locate in your area. The advertisement must clearly identify the benefits that would appeal to firms considering relocation or setting up initially in your locality. Give reasons why you feel your advertisement could prove effective in the long-term. (6)

3 The following questions are all related to the use of bar codes in businesses which are shown on page 44.

    (a) What is a bar code? (1)

    (b) How does a computer 'read' a bar code? (2)

    (c) In what way does a bar code help a supermarket to easily provide a customer with an itemised bill? (2)

    (d) How could a supermarket use its bar code system to update its stock records? What would be the main advantage of doing this? (3)

    (e) Describe two examples of the ways that a supermarket would use data collected from bar codes for 'sales analysis'. (4)

    (f) Libraries combine bar codes on books and on membership cards to control the issue and return of books. Describe in detail how a business offering the hire of video cassettes could usefully operate a similar system and what the benefits would be compared to a manual system. (8)

4 Look at the diagram on page 45 of a computer system. If consists of the following parts: mouse, VDU, processor, keyboard.

    (a) What do the letters VDU stand for? (1)

    (b) List the names of each of the four parts of the system shown and beside each give the identifying letter A, B, C and D shown in the diagram. (2)

    (c) Describe the function of any three of the items of equipment contained in your list in Part (b) above. (3)

Comprehensive Business Studies

The bar code reader reads the following code into the computer

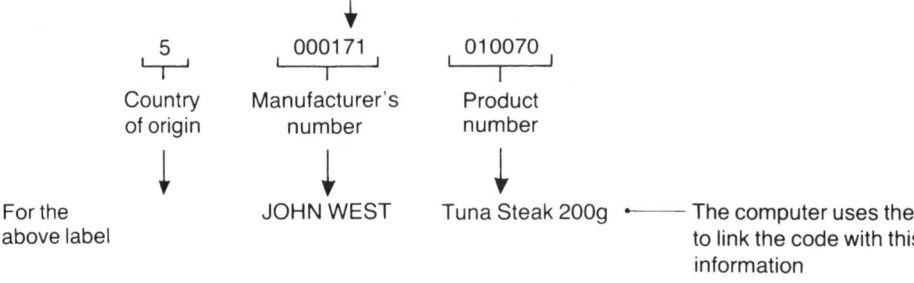

Bar codes and supermarkets.

Bar codes were introduced:
- *to record which goods have been sold*
- *to speed up customers checking out at the tills*
- *to replace price labelling of goods.*

They also provide:
- *the customer with an itemised bill*
- *the supermarket with accounts*
- *the supermarket with data for sales analysis.*

This illustration is referred to in Question 3 on page 43

Organisation of Production

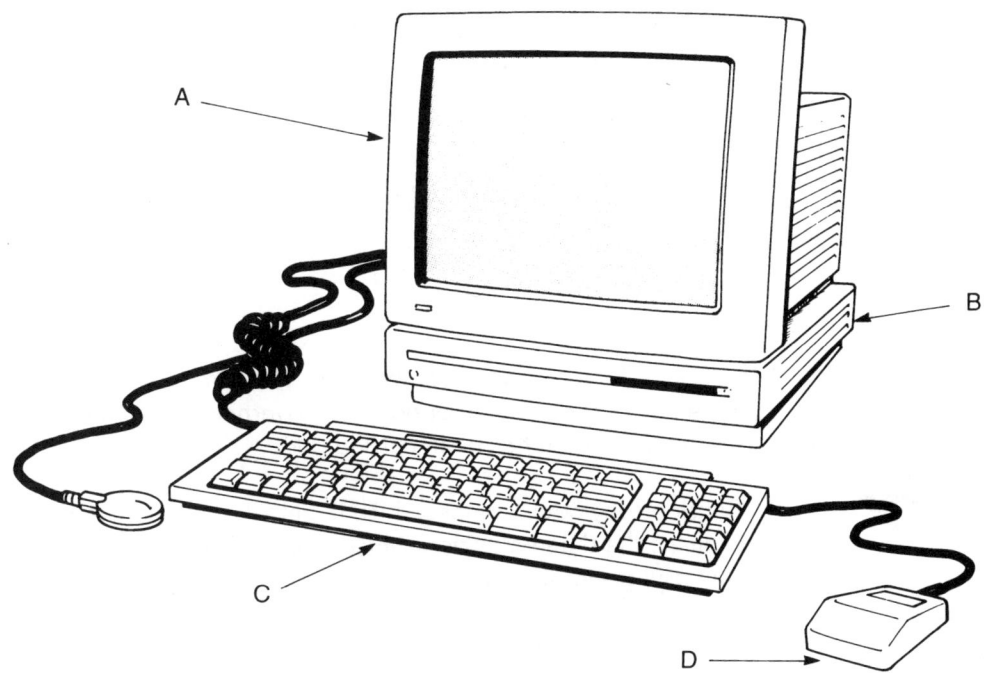

(d) *Hardware* is the name given to any device which is part of a computer system, e.g. VDU, mouse, processor. *Software* is the term given to the programs that are used on the computer. They are stored on either a floppy disk, hard disk or on a network fileserver.

Complete a table similar to the one below placing the software and hardware terms listed in the correct column:
- laser printer
- personnel records
- keyboard
- customer accounts
- bar code reader
- address file
- graphics scanner
- spreadsheet.

Hardware	Software

(4)

(e) The six main areas of computer software are:
   (i)   word processing   (iv) graphics
   (ii) control   (v) desk top publishing
   (iii) databases   (vi) spreadsheets.
   Choose any fine of these aspects of computer applications and for
   each describe a different specific business application. (10)

Research Assignments

1 Consider the extent to which the siting of businesses in your area can be seen to be influenced by local or national government. Provide evidence to show personal research has been carried out.

2 Consider any new business which might wish to locate in your area and examine the different factors which would help them to choose between two contrasting sites that you have personally investigated.

3 Take any vacant business premises in your locality and put forward rational arguments for starting a new type of business in those premises.

4 Use a relatively local map to illustrate the main area of location of primary, secondary and tertiary production. Make observations on the reasons for site choice in each case.

5 Your school art department has decided to start a mini-enterprise which will produce ornamental pottery for marketing locally. A local bank has offered to finance the rent of a small shop in the town, if it is not too expensive. What are the cheapest but most practicable premises you can identify? Give reasons for your choice.

6 Investigate two contrasting businesses in your locality that are involved in manufacturing. Make a comparison of the extent to which they use information technology in their production processes.

7 Produce personal research evidence that proves at least two businesses you have personally investigated achieve 'technical economies of scale'.

8 Choose a vacant business premises in your local area. What type of business would you recommend being opened on the site? Give reasons for your answer.

3. Business Organisation

3.1 The role and functions of a business

Business aims and objectives

A *business aim* is the overall goal the business is trying to achieve. It is the broad general direction in which the business is heading. A business can have several aims. For example, a business might want to:

- increase its share of the market
- increase its profits
- reduce its production costs.

A business will also have objectives. *Objectives* are shorter-term goals or specific targets that a business uses to help it achieve its aims. Objectives give direction to the firm's organisation and its operations. They can be used to assess how effectively the business is operating. For example, if a company aims to reduce its operating costs through an objective of increased use of technology, it can be judged in due course how close it came to achieving its aim. If operational costs have not been achieved it may be decided that the purchase of new equipment was not justified.

The main aim of any business is to make profits in order to give the best possible return to the owners for the money they have invested in the company. Businesses achieve this aim mainly through their major functional areas of production, finance, marketing and personnel.

Production

The broad function of production is to satisfy human wants. In order to do this through the production of goods and services the firm will have to co-ordinate:

- the purchase of stocks and raw materials;
- the design of goods;
- research, development and experimental work;
- the manufacture of the company's products;
- control of the quality of production;
- storage of the raw materials and finished goods.

We can see this reflected in the production of furniture. The firm may design prototype furniture from raw materials it has purchased. It will research the market to investigate the best ways to market such items. This research will also reveal what need there may be to amend the design of the prototypes, and to produce samples to show prospective customers and obtain orders. Only then will full-scale production take place, during which quality control will be maintained to ensure that what is produced is of the required standard, and workers called *progress chasers* will make sure that goods are produced within the timescale required. The finished products will then be stored until they are required for the intended market. Chapters 8 to 11 give further details on marketing.

Finance

Finance is required to form a business and to fund its operations. It is required, for example, to purchase plant and machinery, raw materials, and to pay wages to workers. A business also needs finance to meet day-to-day running expenses and maintenance costs.

There are four main sources of business finance (also called capital): (a) savings of the entrepreneur(s); (b) capital borrowed from a bank or some other financial institution; (c) capital raised by the sale of shares in the business; (d) profits of the business reinvested ('ploughed back' or 'retained').

The finance of business is examined in more detail in Chapters 15, 16 and 17.

Marketing

The marketing function of a business aims to anticipate consumer demand in order that the right products are manufactured. Once the commodities have been produced it is then the function of marketing to promote sales to the consumer. Marketing is not confined to goods alone; labour, capital, land and buildings must also be marketed as well as the many services that are needed. Chapters 8 to 11 examine marketing in detail.

Personnel

The personnel function of a business is concerned with recruitment, selection, training and welfare of employees. Theoretically, the more businesses that exist, and the more successful they are, the greater is the number of personnel needed. However, in reality the provision of employment is far more complex than this simple view. For example, technological developments which lead to increased efficiency and business growth can also result in a reduction of the number of employees needed in a particular industry.

The integration of the two broad technologies of computers and telecommunications has led to increased efficiency and business growth. The revolution in electronics has transformed many of the traditional areas of employment. For example, many of the functions of office workers have been by-passed by computers and word processors; methods of communication have rapidly changed with telecommunication making an even greater contribution. And the automated factory is now becoming more commonplace.

Part of the personnel function of business is the management of these aspects of the business: to recruit people with appropriate skills, care for their welfare, and ensure that where necessary in-service training is provided to update their skills. The personnel function is examined in Chapters 5, 6 and 7.

Business Organisation

Management

Responsibilities of management

The foregoing functional areas of a business have to be co-ordinated and managed to ensure that the resources of the business are used to the best advantage.

All members of an organisation have some responsibility, even if it is only to

PRODUCTION

FINANCE

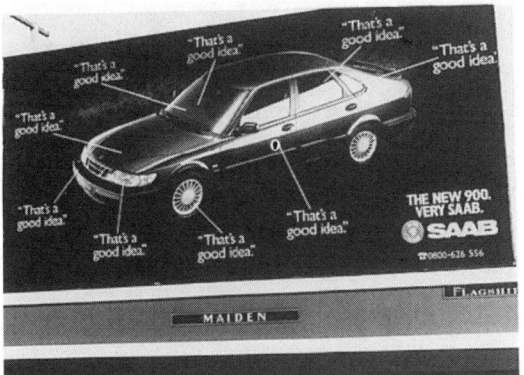

MARKETING

PERSONNEL

The functional areas of a business

have regard for their own safety and that of their work colleagues. But the higher in the hierarchy of the organisation that a person is, the greater will be that person's responsibility. Consequently, the greater degree of responsibility lies with the managers of an organisation, whether they are managing directors, or managers of departments. Managers in this respect are those who have the responsibility to direct, control and co-ordinate others.

The management of an organisation are responsible to the firm's:

- *owners* – to achieve the best possible return for the capital they have invested and to re-invest or 'plough back' sufficient capital in order to ensure sound future growth and development of the business;
- *customers* – to provide goods or services of good quality, within the agreed period of time, and at a fair and economic price;
- *employees* – to provide the safest and most comfortable working conditions possible, to pay a fair wage and to secure future employment as far as possible.

The management also have some responsibility to the government, and to society. The responsibility to the government is to ensure that the company abides by the law, and behaves in a manner that is compatible with the country's trading practices both at home and overseas. The responsibility to society is to ensure that the firm's operations do not cause harm to the general public, e.g. through being environmentally aware.

In order to meet these responsibilities the management must organise and co-ordinate the work of others. The manager will, therefore, at times be required to:

- appoint and train new staff;
- communicate company policy;
- give instructions and set tasks;
- assess performance;
- discipline and dismiss staff.

Superiors are expected to be responsible for the actions of their subordinates. Although they can delegate the power or authority to carry out tasks to subordinates, the responsibility for actions cannot be delegated and ultimate responsibility always remains with the manager.

Management functions

The functions of management can be grouped into six areas:

1 *Planning*. This involves methodically looking ahead, making decisions, and formulating policy on the intentions and objectives of the organisation and the methods to be used to achieve these objectives. It assists the efficient utilisation of the firm's resources and it emphasises preventative rather than corrective measures.
2 *Direction*. This involves giving instructions to workers so that they are clear as to how their work should be done to best benefit the organisation.
3 *Delegating*. This involves assigning tasks or goals to subordinates while at the same time granting them the necessary authority to carry out those tasks. The

subordinates must recognise their responsibility and accept their accountability for the expected performance.
4 *Controlling*. This involves supervising and checking the activities and performance of subordinates to ensure that instructions are being carried out properly and plans and methods are being followed.
5 *Organising*. This involves ensuring that workers can get on with their jobs by making sure that people, materials and machinery are available in the right place at the right time. Good organisation involves planning of what is to be done, who is to supervise it, time frames and the most efficient method of doing it.
6 *Co-ordinating*. This involves directing and integrating the activities of the team under their direct supervision and contributing to the overall co-ordination of the activities within the organisation in order to form a united strategy of operations to achieve the organisation's objectives.
7 *Motivating*. This involves encouraging other members of the organisation to carry out their tasks properly and effectively. Although extrinsic incentives such as wages help to motivate people, the ability to motivate others is very much dependent upon leadership qualities which are discussed later. Intrinsic incentives such as job enlargement and job satisfaction also help to motivate people.

The business plan

The management of a business is helped in achieving the firm's objectives by the business plan. This is an explanation of what the business is intending to do (its aims) and how it is going to achieve its aims (through its objectives). A business plan is often presented to a bank or some other financial institution when the business is applying for a loan. The business plan is also important in helping the owners or managers to clarify what they are trying to achieve. In due course it can also be referred to in order to assess how successful the business has been in achieving its aims and objectives.

The business plan will state the aims and objectives of the business, and it will explain how these are to be achieved. The business plan will state:

- what the business intends to make or sell
- who the intended customers are
- the way customers will learn about what is being sold
- how much will be charged for the product or service
- in what ways competitors will be beaten
- how the business will be financed and cash flow maintained
- in what ways the business is expected to develop and grow.

Leadership

People who are in a supervisory position in business need to have some understanding of group dynamics, that is the way that people interact in a group situation. The extent to which people work effectively (or not) together affects the overall success potential of the business. In the business sense there are four basic elements of group behaviour: the group, an objective, the individual and the leader.

The group

Groups can be divided into two categories:

1 *Informal groups* have usually come together voluntarily (e.g. a music group) and the purpose of the group is not defined too specifically. There are no set rules (although an informal group may have an objective, e.g. to raise money for charity) and the leader will be chosen by the members of the group. Informal groups just develop because those involved recognise they have some common interest, e.g. interest in a particular sport.
2 *Formal groups* are usually created for a specific purpose, e.g. a department in a firm. This type of group has a formal structure, a specific objective, and an appointed leader. In fact, the leader may be the one who chooses the members of the group, and consequently enjoys the power of authority. People in businesses and factories generally work in formal groups, with expected standards of production and behaviour.

An objective

Because most groups in business are formal ones they required a clear objective, e.g. to formulate a marketing campaign for a new product. Unless the objectives are clearly defined (i.e. by the leader) the group will lose direction; the objective will be liable to be misinterpreted.

The individual

Even though they are part of a group each person still has to work as an individual in order to make their contribution to the group objective. However, this can result in a problem if the views of the individual or their attitude or behaviour are not in harmony with the rest of the group. Under such circumstances the importance of the objective may be sufficient to solve the conflict. Alternatively, it may be the skill of the group leader that will be the deciding factor.

The leader

Whereas the leader of an informal group may be chosen by the group members, with formal groups the leader is often appointed, e.g. managers, chairperson, etc. In this position the leader may have the power to regulate the group behaviour (e.g. in a position to be able to direct someone to do something), but to use their authority in this way may adversely affect the group morale and attitudes. For this reason a good leader will try to identify the parameters within which the group can operate, often delegating some responsibility to members of the group.

The main function of the leader in a business is to ensure that the group works effectively and carries out the tasks assigned to it. It is often the case in formal groups that it is part of the leader's role to supervise the work of individuals and make recommendations to superiors. In informal groups. however, the leader may be the reason why the individual has chosen to join the group. Whilst the latter is an example of group harmony it can also be a source of discontent when some individuals see themselves as alternative leaders.

Earlier in this chapter we saw that it is important that workers feel motivated. Wages are often assumed to be a motivating factor, but an unlimited amount of capital to provide wages cannot be guaranteed, and wages alone are limited in the extent to which they can be relied upon to encourage people to work hard and effectively.

The success of management and the ability to motivate others very much depend upon the ability to lead. But leadership qualities are difficult to identify and to define, firstly because they depend on the manager's own attitude towards the responsibilities delegated to him or her and to his or her subordinates. Secondly, the ability to lead is considerably influenced by the attitude of the manager towards the problems of his or her subordinates. Thirdly, some of the qualities required to lead others differ from one occupation to another.

To be able to motivate others managers must also be inspired. They need to be committed to their organisation and must have interest and pride in the products or services which they produce or sell. Leadership qualities are particularly revealed by the willingness of superiors to listen to, and understand, problems from their subordinates' point of view.

Styles of leadership

There are four basic styles of leadership and a leader may combine any of these:

1 *Authoritarian or autocratic*. Such leaders are the absolute authority on all matters. They decide what to do and, whatever others may think, it is done. It is often the case that this type of leader frequently uses his or her position in authority to exert his or her will over others.

   Such an approach to leadership is often effective, but not necessarily the most efficient. Although work may be completed in the way that the leader has specified, at the same time employee input and innovation is discounted.

2 *Participative or democratic*. The leader will consult with those likely to be affected before making a decision, although the leader will reserve the right not to act on a majority view.

   This style of leadership is popular because it enables workers lower down in the hierarchy to participate in the decision-making process. Consequently, they are more highly motivated and need less supervision.

3 *Laissez-faire or free-rein*. In this style of leadership the leader gives limited directions to workers. They are given general directions on the tasks to be tackled and then left to achieve them in the way they think is best.

   There are circumstances where this type of leadership is appropriate (e.g. where the employee acts in a consultancy capacity), but generally, most employees prefer to work under some degree of authority from a superior.

4 *Charismatic*. A charismatic leader is one who influences and motivates others because he or she has an outstanding personality or character. This type of leader is relatively rare but can be very successful in the extent to which they can motivate others to do things to support them.

Management communication

The success of any organisation is greatly influenced by the participation of all its members in its activities. We have seen earlier in this chapter that managers have an important part to play in co-ordinating and motivating all workers to achieve a common goal. But for all the workers to make a contribution they need to know what goals they are expected to achieve. Experience has shown that people are more committed to involvement in an organisation where they are well-informed of policies, and even more so when they have participated in making decisions.

Good communication is important in involving all members of an organisation in its activities. The most effective management communications require a two-way flow of information – downwards from management and upwards from employees.

Downward communication is initiated by management and is used to inform employees of the company's proposals, policies, decisions and progress. There are two main methods of downward communication, oral and written:

- *oral* – direct command, discussions, meetings, loudspeaker, intercom, closed circuit television, telephone;
- *written* – letters, memoranda, notice-boards, reports, company magazine, hand-books.

Upward communication may be initiated by employees but it is often 'collected' by management. For example, management may well require specific information from employees. This feeds back to management the views, suggestions, pro-

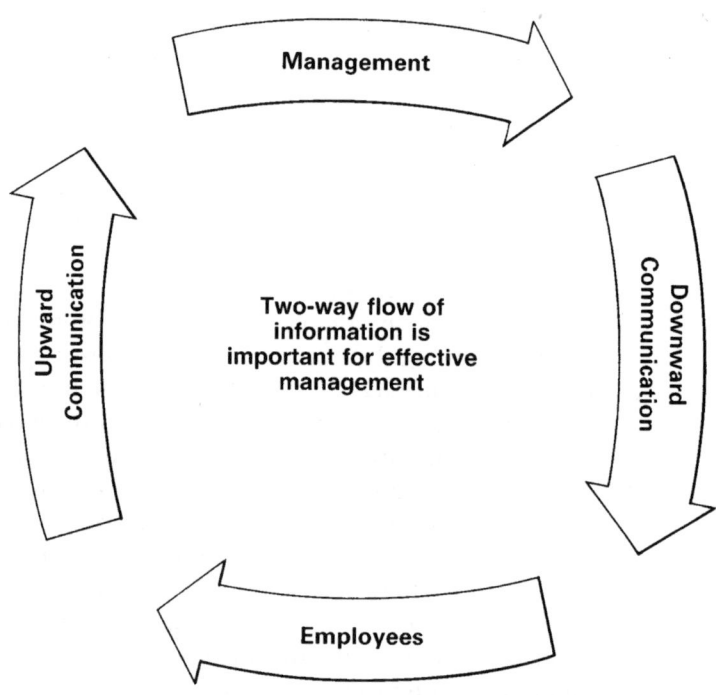

Business Organisation

posals and problems of employees. Upward communication can be 'collected' by direct and indirect methods:

- *direct* – by managers talking to employees and elected representatives;
- *indirect* – suggestion schemes, attitude surveys.

3.3 Small and large businesses

The internal structure of a firm is influenced by its size. The small business is organised fairly simply, whereas the larger company has a more complex structure and more divisions.

Small businesses

Small businesses cannot easily be divided into departments because they do not have the people or floor space to organise in this way. Consequently, workers in small firms tend to specialise less and they are required to have a wider range of skills and a broader knowledge of the way that the business is organised. This is because the workers are required to be able to carry out a wider variety of tasks, whereas in a large organisation they would have more opportunity to specialise in a particular activity. However, the variety of the work in a small organisation is considered to be an advantage by some workers.

Large businesses

Large businesses are generally private or public companies which are dealt with later in Chapter 4. These types of organisation are owned by shareholders. These shareholders elect a board of directors to decide the general policies that the firm will follow. The board of directors will appoint a managing director to supervise

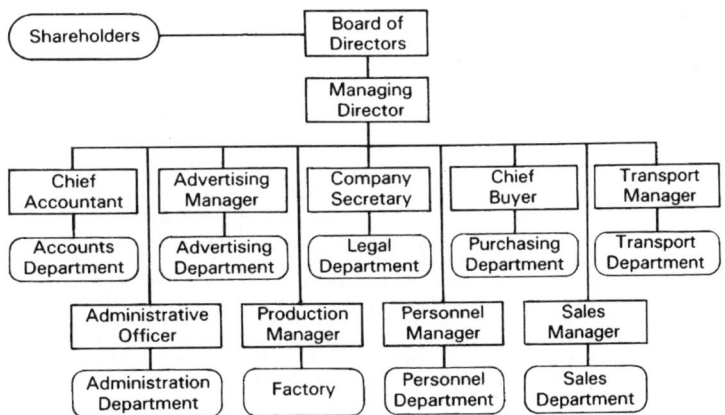

A large business can be divided into separate departments, each with its own manager and internal structure.

Comprehensive Business Studies

ACCOUNTS
Records all payments in and out of the firm. It is particularly concerned with incoming and outgoing invoices, and maintaining the firm's money flow. Payment of wages is frequently included in the responsibilities of this department. The modern accounts department has an extensive data processing system backed up by computers.

SALES
To plan and organise the selling of goods or services offered by the firm. This department is one of the most essential because without it other departments would not be needed. Sales representatives provide an important link between the company and potential customers.

LEGAL
Most legal matters are dealt with by the company secretary, although a very large organisation might have a legal department. The department's activities include legal matters such as contracts, guarantees, insurance, compensation, etc.

ADVERTISING
May be a separate department or it can be incorporated into the sales department. The aim of this department is to make potential customers aware of the goods or services the company offers and to encourage custom. Smaller firms may employ the services of an advertising agency to carry out this work for them.

PURCHASING
The purchasing or buying department is responsible for all items bought by the firm. It obtains quotations from suppliers and issues orders, ensuring delivery is made on time. It also checks that prices, quality and quantity delivered correspond with the quotation and order. This department also deals with 'requisitions' which are written requests for supplies from other departments in the firm.

TRANSPORT
May operate the company's own fleet of vehicles, or alternatively it organises other forms of transport using agencies outside the firm. The function of this department is to arrange for delivery of goods to customers on time, in good condition, at home or overseas, and by the most economical method and route applicable.

ADMINISTRATION
Many firms have a general office concerned with co-ordinating the activities of the various departments of the firm. The administration department may include back-up facilities such as centralised filing, typing pool, mail room, reprographics and data processing. The administration department is frequently closely related to the managing director.

PRODUCTION
Where the company is involved in production of some commodity, a production department may be used to co-ordinate the work of the factory unit. 'Progress chasers' may be employed to ensure that delivery schedules are adhered to, and 'quality controllers' can be used to maintain production standards and investigate complaints or deal with goods returned as faulty.

HUMAN RESOURCES
Concerned with finding the right person for vacant jobs, dismissing unsuitable workers, dealing with resignations and providing references. It is involved directly in any induction training or staff training school the company operates. It maintains personal records of all employees and is involved in the welfare and happiness of all personnel.

The departments of a large firm.

the day-to-day operations of the business, and to ensure that the policies decided by the board of directors are carried out. A company secretary is also appointed to deal with legal matters such as contracts of employment, product guarantees and government legislation.

3.4 Organisational structure

Chain of command

Many companies are organised in the form of a pyramid. The person at the top of the pyramid has the most authority and the steps down the pyramid indicate less authority. Each person in the pyramid is responsible to the person immediately above them (sometimes referred to as their 'line manager'). The sections of the following pyramid show the person in the managing position is at the top of the chain of command. This shows the lines of communication between the person in the supervisory position and his/her subordinates. Each manager delegates work to the people below him/her in the chain.

Span of control

This is sometimes also referred to as 'span of management' because it refers to the number of subordinates a manager supervises, or the effective limit to the number of others that a manager can supervise efficiently. There are a number of factors that influence the span of control and they include the following:

- *The complexity of the work.* Some work is easy to check whilst other work demands closer supervision by the manager.
- *Self-discipline of workers.* Where workers are well motivated and have a professional approach a greater number can be supervised.
- *Method of communication.* Some methods of communication (e.g. face-to-face) are more demanding than others (e.g. electronic methods).

FACTORY PERSONNEL

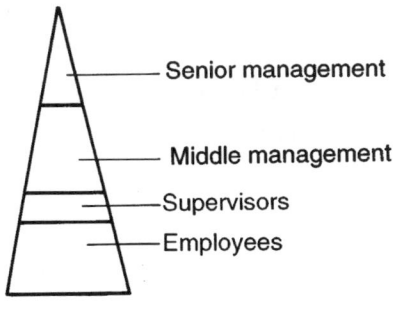
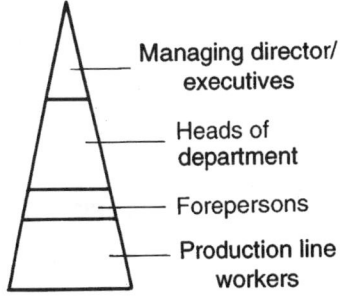

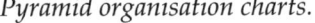

Pyramid organisation charts.

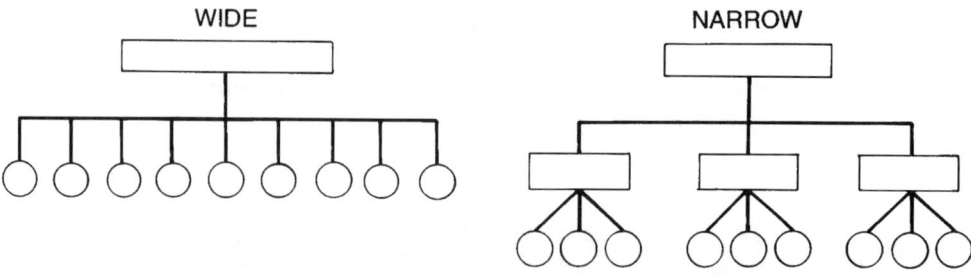

Span of control.

- *Frequency of supervision.* The more frequently that a manager needs to see subordinates the more limited will be the span of control.
- *Capability of the manager.* Some managers have more ability to lead and motivate than others and this will extend their span of control.

If workers do not need close supervision then the span of control can be wide and flat. Where there is a need for closer supervision the span of control will be narrow and contain more people in sub-supervisory positions.

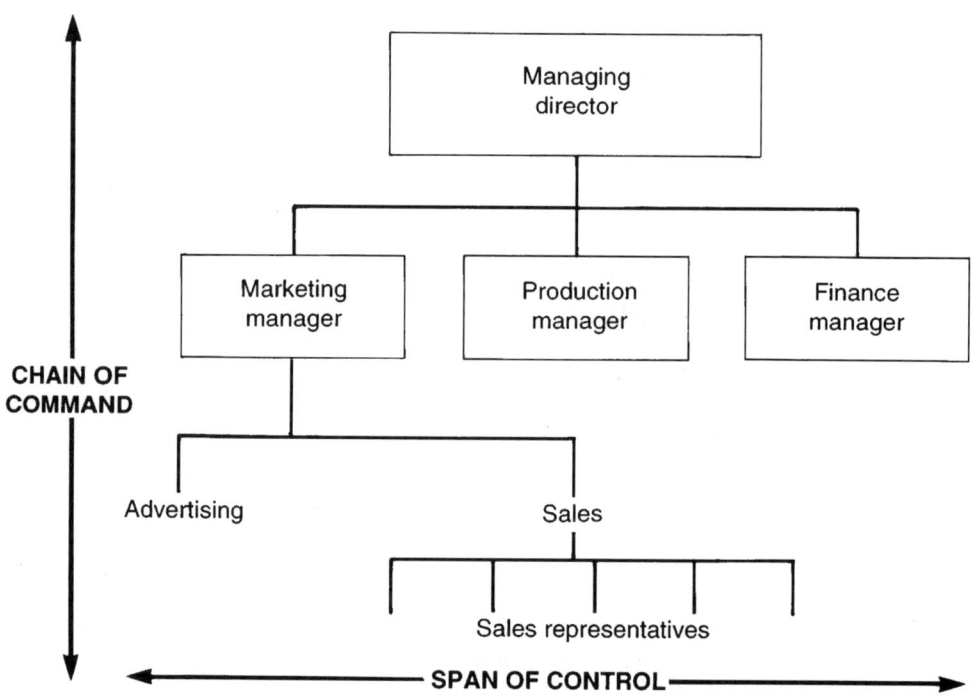

Combined chain of command and span of control.

Organisational structure

To enable a firm to achieve its objectives satisfactorily it relies on two types of relationship between personnel. One type is 'formal' and the other 'informal'. Together these relationships are called the 'organisational structure' of a firm.

Business Organisation

Formal organisation

Formal organisation is concerned with the official lines of communication followed by employees to carry out management decisions. It allows those in charge to define objectives for each section/department to enable the organisation to achieve its corporate aims. It helps to define responsibilities and to ensure that tasks are not duplicated but are co-ordinated between functions within an organisation, so that each department blends its activities with those of other departments to form a corporate strategy.

A formal organisation chart shows the structure or relationships through which a firm intends to work. But in addition to this *formal structure* there usually exists *informal links*. These links can be useful to a firm because they can help to support the organisation; for example, if a group of workers organise social events it can have the beneficial effect of motivating workers. However, informal contacts can also be damaging; for example, groups of workers meeting outside the business may discuss aspects of the firm's operations and promote mistrust and ill-feelings based on rumour rather than fact.

The functions found in organisations will vary depending on their type or size, and this will affect the organisational structure used.

There are basically four types of formal organisational structure and a business might incorporate more than one:

1 line organisation
2 staff organisation
3 functional organisation
4 committee organisation.

Line organisation

This is a traditional form of organisation which involves a direct flow of authority, and responsibility is dispersed and delegated from top to bottom. The owner, or chief executive, will instruct those below him, e.g. the departmental managers. They, in turn, will instruct the employees who then comply with the instructions. (This is looked on as a narrow span of control.)

Within this hierarchical form of organisation everyone has some responsibility. The higher the position in the hierarchy the greater is the responsibility, and this responsibility cannot be delegated. Tasks or objectives, however, can be delegated, and so can authority or the right to use power. This right is defined by the hierarchy and should correspond with the delegator's position in the hierarchy.

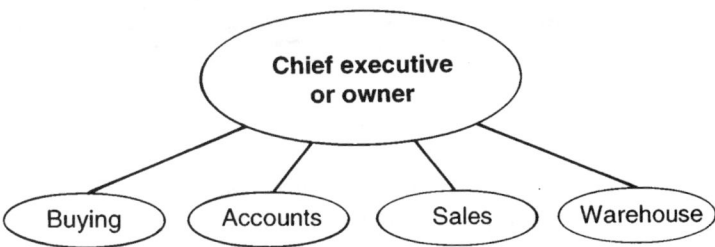

Line organisation in a small firm.

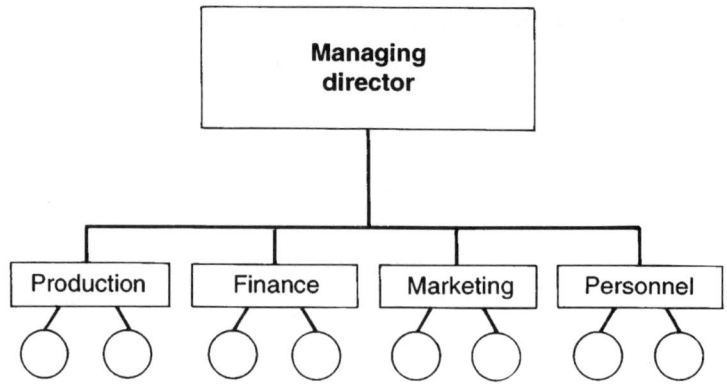

Line organisation in a larger firm.

The benefits of this method of organisation are that it is easy to understand and has an uncomplicated chain of command. Decisions can be reached quickly. It is particularly suited to a small business. However, this type of structure ties up the owner/chief executive with administration, leaving little time for policy-making and planning. It also restricts the inclusion of specialist personnel where services are required by more than one department. A small firm could 'buy in' these services, e.g. legal advice and the information offered by research agencies, but this would be uneconomical for a large firm which would prefer to employ its own specialists. For this reason the line organisation tends to be less suited to a large firm.

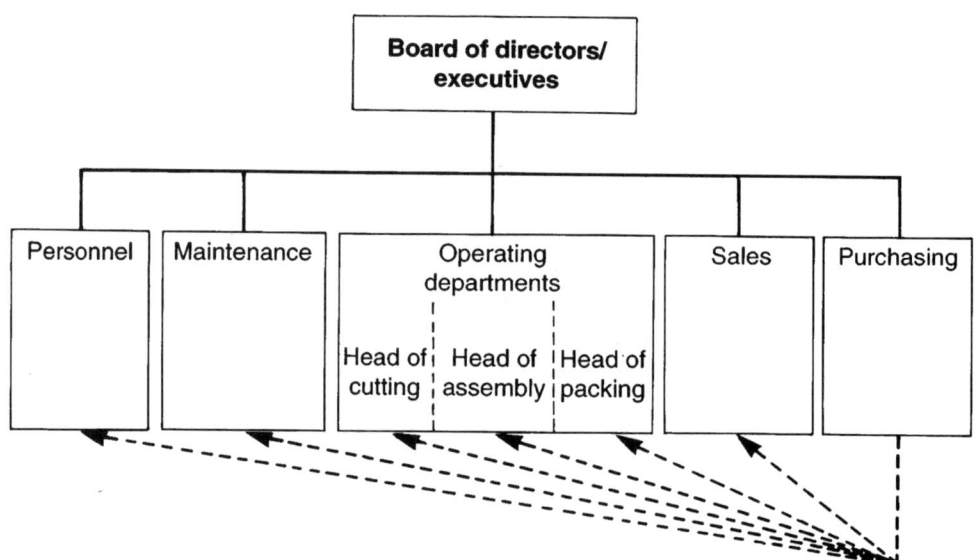

Staff organisation: the service departments supply facilities to the operating departments and also to the other service departments. The dotted lines show how one department of an organisation might provide a service to all or many other sections.

Business Organisation

Staff organisation

Staff organisation is a development of a line organisation. Some activities of a business cut across the departments of a linear structure because they offer a service facility (e.g. legal or research activities) to several if not all departments. As mentioned earlier when looking at line organisation, a large firm would find it more economical to employ specialist staff to offer these services and advice to other departments. Staff of these 'back-up' services can advise, but generally not direct or control, the other departments.

A major advantage of this system is that it allows employment of specialist workers. The main disadvantage is that the lines of responsibility and authority are less clear and this can result in disputes between specialist personnel and heads of departments.

Functional organisation

This type of organisation is set up in departments to carry out the basic functions of the business, e.g. finance, production, sales, warehouse/delivery, etc.

The head of each specialist department supervises, controls and is responsible for just the one function with which it is involved. However, a subordinate employee, carrying out a task, will be in the unenviable position of receiving orders from, and being accountable to, possibly all the specialist department heads.

This is a wide span of control and this type of organisation requires a lot of co-operation and common sense to avoid confusion and conflict in the workforce.

This method of organisation has its place in a business which has branches located around the country, or in a situation in which there is the need to have specialist functions based at a suitable location, e.g. a shipping office or warehouse positioned near docks. Under these circumstances the specialist departments would probably be based at the head office and control of the branches would emanate from there. However, the branch managers would retain a certain amount of autonomy whilst also being able to draw on the functions and expertise at headquarters.

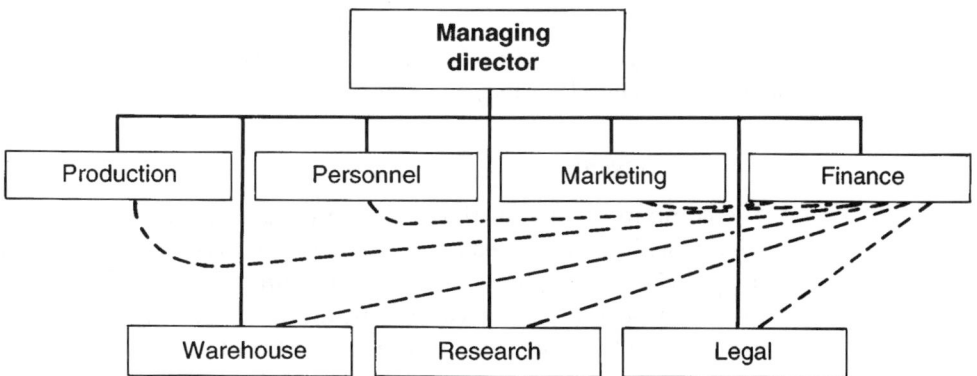

Functional organisation: within a functional organisation's structure a member of a department might receive instructions from many or even all of the other departments.

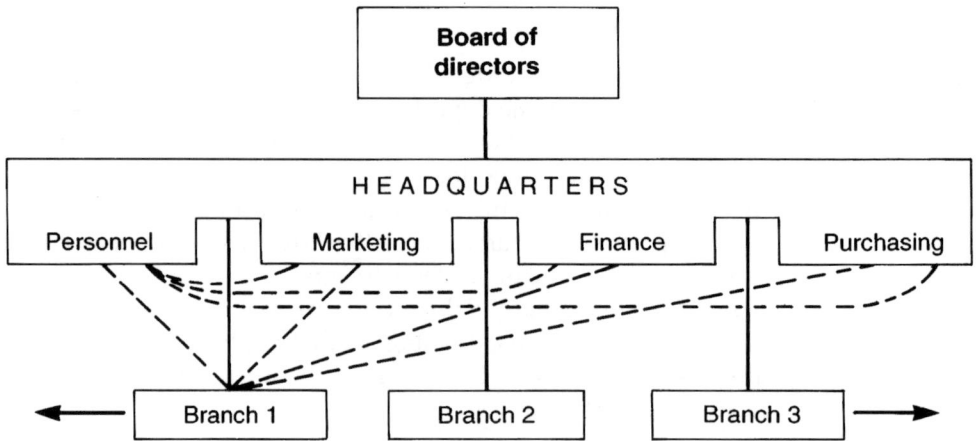

Functional organisation: in a large functional organisation structure the branches might use any of the departments at headquarters, and those departments might also use each other.

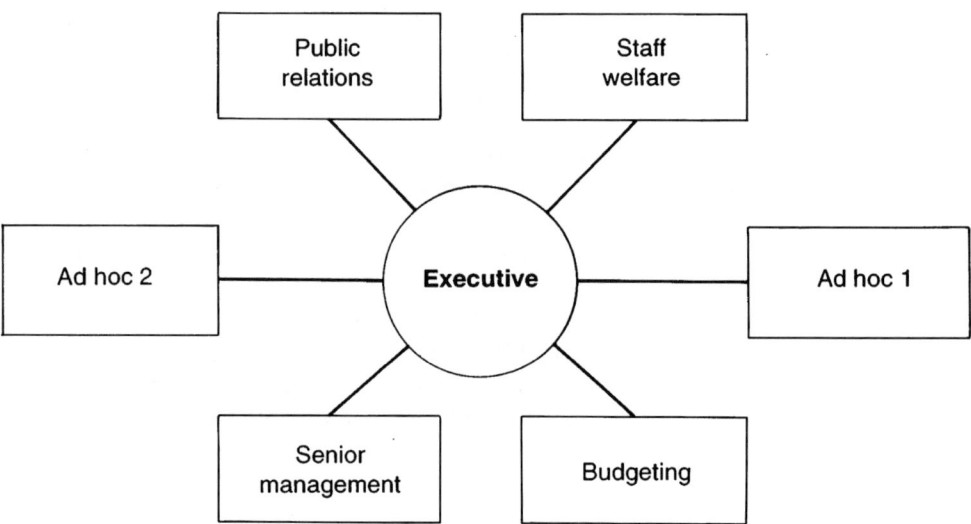

Committee organisation: a group of specialists is brought together to advise top executives and help them develop policy and procedures.

Committee organisation

The committee organisation is based on the management principle of grouping specialists in committees to advise the executives and to assist them in developing policies and procedures. Some committees will have authority to recommend to supervisors (upward communication), others are formed purely to receive information (downward communication), and some will undertake management functions, e.g. policy-making. Some will be permanent working groups whilst others will be 'ad hoc', i.e. set up to examine a particular problem, and then dissolved once they have achieved their goal.

Business Organisation

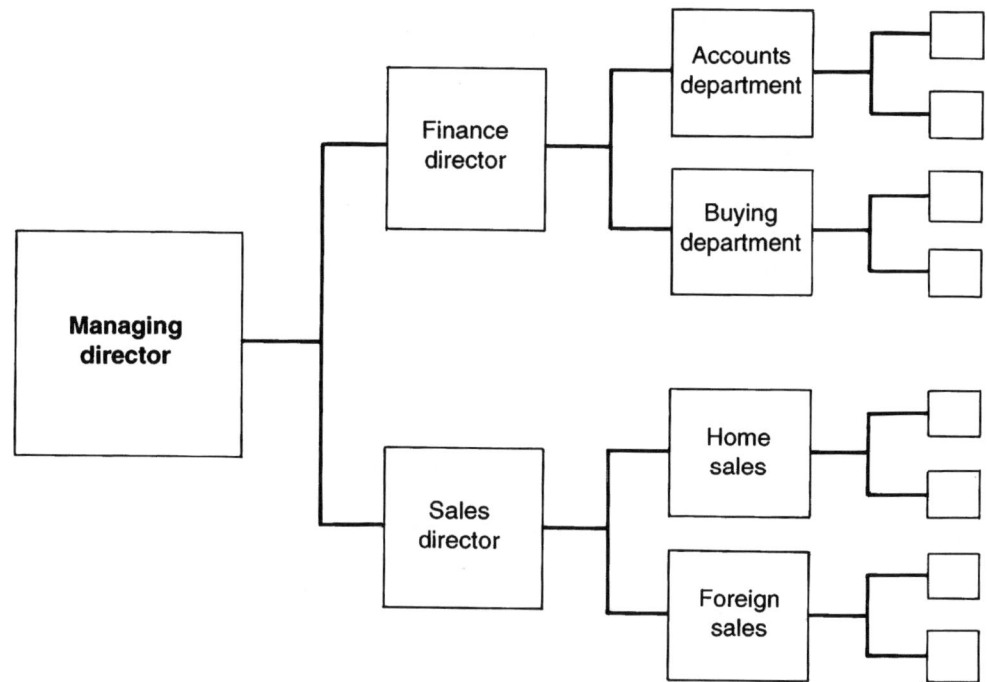

A horizontal organisation chart.

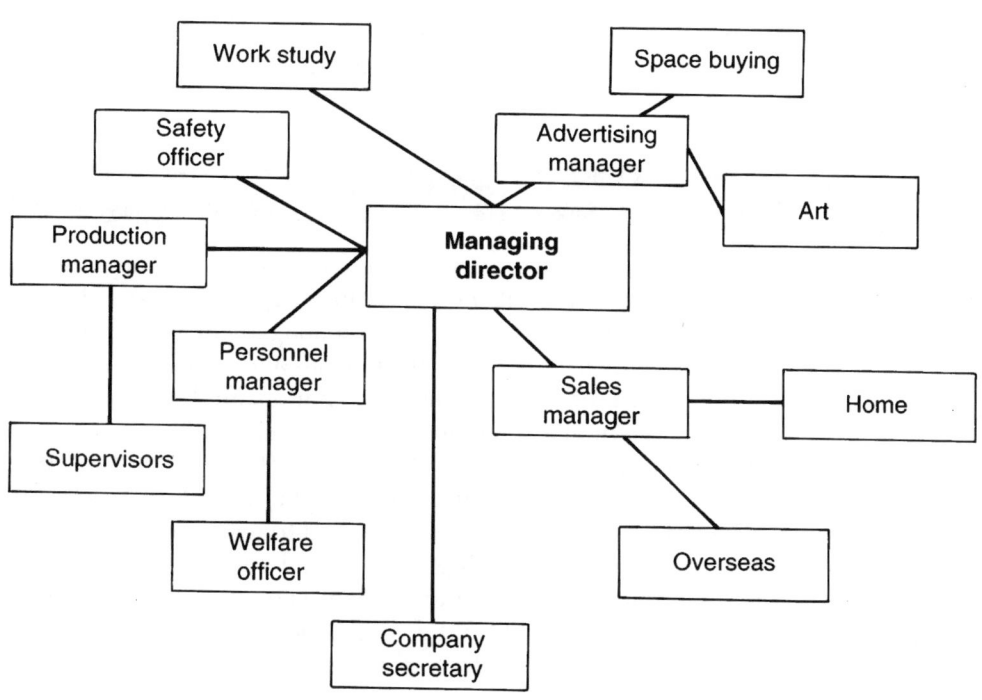

A circular organisation chart.

Committees invariably slow up the decision-making process, but they improve morale by allowing employees to participate. The combined judgement of several specialists in similar or diverse areas also promotes sound decision-making.

Informal organisation

Some groups have an influence on an organisation but do not necessarily have the interest of the business directing their actions. Workers tend to form into informal groups based on their interests or skills. For example, a group of workers might get together to organise a social function. The reason for this grouping is not intended to benefit the organisation, although it may well have a good influence on morale which is in the firm's interest. In another example, workers might form a group of people concerned about a new development the firm wants to undertake and in which they want to express an adverse opinion.

It is important for management to recognise the way in which informal groups work if they are to minimise the damage they can cause, or to maximise the benefits to be gained by utilising such groups wherever possible.

Organisation charts

Organisation charts are illustrations which show the formal structure of an organisation. The chart shows the different positions in the business and indicates what is done by each part, or shows the links between various parts of the organisation.

The size of a business will obviously influence the structure and complexity of the chart. There are a variety of ways of presenting organisation charts. The method shown on page 55 is a vertical organisation chart. This is the most popular, but there are others, for example a pyramid organisation chart is shown on page 57, and illustrated on page 63 are horizontal and circular charts.

3.5 Centralisation and decentralisation

Centralisation refers to an aspect of business organisation where the firm is organised in such a way that the main authority, control and decisions are made by some central group, such as a senior management or executive group.

Decentralisation exists when the policies and decisions of a business are made at various levels of the organisation. For example, individual departments or branches may make some decisions independently, but taking into account and perhaps interpretating the firm's general policies. Decentralisation implies *delegation* – in other words, the authority to make some decisions is spread.

The term centralisation can be applied to resources as well as organisation and decision making. The equipment related to several departments or branches could be centralised in a kind of 'pool'. For example, a building company with several divisions might hold a central pool of plant machinery that the various parts of the business can draw on.

Business Organisation

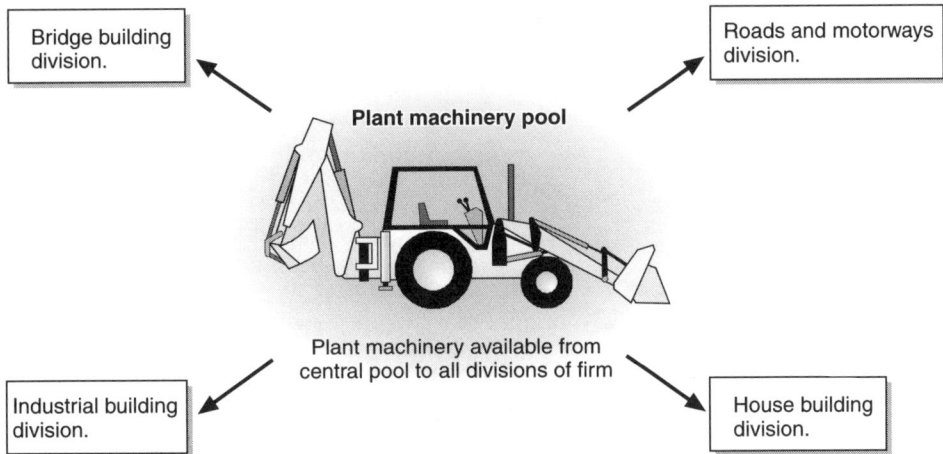

An example of decentralisation of administration, but centralisation of resources.

3.6 Activities

1. How do business aims differ from business objectives?
2. Give two examples of business aims, and for each give three appropriate objectives.
3. What is the main aim of a business?
4. How do the four functional areas of a business help it achieve its general aim?
5. Why is management an important aspect of a business?
6. Briefly describe the responsibilities of management.
7. Why do managers have more responsibilities than their subordinates?
8. Give at least three examples of responsibilities you think a manager has to the government and society.
9. In what ways do management meet its responsibilities?
10. Describe the main functions of management.
11. Why is it important for a manager to have an understanding of group dynamics?

65

12. Explain the difference between informal groups and formal groups.
13. Why is it important that a firm's objectives are clearly understood by its employees?
14. Why is it that wages are limited in the extent to which they can be relied on to encourage people to work hard and effectively?
15. Why is it difficult to define the qualities needed to lead others?
16. List in your own order of priority ten qualities you would look for in a potential manager of a medium-sized manufacturing company.
17. Briefly describe each of the four styles of leadership.
18. Why is communication an important factor of management?
19. 'Effective management requires a two-way flow of communication.' Explain this statement.
20. Make an outline comparison between the organisational structure of a small business and that of a large business.
21. How does the function of a managing director differ from that of other directors?
22. Describe the functions of six departments of a large company.
23. Why are there so many variations of span of control?
24. How does chain of command differ from span of control?
25. Describe the four types of formal organisational structure.
26. Produce simple diagrams and concise explanations to illustrate the four types of organisation chart shown in this chapter.
27. Explain the difference between centralisation and decentralisation.
28. In what ways might a firm employ both centralisation and decentralisation?

Business Organisation

Structured Questions

1

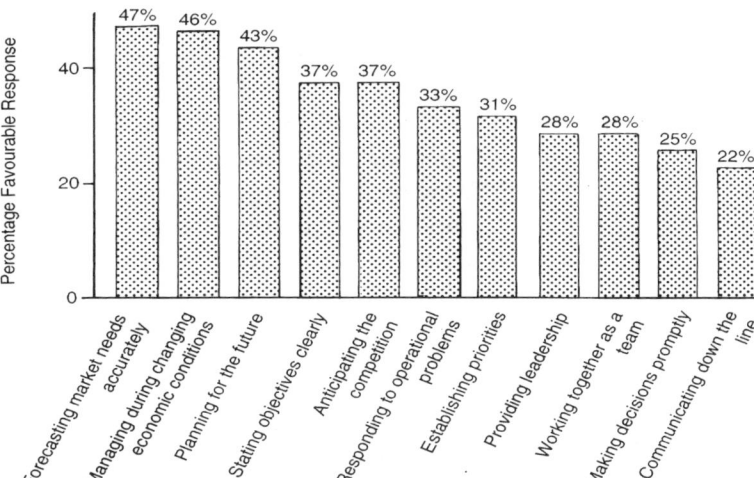

ATTITUDES OF UK MANAGERS TOWARDS BUSINESS PERFORMANCE

PEOPLE MANAGEMENT SKILLS TOP OF THE AGENDA FOR TODAY'S MANAGERS

The Institute of Management issued a news release in which they claim that their research shows that today's managers are increasingly taking responsibility for nurturing and developing their people. As the information age unfolds, managers are also seen as recognising the importance of how to share knowledge and expertise within organisations.

In a time of continual change, top priority is given by managers to developing leadership and team-working skills in their people (87%). Over three quarters (77%) also see coaching and mentoring as vital.

The Institute also states that the changing nature of work and the 24 hour economy mean that new ways of working are high on the agenda for today's managers and 40% believe that new initiatives on flexible and mobile working are likely to be introduced in their organisations over the next year. A further 34 % think that this is likely to happen within the next five years.

These findings are held to reflect the importance of managers developing good communication and people management skills.

Reference: Institute of Management, News Release, 26 April 2000

(a) When developing staff, what do managers see as 'top priority'? (2)
(b) Why do you think this is considered to be the top priority? (2)
(c) Why do you think coaching and mentoring is considered vital? (4)
(d) What is meant by 'flexible and mobile working'? What are the advantages and disadvantages of this style of working to an organisation? (6)
(e) Why is it important for managers to develop good communication and people management skills? (6)

67

2 Refer to the diagram on page 56 and answer these questions.

(a) Name the department of a company that would be particularly concerned with the firm's money flow. (1)

(b) Give two examples of matters that are likely to be dealt with by a company's Legal department. (2)

(c) Why are larger organisations more able to divide into a departmental structure than smaller ones? (2)

(d) Give three examples of work carried out by a Purchasing department other than buying items. (3)

(e) The Sales and Advertising departments have a close association and they are sometimes incorporated in a larger department called Marketing. What is the important association between these two departments? (4)

(f) The Human Resources Department is stated to be involved in 'induction training or staff training'. Give specific descriptive examples of what this may involve and explain why it is important to business operations. (8)

3 Look at the diagram on page 55 showing a typical example of the structure of a public limited company and answer these questions.

(a) Which of the labels in the diagram refers specifically to the owners of the business? (1)

(b) The chairperson of a board of directors is an 'elected' position whereas the managing director is an 'appointed' position. Explain the difference between the words in inverted commas in relation to these positions in an organisation. (2)

(c) How does the work of a managing director differ from that of other directors? (3)

(d) Why is the Transport department particularly important to both the Sales department and the Factory department of a large organisation? (4)

(e) Describe the work of two of the following business occupations, including mention of who their line managers would be in the diagram:
  (i) wages clerk;
  (ii) progress chaser;
  (iii) sales representative. (4)

(f) Clearly describe the work of three managers in the diagram and in each case say to what extent they need leadership qualities. (6)

4 Consider the article that follows on page 69:

(a) What is a multinational company? (1)

(b) Why is the question of centralisation and decentralisation particularly relevant to large organisations rather than small ones? (2)

(c) List at least three benefits you feel a firm gains from centralisation. (3)

(d) List three advantages that can occur as a result of decentralisation. (3)

Business Organisation

> **Centralisation** refers to a situation when a business is organised in such a way that policies and decisions for all branches of the firm are made by a central body. It is also used to describe a situation whereby internal services of a firm, e.g. reprographics or filing, are carried out by one department for the whole of the organisation.
>
> **Decentralisation** exists when the policies and decisions of a firm are made away from the central control. Each branch of the firm makes its own decisions on how it will operate.
>
> A major problem large organisations face is the degree to which control is centralised or how much decentralisation there should be. Most firms such as multinationals use a mixture of centralisation and decentralisation.

(e) How would centralisation of a company's reprographic services save in the overall cost of equipment if the firm consists of 15 departments? (4)

(f) Discuss the view that decentralisation of control of the decision-making process can have the effect of motivating those with management responsibilities. (7)

Extended Answer Assignments

1. Make a diagrammatic 'map' of the organisation structure of a small and a medium-sized local firm with which you are familiar. Comment on the differences observed.

2. Make a comparative study of the organisation structure of a local department store and that of a local manufacturing unit. Explain the reasons for the differences you observe.

3. Select two competing businesses situated within your locality and show:
   (a) how they compete;
   (b) why they are both able to survive in spite of the competition they are part of.

4. Write to two multinational companies with questions that aim to find out which policies are decided centrally. Produce a report that summarises your findings and suggest reasons for the decision process of each firm.

5. If you were the managing director of a bakery firm with a central bakehouse and 20 shops selling your products, what kind of organisation structure would

you have? Give your reasons and describe other possible forms of structure and comment on their likely suitability.

6 Produce an organisation chart to represent the structure of your local council. Explain why you think it is divided into departments and describe the function of six of the departments. Comment on the similarities and the differences between the council organisation when compared with the organisation of a business.

7 Make a survey of at least two local businesses to investigate the statement, 'All managers are required to lead, but not all managers are leaders.' Discuss this statement using specific examples to illustrate your answer.

8 Investigate a business to which you can gain relatively easy access. Describe the extent to which the firm achieves its aims through the functional areas of production, finance, marketing and personnel.

9 Choose a suitable local or national business, or mini-enterprise within your school/college, and evaluate whether the business has succeeded in meeting its aims and objectives.

4 Types of Business

4.1 Private and public enterprise

Britain is said to have a 'mixed' economy because it consists of both private enterprise and public enterprise.

Private enterprise refers to businesses that are owned by private individuals (some of the public) engaged in the production of goods or services. There are four main forms of business ownership in the private sector of the economy:

1. sole traders
2. partnership
3. private limited companies
4. public limited companies.

There are also some private organisations which have a special relationship with the owners of the business. Co-operative societies and holding companies are examples of these special forms of private enterprise. These special relationships are examined later in this chapter.

Public enterprise refers to industries and services owned by the state (all of the public) and run by central or local government.

Business aims and objectives

Aims are the general overall goal that a business is trying to achieve – it is the general direction the business wants to work towards. *Objectives* are the smaller goals that a business chooses to help it achieve its aims. For example, a business might aim to increase its share of the market, and it could try to achieve this aim through the objectives of increasing its spending on advertising, employing more sales staff and broadening range of products it markets.

Sometimes business will have different aims and objectives depending upon what type of business it is. For example, a *state-owned enterprise* may be more interested in the service they provide (e.g. refuse collection) than achieving a profit. The following are just a few examples of other differences between business aims and objectives.

The owner of a *small business* (e.g. a sole proprietor or partnership) may be willing to accept a smaller profit than a larger business because the owner(s) get satisfaction from being their own boss, or because they need lower prices in order to break into the market.

Whilst the owners of a small business are likely to actually work in the business, in a *larger business* (e.g. a limited company) those who own the business (the *shareholders*) are not generally the employees, and these two groups may well have different aims and objectives within the same business. The shareholders will want the best return they can get from their investment, whereas their employees will be more interested in what they can earn, working conditions and security of employment.

Limited liability

The business entrepreneur faces many risks when participating in business activity, especially if the firm has unlimited liability. This means that if the business goes bankrupt and cannot pay its creditors, the owner's personal possessions such as car or home and its contents can be taken and used to pay the debts owed.

Although many small firms do have unlimited liability, larger organisations face so much greater risks that only some form of security for personal assets encourages people to invest and accept the greater risks involved.

The status of limited liability allows people to invest in a business without having to face the risks of unlimited liability. Limited liability indicates that the liability of shareholders for the debts of a business is limited to the amount they have invested in the business and not their personal assets.

Limited liability can be applied to the shareholders of a private or public limited company and a limited partnership. The private company and limited partnership must show the letters Ltd at the end of the company title. The public company must indicate limited liability by the letters plc (public limited company) at the end of the company title.

Limited companies are said to have a 'separate corporate identity', in other words, an identity separate from their shareholders. They can sue and be sued in their title name.

Types of Business

4.3 Private ownership

The sole proprietor

This type of firm is owned by one person who provides all of the capital needed to form, operate, or expand the business. The sole proprietor (sole trader) is the simplest and most common type of enterprise. It is the easiest form of business to set up and it is also more likely to fail than any other.

Such businesses as sole proprietors tend to have only a few employees and less machinery or capital than larger businesses. They also have less plant facilities and fewer opportunities to make economies of scale. Their market tends to be less diversified than that of larger businesses because their levels of operations limit their output.

The sole proprietor has the following advantages:

- The size of my business means that I need less capital (money to start the business).
- I have independence and need not consult anyone when making decisions.
- I need not share my profits with anyone else.
- I have personal contact with the whole business and all my customers.

The sole proprietor has the following disadvantages:

- I have unlimited liability. This means that if the business and I am unable to pay my creditors, they can take my personal possessions, such as my car or house and its contents if I own them.
- I can suffer from lack of continuity. This means that if I am unable to run the business, even temporarily, perhaps through ill health, then often there will be no one to run the business.
- I have to provide all the capital.
- I will often find it difficult to obtain loans of capital because I am a bigger risk than a large business.

Partnerships

Some of the problems faced by the sole trader can be overcome by incorporating more owners into the business to form a partnership.

Partnerships are regulated by the Partnership Act. This Act allows partnerships to have from two to twenty members although there are two exceptions to this rule.

1. Banks which operate as a partnership are not allowed to have more than ten partners.
2. Some professional partnerships are allowed to have more than twenty partners (e.g. accountants, solicitors, members of the Stock Exchange).

A deed of partnership sets out the rights of each partner, such as the way in which profits are to be divided. If there is no partnership deed, the provisions of the Partnership Act are assumed to govern the partnership, and that Act provides for equal sharing of profits.

All partners are equally responsible for the debts of the business. A 'sleeping' partner is one who invests in the business but takes no active part in running it, but such a partner is fully liable with other partners for debts incurred by the business.

It is possible to have a limited partnership but at least one partner must accept unlimited liability. Consequently, limited partnerships are relatively rare.

Some professional bodies prohibit their members from forming a limited company and, therefore, the partnership is particularly suitable for them. Solicitors, doctors and accountants are examples of professions that are not allowed to have limited liability status.

Advantages

- Easily formed.
- Greater continuity than sole trader.
- More people are available to contribute capital to the business.
- Expenses and management of the business are shared.

Disadvantages

- Generally unlimited liability.
- Possible conflicts between partners.
- Each partner is fully liable for the debts of the business.
- Membership limit of twenty restricts resources of business.

Private limited companies (Ltd)

Any company which is not registered as a public company is a private limited company. This type of business must include Limited (or Ltd) in its title name.

Both private and public limited companies are sometimes referred to as joint stock companies. This is because the money contributed by many shareholders is combined to form a joint stock of capital assets, which is used in some form of business enterprise to generate further wealth or profit which is divided between the shareholders.

The private company is allowed from two to an unlimited number of members (shareholders). The capital of the firm is divided into shares, but the shares are not sold on the Stock Exchange and they cannot be advertised for sale publicly. Consequently, shares have to be sold privately – hence the name 'private'.

Some firms may wish to keep ownership within a particular group of people, for example, within a family or a religious group. The private company may restrict share transfer if it wishes by writing a rule into its articles of association requiring members to offer shares to existing shareholders before attempting to sell them to non-members.

The private limited company has the following advantages:
- We can have more people contributing capital than the sole proprietor or partnership.
- We have greater continuity than smaller businesses.
- We have limited liability

The private limited company has the following disadvantages:
- We may be limited in the capital we can raise because our shares cannot be offered for public sale.
- Our capital raising possibilities can be further reduced if we restrict share transfer.
- Our audited accounts have to be available for inspection.

Public limited companies (plc)

The public limited company must indicate its public status by including the letters plc (public limited company) in the title name.

The public company in formation must have at least the minimum amount of share capital laid down in the Companies Act 1985. It is allowed from two to an unlimited number of shareholders, and it can advertise shares and debentures for public sale. Capital raising is also helped by the fact that public company shares are listed on the Stock Exchange. This encourages people to contribute to the original share capital because they know they can easily sell their shares second-hand on the stock market. Consequently, this type of business organisation can raise almost limitless funds.

When an investor buys shares in a limited company they become a part owner. This not only entitles them to a share of the company's profits, but also gives them the right to some say in the way that the company is operated. It is usual for the shareholders of a company to elect a small committee called a *board of directors* to decide overall company policy on behalf of the shareholders. A chairperson is also elected to regulate board meetings.

Even a board of directors consists of too many people to take an active part in the day-to-day operation of the firm so the board appoint a managing director to carry out this function. Both private and pubic companies elect a board of directors and a chairman and appoint a managing director.

Advantages

- Have limited liability.
- Enjoy maximum continuity.
- Can raise large sums of capital.
- Large size enables them to enjoy 'economies of scale', such as being able to buy supplies in bulk.

- Size allows them to buy special equipment which will save in labour and expense.
- Find it easier to borrow money than smaller businesses because they are less risk than smaller firms.

Disadvantages
- Formation involves considerable documentation and expense.
- Company, employees and shareholders become too detached from one another because of large size.
- Ease of transfer to share ownership can lead to 'takeover' bids for company.
- Tend to develop too many rules ('red tape').
- The annual accounts of the company are open to public inspection which reduces confidentiality of the firm.

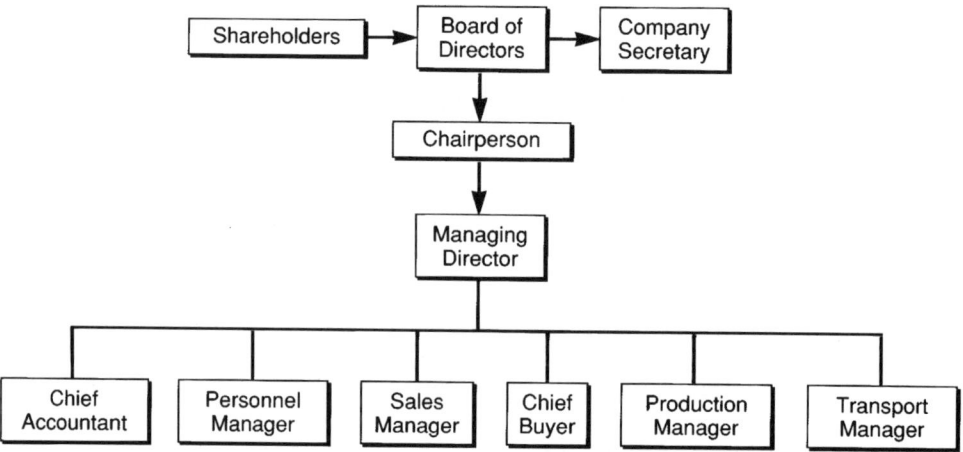

Forming a limited company

All types of private businesses, including sole traders, partnerships and private and public companies, must register with the Registrar of Business Names if they wish to operate under a name other than that of the owner.

When a limited company is being formed it must register with the Registrar of Companies. This registration is carried out mainly by presentation of two completed documents, the memorandum of association and the articles of association, by those initially forming the company. Both the private and the public company follow a similar procedure, except that the private company passes through fewer stages than the public company.

Memorandum of association
This document states the external relationships of the company, for example the relationship between the company and others. The memorandum of association consists of a number of clauses.

Types of Business

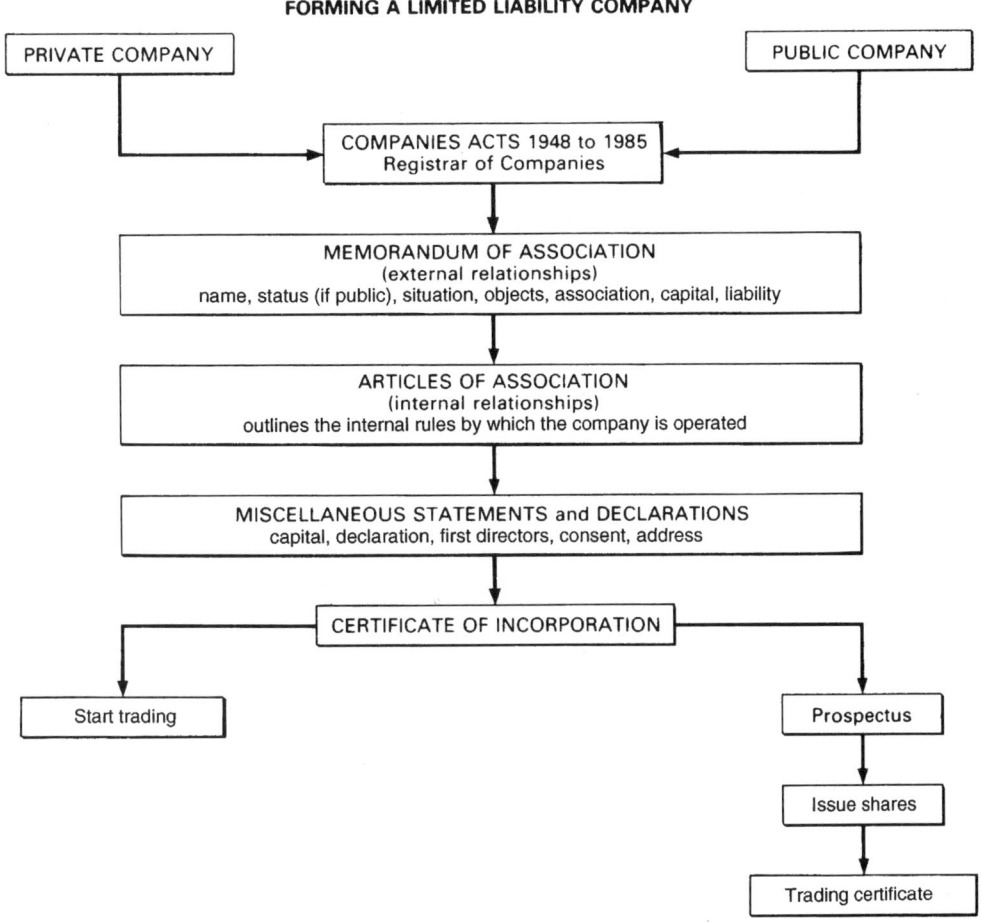

FORMING A LIMITED LIABILITY COMPANY

Name clause

This states the trading name of the company. The Registrar of Companies ensures that no two companies are formed bearing the same name. The Registrar of Companies also looks for misleading names, suggestive names (i.e. of a connection with, say, the Royal Family) and similar names.

Status clause

The memorandum of a public company has to state that it is to be a public company. The public company indicates its status by the letters PLC (or plc) at the end of its title name, whereas the private company ends its title with Limited (or Ltd). The Welsh equivalent 'ccc' is also acceptable under relevant circumstances.

Situation clause

This identifies the country where the registered office of the company is situated. The company can move its registered office within the stated country.

Object clause

This clause states the object for which the company is established, for example to manufacture toys, or to publish books.

Liability clause

This states that the liability of shareholders is limited to the amount they have invested in the company.

Capital clause

This is a statement of the amount of capital with which the company is to be registered and the manner in which it is to be divided into shares, for example £500 000 divided into 25p shares or £1 shares. A public company must have a nominal share capital of at least £50 000.

Association clause

This is a declaration implying that those signing the memorandum wish to form the company and that they are prepared to take up and pay for the number of shares shown on the form by their name. The minimum number of signatories is two.

Articles of association

The articles of association outline the internal relationships of the company, that is the broad way in which the internal organisation will operate. This document must be signed by the same people who sign the memorandum of association.

The contents of this document are more flexible than those of the memorandum of association and they can easily be changed by the shareholders. However, any alterations to the articles of association must not conflict with the memorandum of association.

Contents of the articles of association

- The rights of shareholders.
- Methods of election of directors.
- The manner in which meetings are to be conducted.
- Division of profits

Miscellaneous statements and declarations

In addition to the memorandum of association and the articles of association the promoters of a company must also make the following statements and declarations to the Registrar of Companies.

Statement of nominal capital

This shows the amount of registered capital and the manner of its division into shares (similar to the capital clause in the memorandum of association).

Types of Business

Declaration

A statement made under oath by the company secretary of a director confirming that all the requirements of the Companies Act have been met.

List of first directors

The names of the first directors of the company are listed.

Statement of consent

Signed by each of the proposed directors confirming that they are willing to act in this capacity.

Address of registered office

This states the precise registered address of the company. Any changes in this address must be notified to the Registrar within twenty-eight days of change.

If the Registrar of Companies is satisfied that all the requirements have been met, a certificate of incorporation is issued. The business now has an identity separate from that of its owners. A private company can now start trading and a public company proceed to raise capital.

Raising capital for a public company

The directors of a public company can now attempt to raise the capital stated in the capital clause of the memorandum of association. This is done by issuing a prospectus, which is a printed circular or an advertisement, giving a frank outline of what the company hopes to do, and detailing the amount of capital required to start trading.

When the Registrar of Companies is satisfied that the company's share capital is not less than £50 000, and that at least a quarter of the nominal value has been paid on each share, a trading certificate is issued allowing the company to begin trading.

4.4 Special business relationships

Franchising

In franchising, a company allows someone to buy the right to use their products or techniques under their trade names. This is one of the fastest growing sectors of the economy and over 20 per cent of retail sales is accounted for by this form of trading, and the trend is growing each year.

Franchising offers a 'ready-made' business opportunity for those who have the capital and are willing to work hard. The potential entrepreneur or franchisee pays to use the name, products, or services of the franchisor who receives a lump sum and a share of the profits of the business.

The franchisee receives the majority of the profits, but must also meet most of any losses. In addition to allowing use of their name, products, techniques, or services, in return for the money they receive franchisors usually provide an extensive marketing back-up.

Fast food giants such as KFC and Burger King are particularly well known in the franchising sector, but the range of franchise activities is much wider than just fast food. The following are a few other examples of this type of business:

- developing and printing films
- home tuning of car engines
- drain clearing
- door to door ice-cream sales
- bakeries

Co-operatives

Co-operation sometimes develops in production when small units of agriculture or manufacturing owned by people with small and limited amounts of capital combine together for the purpose of sharing labour and buying or hiring equipment which individually they would be unable to afford.

By co-operating in this manner the members of the co-operative not only have access to the economic use of equipment purchased or hired through their pooled resources, but they can also enjoy economies of scale such as bulk purchasing of supplies and wider advertising and marketing possibilities.

Productive co-operation is less familiar in Britain than it is in many other European countries, and in this country most examples of co-operatives are found in distribution (*see* Chapter 10) rather than in production.

Holding companies

For a variety of reasons, businesses sometimes form a temporary or permanent combination to achieve a certain aim. For example, the combination of three or four businesses might usefully bring together several separate processes into one production unit.

This kind of partnership of companies is usually incorporated as a holding company. Each member company retains its legal entity, but overall control lies with the holding company.

Building societies

Building societies are a further example of a special business relationship. They operate on a non-profit-making basis. They are concerned with personal rather than business matters and, consequently, they are considered to be on the fringe of commercial activities.

Building societies are intermediaries between 'small' savers who wish to invest funds and people who wish to borrow money to purchase or improve property. Building societies lend by means of a *mortgage* which is a long-term loan, often repayable over a period of twenty years or more. Most of the deposits to building societies are lent out in this manner, but some of their funds must of course be retained to meet demands for cash withdrawals.

It is usual for the deeds of the property purchased by a borrower to be held by the building society until the mortgage has been repaid. If the borrower defaults in repayment of the mortgage, the society can sell the property to recover the debt.

Building societies have always competed with the commercial banks to obtain deposits from savers. Since the Building Societies Act 1987 the societies have been allowed to compete more openly with the banks, offering many of the financial services that have traditionally only been provided by the banks. Recently many building societies have changed their status fully into banks. Some banks have also begun to provide mortgages and these developments are providing the basis of healthy competition between building societies and banks.

4.5 Business growth

Reasons for growth

Most of the large firms that exist today started as a small business and have grown. Many of today's small firms are tomorrow's big businesses. Businesses grow and expand for a variety of reasons:

- they are successful and expansion is necessary to meet the demand for their product;
- they wish to make a greater level of profit;
- they are trying to gain economies of scale;
- they wish to reduce competition and become market leaders, maybe even gain a monopoly;
- they wish to secure their sources of supply or outlets for their products.

Expansion will only take place if the business can benefit and make extra profits.

Methods of growth

Basically firms can grow in four ways:

- by working existing plant and machinery harder, pushing it towards full capacity;
- by extending existing capacity or moving to a new bigger site;
- by a *merger* with another company – mergers take place when both businesses involved are in agreement about joining together;
- by a *takeover* of another company – a takeover occurs when one company gains control of another against its wishes by buying the existing owners out.

Directions of growth

Businesses need not expand simply by doing more of what they are already doing. Depending on the motives for expansion they can grow or integrate in a number of directions.

Horizontal integration

This is when a business extends its current operations, doing more of what it already does. It expands at the same level in the chain of production (e.g. a car manufacturer expands and builds another plant to produce more cars).

Chain integration

This is expansion to produce the same product, but for a different market (e.g. a car manufacturer producing more cars to sell in a new overseas market).

Lateral integration

This is expansion into a similar area of production, using similar techniques and processes, but making something different (e.g. a car manufacturer expands to produce tractors).

Vertical integration

Vertical integration may be 'backwards' or 'forwards', or in both directions.

- *Expansion backwards* along the chain of distribution occurs, for example, when a business begins to produce the components and raw materials the business needs (e.g. a car manufacturer begins to produce tyres or windscreens for use in its own cars).
- *Expansion forwards* involves extending along the chain of production, for example taking on the selling of the products (e.g. a car manufacturer opens up its own car showrooms).

Conglomerate integration

This is expansion into an area that has nothing to do with the current operations of the business (e.g. a car manufacturer begins to produce furniture).

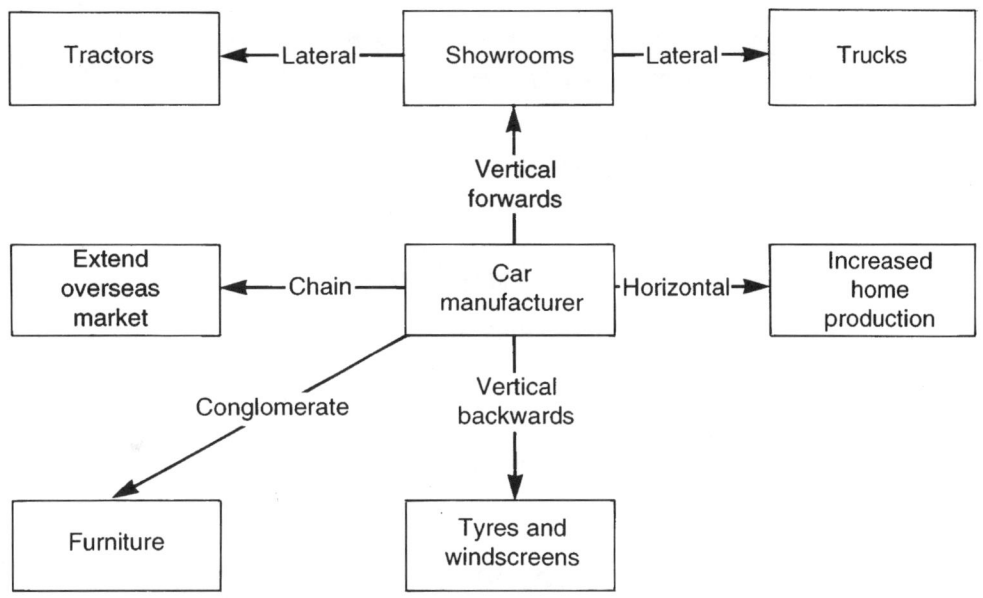

Multinationals

It is not unusual for expansion to take place across international borders. In other words, companies sited in different countries may combine to form a multinational company. The multinational is an enterprise that has subsidiaries or branches in more than one country.

The main objectives of a multinational are to expand its operations into other profitable areas. It will do this in order to gain as large a share of the world market as possible, and to use its expertise and skills to the benefit of all the companies in the group.

The decision-making process is controlled by the parent company and implemented through its foreign subsidiaries. These subsidiary companies are firms that have either been set up by the parent company, or they are foreign businesses which have been taken over. The parent company may own the subsidiary completely, may have a controlling interest (own a majority of the shares), or may just own a large and influential number of shares in the subsidiary.

Monopoly

Business in most democratic societies is based on the concept of free competition. firms do not have the right to compete unfairly with rivals.

A possible result of the expansion of organisations is that they may end up in a monopolistic position. A monopoly exists when a company has so much control over the supply of a commodity or service, that it is able also to control the price. In law, a monopoly exists when a company controls 25 per cent of the total supply of a product. Whilst such a situation is beneficial to the firm, it can be against the interests of the consumer if the company abuses its power.

4.6 Public enterprise

Public enterprise refers to the various forms of business organisation in public ownership. These fall into two broad categories: municipal undertakings and state undertakings.

Municipal undertakings

Municipal undertakings are businesses or services operated on a commercial basis by local authorities. They are financed by local taxation such as the Council Tax and charges are usually made for the use of the service. Sometimes municipal undertakings are subsidised by grants from central government. Examples are sports centres, theatres, bus services, conference halls, art galleries, museums and street markets.

State undertakings

State undertakings, state ownership, public ownership, public enterprise, public corporation, nationalised industry and municipal undertaking are all terms that are used to refer to some form of enterprise that is operated by central or local government on behalf of the public. From these titles you will gain insight into a common mistake made by many students: confusing the terms 'public company' and 'public corporation'. The latter is the type of organisation that is run by the government.

Some public enterprises were set up by the government in the first place, whilst others have been taken into public ownership having at one time been in private ownership. When a privately owned business is taken over by the state it is said to have been *nationalised*. When the reverse has taken place and a state-owned business is sold into private ownership, it is said to have been *privatised*.

Most countries in Western Europe have a *mixed economy* – made up of both private and public enterprises. There has been a relatively recent trend in the UK and other European countries to privatise many of the state-owned enterprises. An extension of this trend has been where some activities previously operated by central or local government have been put out to *competitive tender*. This means that the government no longer directly employs the people to do some of the work they are responsible for (e.g. refuse collection), but instead advertises for businesses to *tender* to carry out the work.

Reasons for public ownership

- To take a monopoly out of private ownership.
- To keep a natural monopoly in public ownership.
- Sometimes the initial capital cost of setting up an industry may be too high for private enterprise.
- Some forms of enterprise may be essential to our welfare but uneconomic for private business.

- National security may have to be protected through state ownership (e.g. atomic energy).
- To standardise equipment and avoid duplication of services (e.g. British Rail).
- To save an ailing industry and protect jobs.

Advantages of public ownership
- Government has the resources to fund a vast industry, even if it is uneconomic.
- Will ensure provision of essential services.
- Reduces possible duplication of equipment.
- Enables large sections of the economy to be planned towards a single strategy.
- Profits benefit the whole nation as opposed to a limited number of private individuals.
- Large size of public corporations allows them to enjoy maximum economies of scale.
- Personnel are appointed and promoted because of proven ability as opposed to personal contact or share of business owned.

Disadvantages of public ownership
- Can be over-cautious due to the fact that they are answerable to the public.
- Bosses are politicians who may not have the necessary business expertise.
- Local issues may be disregarded in favour of policies of national importance.
- State monopoly can lead to inefficiency and insufficient profit motive.
- Losses have to be met by taxpayer.

4.7 Activities

1. Why is Britain said to have a 'mixed' economy?
2. How does private enterprise differ from public enterprise?
3. How do business aims differ from business objectives?
4. Why might state-owned enterprises have different aims and objectives from businesses in the private sector?
5. In what ways could the aims and objectives of small businesses differ from larger organisations?
6. Explain the meaning of limited liability.
7. Why is the sole proprietor the most common type of business? What are the advantages and disadvantages of this type of business?
8. What advantages would a sole proprietor gain by becoming a partnership?

9. Why are limited partnerships relatively rare?
10. Make a detailed comparison between private and public limited companies. Include a list of the advantages and disadvantages of each of these forms of business ownership.
11. Give a description of the process followed in forming a limited company.
12. Give a brief description of the various forms that co-operatives may take.
13. Why can a franchise be said to be a 'ready-made business'?
14. Why are building societies an example of a special business relationship?
15. What is a holding company?
16. What are the reasons for business growth?
17. Explain the difference between a merger and a takeover.
18. Describe the different forms of integration.
19. What is a multinational company?
20. Why are monopolies generally not in the public interest?
21. Explain the difference between municipal undertakings and state undertakings.
22. What is nationalisation? Why might government decide to nationalise an industry?
23. List the advantages and disadvantages of public ownership of business.

Structured Questions

1. (a) Explain the words 'founder' and 'entrepreneur' used in the following newspaper article. (2)
   (b) Why does the owner of the business tend to be carrying out all the managerial functions at the 'existence' stage of business development? (2)
   (c) Advertising tends to become an important feature of a business at the 'survival' stage. Why is this so? (3)
   (d) What does it mean in the article when it says that the business 'credibility and technical feasibility has been established' at the 'success' stage? (3)
   (e) What 'economies of scale' are likely to be introduced during the 'success' stage of development? Why are these not likely to be introduced earlier in the development of the business? (4)
   (f) Why do the skills required of a business person change as the business grows? (6)

Going it Alone

There has never been a better time to start a business of your own, but our Business Correspondent Amira Shah reports, it's a rocky road before you can hit the big time.

Instant success is rare in business and budding entrepreneurs need to be aware of the five stages of growth of a business:

Existence At the existence stage the founder is technically orientated and using all the energy to design and manufacture a product (or provide a service). The business is run by the owner who often performs all the managerial functions.

Survival At the survival stage the business becomes more aggressive in seeking new customers and a small standardised product line appealing to a wider set of customers is developed. The number of employees starts to expand and the owner becomes much more burdened with management responsibilities.

Success At the success stage the business credibility and technical feasibility has been established. Economies of scale are introduced in the production process. The owner has to make a decision, either to concentrate all his or her energies on expanding the company with the consequent risks or to keep the company stable and profitable and provide a basis for alternative interests.

Take off If the owner decides on the expansion route and is successful then he or she should reach the take off stage. At this stage there are multiple product lines and a divisionalised organisation structure to cope with the increasing complexity of the business.

Resource maturity At the resource maturity stage, the business is now very well established. It is successful and the owner and the business have become quite separate financially and operationally. However it can become very bureaucratic and stifle innovation.

One of the major challenges for independent business people is that both the problems faced and the skills necessary to deal with them change as the business grows. You need to anticipate these changing factors based on the stage of development of your business.

Similarly at the success stage, you have to decide whether or not to commit all your time and risk everything you have worked for to date in order to grow further.

2

> Dai Evans holds a majority shareholding in Easy Electronics plc, a company that owns a large chain of shops that sell a wide range of household electrical goods. Hightec Electrical plc produces a range of electrical items such as kettles, irons, hairdriers, etc. Hightec have been trying to take over Easy Electronics for some time. They have been openly buying ordinary shares on the Stock Exchange over the last year, but they have not managed to obtain sufficient shares in order to make a bid for the company. They have now offered to buy Dai Evans' shares at a price above the current market price.

(a) What do the letters plc stand for? (1)
(b) What implications do the letters plc have for companies? (2)
(c) What is meant by the wording 'Dai Evans holds a majority shareholding'? (2)
(d) What do you understand by the term 'takeover' as used here? (2)
(e) State at least three ways that the takeover could affect the workers of Easy Electronics if it were to take place. (3)
(f) What factors might Dai Evans take into account before agreeing to sell his shares? (4)
(g) Suggest reasons why Hightec would want to take over Easy Electronics. (6)

3 Refer to the article about franchising on page 89.

(a) In your own words explain what franchising is. (2)
(b) Explain the terms franchisee and franchisor. (2)
(c) What is meant by 'start-up costs'? (3)
(d) The article says that profit projections generally show that franchisees should get their money back in 3–4 years. What are 'profit projections'? (3)
(e) State four disadvantages of being a franchise holder. (4)
(f) Why is a franchise business seen by banks as more likely to be successful as a form of self-employment that starting out on your own? (6)

4 Answer the following questions which are related to the illustration on page 77 showing the procedure involved in forming a limited liability company.

(a) At which of the stages in the flow diagram shown is a business given an identity separate from its owners? (1)
(b) How can the general public readily tell whether a business is a private or a public company? (2)
(c) If two limited companies were formed with the same name this could cause confusion. How is this avoided? (2)
(d) What are the implications of a business having limited liability? (2)

Types of Business

Franchising can offer success in self-employment

FRANCHISING is a method of starting up on your own by buying, not a business as such, but a licence from a franchisor to use his name and his tested operating methods and the exclusive rights to sell his products or service in a privileged territory for a fixed but renewable period of time.

The idea is that if you follow the methods that he lays down and that other franchisees have followed, you will achieve a predictable level of results.

The start-up costs vary from under £10,000 to over £250,000, but the average is around £40,000-£50,000 and profit projections generally show that you should get your money back in 3-4 years. Furthermore you can borrow up to 70% of the cost of an approved scheme from the bank.

There are about 350 franchises on the market and a number of them are household names: Tie Rack, Prontaprint, Pizza Express, Budget Rent a Car and Body Shop, are just a few.

Rapid expansion

In the USA, franchising accounts for 30% of all retail sales, and though it has a long way to go to reach anything like that figure here, it is expanding even more rapidly. Latest figures show that annual UK sales are at £2.2 billion and that they are expected to top £5 billion comfortably by the end of 1990.

Franchising is seen by the banks and, increasingly, the government, as one of the major avenues into self-employment, because using a business format in this way has proved to have a high success rate as compared to starting out entirely on your own.

Source: *Executive Post*, June 1988.

(e) The diagram shows that a public company raises its capital eventually by issue of shares. How does a private company raise its capital? (3)

(f) Briefly state the differences in function of the memorandum of association and the articles of association, giving a separate example of an item included in each that is not contained in the other. (4)

(g) Explain the differences between a private limited company and a public limited company. (6)

Research Assignments

1. Make a survey of all (or a section of) the businesses in your high street and discuss the appropriateness of the various forms of legal identity for the nature of the business enterprise. Can you give reasons for any differences you can identify?

2. Carry out a survey of municipal undertakings in your locality and assess to what extent it would be more appropriate if they were in private ownership.

3. Make a study of any local issue which has implications for local businesses, e.g. introduction of a one-way system or parking restrictions. What is your view of the effect the development may have on local businesses?

4. Form a diagrammatic 'map' of the organisation structure of a small and a medium-sized local firm with which you are familiar. Comment on the differences observed.

5. Locate a well-established local entrepreneur who started his or her business from 'scratch'. What factors can you identify as making contributions to its apparent success?

6. Complete a survey of all the public sector activities within your locality which are controlled by a public corporation, central government or local government. To what extent do you consider the source of control appropriate to local needs?

7. Choose one of the nationalised (or one that has been privatised) industries and trace its development from the time of nationalisation to its present status.

8. Interview the owners of any relatively recently established business in your locality:

    (a) Discover what are the main problems faced by the owners.
    (b) How did they overcome the difficulties?
    (c) What problems are they still faced with?

9. Imagine that you are a skilled craftsman who has recently been made redundant and you have been awarded £30 000 redundancy pay. What local help is available to assist you to set up your own business?

# 5 Recruitment, Selection and Training

5.1 The Human Resources department

The functions of the department

The Human Resources Department is sometimes called the Personnel department in some firms. This is because it is concerned with the personnel (people) employed by the business. The department is responsible for finding the right person for vacant jobs. This involves advertising the vacancy in the most appropriate way, interviewing applicants, offering the best candidate an appointment, inducting them into the organisation, and providing training and further development opportunities for them. The department is also concerned with the welfare or well-being of employees. It will also be involved in dealing with resignations of workers, providing them with *testimonials* and *references*. It may also be involved in the dismissal of workers, perhaps involving redundancy.

Publicising job vacancies

Employers want to get the best person possible to fill a vacancy and those seeking employment will want to investigate all available possibilities. The following are the main sources of information for people seeking job vacancies:

- school or college careers advisers
- job centres run by government agencies
- employment agencies run by private firms
- local careers officers
- newspaper advertisements
- people who already work for the firm.

The Human Resources Department is helped in attracting and selecting appropriate staff by a job specification and a job description.

Job specification

The *job specification* identifies the *qualities* required of candidates for a particular job. It will vary in accordance with the job but may include items such as:

- personal characteristics required
- qualifications or past experience necessary
- physical fitness required
- skills needed.

Job description

The *job description* will vary depending on the job. It is a broad general statement which will usually include:

- the job title
- a description of the work and responsibilities
- special skills or features of the work
- the department where the employee will work
- who the employee will be responsible to.

Advertisements are the most common way of publicising a job vacancy and inviting applications. These advertisements are important to the firm because they must be carefully formulated so that they attract the right sort of applicant. They must clearly state what is required otherwise valuable time will be wasted investigating the suitability of applicants. They are also important to the job hunter because they help to ensure that they only apply for the kind of job they really want. The people that the firm is trying to reach with their advertisement are referred to as the *target audience*.

Letters of application

In some cases it may be acceptable to type a letter, in others the advertisement may state that the application should be in 'first hand', in which case the letter should be handwritten, preferably on plain paper. It is sensible to make a rough draft of the proposed letter before writing it out in detail.

Curriculum vitae

Job advertisements today frequently ask for a curriculum vitae (CV) from appli-

Advertisement	Question
OFFICE JUNIOR £4500 pa to	Is the pay suitable?
check invoices and calculate insurance and freight costs.	Will you enjoy the work?
Experience preferred, but school leaver with Business Studies background considered. Neat handwriting, aptitude for figure work and minimum GCSE Grade	Have you the qualities required?
C in English and Mathematics required.	Do you have the right qualifications?
• Luncheon vouchers • Flexible hours • Sports and social club • Pleasant offices near railway station	Are there any fringe benetifs?
Applications in writing to: Mr B Mason, The Personnel Officer, Astor Publications PLC,	What form of application is required?
7 Pleasant Street, BIRMINGHAM B10 9UB	Is the job within convenient reach?

Factors a job applicant will take into account when considering making a job application.

Recruitment, Selection and Training

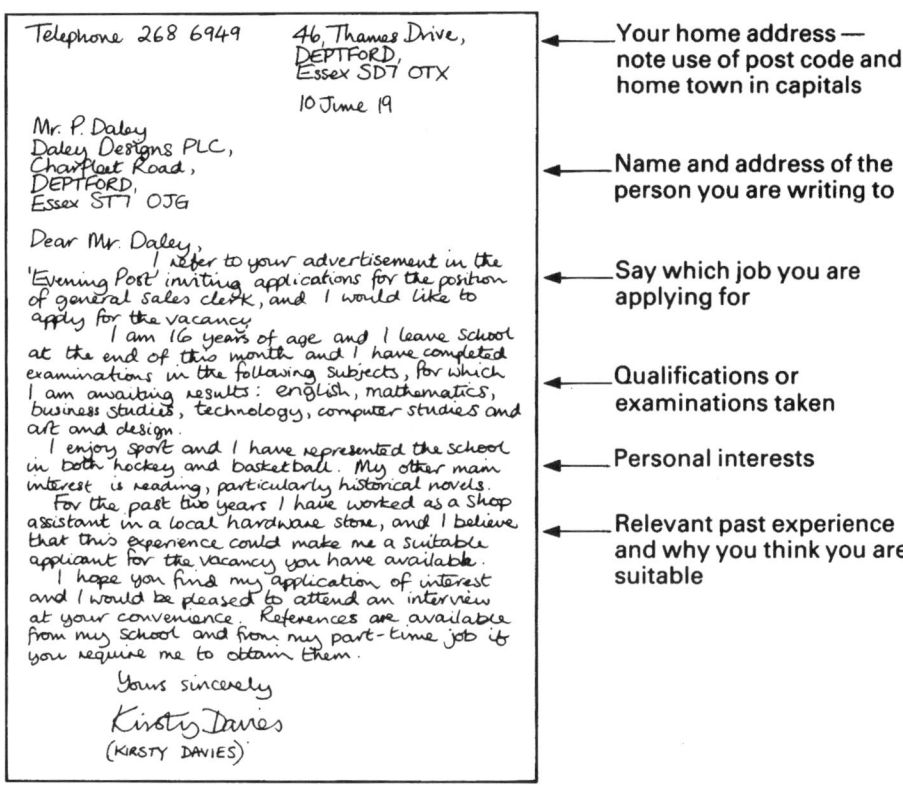

Employers will be influenced by a letter that is clearly worded and presented in the correct manner.

cants. A CV is a brief history of the applicant, for example school, qualifications, relevant experience, etc. This should be typed to accompany the letter of application, thus making it possible to make the letter shorter and more concise. Sometimes names, addresses and telephone numbers of the referees are included at the end of the CV.

Application form

These are standard printed forms which are sent out by firms for applicants to fill out providing specific information to support their application. The form may be sent to the applicant for completion prior to interview, or it may have to be completed under supervision at the interview.

There are two main reasons why firms use an application form as part of the recruitment and selection process. First, it acts as a check on personal details, qualifications and experiences, and it ensures that key information is included in the minimum space. Second, it allows selection panel members to easily make comparisons between candidates.

```
               CURRICULUM VITAE    SUNILA PATEL

               ADDRESS             21 Courtfield Road
                                   Nottingham

               DATE OF BIRTH       12 October 1969

               SEX                 Female

               PLACE OF BIRTH      Nottingham

               NATIONALITY         British

               EDUCATION           St Martins School
                                   Ladyfield Road
                                   Nottingham

                                   1981 to 1986

               GCSE                English language
                                   Mathematics
                                   French
                                   Biology
                                   History
                                   Business studies

               INTERESTS           Reading
                                   Outdoor sports
                                   Music

               WORK EXPERIENCE     Saturday job in family general store
```

Example of a curriculum vitae.

References

Most employers will require applicants to provide the names of persons (*referees*) willing to testify as to the character of the candidate, or written declarations (*testimonials*) from reliable persons testifying to the good character of the applicant. Referees should be contacted by the applicant for permission before using their names on the CV.

5.2 Short-lists and interviews

Short-lists

Applications for employment are received by the Human Resources department. It is often not practical to interview all the applicants for a job. Instead, the number of applications are reduced to form a *short-list* of the most suitable applicants for the vacancy. Those involved in drawing up the short-list will obviously be seeking the most suitable applicants, but they will take care to ensure that laws such as the *Race Relations Act* and the *Sex Discrimination Act* are not broken.

Recruitment, Selection and Training

Interviews

Short-listed applications for employment are invariably interviewed (usually in the Human Resources department) before any job offer is made. The aim of the interview is not only to assess the suitability of the candidate for the vacant position, but also to give the applicant the opportunity to seek further information about the job. During the interview the applicant may be required to complete an *aptitude test* designed to assess their suitability for the job available.

The interview is crucial for the applicant because it is at this time that the interviewer assesses the candidate's appearance, ability to communicate and general manner. Consequently, it is important to be thoroughly prepared for the interview.

Preparation for the interview
- Do a little homework about the job for which you have applied.
- Use your common sense about your appearance.
- Remember the name of the person you have to see.
- Know exactly where the interview will take place.
- Plan the route to get there.

During the interview
- Only sit down when invited to.
- Do not smoke.
- Try to be relaxed and confident.
- Concentrate fully on the interviewer.

Crossing your fingers will not get you a job.

- Be prepared to answer questions.
- Try to ask some sensible questions when you are invited to do so.

At the interview
- Dress carefully.
- Take the letter inviting you for interview.
- Arrive promptly.
- Appear confident but not flippant.
- Do not be over-familiar.

Questions to be prepared for
- Why do you want the job?
- What qualities do you have to offer?
- What is your future ambition?
- What do you do in your spare time?
- What do you read?

Questions you could ask
- What does the job involve?
- What hours are involved?
- What is the salary?
- What are the opportunities for promotion?
- What are the holiday arrangements?

Carrying out an interview effectively

It is important that the interviewer carries out their function correctly if the best person is going to be recruited. The interviewer will be helped to some extent by the contents of the job specification and the job description, because these contain the criteria they are trying to match the candidate to. Before they commence the interview the interviewer needs to have a clear idea of:

- what they are trying to find out about the candidate
- how they are going to find out what they want to know.

An import skill in interviewing candidates is the ability to put them at ease during what can be a stressful situation. The skilled interviewer will:

- encourage the interviewee to reveal something of their true personality
- ensure that their questions help to judge the candidate's fitness for the job
- ask 'open-ended' questions, rather than 'closed' questions that require only a 'yes' or 'no' answer.

A good interviewer will be wary of the *'halo effect'*. This refers to the danger of allowing one impressive, favourable candidate to influence your consideration of other candidates. A good interviewer will also be mindful of the effect on an unsuccessful candidate of not offering them the job. They will take care that this person does not see not getting the job as a personal failure.

The person who has been selected to fill a vacancy is in due course given a *contract of employment*. This gives the employee particulars of their *terms of employment* in the form of a contract. The details of the content of the Contract of Employment can be found in Chapter 6.

5.3 Staff orientation and development

Induction

All new members of a business need help in becoming familiar with the organisation of the firm, to learn about their new job, and to become acquainted with their work colleagues and other people in the organisation. The sooner that new employees are working effectively, the quicker they will be making a useful contribution to the business. Many firms operate an induction programme to help new staff to settle in quickly. Some organisations issue employees with a staff handbook containing basic information about the business and the rules or principles it expects employees to follow.

The induction programme may include visits to various parts of the organisation so the employee becomes familiar with the work of colleagues. Sometimes a new employee will be attached to a *mentor*. The mentor is an experienced member of the staff who helps to familiarise them with their new job.

Appraisal

Appraisal is a system of identifying staff development needs and evaluating the progress an employee has made in their professional development since the last appraisal was carried out.

There are no specific requirements for an appraisal process, and each organisation will tailor its appraisal programme to its own requirements. But a typical appraisal programme will include the person being appraised (the *appraisee*) being guided through the process by another member of the organisation (the *appraiser*). The appraiser is often the person the appraisee is responsible to – their *line manager*. A typical appraisal programme will include evaluation of:

- the appraisee's progress over the period since the last appraisal
- targets for the appraisee to achieve during the next period
- training needs of the appraisee
- improved performance likely to occur from the development
- how improved performance will be measured
- the date the next review will take place.

The appraisal process will often be part of a wider programme in a large organisation, where there may well be a *staff development plan* which will supervised by a senior member of staff, such as the Human Resources Manager.

 ## Training

Many employers recognise the benefits of helping staff to improve their skills and experiences and try to promote this through a *staff development programme*. Training is an important part of staff development and it may be carried out *internally* or *externally*.

Internal training is sometimes called 'in-house' training because it takes place within the organisation, e.g. courses run by the firm, or *on-the-job-training* which involves the employee learning new skills within the working environment.

External training is provided by organisations outside the firm, perhaps by a local college. Sometimes the employer will give an employee time off work to attend approved courses.

Vocational qualifications

Vocational courses have become an increasingly important aspect of business training and staff development. *National Vocational Qualifications (NVQs)* are qualifications awarded to workers and related to the work they do in their place of work. They are divided into units, each of which addresses a particular skill relevant to the person's work. NVQs aim to give people the ability to do a specific job – known as competency. An important aspect of NVQs is that they encourage an employee to examine closely the work they do and, therefore, promotes good working practices.

General National Vocational Qualifications (GNVQs) provide a broader training than NVQs and they cover a broad vocational area including a collection of subjects related to the world of work. A person following a GNVQ programme learns general skills, as well as studying the knowledge and ideas that are used in a vocational context. GNVQs are also split into units, but they are largely classroom based.

Investors in People is the National Standard for effective investment in people. In order to meet the Standard, organisations have to demonstrate they are ensuring

Reproduced by permission of Investors in People UK.

Recruitment, Selection and Training

that their employees have the skills and motivation to carry out the work they are required to do. Organisations which meet the Standard provide a variety of training and development opportunities for their staff, and they are allowed to display evidence of recognition that they meet the Standard through use of the Investors in People logo.

5.5 The welfare of employees

Looking after employees

Welfare refers to the concern for the physical well-being of people. Social facilities, lighting and heating, hygiene and canteen services are all examples of things that contribute to the welfare of employees. These all come within the functions of the Human Resources Department in a large firm.

The Human Resources Department may be responsible for the operation of the company's sports and social club, organising activities and events which encourage employees to mix socially. A member of this department may also have the responsibility of visiting employees who are sick, or those who have retired.

The firm may have its own house newspaper or magazine which is used to keep the workers up-to-date with events in which the company is involved, as well as providing a means of general communication.

Most firms recognise that good working conditions not only keep the employees happy, but also help to make them more productive and efficient. For this reason, firms try to provide good working conditions, but there are a number of Acts which are particularly concerned with staff welfare. These are dealt with together with other aspects of working conditions in the next chapter.

5.6 Staff records

The letter of application for employment, the curriculum vitae or the completed application form, together with the results of any *aptitude tests* taken when the new employee joins the firm, form the basis of the record of the individual held by the employer.

Over the years of employment the file held is added to by progress reports from other more senior members of the firm. These reports and other records of progress will include reference to the following aspects of the employee:

- punctuality
- health
- academic progress
- promotions and salary increases
- suitability for further promotion
- misdemeanours.

From the foregoing it will be obvious that the contents of personnel records are highly confidential. For this reason, people who work in the Human Resource Department are expected to be discreet. In addition, security of personnel records is of utmost importance.

5.7 Resignations, dismissal, redundancy and grievance

Resignation

Employees may *resign* their job. That is, they may leave one employer and go to another. Where this is the case, they are required to give *notice*. This means they must tell the employer in advance that they intend to leave. The period of notice to be given will be stipulated in the contract of employment. When leaving one employment for another the worker may be given a *reference* (sometimes called a testimonial) as a testimony of their character and quality as a worker. The person providing the reference is call the *referee*.

Dismissal

In the following chapter reference is made to the Contract of Employment Act which requires all employees to be given details of the terms of their employment. The contract of Employment includes the length of *notice* (length of time as notification of ceasing employment) to be given by the employer and the employee. When a worker wishes to take up new employment elsewhere they are required to give a period of 'notice' which allows the employer to look for a new employee. Similarly, if the employer wishes to dismiss the worker a period of notice is generally observed, although there are exceptions to this, such as when the employee has been guilty of a serious misdemeanour. In such circumstances it is usual that certain steps will have been followed:

1 oral warning
2 written warning
3 suspension
4 dismissal.

Obviously the employee may get instant dismissal for breaking substantive rules of the organisation, e.g. stealing, or putting other employees in danger.

Today workers are protected against unfair dismissal by the Employment Protection Act which requires an employer to show that there are good reasons for terminating employment. An employee who feels that they have been unfairly dismissed can complain to an Industrial Tribunal. If the Tribunal finds that the employer has acted unfairly or unreasonably, it can order reinstatement of the employee. If this is not practicable, the Tribunal can award compensation against the employer.

Recruitment, Selection and Training

Redundancy

This refers to a situation when an employee loses their job because it no longer exists. This may occur because the business has been forced to cease trading, or when the firm no longer has the capacity to employ the same number of workers.

When an employee loses their job as a result of redundancy they need financial help to enable them to make the transition to new employment.

The Redundancy Payments Act requires employers to make a lump sum payment to employees being made redundant (so long as they have served a minimum period of time). The amount of redundancy compensation depends upon the age, length of service, and pay of the employee.

Grievance procedure

An employee has a 'grievance' in the following situations:

- an existing employer/employee agreement has been broken;
- a labour law has been violated by the employer;
- the employer has acted in an unfair manner;
- the health or safety of the employee has been put at risk.

The first point of contact for the employee is their *work supervisor* who may be willing and able to offer a remedy for the circumstances. Certainly this person would be the point of contact between the aggrieved person and the firm's management.

Should representation through the supervisor be inappropriate or unsatisfactory, the worker will contact their *union representative*, often another employee of the company. This person will be familiar with the rights of the worker and will act on their behalf, or direct the grievance to the union for advice and guidance. The union may even decide that the employee does not have a real grievance, and it is part of their function to advise the worker of this.

5.8 Activities

Make a note of it

1. Why is the Human Resources Department sometimes referred to as the Personnel Department?
2. Summarise the main functions of the Human Resources Department.
3. List five sources of information about job vacancies.
4. In what ways can a job specification help in the formation of a job advertisement?
5. What information does a job description contain?

6. Why are job advertisements important to both the firm and the applicant?
7. List four specific pieces of information that the job applicant can obtain from the advertisement.
8. What does it mean when an advertisement states that applications must be in 'first hand'?
9. Make a list of six suggestions you would give someone to help him or her write a letter of application for a job.
10. What is a curriculum vitae? What information does it contain?
11. In what way does an application form differ from a CV?
12. What is the function of 'referees' and 'testimonials' in relation to applications for employment?
13. What is a 'short-list'?
14. What is the main purpose of the interview?
15. Why might a job applicant be required to complete an aptitude test?
16. In what way can someone usefully prepare for a job interview?
17. List six points the candidate should observe during the interview.
18. Give four examples of questions that might be asked of an applicant at the interview.
19. Suggest four questions the job applicant could ask when invited to do so.
20. What is the aim of an interview?
21. Why is it important that an interviewer carries out their function effectively?
22. What will help an interviewer to appoint the best person?
23. What is the purpose of an induction programme?
24. Why do you think the work of a 'mentor' is important?
25. What is appraisal?
26. Explain the following terms: appraisee, appraiser, line-manager.
27. Why are vocational qualifications so relevant to both employers and employers?
28. What is 'Investors in People'?
29. Why would a firm be interested in the welfare of its employees?
30. In what way might a firm show its care for the welfare of its employees?

Recruitment, Selection and Training

APPLICATION

Surname: McMeakin (Mr/Mrs/Ms)
Forename(s): Richard David
Address: 10 Juniper Close, CATERHAM, Surrey CR3 6SZ
Nationality: British
Date of birth: 24/12/79

EDUCATION

School or college	Dates	Examinations taken
King Edward, Caterham, Surrey	1992 – 1997	GCSE: English, Maths, Science, Business Studies, Geography

PREVIOUS EMPLOYMENT

Name of employer	Dates	Position held
The Bargain Shop, High Road, Caterham	1995 to present	Part-time shop assistant, some experience on cash till.

Other relevant experience: Two weeks of work experience arranged by my school in a local estate agents. I answered the telephone, did some duplicating, and prepared mail for the post. Sometimes I went out with one of the agents visiting properties.

Hobbies and other interests: I belong to a local drama group presenting small shows for charity.

Referees

Name: Dr. K. Beasely
Position: Headmaster
Address: King Edward School, Southwick Road, Caterham.

Name: Mrs. B. Rose
Position: Manager
Address: The Bargain Shop, High Road, Caterham.

Signature: R. McMeakin
Date:

OFFICE USE ONLY

Medical Report	References received
Date appointed	Department	Position

31 How would the Personnel department in particular be involved in the welfare of employees?

32 Briefly describe the kind of information likely to be found in personnel records. Why is security and confidentiality important to personnel records?

33 Explain the difference between resignation, dismissal and redundancy.

34 When does an employee have a genuine grievance?

35 What action can an employee take when they have grievance?

Structured Questions

1 The questions below are all related to the application for employment on page 103.

(a) Name the person who is applying for employment. (1)
(b) How important is it to the employer to know about details of the applicant's previous employment when it was only done on a part-time basis? (2)
(c) Why is the employer interested in the applicant's 'hobbies and interests' even though they may have no relevance to the vacant position? (2)
(d) What is the purpose of 'referees' and why are two requested? (4)
(e) Briefly state the purpose of each of the small sections within the part of the form marked 'office use only'. (5)
(f) What is a 'short-list' and what factors might an employer take into account in deciding whether this particular applicant should be short-listed? (6)

2 Refer to the newspaper article on page 105 related to a sales career and answer the questions below.

(a) What work do you think a careers' counsellor does? (1)
(b) Why is it in the interest of both the employer and the employee that the salesperson is successful? (2)
(c) What do you understand by the word 'extrovert' in the context that it is used in this article?
(d) Why does age and previous job experience affect a person's chance of success in a sales career? (6)
(e) The article states that the type of person most suited to sales work is determined by the type of business or product involved. Take two contrasting types of business and explain why they require a different type of salesperson. (8)

3 Questions a–e are all related to the 'sales career' article below.

(a) Why do salespeople need to be able to 'understand and manipulate numerical data and to be able to read and understand product information'? (2)

(b) The article says that 'sales effectiveness tends to increase up to the age of about forty and to decline in later years'.
   (i) Give two reasons that support this statement. (2)
   (ii) Give one example of the type of sales where this statement may not apply, giving reasons for your choice. (3)

(c) 'Most recruiters who are looking for salespeople refer to the importance of motivation – by this they usually mean the motivation induced by monetary rewards.' Briefly explain how most firms motivate their salespeople. (3)

(d) Salespeople need to be able to work on their own initiative. What does this mean? Quote from the article to support your answer. (4)

Discover if you've got what it takes for a sales career

By ROGER LAY

THE EXPERIENCE of careers' counsellors is that very few people have in mind a sales career as their first choice.

But the sales team is an essential element of any commercial enterprise. Quite a lot of people therefore, find themselves in selling roles.

Clearly, if you are faced with the prospect of a sales career, it is in both your interests and that of your future employers that your chances of success be as high as possible. How can you tell if you are likely to make a successful salesperson?

The popular image of the successful salesperson is of someone who is highly extroverted or outgoing, socially confident and who tends to be fairly agressive in their approach to people.

Although there would appear to be an element of truth in this, research into the question reveals a far more complicated picture.

Some of the factors which determine the type of person most suited to sales work are;
- The type of business or product involved.
- The selling techniques used (telephone sales, face-to-face contacts, cold calling, maintenance of major accounts etc.).
- The extent to which technical product knowledge is required.

Age and previous job experience also affect a person's chance of success in a sales career.

Although the factors which determine success in sales are complex, it is clear that personality type is important.

The difficulty in predicting what type of person is likely to be successful, is that even where the type of business and selling techniques are known, there are still quite wide variations in personality type. Nevertheless, there are some common factors:
- Social confidence or social sophistication, and the ability to relate easily to others.
- Organisational effectiveness and independence, and the ability to formulate and carry out a plan of action without close supervision.
- Emotional resilience, and the ability to keep going even when the customer says 'no.'
- Energy, enthusiasm and competitiveness, and the ability to go out looking for a sale rather than waiting for the telephone to ring.
- Persuasiveness, and the ability to change a person's inclinations, opinions or decisions.
- Lack of modesty also appears to be a characteristic of some successful salespeople.

It is perhaps worth noting that there is little support for the idea that successful salespeople need to be outgoing in nature and aggressive in their approach (although some people with these characteristics do in fact succeed in sales work).

Most recruiters who are looking for salespeople refer to the importance of motivation — by this they usually mean the motivation induced by monetary rewards.

However, research evidence suggests that financial motivation is only significant where a commission pay system operates.

As far as abilities are concerned, successful salespeople tend to be above average in intelligence. More specific aptitudes which are relevant include the ability to understand and manipulate numerical data (eg: price lists, numerical tables) and to be able to read and understand product information.

Where the product or service being sold is highly technical in nature, a salesperson is likely to be more effective if they have a good familiarity and understanding of technical aspects.

A number of special psychological tests have recently been developed to assess sales potential. These tests typically concentrate on evaluating personality factors relevant to selling.

Age is another factor related to sales success — sales effectiveness tends to increase up to the age of about forty and to decline in later years.

A final observation — although as observed earlier, quite a wide range of personalities can be successful in selling roles, sales managers (having almost always been successful salespeople themselves) usually believe that only people in their own image will be successful and recruit accordingly.

Source: *Executive Post.*

(e) If you refer to the list of common factors identified as likely to influence a person's success as a salesperson, some of these tend to contradict the later statement – 'There is little support for the idea that successful salespeople need to be outgoing in nature and aggressive in their approach.' Discuss this observation. (6)

4 Look at the 'Situations Vacant' advertisements below and answer the following questions.

(a) Considering that a typed application is easier to read, and a telephone application quicker to deal with, why do many job advertisements ask for applications in writing? (2)

(b) Why do all the jobs here quote reference numbers and no individual addresses? (2)

SITUATIONS VACANT

PERSONNEL ASSISTANT
AGE 17+ £7500 pa
Excellent benefits

Additional team member to join this busy personnel environment. Sense of humour, bags of stamina, good typing/administrative skills essential. Good telephone manner. Ref 134

RECEPTIONIST
TO £6000 pa Age 16/18
Young, bubbly, well presented young lady required for superb reception area. Excellent benefits to include gym, subsidised restaurant. Typing an advantage, pleasant personality essential, willingness to learn PABX switchboard as relief operator. Ref 166

TELEPHONIST/TYPIST
We require a Telephonist Typist for our large car showrooms. Will train on switchboard but accurate typing is essential – 40 wpm. Some clerical work involved. Good salary and some perks. Ref 281

SHORTHAND SECRETARY
£9000. Good s/h skills/audio. Working on a one-to-one basis for partner. Lots of variety. 5 weeks' holiday. Early finish Friday (4.30). Ref. 294

SALES OFFICE CLERK
We are an extrovert team working in a busy sales office and we need help! If you enjoy dealing with people, have legible handwriting, numeracy skills and a good telephone manner – contact us now. Salary negotiable. Ref 207

ACCOUNTS CLERK
LVs, pension scheme ideal opportunity for a person with all-round knowledge of accounts and experience of computerised systems. Immediate interviews. Salary £6250. Any age.
Ref 222

AUDIO TYPIST
£6000 Age 16+
Busy office needs extra pair of hands typing correspondence, reports, etc. Duties will include client/telephone liaison. Solicitors. Good salary offered. increments for RSA/LCCI qualifications at higher levels. Apply in writing in first instance.
Ref 285

WP SECRETARY – LOCAL £8000
Lovely position for a confident secretary with a flair for admin. Meeting and greeting clients, cross-train on our WP system and Telex. Never a dull moment! Qualifications required in word processing. Ref 298

All applications quoting reference number to:
Topline Employment Agency
17 Primrose Park
UXBRIDGE
Middx
UB10 9TZ

Recruitment, Selection and Training

    (c) What is meant by 'a good telephone manner' and why is this important to both a firm and its clients? (3)

    (d) One of the advertisements shown states 'good salary and perks'. What are perks? Give some examples. (3)

    (e) These jobs are all advertised through an employment agency. What services would such a business provide to help a firm to obtain appropriate new employees? (4)

    (f) Applicants for jobs would be 'short-listed' by the firm looking for new staff. What is a 'short-list' and what factors might the employer take into account when deciding who to include in the list? (6)

5 The questions below are also related to the 'Situations Vacant' advertisement on page 106.

    (a) What is meant by the wording apply 'in the first instance'? (2)

    (b) Take any two *contrasting* job advertisements shown here and briefly explain the work involved. (2)

    (c) Choose any one of the jobs advertised and draft a letter of application for yourself. (6)

    (d) All of the following terms have been used in the job advertisements shown here. Briefly explain each one:

        £6000 pa   PABX
        Salary negotiable   LVs
        S/h skills   Increments
        WP system   Subsidised
        One-to-one   40 wpm (10)

6 Look at the following job description and answer these questions.

    (a) What is the purpose of a job description? (1)

    (b) Say, in no more than 25 words, what work a sales representative does. (2)

    (c) Most job descriptions include details of hours of employment but this one shows none. Give two possible reasons why no hours are included in this description. (2)

    (d) Why do you think this company holds its annual sales conference at weekends? (2)

    (e) Give three examples of the sort of advice a sales representative might give to customers. (3)

    (f) What do you understand by 'induction training'? (3)

    (g) This sales representative sold £32 000 of the company's products during the first four months of employment, and a further £25 000 in sales in the following two months. How much commission would the person receive in the first six months, and what would be their total gross earnings for the period? Show all calculations. (3)

    (h) In what ways could both the employee and the employer gain from payment by both a basic wage and commission rather than by basic wage alone? (4)

Comprehensive Business Studies

> **JOB DESCRIPTION**
>
> **Job title:** Sales Representative
> **Salary:** £10 000 P.A. + 10% commission
> **Car allocation:** Grade C
> **Department:** Marketing
> **Responsible to:** Sales Manager
> **Duties and responsibilities:**
>
> 1. Visit existing customers to obtain orders and offer advice
> 2. Make contact with new potential customers and solicit orders
> 3. Submit monthly sales analysis reports
> 4. Attend bi-monthly sales meetings at Head Office (Saturday a.m.)
> 5. Participate in annual sales conference weekend at various venues.
>
> **Supervision procedures:** Induction training initially supervised by Sales Manager for two months. Further two months supervision by Senior Sales Representative. Commission at half rate during this induction period, thereafter at full rate. Review of Job Description and salary after 12 months.

Research Assignments

1. How do local employers attract staff? Provide evidence to support your findings.

2. Select four contrasting advertisements for business jobs and describe how you would ensure that you accept the most appropriate applicant for the vacancies.

3. Make a study of the induction programme of a firm with which you are familiar or can gain access to and suggest ways in which it might be improved.

4. Design an induction programme to introduce pupils new to your school/college, or those joining a business with which you are familiar.

5. Describe the facilities the government provides which help people who want to train for new employment.

6 While out on work experience make a comparative study of your job and another in the same organisation.

7 Make a survey of job vacancies at your local Job Centre and find out from the Centre how many local people are unemployed. Give suggestions why such jobs remain unfilled while there are people unemployed

8 Using examples from your local area, evaluate the methods used by different companies in the recruitment and retention of staff.

Motivation of Employees

6.1 Job satisfaction

People spend a large percentage of their life at work. Therefore, it is important that they get some satisfaction from their job. Not all jobs can give satisfaction, and people have different ideas of what constitutes a good job. For some people pay is the most important factor, others will have some other priority. Often it is a combination of many factors which makes a job satisfying. The following are just some of these factors. What others would you include? What would be your order of priority?

- Pay and opportunity for wage increases.
- Promotion prospects.
- Working hours and times of attendance.
- Holiday arrangements.
- Job security.
- Friendship and relationship between employees.
- Conditions in which work is carried out.
- Fringe benefits or 'perks' given.

Most jobs will include a combination of the above factors. Some are within the influence of the employee, but the employer has by far the greater effect on working conditions. There are, however, laws which ensure that working conditions do not fall below an agreed minimum standard. Some of these laws are examined later in this chapter.

There are various specific strategies that are used by employers to positively promote job satisfaction. Two of these are job enlargement and job enrichment:

- *Job enlargement.* This is where additional tasks are built into a job in order to make it more interesting or more satisfying for the worker and perhaps to relieve monotony by making it more demanding.
- *Job enrichment.* This is where the management of a business attempt to make a job satisfying, and more motivating for the worker, by changing the tasks and responsibilities it involves.

Appraisal of employees

Appraisal is a method of assessing how well an employee is carrying out his or her work. Performance is often rated against predetermined or negotiated criteria and usually targets are identified for achievement in the future. If managed effectively, appraisal is an important motivating tool. It recognises the achievement

Motivation of Employees

and the effectiveness of the employee, and it also gives them a direction for future development. Appraisal is dealt with in more detail in Chapter 5.

Wages

Wage Differentials

Wages are the reward paid for labour. Not surprisingly wages are considered more important to most people than many other things in life. This is because the level of earnings has such a considerable effect on the quality of life. The amount of income received influences the type of house and furnishings one can have, the quality of car owned and where and for how long holidays are taken. The poorly paid person cannot hope to compete with the highly paid person with regard to standard of living and leisure facilities. But for a variety of reasons some people are better paid than others, and it is important to understand why this is so.

The key to the reason for wage differentials is demand and supply. For the purpose of comparison we can take the wages of doctors and bus drivers as examples of where differences in wage levels exist. Both of these occupations are important to the community, but the doctor's wage is considerably higher than that of the bus driver. In other words, the cost of the doctor's services is far higher than the cost of the bus driver's services. Alternatively, we could say that the supply of doctors is smaller than the supply of bus drivers, forcing up the price of the doctor's services.

The supply of doctors is smaller than that of bus drivers for the following reasons. These same reasons can also be applied to many other examples of occupations where wage differences exist.

- The occupation requires a high degree of skill and academic ability.
- The training period is too long for many people.
- There is a degree of risk involved (e.g. infection).
- The work requires a special aptitude.

What other reasons can you think of for wage differentials?

Productivity deals

These are negotiated by the employer with employees (or their representatives).

They are agreements where targets are set or changes in working practices are implemented in order to achieve improved productivity. In return for the increased output employers give increases in wages.

Job evaluation

This refers to ranking jobs in order of importance, particularly for the purpose of deciding rates of pay.

Rates of pay

There are several ways that wages may be calculated, and sometimes a wage payment may combine more than one of these.

Flat rate
A set rate of pay per week or month based on a standard number of hours. Many workers are paid by this system but it does not always provide incentive to give extra time or effort.

Time rate
The worker is paid a set amount for each hour worked. The worker is paid 'overtime' at a higher rate of pay for additional hours worked.

Piece rate
This is not as common today as it has been in manufacturing in the past. A payment is made for each good quality item produced to encourage the production worker to give maximum effort.

Commission
A payment made additional to a flat or time rate as a percentage of the value of sales or business promoted.

There are various ways that rates of pay are established, two of these are *productivity deals* and *job evaluation*.

Deductions from pay

Gross pay is the total amount earned by the employee before any deductions have been made.

Net pay is the amount received by the employee after any deductions have been taken away. This figure is particularly important because it represents the actual income the worker receives.

Statutory deductions
These are compulsory deductions enforced by law:

- *Income Tax* – deducted from each wage payment through the PAYE (Pay As You Earn) system;
- *National Insurance* – weekly contributions to the state welfare scheme (e.g. health services) taken from each payment of wages.

Voluntary deductions
These are deductions that the wage earner can decide whether or not to have deducted automatically from their wages, for example:

- union membership fees;
- contribution to company social club;
- payments to private pension schemes;
- private medical schemes (e.g. BUPA) payments;
- transfers to the state savings scheme (SAYE – Save As You Earn).

Problems with payment systems

There are some problems associated with most of the rates of pay systems summarised earlier. For example, the 'flat rate' system does not reward the person who works harder than others, and the 'piece rate' system can result in rushed and poor quality work. Most wage systems rely on the conscientiousness of the worker, and this varies. It is for these reasons that firms sometimes use a combination of more than one rate of pay system and other 'back-up techniques'.

Share ownership Businesses sometimes use this system to motivate employees and to encourage loyalty. The employee is awarded shares in the company as an addition to their wages. This motivates them to work to achieve profitability for the company.

Profit-sharing The business encourages employees to work effectively by sharing the profitability of the business with them in some way.

Productivity deals A productivity deal is an arrangement whereby the employer agrees to improve the level of wages in line with an improvement in output. A productivity deal is sometimes linked to the piece rate system or a bonus.

A bonus is a way that employers can reward workers for improved profitability. A bonus is paid to employees as a share of additional profits gained by the employer due to increased effort, output or efficiency on the part of workers.

Fringe benefits Some employers provide their employees with these 'invisible' additions to their wages. They are sometimes referred to as 'perks'. The following are just some examples of fringe benefits, but there are many others

- free or subsidised meals
- a company car
- free membership of private medical schemes
- low-interest loans
- discounts off company products or services
- assistance with house-moving expenses.

Payment of wages

A wages or payroll department is responsible for the payment of wages. People employed in this department need an aptitude for work with figures and are often required to be familiar with the use of a computer.

When an employee is paid at a time rate, they will have a time card (clock card) which is kept in a rack near a time clock. As the employee arrives and leaves work they 'clock' on and off by inserting their card into the time clock. The times printed on to the time card are used by the Wages department to establish how much the employee should be paid.

Whether payment of wages is made by cash, cheque or credit transfer, the employee receives a pay advice. This is usually a slip of paper which is filled in by the Wages Department, often by computer, so that the employees can see how their net pay has been reached. The pay advice will contain the following information

- employee's name and work number
- tax code
- national insurance number
- gross pay
- bonus, commission, overtime
- compulsory deductions
- voluntary deductions
- net pay.

Much of the Wages Department work of calculating wages and producing pay advices can be assigned to computers. When the worker 'clocks' in and out the time data can be recorded on the time card by punch holes or magnetic ink characters. The data can be 'read' by computer and used to automatically:

- calculate gross and net pay;
- print out pay advice;
- maintain cumulative records for the production of:
  - *Form P45* – statement provided to an employee changing jobs to inform the new employer of the amount of income tax paid to date;

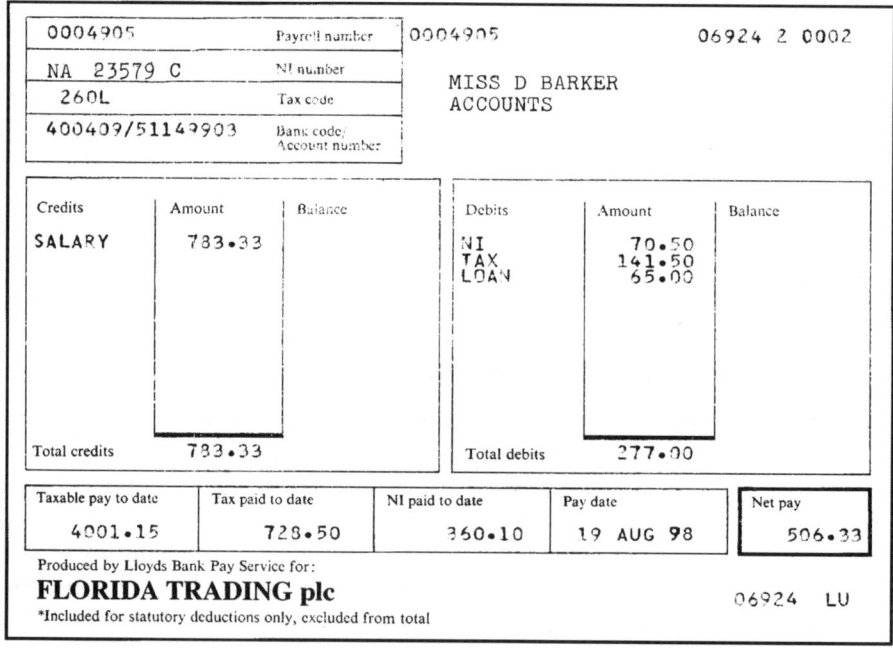

Pay advice.

- *Form P60* – annual certificate or statement notifying employee of gross wages, gross tax, and net wages paid for the whole year.

Fringe benefits

Some firms offer 'invisible' additions to the wages of their employees. These are called 'fringe benefits' or 'perks'. The following are examples of the kind of benefit given by the employer in addition to wages:

- free or subsidised meals (e.g. luncheon vouchers – LVs);
- company car;
- free membership of private health schemes;
- low interest rate loans for house purchase, etc.;
- reduced prices for company products or services;
- assistance with expense of moving house;
- help with payment of private education fees.

6.3 Working conditions

Terms of employment

The terms of employment are the arrangements or agreement between the employee and the employer of what task or responsibilities the employee is expected to carry out, and what reward they will receive for doing so. Information relating to this can be found in the job description, the job specification and the contract of employment. The job specification and job description are examined in Chapter 5.

Contract of Employment Act 1972

This Act requires employers to give employees particulars of their terms of employment. This contract must either be given to the employee or kept where they have access to it. The contract includes:

- job title;
- hours of work;
- holiday arrangements;
- rate of pay and how frequently paid;
- period of notice to be given by either side;
- person to contact in event of a grievance;
- legal rights such as belonging (or not belonging) to a union.

Hours of employment

One of the most important terms of employment is the hours of work. This refers not only to the total number of hours to be worked, but also what times of the day or night the hours have to be worked.

Although some people work shift work, most people work fixed hours. Consequently, most people are travelling to and from work at similar times. This results in traffic jams and congestion on public transport, and discomfort for travellers. It also means that public transport is not being used economically.

Not everyone finds it convenient to work the same hours as others. Workers sometimes need periods of time when they are not required to be at work. In addition, many businesses have periods of the day when not all members of staff are required to be present. At other busy 'core' times, everyone is needed at the same time.

Flexible Working Time (FWT)

Flexitime, FWT or flexible working time are the names given to a system of arranging working hours so that at 'peak' or 'core' times all members of staff are at work. Outside core time employees are allowed to choose the hours they work, so long as they complete the required number of overall hours in the week.

The working day of the firm is defined in three ways:

1 *Band time* – this is the total period of time the business operates, for example, 8.00 am to 6.00 pm.
2 *Core time* – this is the period of time when all members of the firm are expected to be at work.
3 *Flexible time* – this is the period outside the core time when employees can choose whether they work or not, so long as they complete the total number of weekly hours they are paid for.

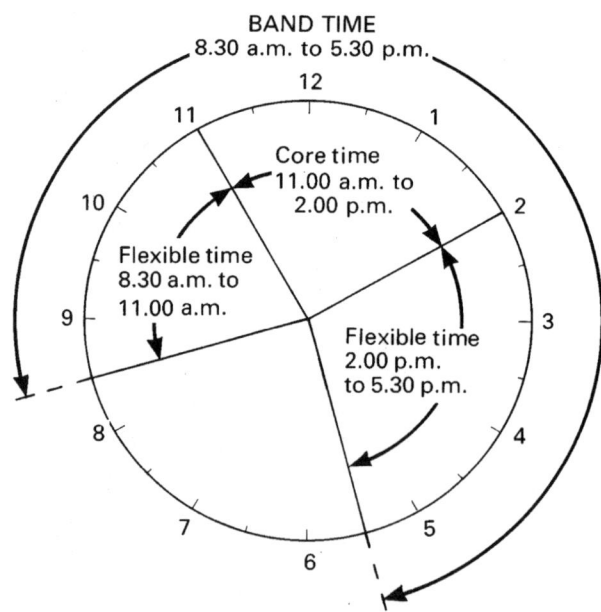

Total hours to be worked by employee = 35 hours

Flexible working time.

To choose their working hours employees first calculate core time. Core time in the above example is 5 days × 3 hours (11.00 am to 2.00 pm) = 15 hours. This leaves 20 hours (35 − 15 = 20) of working which can be chosen from FWT. Before choosing the hours of flexitime, employees will have to take into account the time they wish to use for lunch breaks. Most firms will insist that the employee takes at least a 30 minute lunch break.

Health and safety

The health and safety of employees is a major aspect of working conditions. The duty of employers to provide safe working conditions is often backed up by statutory requirements. The three main Acts which relate to health and safety are the Factories Act 1961, the Offices, Shops and Railway Premises Act 1963 and the Health and Safety at Work Act 1974.

Factories Act 1961

The Act in fact covers more than factories in the normal sense of the word. It includes brickworks, cement works, construction sites, dry cleaners, garages, gasworks, laundries, potteries, printing works, slaughterhouses and many other businesses which use mechanical machinery. The Act includes the following rules:

- work places must be properly lit and well ventilated;
- sufficient toilet and washing facilities must be provided;
- moving machinery must have a fenced surround;
- hoists, lifts, etc. must be properly constructed and maintained;
- floors, passages and stairs must be kept unobstructed;
- floors must not have slippery surfaces;
- fire-escapes must be provided and maintained.

Offices, Shops and Railway Premises Act 1963

This Act represents the principal legislation affecting working conditions in offices. Included within this Act are the following provisions:

- rooms must not be overcrowded (twelve square metres of floor space per person);
- temperature must not fall below 16°C;
- there must be adequate supplies of fresh or artificially purified air;
- suitable natural or artificial lighting;
- suitable and sufficient sanitary conveniences must be conveniently accessible, clean and properly maintained;
- accessible washing facilities with running hot and cold water, soap and clean towels.

Health and Safety at Work Act 1974 (HASAWA)

This Act sets out the duties of both the employer and the employee relating to health and safety.

- The employer's duty can be summed up as the responsibility to provide a safe workplace, including arrangements for hazards such as fire, and the maintenance and safety of machinery and equipment.
- Employees also have the duty to take reasonable care for the safety of themselves and other working colleagues at all times, and to cooperate with the employer on all matters of safety.

Other important employment-related Acts

Sex Discrimination Act 1975 – makes sex descrimination illegal in education, employment, training and the provision of goods, facilities and services.

Race Relations Act 1976 – makes racial discrimination illegal in employment and other activities such as education, housing, clubs and consumer affairs.

Equal Pay Act 1970 – aims to ensure equal treatment between women and men in respect of pay and terms of employment.

Data Protection Act 1984 – gives people the right to see information about them that is stored on computers.

6.4 Activities

Make a note of it

1 Why is it important that people gain satisfaction from their jobs? List six factors that you think make a job satisfying.

2 How can job enlargement and job enrichment help to motivate employees?

3 What is appraisal?

4 Why are wage differentials often the source of envy and discontent between workers?

5 List five factors which influence the supply of people suitable for a particular form of employment.

6 Briefly describe each of the following ways of calculating wages: flat rate; time rate; piece rate; bonus; commission.

7 What is a productivity deal?

8 How does job evaluation assist in establishing rates of pay?

9 Explain the differences between gross pay and net pay.

Motivation of Employees

10 If you have earned a gross wage of £210.28 and must pay deductions totalling £57.36, what will be your net pay?

11 Give examples and explain the difference between statutory deductions and voluntary deductions.

12 Cash is one way of paying wages. Name two others.

13 What is the purpose of a time card system? How can this system be of help to the Wages department of a firm?

14 List at least six items of information likely to be found on a pay advice.

15 Briefly describe the way that a computer could be employed in the Wages department.

16 Explain the purpose of forms P45 and P60.

17 What are fringe benefits? Give six examples.

18 List the kind of information that is contained in the contract of employment.

19 Why are hours of employment important to the working conditions of an employee?

20 What is flexible working time? Why is it possible to operate this system for people working in a restaurant, but very difficult to adopt for a school?

21 'The Factories Act 1961, the Offices, Shops and Railway Premises Act 1963 and the Health and Safety at Work Act 1974, all aim to protect working conditions, but they each have differences in their application.' Explain this statement.

Structured Questions

1 The newspaper article on page 120 is related particularly to 'personnel professionals'. These are people who work in the Human Resources Department of a company.

(a) What do you understand by the term stress in relation to working? (1)
(b) Why have the new responsibilities of personnel professionals contributed to their stress? (2)
(c) What do you understand by the term 'redundancy programme'? (2)
(d) Why would a redundancy programme result in stress for personnel professionals? (3)
(e) Briefly describe two forms that industrial action could take and say why such action would contribute to the stress of workers in a Human Resources Department. (4)

Personnel stress

THE MOST stressful activity for personnel professionals is the closure of a plant or the announcement of a redundancy programme. The second most stressful situation is the firing of a senior executive.

This is in contrast to the threat of industrial action, which rates only as a 'fairly stressful' situation. These are the findings of a recent survey in Personnel Today.

The survey asked the heads of personnel departments in some of Britain's largest companies to name the areas of their work which they found most stressful. A second survey, also looked at the new responsibilities which personnel departments are facing.

The responsibilities identified reflect the profession's increasing involvement in corporate activities, with 58% of those questioned noting their increased involvement in business strategy.

In the traditional area of trade union negotiations, however, 24% felt that they are now much less involved.

New responsibilities have included the use of computers and the administration of company pension schemes. The latter has become especially complex following changes in legislation.

Another major area has been the introduction of new staff evaluation and grading schemes, and employee share or profit-related pay. The introduction of such schemes now involves 59% of those asked.

"The findings of this latest survey reflect the changing business environment in which the personnel professional is working," explains Helena Sturridge, editor of Personnel Today.

"Their growing responsibilities have brought with them the need to cope with a number of stressful situations, and to manage a workforce in a far more sophisticated nature than ever before."

Source: Executive Post.

(f) What is a 'staff evaluation' and grading scheme' and why can this contribute to stress levels for personnel professionals in particular? (4)

(g) One way that a personnel department might be involved in business strategy is through public relations work. What does this involve? (4)

2 Refer to the newspaper article on page 121 and answer the following questions.

(a) Why would a management consultant be particularly useful to a small firm? (1)

(b) What service would a management consultancy give its clients? (2)

(c) Briefly say what an executive is and give two contrasting examples. (3)

(d) What is executive leasing and how does it differ from management consultancy. (3)

(e) Executive leasing is often used for handling 'one-off' assignments. Give three examples of 'one-off' assignments where an executive might be leased. (3)

(f) Why does executive leasing demand people with 'proven experience at middle or senior management level'? (4)

(g) State one advantage of executive leasing from the point of view of the executive. (4)

Motivation of Employees

3 Refer to the pay advice illustrated on page 114 and answer these questions.

(a) Name the employer and the employee related to the pay advice shown. (1)

(b) Give one reason for giving employees a payroll number. (1)

(c) What do the letters NI shown stand for? (1)

(d) What is the purpose of showing a bank code and account number? (2)

(e) This pay advice shows two statutory deductions from pay. What are they? (2)

(f) How much is this employee allowed to earn tax free in a year and how can you tell this from the pay advice? (3)

(g) List three possible voluntary deductions the employee could choose to pay. (3)

(h) Use information contained on this pay advice to help you explain the difference between gross pay and net pay. (3)

(i) This pay advice relates to just one calendar month of employment. Assuming that the employee's rate of pay and monthly deductions do not change, what would be the figure for gross pay and net pay for a 12-month period? Show all calculations. (4)

Dramatic Leap in Executive Leasing Now Seen as a Credible Professional Career

There has been a dramatic recent increase in the number of firms offering management consultancy services. These services are particularly useful for smaller firms with insufficient funds to employ suitable management executives.

This trend has been accompanied by the development of executive leasing: the engagement of an executive for a limited period to fill a particular short-term gap; for example, handling a 'one-off' assignment, or bridging a gap between one senior executive leaving and a successor starting.

Executive leasing offers one of the best ways of handling specific but short-term problems.

Executive leasing is now increasingly seen as a credible professional career, but success requires the executive to have had proven successful experience at middle to senior management level.

Research Assignments

1 Use personal interviews with workers in a variety of occupations to examine to what extent job satisfaction is important.

2 Make a comparative study of wages for different occupations in the same industry giving reasons for differences that exist.

3 Make a comparative study of wages for the same occupation in different industries giving reasons for differences that exist.

4 What evidence can you find that indicates the effectiveness of legislation on equal pay for women in your locality?

5 Interview a cross-section of office workers and people involved in some form of production. Find out how informed they are about the aims of their employers. Comment on your finds.

6 In many organisations there are often people who are keen to be promoted, and there are others who are not interested in advancement. Interview a cross-section of people in employment with the aim of establishing why these attitudes exist.

7 Visit your local Job Centre. Identify at least three contrasting job vacancies which illustrate wage differentials. Give a detailed explanation of the reasons for the different wage levels.

8 Obtain an example of a completed P45, P60 and P2 and clearly explain the function of each, identifying the purpose of particular data on each form.

Industrial Relations

7.1 The importance of industrial relations

People are not only the most important resource of an organisation, they are also the most costly resource. It might, therefore, be considered almost impossible to avoid at least some conflict between the employer and the employee. The employees will want to achieve the highest pay they can, while the employer will want to minimise the firm's wage costs. But there are other reasons linked to wages that can work against industrial peace and these are not necessarily directly related to the employer/employee relationship. For example, wage differentials (examined in detail in Chapter 6) can result in conflicts between groups of workers, and these conflicts can have an adverse effect on good working relationships.

The term 'industrial relations' is generally used when statements are made which refer to the extent to which conflict or peace exists in industry, as well as between employers and employees.

7.2 Trade unions

Trade unions are associations of people who join together in their common interest to regulate the relations between employees and employers.

Unions are important from the point of view of workers because they enable them to pay a small subscription each, which the union then uses to employ skilled officials to act on the workers' behalf. Unions are also important to employers because they enable them to have discussions and negotiations with a small number of people rather than many.

Trade union aims

Trade unions aim to secure for workers:

- improved wages and reduced working hours;
- improved working conditions;
- full employment and national prosperity;
- job security;
- benefits for members who are sick, retired or on strike;
- improved social security schemes such as unemployment, sickness benefit and pensions;

Comprehensive Business Studies

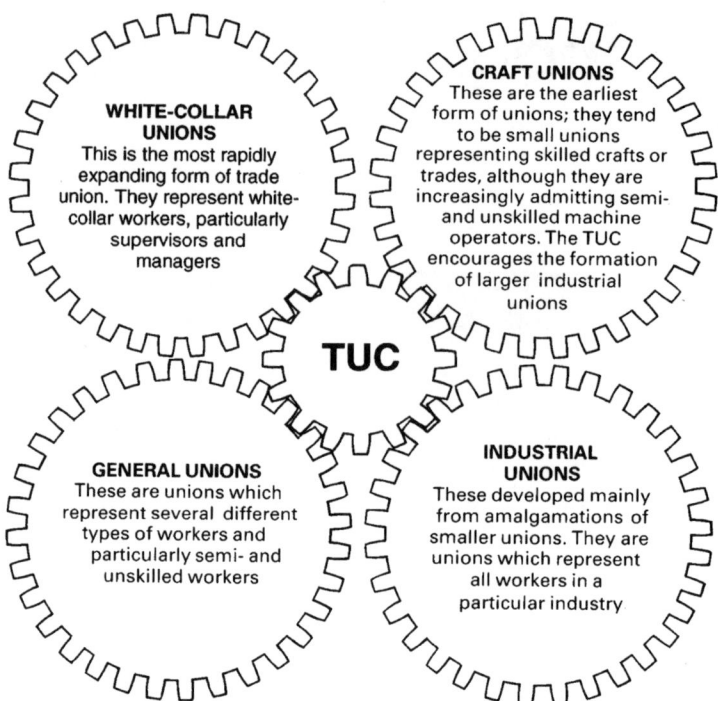

There are different types of unions, classified according to the type of workers they represent. In many countries trade unions have joined together to form congresses or councils. In the UK the Trades Union Congress is an example of this type of 'union of unions'.

- a say in government;
- participation in company decision processes;
- a reasonable share in the wealth of the country;
- improved public and social services.

Trades Union Congress (TUC)

The TUC is the central body of the trade union movement. It is the representative voice of the many member trade unions, and consequently the government often discusses industrial policies with the TUC and attempts to obtain its co-operation. The TUC tries to promote the aims of the unions and to encourage support for them.

Although the TUC is an important part of the industrial scene, people often overestimate its powers. The TUC's powers are in fact very limited. The real power in the TUC lies with the member unions and a democratic process which produces overall union views and policies.

Most of the main unions are associate members of the TUC, and the amount of power each union has within the organisation is determined by the size of its membership.

At the TUC Annual Congress, which usually takes place for one week in September, the General Council is elected to carry out TUC policies and work throughout the year. It is responsible for most of the main decisions and actions, whilst taking into account the wishes of the associated unions.

Each member union can send a number of delegates with voting power to the Annual Congress. The number of delegates is related to the size of the union's membership. The Annual Congress provides an important public platform for the unions to discuss important issues affecting the economy.

Criticisms of trade unions

One of the main criticisms of trade unions is that the typical member does not actively participate in its activities until there is some crisis or conflict which affects them personally. During the absence of active interest by the majority of the union's members, those with more positive and sometimes extremist political views can move into positions of influence and control in the unions. In such circumstances, the union could be open to abuse by persons using conflict situations for their own political ends.

7.3 Collective bargaining

The main function of trade unions is to obtain improved wages and working conditions for their members. Sometimes the employer reaches a satisfactory wage agreement with individual employees, but wage settlements are often the result of collective bargaining. This refers to talks between representatives of employers and trade unions to decide pay rates and conditions of employment.

The union represents a group of workers and negotiates a settlement on their behalf with an employer or a group of employers. It is just as much in the interest of the unions as it is in the employers to reach a speedy settlement, because both sides can only benefit if there is continuity in working.

Although pay is one of the main topics of collective bargaining, many other issues can be involved, including;

- hours of work
- holiday entitlement
- sick pay
- pensions
- maternity leave
- working conditions
- training
- promotion prospects
- redundancies
- recruitment.

Although negotiations between employers and employees may not reach an agreement, there are other possibilities to solve the deadlock.

Conciliation

Conciliation is where a third party is appointed (sometimes by the government) to try and help find a solution acceptable to both sides. The Advisory,

Conciliation and Arbitration Service (ACAS) is particularly used to attempt to bring the two sides of a dispute nearer together. The work of ACAS is examined in more detail later.

Arbitration

This is where both sides of a dispute request that the dispute goes before an arbiter. Both sides agree to accept the verdict of the arbiter.

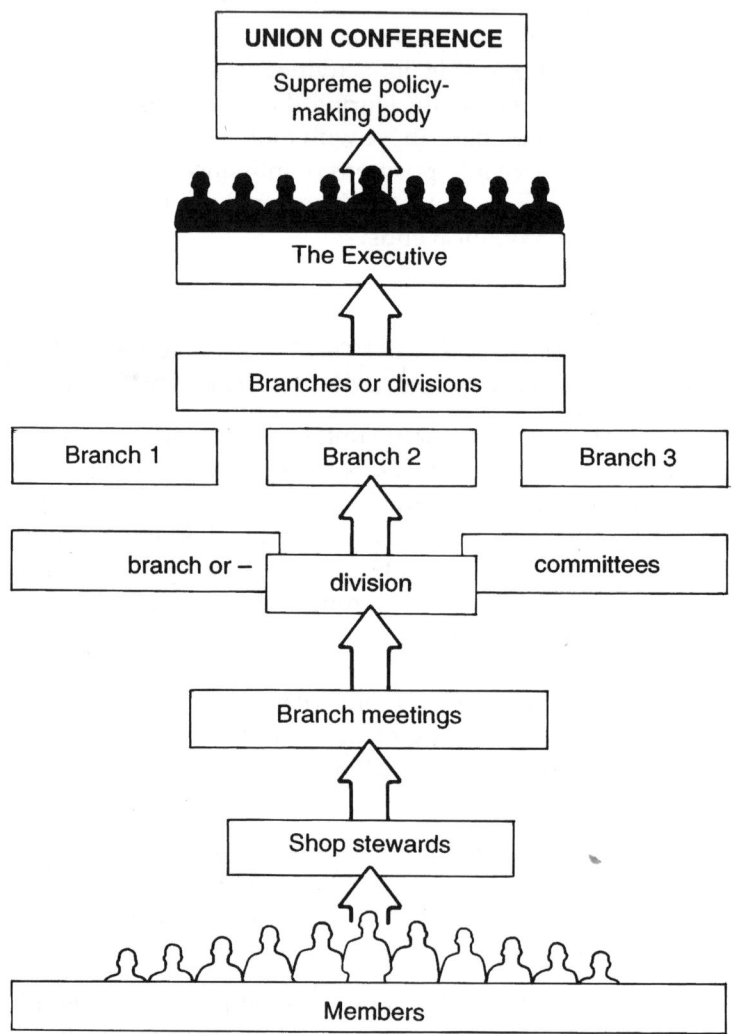

A typical union structure.

Industrial Relations

7.4 Industrial disputes

When there is a major disagreement between an employer and their workers, it is sometimes referred to as an 'industrial dispute'. *Negotiations* may result in an agreement or a compromise between the parties. Where a compromise cannot be reached, the employees may decide to take some form of *industrial action*.

Industrial action

Industrial action refers to the methods workers use during an industrial dispute. The following summarises the most commonly used methods of industrial action.

Strike

- *Official* – on advice, in consultation or with union approval and backing, workers cease work (withdraw their labour). Under these circumstances the union may provide strike pay from the funds contributed by members.
- *Unofficial* – sometimes called a 'wildcat' strike' the workers cease work without union backing.
- *No-strike agreements* are arrangements where workers agree not to take strike action in return for certain contractual agreements with their employers.

Demarcation dispute

A demarcation dispute is one where 'who does what' is in question, and is often a dispute between unions. This is a situation where one group of workers objects to another group doing particular work. Often this sort of dispute is the result of differences in rates of pay between one group of workers and another. It may be that one group of workers is doing work thought to 'belong' to another group, and for a lower rate of pay.

Overtime ban

Overtime provides a convenient way for employers to obtain extra working hours without taking on additional employees. When an overtime ban is in force the workers refuse to work additional hours.

Work to rule

Workers follow the rules and regulations of the company exactly. By adhering strictly to the rules in this way work is slowed down and productivity is reduced.

Go slow

This is similar to a work to rule. The workers do their work thoroughly, but at a slower pace than normal, causing a fall in output.

Closed shop

A closed shop means that all workers in a firm belong to one union and they refuse to work with anyone not a member of that union.

Picketing

In order to maximise the effect of their industrial action, a group of workers on strike may stand outside the firm's entrance and try to persuade other workers not to 'cross the picket line', i.e. not enter the premises.

Sit-in

Workers occupy the premises ensuring that no goods enter or leave, and preventing the operation of the firm. Sometimes, such as when a factory is threatened with closure, the sit-in becomes a 'work-in'. Workers occupy the factory and keep it in operation without the presence of the management.

Boycott

Within a boycott action union members may refuse to work with certain other people, or work or move certain machines or equipment. They may decide to take this kind of action when they feel that jobs are at risk of being lost. Someone who goes against the union wishes by working during such a boycott is sometimes called a *'union buster'*.

7.5 Assisting industrial peace

From the foregoing description of the ways in which trade unions organise their activities, it can be seen that a large and powerful union could easily put a small firm at a disadvantage. For this reason firms also need to get together and form associations to protect and promote their interests. By combining in this way the employers are able to match the power of the trade unions. In addition, employers' associations can act as a single voice for many employers. They also provide a means of industrial research and the communication of ideas and information.

Confederation of British Industry (CBI)

The CBI is the major employers' association in Great Britain and it is the opposite number of the TUC. The CBI represents employers in a similar manner to that in which the TUC represents the trade unions.

Industrial Relations

Although they disagree on many issues, the CBI and the TUC are frequently in consultation with each other and their combined co-operation on many matters related to industry results in useful contributions to industrial policies and plans.

Like the TUC, the CBI has some permanent staff led by its Director General. Also similar to the TUC, the real power of the CBI lies with its members and this is also focused at the Annual Conference.

Advisory, Conciliation and Arbitration Services (ACAS)

ACAS is a body available for use by both the employers and employees. The function of ACAS is to conciliate (pacify) and arbitrate (mediate) on matters related to industrial relations. It is managed by a council of nine members, three of whom are independent of it, three are appointed in consultation with the CBI and three are appointed in consultation with the TUC.

Where the parties to a dispute are in a 'deadlock' position, some progress may be made with the help and consultation of a third 'outside' party such as ACAS. In such circumstances an officer of ACAS examines the issues involved and tries to conciliate the parties.

Another avenue that can be explored through ACAS is to seek arbitration, that is to allow a third party to act as a kind of referee. ACAS will provide arbitration facilities, but only if both parties to the dispute agree to go to arbitration, and both also agree to accept the conclusions reached.

Industrial tribunals

Industrial tribunals are independent bodies whose verdicts are legally binding. They deal with individual conciliation cases. For example, where an employee has a grievance against their employer, such as for unfair dismissal.

A tribunal consists of a lawyer (the chairperson), one representative of the employer, and a representative of the employee (often a trade union representative). The tribunal listens to the evidence put by the parties involved and reaches a verdict. The tribunal has the power to award compensation to the employee, and it can even order a company to reinstate a person they have dismissed. Tribunals deal mainly with cases of unfair dismissal but also other breaches of employees' rights.

The Employment Act 1988

The Employment Act 1988 gives union members rights which they can use to prevent abuses of union power against them. Members of some unions already had similar rights in their union's rules, but this law now guarantees all union members the same rights.

- Union members can restrain their union from calling them to take industrial action without support for the action from a properly conducted secret ballot.

- Union members have the right not to be unjustifiably disciplined by their union, e.g. for deciding to honour their employment contract and go to work or cross a picket line rather than take part in industrial action.
- Industrial action to enforce or maintain any kind of closed shop is unlawful and dismissal from employment for not being a member of a union is not acceptable.
- Postal voting subject to independent scrutiny is required for many of the situations where union members are required to make decisions.

7.6 Role of the government

The activities of the government obviously affect the lives of workers in a variety of ways, not only through their success or otherwise in managing the economy, but also through the laws which are brought into being. Some of these laws may be seen by trade unionists as being against the interest of their members, especially those laws which aim to place restrictions on what a union can do. Consequently, the unions see part of their responsibilities as to try to prevent such laws from coming into existence. This of course brings the union movement into direct conflict with the government and can contribute to a deterioration in industrial relations.

Traditionally, the trade union movement has always supported the Labour Party and, generally speaking, the movement has always been suspicious of the Conservative Party. Although there do appear to be more conflicts between trade unions and Conservative governments, this is not always the case, and there have

These protest notices are all related to general issues pressure groups might wish to influence. Design some notices that might be used to influence businesses.

been occasions when Labour governments have not been able to rely on the full backing of the trade unionists.

While we have acknowledged in this chapter that trade unions aim to improve conditions of work for their members, unions cannot do this without taking into account government policy. Workers can only hope to achieve full employment and choice of occupation and place of work, if the government is able to plan the economy. For this reason, governments have an important role to play in industrial relations by producing imaginative ideas, and communicating them in a way that is open, honest and clear.

Enlisting the co-operation of the unions in implementing government policies has become an important feature of modern society. This entails involving the trade union movement in matters of economic policy formation, primarily through consultation. It is in this aspect of government that the roles of the CBI and the TUC can prove valuable.

7.7 Pressure groups

Pressure groups are voluntary organisations which seek to encourage the government, local council, or some other organisation to recognise their views and respond to them. They try to influence the decision-making process by demonstrating the strength of their feelings.

Perhaps one of the most well-known pressure groups in Britain are trade unions. The TUC acts on their behalf to influence the government's thinking on issues that concern trade unions (particularly those connected with pay and working conditions). The TUC also acts in a similar way as a pressure group on employers. The CBI acts on behalf of employers and tries to influence the government from their point of view.

Pressure groups are not all formal ones such as those examined so far. Sometimes an informal group will form spontaneously, perhaps due to a passing situation, e.g. a no waiting system in the local town.

Although pressure groups are often portrayed in the media as trying to influence local or central government, they do at times try to influence business also. Apart from workers trying to influence pay awards, the general public may try to put pressure on businesses to protest about issues such as advertising techniques, building expansion, or use of certain raw materials.

Governments and businesses are subjected to pressure from groups of people or organisations who are trying to influence policies to be adopted. Sometimes continual pressure is put on the government, industry or specific businesses to acknowledge or make concessions to the views of the pressure groups. The pressure may be exerted through the press or TV propaganda, or it may be less formally organised.

Firms face pressure from groups both internally and externally. Internal pressure sometimes comes from groups of shareholders trying to influence company policy. However, the main pressure on firms tends to be external – that is consumer pressure.

The most basic form of consumer pressure is the opportunity customers have to take their custom elsewhere, although where the firm is in a monopolistic position (e.g. supply of electricity or gas) this possibility may be limited.

The Consumers' Association plays an important role as a pressure group. The group obtains funds from members who buy the magazine called *Which?* The funds are used to test a variety of products and to publish comparative reports in the magazine. These reports are frequently quoted in the press and on TV and radio and consequently they influence producers and traders. The Association also publishes books of consumer-related interest.

Some television and radio programmes also act as watchdogs to expose firms who are guilty of malpractice. Many newspapers and magazines also publish details of investigations carried out by their 'Consumer Watchdogs'.

Many of the national organisations providing domestic supplies and services who are in a largely monopolistic position are subject to the scrutiny of consumer councils. For example, the Post Office Users' National Council investigates complaints about the postal service, and there are similar councils for other large domestic suppliers and state-owned industries.

Trade unions and the CBI also act as pressure groups. They not only represent the interests of their members, but they also put forward views on a wide range of issues such as trade, education and consumer affairs. Other organisations such as the AA and the RAC represent the interests of motorists.

There are also environmental pressure groups who represent those who are particularly concerned about the environment. Currently the organisation called Greenpeace is gaining a lot of attention worldwide in its attempts to get government and industry to recognise the need to protect the environment.

7.8 Activities

Make a note of it

1. What do you understand by the term 'industrial relations'?
2. To what extent would you say that it is inevitable that employers and employees will come into conflict?
3. What is a trade union?
4. List the aims of trade unions. What part does the TUC play in putting across the aims of the unions to others?
5. What is the Trades Union Congress? Why do you think that the government often discusses industrial policies with the TUC?
6. Describe the organisation and functions of the TUC.
7. Give a brief description of the four main types of trade union in the United Kingdom.
8. What are the main criticisms of trade unions?
9. What is the main function of trade unions?

10. Say what you understand by the terms 'collective bargaining', 'conciliation' and 'arbitration'? What is the relationship between these terms?
11. What do you see as the main function of an industrial tribunal?
12. What are restrictive practices? Why are they adopted?
13. Explain the difference between an official and an unofficial strike.
14. Shop stewards are ordinary full-time workers who are elected by a group of union members to represent them to the union and also to the management. Bearing this in mind, why do you think that it is often shop stewards who call a 'wildcat' or unofficial strike?
15. What is a demarcation dispute?
16. Trade unions use a variety of methods to try and persuade employers to agree to wage claims. Explain how the following methods operate:
    (a) overtime ban
    (b) work to rule
    (c) go slow
    (d) sit-in
    (e) blacking.
17. Two controversial aspects of trade union activity are:
    (a) picketing, and
    (b) the closed shop.
    Describe these two forms of action. Why do you think they are controversial? Do you think they should be allowed? Give reasons for your answer.
18. Why do employers need representatives just as much as employees?
19. Describe the functions of the Confederation of British Industry. Explain the relationship and similarities between the CBI and the TUC.
20. What is the function of the Advisory, Conciliation and Arbitration Service (ACAS)?
21. Explain the role of the government in industrial relations.
22. What is a pressure group?
23. Why are pressure groups important to consumers?

Industrial Relations

Structured Questions

1 Refer to the article about firefighters below.

   (a) Who are 'public sector workers'? (1)
   (b) Why would the Chancellor of the Exchequer want to interfere in the pay awards of public sector workers? (2)
   (c) Why should possible action by the firefighters concern local businesses? (2)
   (d) Explain what you understand by 'industrial peace'? (2)
   (e) What is the function of shop stewards? To what extent can they contribute to industrial peace? (3)
   (f) Describe two forms of industrial action that firefighters could take other than striking. (4)
   (g) In what ways can bodies outside of those involved in an industrial dispute help in resolving the differences that exist? (6)

FIREFIGHTERS FIRE THE FIRST SHOT

The country's firefighters have fired the opening shot in the dispute by public sector workers who are incensed by the Chancellor of the Exchequer's decision to restrict the wage rises of public service employees. Local businesses have expressed concern over possible loss of fire cover.

The Fire Brigades Union is on the brink of calling a strike over pay for the first time in 15 years.

The union was meeting employers today in London in a last ditch bid to hold on to a pay formula which has kept the industrial peace since 1987.

But the government wants to scrap that agreement for a year and pin firefighters' wages to a public sector pay ceiling of 1.5 per cent.

If today's talks reach stalemate an immediate ballot and then a strike is on the cards, and shop stewards will begin to organise local action.

2 (a) What do the letters CBI stand for? (1)
   (b) Define the term 'collective bargaining'. (2)
   (c) Describe three of the peaceful ways in which trade unions can try to obtain better wages and working conditions for its members. (3)
   (d) Describe four benefits of belonging to a union. (4)
   (e) How does the function of the CBI differ from that of the TUC? (4)
   (f) In what ways does 'collective bargaining' benefit both the worker and also the employer? (6)

Today many workers in the same, or similar, trades join a trade union. The union tries to obtain better wages and improved working conditions for all of its members. This saves each employee struggling individually with their employers. This is called 'collective bargaining'.

Union officials representing the employees meet representatives of the employers at a national level. Any agreement they reach applies to everyone in the union or group of unions in the whole country.

3 The following questions are all related to the industrial actions referred to in this chapter.

    (a) What do you understand by the term industrial action? (2)
    (b) Why can industrial actions cause damage to businesses? (2)
    (c) What part do shop stewards play in industrial action? (2)
    (d) Describe four main kinds of industrial action that workers might take. (4)
    (e) Explain the difference between an official and an unofficial strike. (4)
    (f) In taking industrial action groups of workers would choose different times of the year to maximise the effect. How would airline pilots and teachers differ in the time of the year they would choose to implement action? Give reasons for your answer. (6)

4 (a) What is a trade union? (1)
    (b) What are the advantages of belonging to a trade union from the point of view of workers? (2)
    (c) 'Shop stewards represent their union members but they are also employed by the firm'. Explain this statement. (3)
    (d) Briefly describe the four main types of union and explain the types of worker they represent. (4)
    (e) Explain the contribution that conciliation and arbitration can make in an industrial dispute. (4)
    (f) 'A productivity deal is a means of giving workers the improved pay or working conditions they seek without sacrificing the profitability required by the owners of the firm.' Explain this statement with particular reference to the importance of productivity deals to both the employee and the firm. (6)

Industrial Relations

Research Assignments

1 Collect at least four newspaper articles containing reports of industrial problems. In each case describe the influence that trade unions might have on the event in question. Comment whether their involvement is likely to improve or worsen the situation.

2 What contribution do you feel trade unions make to the economy of our country? Provide evidence to support your answer.

3 Describe the work of trade unions. Considering the fact that they have similar aims why are there sometimes disputes between unions? Give examples from the current press to illustrate your answer.

4 Design a questionnaire that can be used to find out the views of the general public on trade unions. Use your questionnaire to survey a representative sample. Present your findings in the form of a report.

5 Approach one of the major trade unions and obtain details of the services and benefits they provide for their members. Design and detail your own leaflet that could be used to attract workers to join the union.

6 Take any current national issue that appears likely to lead to industrial unrest. Describe in detail the steps you would take as an employer to try to deter your employees from taking strike action which would damage your business.

7 An industrial tribunal is an independent body dealing mainly with the claims of unfair dismissal and other alleged breaches of employees' rights. Write a summary of two industrial tribunal cases reported in the press or obtained from a tribunal. What other support is there for employees who feel they have a grievance against their employers?

8 The Marketing Department

8.1 What is marketing?

Marketing refers to all the processes involved in selling goods or services in the most efficient and profitable manner. It begins with an examination of what people want from a product or service (*market research*). This is followed by an assessment of how to produce the product or service (*product development*) that will satisfy that requirement, and at the same time make a profit in the process. The next stage is to develop a *marketing strategy* that will get the product to the appropriate market at a competitive price. This will involve creating an advertising campaign that is backed by selling and distribution procedures.

The following flow chart shows the way that the marketing process is developed.

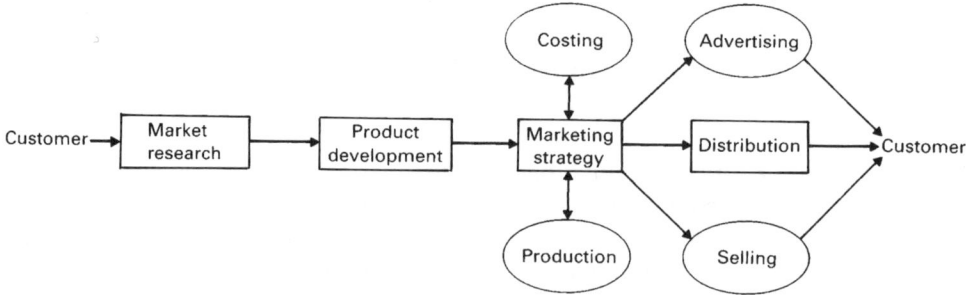

Marketing in this sense is a two-way process. It connects those who produce goods and services with potential buyers. It also finds out what products and services consumers want and relays the information to the producers. This enables them to make the right things available.

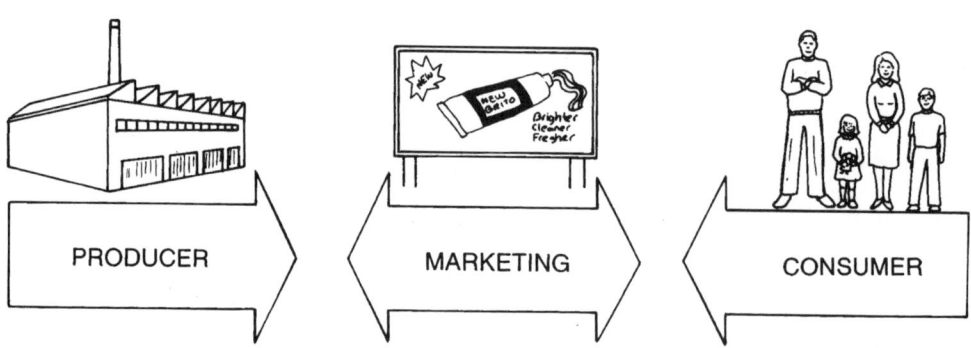

Marketing is a two-way process.

The Marketing Department

Marketing concepts

Marketing concept refers to the typical business goal of satisfying customers' wants and trying to make a profit in the process.

We say that a business is pursuing a *sales concept* when it tries to sell something before learning what the customer wants. Sometimes it suits a producer to operate in this way. For example, if a manufacturer is well equipped to produce a particular product he or she might go ahead and manufacture and rely on their salesforce to persuade the consumer to buy.

By following a *marketing concept* a business will firstly find out what customers want and then try to meet this demand. What the customer wants is known as the *customer concept*, i.e. the business may well do what the customer wants, although it might prefer to do otherwise. For example, a store might stay open until late in the evening to please its customers, even though this adds considerably to its wage bill.

The way that a business finds out what the customer wants is by *market research*. This is the systematic and continuous evaluation of all the factors involved in the transfer of goods and services from the producer to the ultimate consumer. It is particularly concerned with the reaction of consumers. (See also Chapter 9.)

Sales is a support system for marketing. In other words, sales is a marketing strategy which facilitates exchange. Therefore, a major part of the work of a marketeer is to choose the best possible methods of sales to match the products being marketed. For example, the sales strategies for a new flavour soft drink would differ from the sales strategies for a property. Market research plays an important role in the development of sales strategies.

8.2 The marketing department

A firm's *marketing department* is concerned with selling its products or services. This can mean disposing of products the firm has produced, but more often it is a case of identifying what customers want (*customer concept*) and then arranging to meet the need that exists, hopefully making a profit in the process.

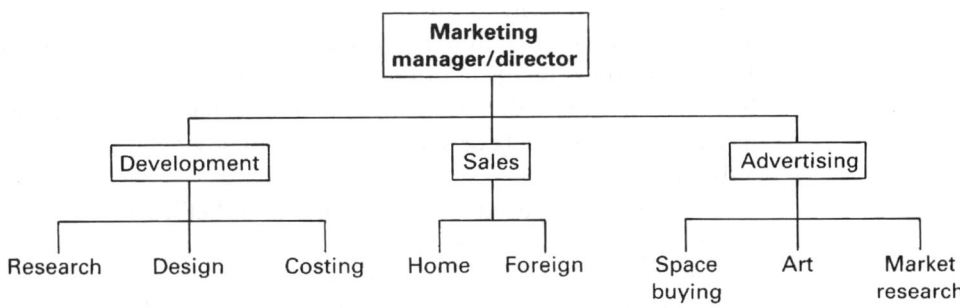

Typical structure of a marketing department in a large company.

There are many ways to organise a marketing department and its structure will be influenced by the size of the firm. In a large company it would be possible to split the department into several subdivisions, each with a specific marketing function. In a small organisation a few members of staff may have to incorporate several of these functions into their duties.

The functions of a marketing department

The marketing department will be controlled by the marketing director or a senior manager. This position entails carrying out sales policies decided by the board of directors, and supervising the work of all the people employed in the department, including the company's *sales representatives* whose job is to visit potential customers and obtain orders.

All documentation related to sales of the firm's products will be dealt with either directly or indirectly by the marketing department. This will include sending out mail shots (sales leaflets), dealing with customers' enquiries and orders, arranging for despatch of goods, and initiating the sending out of invoices and statements of account (see Chapter 12).

A major part of the work of the marketing department is to choose the method of sales to be employed. This will vary according to the product or service being marketed. For example, the method of marketing a new chocolate bar will differ from that used to sell a valuable antique.

The way that products are to be distributed will be given careful consideration. This will involve decisions with regard to which channels of distribution will be used and whether trade will be directed through wholesalers and retailers, or by direct marketing such as by mail order.

The marketing department will obviously be involved in advertising the firm's products. Where the firm is large it may have a separate advertising department. This department will carry out the instructions of the marketing department, and will also offer advice on marketing strategies, including market research. These aspects of marketing are covered in more detail later in this book.

8.3 Marketing mix

Those directly involved in marketing generally follow the *customer concept* defined earlier; that is, they try to see things from their customers' point of view. Where a business wants to influence a specific group of customers (e.g. teenagers) they are its *target market*. A business will often have many target markets, e.g. one for each of its products or services, and it may well approach each target market in different ways.

Once a business has identified its target market it will select what it considers is the most appropriate marketing mix. The *marketing mix* is a collective term that is used to refer to the whole range of marketing activities, techniques and strategies that a firm uses to reach its target market. The variables of a marketing mix can be easily remembered by referring to the 'four Ps' – *product, price, place* and *promotion*.

The Marketing Department

The four Ps that make up the variables of the marketing mix enable the seller to reach the target market.

Product

Obviously the product, good or service, or even an idea, plays an important role in marketing. There is little point in trying to market something that the consumer doesn't want. For this reason, the needs of the consumer must be focused on. The business will need to find out what potential customers want from products or services, and they will take into account:

- how the customer will *use* the product or service
- the *range* of products or services needed
- the standard of *quality* wanted
- the *unit size(s)* required
- what *after-sales* back-up will be needed
- the likely level of *demand*
- what *competition* currently exists
- specific *features* the product or service needs to have
- what aspects of *packaging* will attract customers.

Packaging is clearly linked with the product. Packaging is the outer wrapping of or container for the goods. Packaging not only presents the product in an attractive way but it also gives details about the contents, any potential hazards, the correct usage, etc. In this respect packaging:

- protects the product
- promotes the product

Packaging presents the product attractively and also gives details about the contents.

A brand name has to be short, descriptive and easy to pronounce, and it must appeal to the target market.

- preserves the life of the product
- prevents health hazards that could result from improper use of the product
- makes it more convenient for the consumer to handle the product
- improves the general appearance of the product.

An old established product in a new and improved package usually enhances the marketing potential of the product.

Branding is another important aspect of the product. Branding refers to giving a good a distinctive name, term, symbol or even a design to enable it to be recognised easily.

A *brand name* (or trade mark) is that part of branding which represents the actual letter, letters, word or group of words which make up the name of the good. The brand name differentiates one product from another similar or dissimilar product. It is a registered symbol or name which can only be used by the firm.

Price

No matter how attractive a product is, a crucial factor in the success of the marketing strategy will be the price. It is important to the seller because it incorporates profit, and it is important to the consumers because it affects their ability to purchase what they want. Having decided what product or service to sell, the business has to decide what price to charge. Most products have a *price plateau* which represents the price the customer expects to pay for a product or service. If a seller's price is too high, customers will not buy. If the price is too far below the plateau, the customer may think the product is inferior, and still not buy. In addition, if the price charged is too low, the seller might not cover their costs.

Sometimes a firm may set a price that is deliberately low (called *penetration price*) in order to gain entry to a new market. In due course it would raise the price to a more profitable level.

Although it is the market that eventually determines the price (see later), it is initially fixed by the seller.

Cost-plus pricing Many firms decide their initial price using this approach. It is the most simple method of deciding a price. It involves taking the unit cost (cost of producing a single item), adding overheads and a profit margin to arrive at the selling price. However, this method does not necessarily arrive at a price the market will accept.

Market-orientated pricing With this method of deciding a price, the seller surveys the market to find out what customers are willing to pay before setting their price. Following this strategy they can make their price more competitive than other firms. However, they must ensure that they cover their costs. *Fixed costs* (e.g. rent for buildings, council tax, insurance, wages of employees, etc) are those that have to be paid whether or not a product or service is sold. *Variable costs* (e.g. raw materials, parts and packaging, etc) are those which change depending on the quantity of a product made or a service provided.

Place

Those involved in marketing a product have to ensure that it reaches a place where consumers can conveniently make purchases. Getting the item to this convenient place is called *distribution*. This involves wholesalers, retailers, importers and exporters. These aspects of distribution are dealt with in Chapters 10 and 11. Distribution also depends on transportation which is dealt with in Chapter 13.

A firm will be asking a number of questions in deciding the *channels of distribution* it will use within this part of its marketing strategy, these questions will include:

- Where do customers expect to buy the product or service, e.g. in shops, in this country or overseas?
- Will the customers come to us?
- Do we have to take the product or service to the customer, e.g. mail order?
- How should the product be transported and who will pay the costs involved?

Questions such as those given here may lead to others, for example, where should the seller's premises be located?

Promotion

This refers to the ways in which consumers are made aware of the availability of the product or service and the qualities it has. Advertising is the most important aspect of product promotion and this is dealt with in Chapter 9.

Sales promotion is any activity that supplements advertising and other aspects of visual promotion. The following are just a few of the strategies used in sales promotion. You should find out about the form these take:

- trading stamps
- loss leaders/discounts
- attractive packaging
- after-sales service
- free gifts/gift tokens
- competitions
- special offers
- sponsorship
- product demonstrations
- free samples
- exhibitions
- displays.

The choice of methods of promotion and the way that they are combined is called the *promotional mix*. Promotion is very much about *communicating*. The business needs to tell potential customers what products or services the firm has to offer. It needs to do this in a way that will encourage interest in what the firm has to offer.

Advertising is the part of promotion that tells the potential customer about what the seller has to offer. Advertising does this through various *media*.

Personal selling refers to the promotion of the product or service through direct contact between the seller and the customer. Personal selling by *sales representatives* or *agents* is frequently used to support advertising. The function of *sales personnel* is to liaise with the firm's customers, and tell them about the company's products or services.

Sales promotion refers to the various ways that the product is pushed in the marketplace, and it includes activities such as display and packaging.

From the foregoing it will have been seen that the marketing mix aims to get the right product to the consumer at the right price and to a convenient place where it can be bought. The consumer is made aware of what is available through product promotion. All the strategies involved in the marketing mix are aimed at meeting the needs and desires of the consumer.

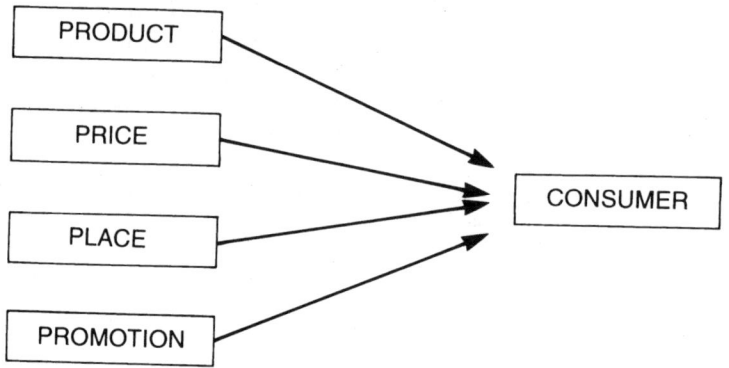

The strategies involved in the marketing mix are aimed at meeting the needs and desires of the consumer.

Product lifecycle

In addition to deciding on the marketing mix a firm must consider how sales might develop. All products move through identifiable stages which are referred to as the *product lifecycle*. Understanding this cycle assists the preparation of a sound marketing plan.

The Marketing Department

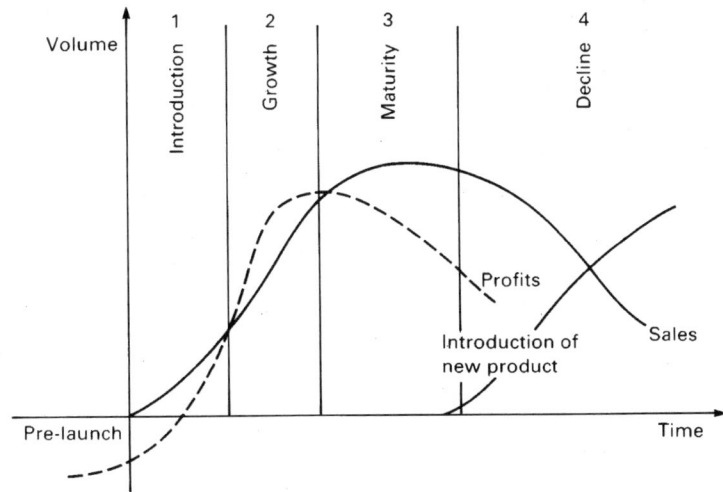

Most products have a lifecycle similar to that shown by this graph which plots a product from its introduction through to its decline. The production and marketing sections of the firm have to be aware of the position of products in their lifecycle in order to maximise profits, and to plan the introduction of replacement products at the appropriate time.

Pre-launch

This stage consists of all the developmental work undertaken before the product is put on the market. During this time the decision has to be taken whether it is worthwhile to pursue the new development. Once it has been decided to proceed, a considerable amount of capital is consumed with no income being earned. The time between the design of a product and its production is known as the *lead time*.

Introduction

In the early stages of marketing sales tend to be low but large amounts of capital continue to be consumed. It is some time before breakeven (see Chapter 16) stage is reached and the product begins to show a profit.

Growth

If all goes well, sales and profits are steadily rising. Marketing becomes more economically viable as an increasing volume of cash comes in from customers. This is a time for vigorous advertising to promote maximum demand for the product.

Maturity

During this crucial period the rate of sales growth begins to slow down. The advent of this is often signalled by prior falling off of profits. The product reaches its ceiling and begins to decline. This is a crucial period for the business because it is important to recognise the signal to improve the product or find a new one.

Decline

This is the period when sales volume shows a market fall. It reveals that the product has lost its appeal or competitive edge. If steps have not already been taken to improve the product it will probably now have to be withdrawn in order to avoid making a loss.

Product range and product mix

From the foregoing examination of the product lifecycle you will realise that if a firm markets only a single product it is at a considerable risk. In fact most products are not marketed on their own but are part of a range of products. For example, a firm might produce a *range* of cake mixes, etc. Many small firms commence their business in this way. A large firm will have a *product mix* which consists of several different products, each with its own range, e.g. cake mixes, biscuits, crisps, instant sauces, dessert toppings, etc.

8.5 Merchandising

Merchandising is an important marketing technique. It refers to the display of goods so that potential customers can conveniently see them and be influenced to buy. The following are just some of the methods of merchandising used by sellers of goods:

- eyecatching window displays, including special offers;
- use of in-house displays to reduce the number of employees needed to sell the goods;
- careful layout of premises that allows customers to get near to goods and move into other parts of the store;
- packaging design that presents goods attractively;
- opportunity for customers to inspect goods closely and perhaps touch them;
- clear labelling and price marking to reduce the need for customers to ask questions;
- eye-level shelf displays for high priority goods.

Packaging and branding are important features of merchandising. Whilst producers will be required to comply with certain regulations relating to information (e.g. contents, weight, etc.) that must be shown on their products, they will also want to put them in containers that will appeal to the consumer.

Branding refers to giving a product a distinctive name that will be easily recognised and identified with the item in question. This is of considerable advantage in advertising a product, because it the brand name is easily recognised then less

The Marketing Department

expense is involved in trying to make the public aware of the qualities of the product.

An obvious example where merchandising is particularly apparent is in self-service stores, but you should not think of merchandising only in respect of retail trade. Merchandising is used by any business that displays goods rather than just keeping them inside their premises.

8.6 Price determination

Profit maximisation

Most firms will want to make the maximum profit possible. This is referred to as *profit maximisation*. This is achieved when the *total revenue* (income) minus *total cost* is at its greatest. In the following table it can be seen that the producer would choose 2,000 as their level of output, because this will maximise their profit.

Output units	Total cost £	Total revenue £	Profit £
1,000	20	40	20
2,000	30	60	30
3,000	60	70	10

In order to maximise profit, a business has to find the right combination of output and price. If the firm charges too high a price, or has its output too high, it will not be able to sell all its products. And it will not be maximising its profits. Deciding the best combination of price and output can be understand through knowledge of the basic rules of supply and demand.

All free markets involving many buyers and sellers operate according to the laws of demand and supply. That is, if the demand for goods and services

increases faster than the supply of them, prices rise. If the supply increases faster than the demand, prices fall. In other words, the price of goods and services is determined by the interaction of the forces of demand and supply and this of course has a direct influence on production.

Demand

The demand for any commodity is the amount that consumers are prepared to purchase at a given price in a given period of time. For each price the demand is different. Usually the lower the price the higher the quantity demanded, and vice versa, although there are exceptions. *Giffen goods* is a name given to those essential and relatively cheap goods for which demand is likely to increase following a rise in price. The term 'Giffen' is given after a nineteenth-century economist of that name who noticed that when the price of bread increased, consumers bought more of it, being unable to afford to buy other more expensive alternatives such as meat and fruit.

The table below shows a possible demand schedule for a fictional commodity at various prices. A demand schedule can also be shown graphically as below right by plotting the data on a demand curve.

This demand schedule and demand curve only refers to an individual consumer, but market demand consists of many people. A market demand curve is obtained by summing the demand curves of all individuals, so we can expect the market demand to behave in a similar way to individual demand.

Both the individual demand curve and the market demand curve express a relationship between the demand for a commodity and the price of it, but there are other determinants of demand:

- price of the commodity;
- price of other commodities;
- income of the buyers;
- population or number of buyers;
- buyer's scale of preferences, i.e. how much the buyer values or prefers the items he or she wants in comparison with other commodities.

If one of the conditions of demand changes the demand curve moves to a new position. For example, a rise in income or purchasing power could increase

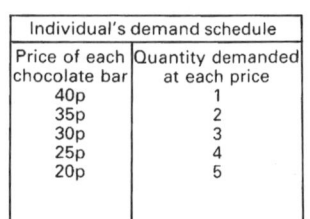 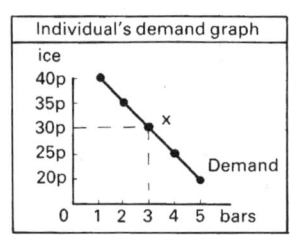 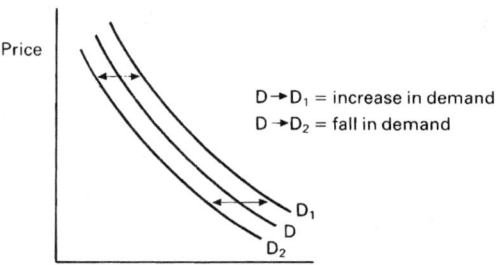

An individual's demand schedule and demand graph for chocolate bars at various prices. The point x on this demand curve indicates that at a price of 30p the person would be likely to buy three bars.

market demand and shift the demand curve to the right (D to D_1). On the other hand, if one of the determinants causes a fall in market demand the curve moves to the left (D to D_2).

Supply

Supply is the amount of a commodity that producers are willing to put on to the market at various prices in a given period of time. For each price the amount supplied is different. Alternatively, we could say that the supply curve shows the price that is necessary to persuade the producer to provide output. Usually the higher the price the more of the commodity the producer will want to supply and vice versa, but in the same way as in the case of demand, there are some exceptions to this.

A supply schedule and graph can be constructed similar to those used to plot demand. Unlike the demand curve the supply curve usually slopes upwards to the right.

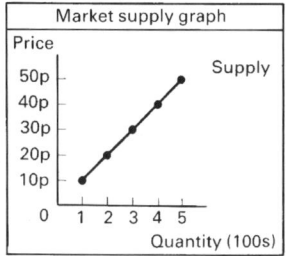

Price

Price is the charge assigned to something, or the *exchange value* for a product or service. The demand for a product or service will be influenced by the price of it.

From our examination of supply and demand so far, it should be clear to the reader that buyers want to buy at the lowest price they can, whilst sellers want to obtain the highest price they can for their goods. Whilst these may at first seem conflicting interests, closer examination shows that it is a combination of demand and supply that determines price.

When any two forces balance each other they are said to be in *equilibrium*. Under the conditions of a perfect market the price of a commodity is determined by the interaction of supply and demand. This can be made clearer by looking at a combined demand and supply schedule which is also expressed graphically for simple observation.

As shown in the table on page 150, it is only at the price of £3 that the number of teddy bears the consumers wish to buy is equal to the amount of teddy bears the producer is willing to supply. This is called the *equilibrium price*, which is the only price at which the amount willingly demanded and the amount willingly supplied are equal.

In the diagram it can be seen that the equilibrium price is at the intersection of

Price	Quantity demanded	Quantity supplied
£5	100	500
£4	200	400
£3	300	300
£2	400	200
£1	500	100

Market for teddy bears – amount demanded and supplied at various prices during one week.

the demand and supply curves: We can also see that if the price is above the equilibrium price, there is an excess of supply and insufficient demand. The result of this is that the price falls towards the equilibrium price. Alternatively, if the price is below the equilibrium price there is insufficient supply and excess demand. This results in the price rising towards the equilibrium price.

Our examination of the laws of demand and supply in this section has been very elementary although sufficient for our purposes. However, it should be understood that in reality the interaction of demand and supply is often more complex. The *economist* is particularly interested in investigating this interaction in greater depth.

8.7 Competition

Competition enhances the efficiency of the economic system. Competition is a major factor in the determination of price.

There are two main types of competition – perfect or pure or free competition, and imperfect competition.

Perfect competition

Perfect competition results from a market situation in which the products of the marketplace are homogeneous, are well known to the participators in the market, and where 'breaking into' the market on the part of both buyers and sellers poses little or no problem. In other words, no one buyer or seller dominates. The competitiveness of the market eventually forces costs and prices to settle at the lowest possible levels, while production will climb to its peak.

Imperfect competition

This market situation results when there are very few producers of goods and services in the marketplace. In other words, there is less evidence of rivalry and excessive exchange in the marketplace. In this atmosphere, monopoly and oligopoly are usually at work.

Monopoly

A *monopolistic* situation results when a single organisation controls an entire line of products and is, therefore, able to determine the selling price. However, the seller is unable to fix both the price and the quantity supplied; he fixes prices at the highest level that he thinks the market will tolerate.

In all EU member countries governments closely monitor monopolistic situations, i.e. when the price of the product is set by a single firm.

Oligopoly

Oligopolistic situations result when a few large suppliers dominate the marketplace. There are many examples of such situations in the UK. The products being marketed are generally homogeneous, e.g. soap powder. Prices are usually tightly structured. The aim is to reduce or even prevent the level of competition that could arise.

Cartels

Cartels are also members of the imperfect market. A cartel consists of a number of firms within a particular industry such as the petroleum industry (OPEC). The firms agree on aspects such as pricing, production levels, sales and the division of the markets.

Government intervention

Governments are sometimes obliged to intervene and protect consumers from the imperfections in the working of the price system. There are two basic methods of government intervention that are used:

1 *Control of prices* through taxation or subsidies. Taxation increases production costs, whereas subsidies reduce them.
2 *Control of demand* by rationing, which is an attempt to influence production and consumption by regulating effective demand.

8.8 Public relations

All businesses care about what the public thinks of their company and will use a variety of ways to try and influence the public to have a high regard for the firm and its employees. The extent to which the public have a good impression of a business is called public relations or 'goodwill'.

In a large company it will be possible to employ a specialist called the *public relations officer (PRO)* who has the responsibility of promoting a good public image. In a smaller business this role would have to be carried out by the owner or a responsible senior employee. But the promotion of public relations is really the responsibility of all employees.

Good public relations may be promoted in direct ways such as making donations to charities, giving away free samples and gifts, operating prize-giving competitions, using famous personalities to endorse the company's goods, etc. These and many other methods are deliberately used to encourage the public to look on the business in a favourable way.

There are also many indirect ways that companies promote their public image, and often these will draw on the help of all employees. For example, potential customers will be influenced by the manner in which employees talk to them on the telephone or at the shop counter. They will also be influenced by the way that their enquiries or complaints are dealt with.

Many companies take particular care with the way that they handle after-sales services because they recognise that this is a vehicle for good public relations. They try to ensure that when a customer has a complaint about a purchase made it is turned to the seller's advantage by showing courtesy and a willingness to put things right quickly.

8.9 Trade associations

Chambers of commerce

Chambers of commerce are voluntary associations of business people. They are sited in towns and cities where commerce is particularly active. Their members come from a wide range of businesses, for example retailing, finance, transport. In other words, a chamber of commerce will consist of people from different types of business. They help to develop and expand business in their locality, and also abroad. They give their members advice on a wide range of matters including legislation, customs regulations, recovery of bad debts and many other important aspects of trading practice.

Chambers of commerce also exist in many overseas countries and today have an important role to play. Through their links with the chambers of commerce in this country they can supply useful information and many contacts for businesses both at home and abroad.

Chambers of commerce also take an interest in education and training for employment. A difficulty faced by educationalists is identifying what skills commerce and industry want students to leave school or college with. The answer to this question can be obtained in part through chambers of commerce and manufacturers' associations.

Manufacturers' associations

A manufacturers' association has many similarities with a chamber of commerce, but in this case each association consists of people from a similar business, for example the Association of British Travel Agents. These organisations provide an ideal forum for the exchange of information between members, and on occasions a common body for carrying out wage negotiations with trade unions.

Such associations have a number of aims but an important one is the formation of codes of practice that are to be followed by their members. In this respect the trade association acts as a focal point for dealing with consumer complaints, as well as promoting goodwill for all their members.

It is not unusual for trade associations to sponsor research and technical information projects for the mutual benefit of all their members. Similarly the trade association may undertake publicity campaigns at home or abroad aimed at creating trade for all members.

8.10 Activities

1. You are employed by a major company that manufactures a range of soft drinks. Briefly describe the process the company would be likely to follow in marketing a new drink.
2. Why is marketing said to be a 'two-way process'?
3. Explain the difference between 'sales concept', 'marketing concept' and 'customer concept'.
4. Describe the functions of a marketing department.
5. What sort of things do you think help a business in identifying its 'target market'?
6. What is meant by 'marketing mix'?
7. What sort of factors might a firm take into account to decide whether to market a particular product or service?
8. Explain the terms 'price plateau' and 'penetration price'.
9. How does 'market-orientated pricing' differ from 'cost-plus pricing'?
10. Describe at least four methods used in 'promotional mix'.
11. Describe the stages involved in a product's lifecycle.
12. How does 'product range' differ from 'product mix'?
13. What is merchandising?
14. List at least six merchandising techniques used by the seller of goods.
15. What are branded goods?
16. What do you understand by demand? What are the determinants of demand?

Comprehensive Business Studies

17 Use the following information to produce a demand graph:

Price per unit (pence)	Quantity demanded at each price (kilos)
45	1
40	1
35	3
30	4
25	5

18 With the aid of a simple diagram explain the effects of changes in demand on the demand graph.

19 List the factors that determine demand.

20 Use simple diagrams to describe the effect of changes in demand on a demand curve.

21 What do we mean by the term 'supply'?

22 What do you understand by price?

23 How does supply and demand help to identify 'equilibrium price'?

24 How does perfect competition differ from imperfect?

25 How does monopoly differ from oligopoly?

26 Briefly describe the work of a public relations officer.

27 Why is public relations an important aspect of a firm's operations?

28 What part do trade associations play in business?

Structured Questions

1 Look opposite at this advertisement placed by Herbal Wonder in a trade magazine. It aims to get those in the hairdressing trade interested in the manufacturer's new range of products. Answer these questions related to the advertisement.

   (a) The advertisement refers to a 'product range'. Name four different items that might be included in the range. (2)
   (b) State four different places to sell this company's products, bearing in mind the target audience. (2)
   (c) How could 'branding' assist the marketing of the product range? (3)
   (d) Name three different marketing occupations that would be involved in the process between the completion of production and eventual purchase by the consumer. (3)

The Marketing Department

(e) Briefly describe four different ways in which the final consumer public might be made aware of this producer range. (4)

(f) What factors would be likely to influence trade customers to purchase Herbal Wonder's products? (6)

2 Read the newspaper article on page 156 'Why is fruit and veg so dear?' and answer the following questions.

(a) Give one possible economic reason why some traders are destroying fruit and veg. (1)

(b) In what way can destroying products affect retail prices? (1)

(c) Use information from the newspaper article to show that the wholesale price of fruit and veg has generally fallen. (2)

(d) Some aspects of this article clearly show that fruit and veg prices have fallen. So what reasons could there be why the fall in prices is not yet reflected in the shops? (4)

(e) Describe the work of the 'middlemen' likely to be involved in the purchase and distribution of fruit and veg. (4)

(f) The supermarket chains say 'shop prices are inflated by transport, processing and packaging costs'. Discuss the validity of this statement. (8)

3 The following questions are related to the chart of a product lifecycle shown on page 145.

(a) Describe some of the work likely to be done during the 'pre-launch' stage of a product lifecycle. (2)

WHY IS FRUIT AND VEG SO DEAR?

Consumer Affairs Consultant

From the dockside to the supermarket, everyone is saying: 'It's not our fault'.

THE GREAT MYSTERY of the fruit and vegetable markets is why are the prices so high to the consumer, when everyone in the trade is saying that profits have been cut to the bone, and competition is higher than it has ever been?

If tomatoes and other salad products are being imported so cheap that some traders are actually destroying some of their imports, why is it so dear in the shops?

Import prices have halved in less than two months, with tomatoes now about 24p a lb. In Superstores yesterday they were selling at 89p.

Cucumbers are just 12p at the dockside … and 68p in the supermarket.

When our Consumer Affairs Consultant tried to discover the answer yesterday, everyone – from shopkeepers to the importers – denied that it was their fault.

Supermarket chains say shop prices are inflated by transport, processing and packaging costs. Supermarket prices are set months in advance.

A Superstore spokesman said: 'Our prices are coming down. Tomatoes have been reduced by 10p a lb in the past two months and we are continually reviewing our prices. In fact we are doing so almost daily'.

Two months ago 1 cwt of imported potatoes sold to the trade in Southampton for £4.48. Yesterday the same quantity fetched only £2.20.

At Manchester bananas have been selling wholesale at around £28 per cwt – less than half of the price six weeks ago. It's a similar story in London.

Fruit and veg goes through a complex chain of middlemen between the grower and the supermarket shelves. For example, bananas are picked on the plantations in, say, the Caribbean, in the green state. They are then transported in refrigerated ships and come in through our docks.

Importers sell them into the wholesale markets, and the wholesalers sell on to the retailers. Sometimes the product may pass through more than one wholesaler before it reaches the retailer. From the wholesalers the bananas eventually end up on the shop shelves, in the yellow condition that most consumers prefer. Timing is a crucial factor in all aspects of the fruit and veg trade.

(b) Why does the 'pre-launch' stage show no profit being made? (2)
(c) Why do large amounts of capital tend to be used during the early stages of marketing? (3)
(d) Why is the 'growth' stage of the cycle the most profitable stage? (3)
(e) What factors influence the introduction of a new product? (4)
(f) How would the profit lifecycle of salt be likely to differ from that of pop records? You may use simple diagrams to illustrate your answer. (6)

4 Refer to the diagram of the possible structure of a marketing department shown on page 139 and answer the following questions.

(a) Why is the diagram shown not likely to be typical of a small company? (2)

(b) How do home sales differ from overseas sales? (2)

(c) What work is carried out in the costing section of a marketing department? (3)

(d) Why is market research an essential feature of marketing? (3)

(e) In what way can the structure shown be said to be illustrative of the 'marketing mix'? (4)

(f) Explain how the development, sales and marketing sections of this hypothetical marketing department are interrelated. (6)

5 Read the newspaper article below and answer the following questions.

(a) What is meant by the following terms used in the newspaper article:
  (i) 'branded name products'; (2)
  (ii) 'turnover of $4 billion a year'. (2)

(b) In what way is television shopping likely to be convenient for consumers? (2)

(c) What marketing techniques are likely to be used by the seller? (4)

BUYING FROM YOUR OWN HOME

Television shopping is about to arrive in some European countries. For one hour, every Saturday morning, families will be able to shop from their TV screens.

Each product will have a four minute slot. During this time viewers can telephone using one of 200 lines, free of charge. They will be able to order a product over the telephone and pay by quoting their credit card number.

The 'Armchair Shopping Show' will follow the pattern of successful shopping shows running in the United States of America.

In the UK, mostly branded name products will be sold, with nothing costing below £200, and presented in an interesting and informative way. Typical items will include clothes, washing machines, cameras, and other goods.

The idea began with the Homes Shopping Network, in America, a 24 hour show. The American show started from nothing in 1986 and by 1990 had a turnover of $4 billion a year.

(d) How will the producers of goods advertised on the 'Armchair Shopping Show' benefit? (4)
(e) What factors will determine whether the 'Armchair Shopping Show' is a success or not? (6)

Research Assignments

1 Visit two different types of local businesses, such as a food store, a clothing store or a furniture store. Compare the merchandising techniques that each use and comment whether differences that exist are related to the nature of the products or are differences in technique.

2 Choose a product or service that is of interest to you. Visit four different stores that sell the product or service. Make a comparison of the way each store markets the product or service.

3 Name a product or service that you purchased recently. Describe the marketing technique that you know helped you to make your choice of purchase.

4 Assume that a major company is planning to build a large sports complex and has asked for your help. You are required to identify different groups of people that would be likely to pay to use the complex, and indicate the features or facilities that should be included in the sports complex so that it will appeal to each of these groups of people.

5 Describe a promotional plan that could be used to market your school or college in order to make as many people as possible aware of the good features of it. How could you evaluate the effectiveness of your plan?

6 Use a particular product, such as a car, and explain why the marketing price demands observation of the product lifecycle.

7 Construct a demand curve to illustrate an analysis of the demand for a particular good or service based on your own personal research.

Market Research and Advertising

Market research

In Chapter 8 we learnt that the marketing concept requires a firm to be aware of the customer's needs, to try and meet those needs, and to attempt to make a profit in the process. Market research assists the firm to meet the goal of the marketing concept by helping the process of finding out what the customer wants – in other words, market research has the effect of identifying the appropriate marketing strategy that will reach the target audience.

Market research investigates what consumers are buying or are likely to buy in the future. The research is normally carried out before launching the advertising campaign. Thoroughly carried out, market research can help to direct advertisers to the most economic and effective way to run their campaign. Sometimes market research is carried out after the product is already well established in order to assess and improve advertising and evaluate product performance.

The aims of market research

Market research has three broad aims:

- *to find out what the public wants* so that the business does not waste resources producing goods or services that are not required.
- *to assess likely volume of demand* to ensure that over-producing does not occur;
- *to discover what will influence consumers* – product name, style and colour of packaging, best target audience, price range, effective hidden persuaders, etc.

In order to achieve these aims the marketeer needs to be aware of the following factors that influence consumer behaviour.

- *Choice*. Where there are several competitors in the market consumers will have several alternatives to choose from. For this reason the marketeer is forced to be competitive.
- *Taste*. People differ in their preference for goods and services and, therefore, the marketeer has to identify these preferences.
- *Tradition*. In some circumstances there may be a long-standing tradition that influences consumer behaviour. For example, some products (e.g. scents) have traditionally been associated with members of only one of the sexes.
- *Income*. The amount of money a person earns clearly affects their ability to purchase. Consequently some highly priced products and services will only be purchased by the higher paid wage-earner.
- *Brand loyalty*. Marketeers often try to create loyalty for their products with

consumers. The hope is that the customer will stay with their existing product because it has satisfied them for some time. Conversely, this brand loyalty also makes it difficult for the marketeer to woo the consumer away from a product that they are satisfied with.

The importance of market research

Market research provides a marketeer with information which will help with decisions about where to sell a product or service, how to sell it, which customers need the product and exactly what they want, how to price the product, how to promote the product, who the competitors are in the market place and the size of the market.

The person responsible for market research has to be able to answer a number of appropriate questions in order to come up with useful information which can aid marketing decision-making in the firm.

Those carrying out market research find out the information they need by asking a cross-section of the public (from all age groups and social backgrounds) a number of carefully designed questions. The questioning is carried out in a variety of places.

In the street, shop or home the researcher will have a set of prepared questions. The answers to many of these questions can be quickly recorded by ticks in boxes marked Yes or No. The telephone is increasingly being used for research in the home.

Questionnaires are also circulated in shops or homes. A carefully constructed questionnaire must be:

- easy to understand;
- simple to answer, perhaps by ticks;
- capable of useful analysis (frequently by computer).

Sampling

- Members of the public may be invited to try the product or compare one more examples and make constructive observations.
- Test marketing may be carried out by selling the product in a small sample area in order to assess likely demand prior to commencing full-scale production.

Types of market research

The following are some of the market research strategies used by marketeers.

Experiments

A product may be developed and marketed in one or two limited geographical areas. During this process data would be collected, tabulated and analysed. The

Market Research and Advertising

MARKET RESEARCH QUESTIONNAIRES

The questions used in surveys have to be carefully constructed to ensure that the data collected is of constructive use. The questions may require:

- **a direct response**
  'YES' ☐   'NO' ☐   'DON'T KNOW' ☐
  e.g. Have you ever read the magazine Which?

- **a scale of responses**
  Strongly agree ☐   Agree ☐   Disagree ☐   Strongly Disagree ☐
  e.g. Do you think smoking should be banned in public places?

- **a range of answers**
  e.g. Which of the following forms of transport have you used in the past week?

Method		How many times?
Bus	☐	☐
Rail	☐	☐
Taxi	☐	☐
Own car	☐	☐

Please indicate your hobbies, sports and interests.

Hobbies and Interests
- ☐ 1 Cooking
- ☐ 2 Gourmet Foods
- ☐ 3 Gardening
- ☐ 4 Knitting
- ☐ 5 Photography
- ☐ 6 Dressmaking
- ☐ 7 Issues of Collectables/Special Editions etc.
- ☐ 8 Home Computing
- ☐ 9 Listening to Music
- ☐ 10 Reading Books

How many magazines do you buy a month?
☐ 11 0   ☐ 12 1-3   ☐ 13 4-6   ☐ 14 7+

Sports and Activities
- ☐ 15 Fishing
- ☐ 16 Tennis
- ☐ 17 Squash
- ☐ 18 Cycling
- ☐ 19 Horse Riding
- ☐ 20 Golf
- ☐ 21 Running/Jogging
- ☐ 22 Shooting
- ☐ 23 Snow Skiing
- ☐ 24 Sailing
- ☐ 25 Water Skiing

☐ 26 Please tick if you normally include your sports and activities as part of your holidays.

Clothing & Fashion
- ☐ 27 Ladies Fashion
- ☐ 28 Mens Fashion
- ☐ 29 Winter/Thermal Underwear
- ☐ 30 Womens Clothes Size 16+

☐ 31 Please tick if you have ever bought anything for your Leisure via mail order.
☐ 32 Please tick if you were satisfied with the purchase.

What do you drink?
☐ 1 Beer   ☐ 2 Wine   ☐ 3 Spirits

Are you interested in buying?
☐ 4 Wine by mail order   ☐ 5 Home Brewing Kits   ☐ 6 Cigarettes/Cigars   ☐ 7 A Pipe

Do you smoke?
☐ 8 Please tick if you would like to stop smoking

A manufacturer of chocolate bars wants to produce a high energy snack bar. Draft out a questionnaire that could be used to find out what would be an appropriate target audience, and the characteristics that should be incorporated into the bar and its packaging to help it sell well.

findings would then be used in deciding whether the *pilot* experiment suggests that it would be worthwhile embarking on large-scale production and distribution.

Observations

Observation is perhaps the most widely used form of market research. The observations may be *formal* or *informal*.

Using the observation approach the researcher watches how people behave or respond to certain situations. For example, does change in packaging design have the effect of improving sales?

Guidelines to be followed during the observations would be set out by the researcher, and appropriate notes made during the period. The information collected would be passed on to the researcher's firm for analysis and decision-making.

Surveys

Sometimes we encounter market research personnel in supermarkets, our communities, in airport buildings, and other public places. These people use questionnaires, personal interviews, or telephone interviews based on carefully constructed questions to establish the views of consumers.

It is of course impossible to survey every consumer and, therefore, a sample is used. This sample has to reflect the whole population. So, the *representative sample* includes both sexes, a variety of age groups, country and town dwellers, and people that are poor as well as those who are not.

The main ways of conducting surveys are:

- *By post*. This is by far the easiest method but it has the disadvantage that many people will not bother to complete and return the questionnaires.
- *By personal interview*. This is the most common method, but it can be expensive because it is very labour-intensive.
- *By telephone*. This approach is becoming increasingly common although it sometimes has a counter-effect on consumers who are 'put off' the product because they object to being disturbed in their homes.

9.3 Market research in action

The market research team

Market research is carried out by specialists called *market researchers*. In a large organisation several such specialists will be used to form a team.

The market research team must ensure that the research is relevant to the needs of the firm as well as the needs of the consumer. Research must be accurate and timely, too, if it is to really achieve the desired result. For example, suppose an organisation that produces clothing for teenagers learns from its research findings that certain types of T-shirts will be popular among teenagers during the summer months. To meet the demands of the teenagers, the T-shirts must be produced to the required specifications in terms of style and colour, they must be produced in sufficient numbers in time for the summer, and they must be delivered to places where the buyers can gain access to purchase them.

If a business is not large enough to employ its own market researchers it can hire the services of a market research agency which is a firm that specialises in this work.

Market segmentation

The potential market for a seller of goods or services can be individuals and also other businesses. Rather than trying to sell to everyone, it makes sense for a seller to identify specific parts of the total market and concentrate on trying to reach those parts. These parts of the market are called **market segments**, dividing the market in this way is called **market segmentation**. The following are examples of market segments, but there are others.

- *Geographic segmentation* – identifying people from a particular country, region, city, suberb or rural area.
- *Demographic segmentation* – targeting people from a population group such as that for age, gender, income or social class (see social grades data).
- *Behavioural segmentation* – people with similar interests, e.g. those in a particular line of business.

Social class categories are based on the occupation of the head of the household as follows:

Class A	Higher managerial, administrative, or professional.
Class B	Intermediate managerial, administrative, or professional.
Class C1	Supervisory or clerical, and junior managerial, administrative or professional.
Class C2	Skilled manual workers.
Class D	Semi and unskilled manual workers.
Class E	State pensioners, casual workers, unemployed.

Table of social grades

Sampling

Having identified a market segment to target for research, it is not realistic or economical to approach everyone in the segment to find out information. Information is usually collected from a *sample* of the market segment. The methods of sampling most frequently used include *random, stratified, quota,* and *cluster sampling*:

- *random sampling* – those to be surveyed (*interviewees*) are picked from some reliable official list such as the telephone directory or the electoral register, at fixed gaps of, say, every 50 or 100 names in the list.

- *stratified sampling* – in this type of sampling researchers deliberately allow bias towards a particular category of person, e.g. females, homeowners, pensioners, or people in a particular profession or type of business.
- *quota sampling* – this is the most common method of sampling. Here, interviewees are chosen randomly, but a certain number of people in specific categories (e.g. social grade or sex) must be included. The number interviewed is in proportion to the total population. For example, if the population contains 10 per cent more males than females, then 10 per cent more females will be included in the sample.
- *cluster sampling* – a cluster sample includes groups of people rather than individuals. For example, the researchers might choose the residents in several towns, randomly chosen, and in certain streets (also randomly chosen) in each town.

Sources of information

The sources from which a market researcher collects information can be classified as primary or secondary.

Primary data is usually drawn from original sources. In other words, none of the data has been collected previously by someone else. This type of data can be collected through experiments, observations and interviews, as described earlier.

Secondary data refers to information that is already in existence in a form different from that the researcher intends to use, but which may be useful to managers in the decision-making process. In other words, secondary data has already been gathered previously by someone else and the researcher's intention is to access the data and make use of it. A firm's files, annual reports, manuals, and brochures, among others, are rich sources of secondary data for the market research team.

Secondary data also includes items such as government statistics, reference books, newspaper articles and even the sales literature of competitors. Because the researcher does not actually have to go out into the field to collect this data first-hand it is often referred to as *desk research*.

Research procedures

The following are typical examples of procedures followed by professional researchers:

1. Identify the problem to be solved or information to be obtained.
2. Set limits to the problem. Focus on one or a few manageable things.
3. Draw on current knowledge (of the product or of the market).
4. Seek out new knowledge. (Current knowledge might be inadequate, irrelevant, or just out of date.)
5. Consider all possible solutions to the problem set (through careful examination of current and new knowledge).
6. Attempt to make suggestions for alternative solutions to the problem set.

7 Select the best solution to the problem. This should always be related to the situation or the environment of the target market.
8 Try out the identified solution, e.g. experiment with a sample/trial run.
9 Evaluate and adjust where necessary.

Research methods

Methods of research are usually grouped into those which are desk based and those which are field based.

Desk research

This method of research refers to collecting *secondary data* from existing sources, and can be largely carried out without going outside the organisation. The researchers may use their own data (e.g. sales records, or replies to previously circulated questionnaires), or some other source of information, such as government statistics or trade journals.

Field research

This involves collecting *primary data*, i.e. collecting new information from surveys outside the firm. There are many ways this may be done, including the following:

- *Postal questionnaires*   This can be an economical way of collecting a considerable amount of data, so long as the questionnaire is carefully worded. An important factor involved in postal questionnaires is trying to find ways of encouraging people to reply.
- *Telephone surveys*   This is a relatively quick way to collect new data without having to actually 'go out into the field'. However, some people are not on the telephone, and those who are may object to being contacted in this way.
- *Direct interviews*   This is a costly method of research because it involves talking to people 'out in the field', and the interviewers need special skills to question people without influencing their answers. However, a skillful interviewer can help to overcome any reluctance on the part of the respondents to reply frankly to questions.
- *Test marketing*   Test marketing involves trying out a new product or service in a small area to assess the public response before full-scale production is undertaken. Testing in a small area can give a producer an idea of what quantity to produce.
- *Observation*   With this technique, researchers watch to see how consumers behave in the marketplace, e.g. how they respond to shop layouts and displays. The information obtained can help businesses (e.g. shop owners) to design the organisation of their premises, and producers to package their goods in the most effective way.

9.4 Functions of advertising

The main functions of advertising are as follows:

- announce new products;
- highlight the unique features of a product;
- build a firm's image around its products;
- highlight special events – concessions, sales, late openings;
- increase market share by stimulating demand;
- educate consumers about the products.

The purpose of advertising

It would be pointless for a business to develop a product or service if there was no way to tell consumers about it. Advertising is a means of communication – it is used to make consumers aware of the goods and services that producers and traders have to offer. An advertisement is a message that uses words, pictures or sound to:

- *inform* potential buyers of the availability of goods and services;
- *persuade* people to buy or behave in a particular way.

Informative and persuasive advertising

Informative advertising gives detailed information about the goods or services available and leaves consumers to decide, without persuasion, if they wish to

Examples of informative advertising.

Market Research and Advertising

purchase. An informative advertisement will contain useful details such as specification, sizes, colour and material. This type of approach can also be employed in public relations and image creation.

Persuasive advertising uses a variety of techniques to persuade people to buy product or service, irrespective of whether they need it or not. These persuasive techniques are sometimes referred to as 'hidden persuaders'.

Advertising's 'hidden persuaders'

One of the ways advertiser may use an advertisement to promote sales is to per-

Look at these examples of persuasive advertisements. Notice how they attempt to try and convince the consumer that they are better than alternatives from other producers. Can you recognise any hidden persuaders?

suade the consumer that the advertiser's product will make the consumer better off in some way. Some of the factors to which this type of advertisement appeals are far from obvious and, therefore, they are sometimes called *hidden persuaders*, for example:

- *sex appeal* – the product is claimed to make the user attractive to the opposite sex;
- *ambition* – the advertisement implies that those who use the product will be successful;
- *personality appeal* – famous personalities are shown using the product to give it an acceptable image;
- *social acceptability* – the advertisement implies that by using the product the consumer becomes more acceptable to others;
- *work simplification* – the product is claimed to make a task easier to carry out;
- *health* – the advertisement suggests that the use of the product contributes to good health.

9.5 Forms of advertising

Advertising media

There is a wide variety of ways in which an advertisement may reach the public, but not all of the ways are suitable for every advertisement. There are many media through which advertising may take place, each of which has a varying degree of effectiveness and cost.

- *Television and radio* are very expensive but are the most effective method of reaching a large audience.
- *National press* reaches a wide area, but is expensive and, therefore, mainly used by large companies.
- *Local newspapers* offer cheaper advertising rates for cover of a limited area. 'Free' local newspapers rely on advertising to meet costs.
- *Magazines or journals* have a more limited circulation but reach a 'selected' audience, offer greater scope for colour advertisements and have a longer life than newspapers.
- *Cinemas* reach a relatively small audience but can be effective, particularly in advertising local shops etc.
- *Posters and hoardings* provide eye-catching signs, sited in public places or on public transport.
- *Point-of-sale* methods provide eye-catching shop counter or window displays to influence the consumer to buy on impulse.
- *Exhibitions* attract large numbers of people who already have at least some interest in the product. Exhibitions also enable specialists in a field to meet and compare products and experience.
- *Circulation* by leaflets (the *mail shot*) can be an effective medium but is very labour-intensive for hand delivery, or costly with regard to postage.

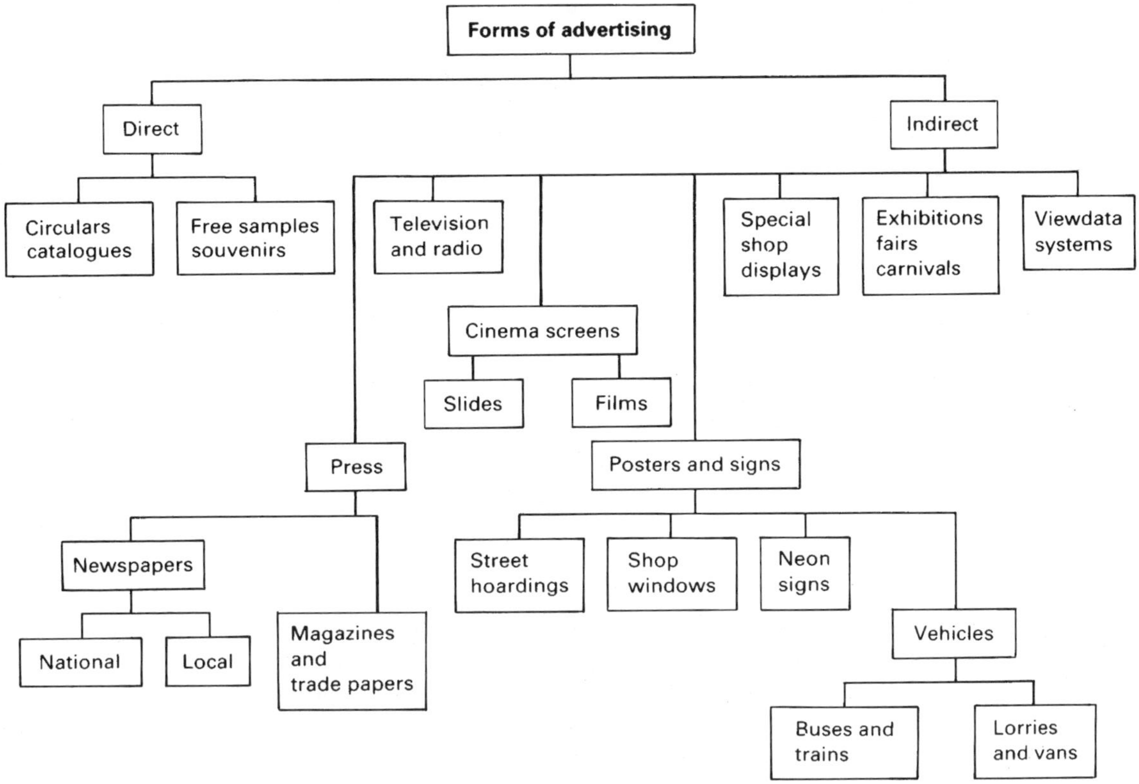

Market Research and Advertising

```
                            Forms of advertising
                           /                    \
                       Direct                   Indirect
```

Direct: Circulars/catalogues; Free samples/souvenirs; Television and radio; Cinema screens (Slides, Films); Press (Newspapers — National, Local; Magazines and trade papers)

Indirect: Special shop displays; Exhibitions fairs carnivals; Viewdata systems; Posters and signs (Street hoardings, Shop windows, Neon signs, Vehicles — Buses and trains, Lorries and vans)

- *Word-of-mouth* (i.e. personal recommendation) is sometimes encouraged by firms carrying out a *whispering campaign* by giving away free samples which they hope the users will talk about favourably.

The marketeer has to decide which of the media is most appropriate for the product or service they are trying to sell. Often a combination of the forms of advertising described above will be incorporated into the seller's advertising campaign.

9.6 The advertising campaign

An advertising campaign is all of the processes a firm employs to sell its goods or services. The campaign will be based on a clearly defined plan, much of which will be formed as a result of the market research described earlier.

Some firms are large enough to have their own advertising department, others may decide it is preferable to employ an advertising agency to carry out an advertising campaign on their behalf. Whichever is the case, the advertiser or agency will have to take many factors into account. The following questions must certainly be answered if the campaign is to be effective.

- Which groups (the *target audience*) of the public is the campaign intended to reach?
- How much money is availabe to be spent on the campaign?
- How extensive is the campaign intended to be – countywide, countrywide or worldwide?
- Which techniques will catch the attention of buyers?

Some of these questions, such as the amount of money to be put into the campaign, can only be answered by the advertiser. Others can be solved through market research.

Advertising agencies

Advertising agencies are businesses which specialise in assisting others with their advertising needs: a service for which they are paid.

The extent of the work that an agency will undertake for its client will depend on how much the client wishes to spend on advertising its product. The agency may work in conjunction with the client's own advertising department, providing advice on how to conduct the campaign, or alternatively it may be employed to organise the complete advertising campaign.

It takes the work of many skilled people to formulate a single advertisement, and the formulation of a complete campaign for a large national company is a vast undertaking. An agency handling such a campaign will employ people with specialist skills associated with marketing.

Apart from market research, an advertising department or an advertising agency would be concerned with artwork and space-buying.

Artwork

This involves the formation of the pictorial display of the advertisement, and includes the creation of wording to go with the advertisement. *Brainstorming* is a typical technique employed in this regard which involves the free expression of ideas until the most suitable wording and visual display is formed.

Space-buying

This is the process of hiring the most appropriate space to display the advertisement. This must be not only the most effective but also the most economically appropriate. For example, although television is one of the most effective forms of advertising it is far too expensive for selling a few inexpensive items.

9.7 Is advertising wasteful?

There is no real answer to this question because it depends on one's personal point of view. Some people argue that advertising benefits the consumer in a variety of ways, whereas others suggest that it causes an added expense to be met by the consumer. What do you think?

Market Research and Advertising

KEY PERSONNEL INVOLVED

CREATIVE DIRECTOR

Carole Stone

I head a team of copywriters and artists who develop the words and visual aspects of the advertisement. My department may buy artwork or film from other specialists if we cannot produce it ourselves.

RESEARCH MANAGER

John Brady

My job is to investigate the potential market for our client's products. The aim is to identify the right 'target audience' for products or services. I try to give the Creative Director ideas about the likes and dislikes of the target audience.

MEDIA MANAGER

Nik Rudge

I decide which type of all the available media is best suited to carry the proposed advertisement. This eventually involves buying 'space' in the media for the advertisement to appear. Obviously I aim to buy space at the lowest price possible.

ACCOUNT MANAGER

Aileen Killick

Whilst I am after the client's money, I do have a wider role. Each of our clients is referred to as an 'account'. Part of my job is to personally supervise all of the work involved in the account. I will be the main point of contact for clients.

How an agency can help in the planning of an advertising campaign.

Arguments for advertising

- It makes consumers aware of the range of choice available.
- It encourages healthy competition between suppliers.
- It promotes demand and makes mass production possible.
- Mass production provides employment and also keeps prices down.
- It helps to pay for sports events and concerts.
- It contributes towards the cost of newspapers and magazines.
- It brightens up town centres with colourful displays.

Criticisms of advertising

- The cost of advertising has to be incorporated into the price of goods or services.
- Most advertising aims to persuade people to buy whether they need the commodity or not.
- 'Hidden persuaders' appeal to emotions and prejudices.
- Some advertising encourages unsociable habits and behaviour.
- Some advertising misleads by making exaggerated claims.
- It encourages people to be wasteful and discard older but satisfactory products for new ones.

9.8 Consumer protection

The need for consumer protection

All firms, people, businesses and even governments are consumers, although we usually refer particularly to individuals when talking about consumers. We have seen earlier in Chapters 1 and 2 of this book that the aim of production is to make things that can be used by consumers. In fact it has been said that 'The sole end and purpose of all production is the consumer.' We have also seen in this chapter that advertising aims not only to inform us about goods and services, but also to persuade us to buy them.

With the growth of large-scale production and the increased spending power of many people, the motivation for firms to obtain and maintain a larger share of the consumer market has risen considerably. This has been further encouraged by technological changes which have not only revolutionised products and the way they are manufactured, but also the manner in which they are marketed.

At one time the attitude of the law in relation to the protection of consumers was *caveat emptor*, or 'Let the buyer beware'. In other words, consumers were expected to protect themselves. Today consumers are protected in a number of ways by legislation and government agencies, but it is still important for consumers to help protect themselves by shopping wisely.

Traders cannot deprive consumers of their rights without facing the risk of legal action. Obviously traders need to know the rights of their customers and the responsibilities that they have to treat them fairly in order to meet their own legal obligation. In addition, the trader has similar rights against his suppliers as his customers have against him, so long as he has not agreed to give up those rights.

The European Union (EU) helps to protect the consumers of its member countries by setting minimum standards of quality and safety. Products which meet the EU standards are allowed to indicate this on their labels.

Consumer law

The following are some of the most important British laws that aim to protect the consumer and guide the businessperson.

Food and Drugs Act 1955 (enforced by public health inspectors)

- Forbids the sale of unfit food.
- States hygienic conditions for production and sale of food products.
- Regulates labelling and description of items.
- Provides minimum standards in food composition (e.g. meat content of sausages, pies, etc.).

Weights and Measures Act 1963

- Requires quantity of pre-packed goods to be shown on the container.
- Makes short weight or false measurement an offence.
- Certain goods must be sold in 'prescribed quantities' (e.g. milk).

Resale Prices Act 1964

- Suppliers are not allowed to impose a minimum price at which their goods must be sold, but they can suggest a manufacturer's recommended price (MRP).
- Suppliers cannot refuse supplies to a retailer who sells below the recommended price.
- Books, maps and medicines are exempt from this Act.

Trade Descriptions Act 1968

This Act makes it an offence punishable by fine or imprisonment to falsely describe goods or services offered for sale. The Act applies to verbal or written descriptions.

Unsolicited Goods and Services Act 1971

This Act makes it illegal to demand payment for goods or services that have not been ordered. Should unsolicited goods be delivered the consumer has two clear courses of action:

1. They can write to the firm giving the name and address from where the goods can be collected. If the trader fails to collect the goods within thirty days they belong to the holder.
2. Alternatively, if unsolicited goods are not collected by the trader within six months, they become the property of the holder.

Fair Trading Act 1973

This Act established a permanent Office of Fair Trading which is a government body with the broad function to keep watch on trading matters in the United Kingdom and protect both consumers and business people against unfair practices.

Prices Acts 1974 and 1975

These Acts gave the government the power to:

- subsidise food;
- regulate food prices;
- require shopkeepers to display prices in a way that does not give a false impression.

Consumer Credit Act 1974

The purpose of this Act is to control all forms of credit services. It includes regulation of credit and hire agreements, licensing of lenders, advertisements, breaches of agreements, extortionate charges and credit referencing. The Act protects the consumer in the following ways:

- All businesses involved with credit or hire agreements are required to obtain a licence from the Office of Fair Trading.
- Consumers can ask a court to reduce unfair or 'extortionate' rates of interest.
- Individuals can ask to see the contents of files referring to them held by credit reference agencies which supply information about the financial standing of people. The individual can ask for wrong information to be corrected.
- All relevant information must be brought clearly to the notice of the borrower. Advertisements offering credit should not be misleading and must advise the consumer of the annual percentage rate (APR), i.e. the true annual rate of interest.
- Compensation may be claimed for goods that are faulty.

Types of credit covered by the Act are as follows:

- *personal credit agreements* – bank loans, overdrafts, personal loans, pawnbrokers, ets.;
- *credit token agreements* – credit cards, chargecards, cash dispenser cards, etc.;
- *hire purchase (HP) agreements* – contracts for the hire of goods for a fixed period of time with an option to purchase for a nominal sum at the end of the period of repayment by regular instalments;
- *credit sales agreements* – similar to HP but goods become the property of the buyer immediately the deposit or initial payment has been made;
- *consumer hire agreements* – these relate to true hire arrangements rather than sales because the items rarely become the property of the person hiring them.

Restrictive Trade Practices Act 1976

This Act aims to safeguard the consumer against the practice of agreements between companies to limit production in order to keep prices artificially high, and to exploit a monopolistic position.

Consumer Safety Act 1978

This Act regulates the sale of goods which may be potentially dangerous, for example toys, electrical goods, cooking equipment, heaters, etc.

Sale of Goods Act 1979

This Act covers all goods (including food) bought from a trader to a shop doorstep seller, and sales by mail order. The seller has three main obligations. Goods must:

1 *Be of 'merchantable quality'*. This means that goods must be reasonably fit for their normal purpose, bearing in mind the price paid, the nature of the goods and how they were described. Thus a new item must not be damaged and it must work properly.
2 *Be 'as described'*. They must correspond with the description given by the seller, or in accordance with labels on the item or the packing.
3 *Be 'fit for any particular purpose made known to the sellers'*. If you ask for plates that are 'dishwasher safe' and the seller assures you that they are, he has broken his contract with you if they are not.

Note: In the case of private sales only obligation 2 applies.

Supply of Goods and Services Act 1982

This Act applies the terms of the Sale of Goods Act to goods supplied as part of a service, e.g. faulty taps provided by a plumber, and where goods are hired or exchanged instead of actually being purchased. The Act also provides that a person providing a service must do so:

- with reasonable skill and care;
- within a reasonable time;
- for a reasonable charge.

Although there is still a need for the 'buyer to beware' when making purchases, modern marketing methods and trends sometimes make it difficult for the consumer to judge fairly the quality and value of purchases. Pre-packed goods are difficult to examine before they reach home. And how can the purchaser (or even the retailer) of a complex computer or hi-fi system know if the equipment is sound?

It is for these reasons that the manufacturer as well as the retailer has responsibilities to the consumer under the Sale of Goods Act.

Consumer Protection Act 1987

This Act makes it an offence to give a misleading price indication for any goods, services, accommodation or facilities. This also applies to 'special offers' which turn out to be false.

Government agencies providing consumer protection

Department of Prices and Consumer Protection

This government department promotes legislation aimed at the protection of consumers, and administers laws related to this. The department also encourages the formation of consumer advice centres and citizens' advice bureaux.

Office of Fair Trading (OFT)

The OFT:

- publishes consumer advice information;
- encourages industries to form associations and codes of practice;
- investigates and prosecutes traders who persistently commit offences;
- checks on fitness of traders who provide credit or hire agreements;
- makes suggestions for changes in consumer law.

Ministry of Agriculture, Fisheries and Food (MAFF)

MAFF administers the law relating to milk production, fisheries, slaughterhouses and the meat trade, and the composition and labelling of food.

Department of Health

This department is concerned with the production and distribution of medicines and also hygiene.

Local Authorities

- *Trading standards* (*consumer protection departments* investigate local complaints about quality description, and the weights or measures of goods supplied.
- *Environmental health departments* deal with complaints related to impure food and food production or selling premises.
- *Consumer advice centres* set up by local authorities deal with consumer problems.

Independent agencies providing consumer protection

Consumers' Association

- A non-profit making association financed by members' subscriptions.
- Carries out comparative tests on goods and services.
- Publishes results in the association magazine *Which*?
- Publishes books on consumer-related matters.

Citizens' Advice Bureaux

Give confidential advice on legal and consumer matters, on a voluntary basis.

British Standards Institution (BSI)

Publishes a series of standards intended to ensure products are fit for the purpose for which they are intended.

- The *kite mark* is awarded to products meeting the required standard.
- The *safety mark* is given to products which pass BSI safety standards.

Design Council

Examines products of British manufacture and issues its own level to those which are judged to demonstrate a high standard in all aspects of design and performance.

Professional and trade associations

Many trade and professions have set up associations to formulate and administer codes of practice which include procedures for dealing with consumer complaints.

Media support for consumers

Media such as television, radio and the newspapers play a valuable part in consumer protection today by investigating complaints, comparing goods and services and evaluating and recommending 'best buys'.

When things go wrong

Of course, things go wrong, and it may not always be the fault of the seller. Before setting off to the shop to complain about faulty goods the consumer should ask three simple questions

- Was it a fault I should have noticed when buying?
- Was it something I was told about?
- Am I expecting too much from something cheap?

If the answer to all three questions is 'No', then the consumer has a reason to complain. They should take along proof of purchase (e.g. receipt), and they should remember to act in a reasonable manner because most respectable traders will want to put things right.

If they have no success at the shop the consumer can write to the organisation's head office. They should keep copies of all correspondence. Should they still not be satisfied they may well then need support from some other agency described earlier.

Activities

1 In what way does market research help a firm to achieve a marketing concept?

2 What kind of decisions does a market researcher hope to be able to make from data collected?

3 Briefly describe the factors that influence consumer behaviour.

4 Where is market research carried out?

5 Describe some of the strategies used by market researchers to gather information.

6 Why is it often important that a market researcher uses a 'representative sample'?

7 Briefly describe three examples of market segments.

8 In what ways can the table of social grades help to target marketing strategies?

9. Describe the four main methods of sampling.
10. Explain the difference between 'primary data' and 'secondary data'.
11. How does 'desk research' differ from 'field research'?
12. Describe at least four methods of field research.
13. What is the aim of advertising?
14. How does 'informative' advertising differ from 'persuasive' advertising?
15. What are 'hidden persuaders'?
16. Briefly describe the various advertising media.
17. What do we mean by the term 'advertising campaign'?
18. What is the function of an advertising agency?
19. List the arguments for and against advertising.
20. Why is consumer protection so important today?
21. What does *caveat emptor* mean and why is this less relevant today?
22. List three aspects of consumer protection contained in the Food and Drugs Act.
23. In which way does the Weights and Measures Act aim to protect consumers?
24. What do the letters MRP stand for? What is the relevance of these letters to consumer law?
25. Briefly describe the purpose of the Trade Descriptions Act.
26. What are the two courses of action open to someone who has received unsolicited goods?
27. Name the important body established by the Fair Trading Act.
28. 'The Consumer Credit Act is the main safeguard for those who buy on credit.' Explain this statement.
29. List and briefly describe the types of credit covered by the Consumer Credit Act.
30. Briefly explain the purpose of the two following consumer protection Acts:
    (a) Restrictive Trade Practices Act;
    (b) Consumer Safety Act.
31. The Sale of Goods Act states that goods must be 'of merchantable quality', 'as described', and 'fit for the purpose'. Explain these phrases.

32 Your friend has recently bought a pair of shoes that are now found to be faulty. Give three suggestions on how she should go about getting the matter put right.

33 State one function of the Office of Fair Trading.

34 Which government department is concerned with the production and distribution of medicines?

35 Briefly describe the work of three types of local authority departments which help to safeguard the interests of consumers.

36 Give a brief description of the contribution that the Consumers' Association makes to consumer protection.

37 The 'kite mark' and 'safety mark' are both symbols that the consumer should look for. Why is this so?

38 In what way do professional and trade associations contribute to consumer protection?

39 In spite of the fact that many of the media rely on advertisers for much of their income, they still try to promote consumer awareness. Give two examples of how they do this.

40 What questions should the consumer ask before they are sure they have a case for complaint?

Structured Questions

1 Consider the advertisement on page 181 from the Peterborough Development Corporation.

   (a) Who do you think paid for this advertisement? (1)
   (b) Who is the target audience for this advertisement? (2)
   (c) What is the aim of the advertisement? (2)
   (d) The advertisement says that 'Peterborough's overheads are amongst the lowest in the country.' What does this mean? (3)
   (e) In what ways do you think that this could be said to be an example of informative advertising? (3)
   (f) State four claims that the advertisement makes as benefits of moving to Peterborough. (4)
   (g) This advertisement was produced by an agency called Deighton and Mullen. Briefly describe how this type of agency assists an advertiser. (5)

2 Lazy Bones Ltd is a manufacturer of household electrical goods. They have decided to produce a new product aimed at the busy working housewife – a remote-controlled vacuum cleaner. The head of the product development

Market Research and Advertising

ONE TRIP TO PETERBOROUGH SAVED THIS TRAVEL COMPANY OVER £3 MILLION LAST YEAR.

In business as well as in travel Thomas Cook have always been going places. But never more so than since they moved their international headquarters to Peterborough.

With Peterborough's overheads amongst the lowest in the country, Thomas Cook annually save millions compared with the cost of operating in London. Yet they're still only 50 minutes by high speed 125 train from the capital.

Peterborough is the ideal choice for companies seeking a new location.

There's an outstanding choice of housing. Schools are first class and people here enjoy unrivalled sporting and recreational opportunities.

If you'd like to join the legion companies who have moved here, cut out the coupon now.

To: John Bouldin, Peterborough Development Corporation, Stuart House, City Road, Peterborough PE1 1UJ. Please send me your free complete guide to relocation.

Name _____ FTT1
Position _____
Company _____
Address _____
_____
Tel: _____

THE PETERBOROUGH EFFECT
IT'S BEEN WORKING FOR CENTURIES.

department has been instructed to produce a prototype with electronic sensors to prevent collisions with furniture, etc.

A name for the new cleaner has yet to be decided; this will be the subject of a brainstorming session. The advertising campaign will be decided following market research and pilot marketing.

(a) Define the term 'prototype' (1)
(b) What is the purpose of a prototype? (2)
(c) What is a 'brainstorming session'? (2)
(d) Describe the kind of market research that would be carried out:
   (i) before the new cleaner goes onto the market; (3)
   (ii) after the cleaner goes on sale to the public. (3)
(e) List four contrasting questions that could be included in a market research questionnaire to help the development of an advertising campaign for this new product. (4)
(f) If the market research clearly shows that there is a need for the planned cleaner, why will there still be a need for an advertising campaign? (5)

3 Read the following information on page 182 about marketing and then answer these questions, which ask you to relate market research to this information.

(a) What does market research tell a business? (1)
(b) In what way would you say that market research helps a firm to set an 'acceptable and profitable price level'? (2)

Market Research and Advertising

WHAT IS MARKETING?

'Marketing is the management process responsible for identifying, anticipating and satisfying customer requirements profitably'

Don't think – as many people do – that marketing is just the smart 'in' word for selling. Selling is a vital, indispensable component of marketing, but only one of several other activities. Marketing thinking and planning begins at or even before, the drawing board and ends only when the company has made certain that the customer is really satisfied with the products or service provided. Because marketing affects so many of the company's resources and activities, it is essentially a team effort.

Good marketing is the end product of a well-led management team fully embracing the marketing concept. The marketing manager is responsible for the marketing plan and the basic information and guidance about prospective markets, their behaviour, size and potential for each product or service supplied by the company.

The Marketing Spectrum

▶ RESEARCH: Identifying, analysing and predicting customer needs.

▶ PLANNING & DEVELOPMENT: deciding on who, what, when and how to meet these needs via new or existing product or service development.

▶ PRICING: setting an acceptable and profitable price level.

▶ PACKAGING: matching physical requirements with visual image.

▶ PROMOTION: generating product awareness and influencing customers' purchasing decisions, e.g. advertising, public relations.

▶ SALES: choosing the most efficient and effective sales approach.

▶ DISTRIBUTION: evaluating the most efficient way of getting the product to your customer, whether directly or indirectly.

▶ AFTER SALES: providing a comprehensive customer care service.

The Marketing Spectrum comprises a number of different functions, many of which are undertaken by specialists. It is the role of the Marketing Manager to co-ordinate the efforts and advice of these people and, based on a view of the situation overall, decide on future action.

Source: *The Chartered Institute of Marketing (UK)*.

(c) How would market research help a producer to 'match physical requirements with visual image'? (3)

(d) Describe two examples of ways that market research can help a business to choose 'the most efficient and effective sales approach'. (4)

(e) 'Marketing thinking and planning begins at or even before the drawing board...' How does market research contribute in this respect? (4)

(f) 'Good marketing is the end product of a well-led management team fully embracing the marketing concept.'
　(i) What do you understand by the phrase 'marketing concept' in the manner in which it is used here? (4)

(ii) Give examples of other wording included in this information that can be directly related to the marketing concept. (2)

4 Answer the following questions about the two advertisements shown below.

(a) 'These two advertisements are aimed at different target audiences.' Explain this statement. (2)

(b) Which of the advertisements shown do you think is probably involved in marketing by mail order? Give a reason for your answer. (2)

(c) What is the significance of the MOPS sign on the bag advertisement? (2)

(d) Which of the advertisements is 'persuasive' and which is 'informative'? Give reasons. (4)

(e) Using any parts of these advertisements as examples, explain how market research could have indicated to the advertiser that it would be advantageous to word the advertisement in the manner shown. (4)

(f) In what way would you say that the Tingle After Shave advertisement uses 'hidden persuaders' to encourage the consumer to buy? (6)

5 Sports Addicts is a monthly magazine selling widely to young people with interests in all kinds of sports. The following advertisement has been published by the magazine to attract potential advertisers.

Market Research and Advertising

Sports Addicts is the most widely circulating magazine in the United Kingdom, with 1.5 million copies sold every month reaching readers with the widest interest in sports, as spectators or active participants. But, did you know you could buy advertising space in any one or more of these 12 areas? Single page, full colour advertisements available at the following rates:

Charge per area Circulation	£ per month
25,000 – 60,000	1,000
61,000 – 120,000	1,800
121,000 – 300,000	2,500

LONDON: 280,000

SOUTH & SOUTH EAST: 110,000

NORTH EAST: 40,000

WALES & WEST: 90,000

MIDLANDS: 160,000

NORTH WEST: 110,000

SOUTH WEST: 45,000

N. IRELAND: 25,000

YORKSHIRE: 110,000

EAST OF ENGLAND: 50,000

REPUBLIC OF IRELAND: 60,000

SCOTLAND & THE BORDERS: 120,000

Special rate for single page advertisement in all regions £12,000 per month. Discount of 10% for any four regions in one month.

Sports Addicts is more than a media, it is a market.

(a) How much does it cost to advertise for one month in the North East Region? (1)
(b) Why does it cost more to advertise in the North West area than in the South West area? (1)
(c) Which area has the highest and which the lowest distribution figure? (1)
(d) Give two reasons why a business might advertise in the North East Region, but not in the West where distribution figures are higher. (2)
(e) Give at least two contrasting reasons (other than distribution figures) why a business could decide to advertise in London and the South East but not in Scotland and the borders. (2)
(f) How much in total would a company pay to advertise in the four regions of London, South and South East, Midlands, and East of England? Show your working out. (3)
(g) How much could a company save by paying the special rate for advertising in all regions for one month compared with the cost if it paid for each of the 12 regions separately? Show all your working out. (3)
(h) What do you think is meant by the statement, 'Sports Addicts is more than a media, it is a market'? (3)
(i) Give two examples of businesses selling contrasting products or services that might benefit from advertising in Sports Addicts magazine. Give reasons for each of your choices, emphasising why the particular product or service is suited for advertising in this media. (4)

Research Assignments

1 You are the advertising manager of a firm that is developing a new soft drink. Describe the way that you would formulate an advertising campaign to promote the launch of your product into a highly competitive market.

2 Advertising is wasteful of resources and causes an increase in the costs of goods. Discuss this statement.

3 Sometimes market research takes the form of 'desk research', that is finding out information about a potential market by referring to reference sources readily available to anyone. Describe the application of some specific reference sources available to market researchers.

4 Using specific examples of marketing techniques employed by companies with which you are familiar, explain why advertising is important to industry, commerce and the consumer.

5 Using a selection of advertisements to assist you, explain why you consider there is a case for consumers to have some protection against the claims of advertisers.

6 With reference to any one consumer good, evaluate the success of the marketing strategy used in relation to that product.

7 Collect and study packaging from a variety of food products purchased by your family. Observe all the details included on the packaging labels. Note the style of lettering, use of colour and graphics, and whether any promotional material is included. Design suitable wrappers (actual size) as alternatives to four of your collection. Write a report to justify the changes you have made.

8 A shoe manufactures plans to introduce a new style of sports trainer into the market. Design a questionnaire that will clearly identify an appropriate target market, and features that would help the trainer to sell well. Test your questionnaire on a representative sample and report on your findings.

 The Home Market

10.1 The chain of distribution

In Chapters 8 and 9 your attention was drawn in various places to the need to distribute goods so that they reach the intended customer. We could divide the target market into two broad categories:

- sales to local markets – *home trade;*
- sales to overseas markets – *foreign trade.*

In this chapter we will concentrate on home trade. We will turn our attention to foreign trade in Chapter 11.

The chain of distribution for home trade links the producer with the consumer through two main *intermediaries* – the *wholesaler* and the *retailer*. Both of these traders are part of *tertiary production* because they add to the value of goods.

Producer ⟶ Wholesaler ⟶ Retailer ⟶ Consumer

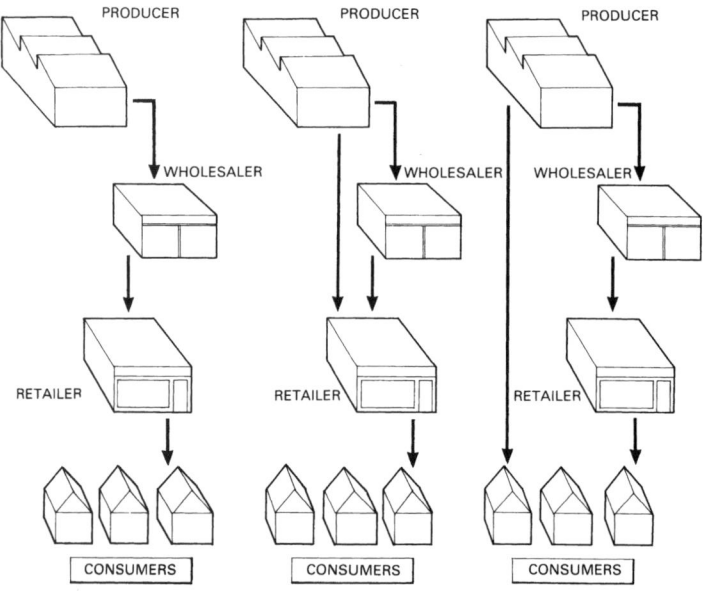

Spot the difference!

The Home Market

10.2 Wholesalers

The wholesaler buys in very large quantities from the producer, thus helping to make mass production possible. If the retailer can order a great enough quantity they may buy direct from the producer, bypassing the wholesaler.

Producers need to sell their products in large quantities to enable them to carry out mass production and enjoy economies of scale. But many retailers cannot buy in the large quantities that the producers and manufacturers want to sell. Wholesalers bridge the gap between producers and retailers by buying in large quantities and selling in smaller, more convenient lots, to the retailer. The retailer in turn sells individual items to the consumer.

The wholesaler's premises are usually a large warehouse divided into sections dealing with specific commodities, and operating on organisational lines similar to a large supermarket.

Retailers may visit the wholesaler to choose their purchases. Alternatively,

Part of a wholesale warehouse.

orders may be telephoned in, or passed to the wholesaler's representatives on their periodic visits to the retailers, and delivered in due course by the wholesaler's own delivery vehicles.

Types of wholesaler

There are two basic forms of wholesaler:

- *General* wholesalers operate from large warehouses sited for convenient access from many local towns. They will allow retailers credit and will also deliver goods to their shops.
- *Cash and carry* wholesalers do not allow credit and do not deliver good. Retailers come to warehouses, select goods, pay for them and provide their own transport.

Sometimes wholesalers will specialise in a particular aspect of trade. For example, one might specialise in supplies in hair care products, whilst another might specialise in clothing and footwear.

Functions of wholesalers

Acting as an intermediary

The wholesaler is positioned between the producer and the retailer. For this reason he is sometimes referred to as a *middleman* or *intermediary*.

Producer ⟶ Wholesaler ⟶ Retailer

But there are exceptions where the producer will sell direct to the retailer, or even straight to the consumer, bypassing both the wholesaler and the retailer.

Breaking of bulk

The wholesaler will buy in large quantities from the producer and sell in smaller lots, usually to the retailer.

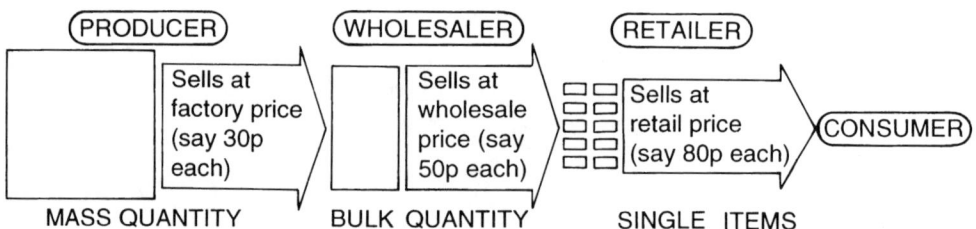

Taking on risks

The wholesaler will predict market trends and buy ahead of demand.

Warehousing

By storing goods the wholesaler saves space for both the producer and the retailer.

Offering credit

The wholesaler may supply goods and allow the retailer to pay at some later date *(trade credit)*. This gives the retailer the opportunity to possible sell the goods before he or she has paid for them.

Services provided by wholesalers

Wholesalers provide some important services to the chain of distribution.

For the producer

- *Reduces transport costs.*
- *Advises producer* of current market trends.
- *Finishes goods* by grading, packing and branding.
- *Makes mass production possible* by ordering in large quantities and therefore reducing production costs.

For the retailer

- *Offers choice* of products from many producers.
- *Supplies small quantities* to suit retailers' needs.
- *Locally situated* providing quick access to goods and open until late in the evening.
- *Advises* latest trends and 'best buys'.
- *Pre-packs goods* ready for the retailers' shelves (graded, labelled, priced, weighed).

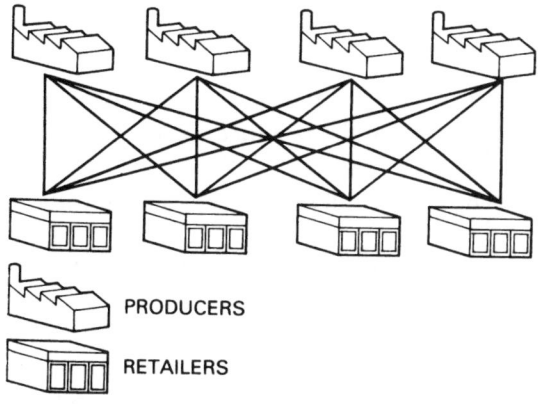

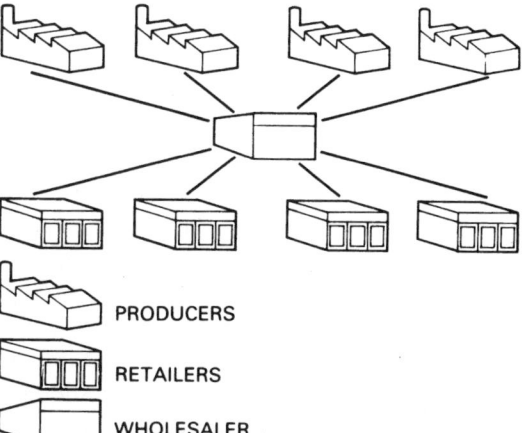

(a) **Without wholesaler**. We can see how the wholesaler saves in transport costs if we take a simple example of four different producers each supplying their produce to four retailers without the use of a wholesaler. Each producer would need to make four journeys to supply each retailer.

(b) **With wholesaler**. If we now introduce a wholesaler between the producers and the retailers each producer now only makes one journey to the wholesaler and the wholesaler makes one journey to each retailer.

The trend towards larger forms of retailers, in particular the big Chain Stores, has resulted in the elimination of many wholesaler businesses. This is because these large retailers can buy in such big quantities that they do not use wholesalers.

10.3 Retailers

The retailer is a trader who provides goods and services to the consumer. They are positioned either between the producers or manufacturers and the consumer, or between the wholesaler and the consumer. In other words, the retailer is the last link in the chain between the producer and the consumer.

The retailer buys in large quantities from the wholesaler and sells in small, convenient quantities to the consumer. If the retailer can order a great enough quantity he or she may buy direct from the producer.

The functions of retail trade

Today we live in a society in which specialisation plays a major part. Most of us concentrate on carrying out our particular specialism and rely on others to satisfy most of our needs. For each of us to be able to specialise in this way requires an intricate pattern of distribution between producers and consumers. This involves a whole range of intermediaries such as banking, insurance, transport, advertising and the many other aspects of commercial activities that are dealt with in other parts of this book. Here we shall concentrate on retail trade which is the final and important link between producers and consumers.

The retailer is the last stage in the passage of goods from the producer to the consumer. In this position the retailer performs a number of important functions:

- *Outlet*. The retailer performs a valuable service to the producer by providing him with an outlet for his products, thus saving the producer from the need to market his own goods.
- *Stocks*. The retailer holds stocks which the consumer can purchase locally in small, convenient quantities.
- *Choice*. The consumer is able to choose from the variety of products of different producers offered by the retailer.
- *Information and advice*. The retailer's expert knowledge and experience enable him to advise and inform customers on quality and suitability of products.
- *Feedback*. The retailer provides a feedback of consumer responses to wholesalers and producers. This helps the producer to become aware of what the consumer market wants, and also helps to ensure that consumers' requirements are satisfied.

Types of retail outlet

Earlier in this Chapter we said that the links between the producer and the consumer are sometimes referred to as the *Chain of distribution*. The methods that are chosen to distribute products to consumers are called the *Channels of distribution*. The various methods of retailing are the most important Channels of distribution.

Door to door

Traders involved in this form of selling generally deal in sales of minor items of goods or services.

- *Pedlars* carry goods from door to door on foot.
- *Hawkers* use some method of transport.
- *Mobile shops* are vehicles adapted to serve as travelling shops, for example the ice cream van or soft drink seller.

Market traders

These operate from stalls in open or covered areas, sometimes in streets or areas specially kept for markets. They are often able to keep prices very low because they avoid expenses *(overheads)* such as electricity, high rent, shop fittings, etc.

Independent shops

This category of retailer is not attached to a large organisation, and for this reason they are referred to by a variety of names, including 'sole trader', 'corner shop', 'unit shop' and 'convenience shop'.

This type of shop is owned by a sole trader or small partnership and is typical of the small shop sited away from town centres. This type of retailer often specialises in offering a single

Comprehensive Business Studies

commodity or service, for example the baker, butcher, confectioner, newsagent, etc. Small retailers such as the independent shop are facing considerable difficulties in larger towns where they have to face up to the competition of large organisations that tend to be more cost-effective.

Multiples (chain stores)

Multiples are chains of shops trading under a single name of common ownership. They are generally controlled from a central headquarters and tend to be sited in town centres and shopping precincts. Examples of multiples are, Woolworths and Tesco.

The multiple shop enjoys many advantages over smaller retailers:

- Their large size enables them to bypass wholesalers and buy in large quantities direct from the producer.
- A single national advertisement can cover all branches nationwide.
- They have the resources to rent or buy stores in prime central sites with large car parking space.
- They can afford to attract customers with *loss leaders* (goods sold at below cost price).

Supermarkets

A supermarket is a large self-service store. A self-service store is defined as a supermarket when it has more than 200 square metres of shopping area and three or more checkout points. Such stores are often organised as multiples.

These shops deal particularly in pre-packed, priced products. Loss leaders are frequently used to attract custom, and customers serve themselves. The provision of shopping trolleys reduces the customers' awareness of the weight of their purchases and encourages *impulse buying* (unplanned purchases).

Because supermarkets are often organised in multiples they usually enjoy the advantages mentioned earlier. They also benefit from economies of scale, for example being able to employ specialist staff such as butchers, bakers and

fishmongers. In addition, they save in staff because the customers do much of the work by serving themselves.

Although this type of shop has many advantages over other retailers it faces some disadvantages:

- large premises in prime areas are expensive;
- pilferage (stealing) levels are high;
- customers receive little personal contact;
- shopping trolleys are stolen.

Department store

This type of shop is sometimes called a 'shop of shops' because it is divided into commodity departments. Each department is operated like a single shop responsible for its own profitability.

Department stores tend to be comfortably equipped with carpets, lifts and a restaurant. Merchandise is attractively displayed, and credit facilities (sometimes interest free) are given to suitable customers. Many have introduced their own charge cards.

Hypermarkets

These are a very large form of supermarket with a shopping area in excess of 5 500 square metres. They offer a very wide range of goods in many specialist departments similar to the divisions in a department store, or parts of the hypermarket complex may be rented out to other approved traders.

Hypermarkets are usually one of many in a chain. They are frequently sited on the outskirts of towns where sites are cheaper and the development of large *retail parks* have proved particularly attractive to them. Hypermarkets provide good parking facilities, and late-night trading is a familiar feature of them.

Mail order

Products are sold in a variety of ways through the mail order method:

Comprehensive Business Studies

Section of a mail order catalogue.

- through advertising in the press, radio or on television, inviting potential customers to buy by post;
- through direct selling with customers choosing articles from a catalogue at home;
- through part-time agents selling to friends from catalogues in return for a commission.

Advantages:

- interest-free credit often given;
- buying in comfort of home;
- goods chosen at leisure.

Disadvantages:

- prices often dearer than shops;
- difficult to assess quality from a catalogue;
- can be inconvenient to return unsuitable goods.

The Home Market

Vending machines (automats) These retail outlets are open 24 hours a day and provide a wide variety of products such as hot and cold snacks, confectionery, drinks, petrol, etc. Vending machines are sited in busy public places and they sometimes suffer as a result of vandalism.

Catalogue shops A catalogue shop (e.g. Argos) publishes a comprehensive catalogue detailing all the products they have for sale in a similar manner to a mail order catalogue. The catalogues are given away free to prospective customers.

Customers who see an item they are interested in buying visit the shop to see a sample. If they like the product the customer can then make the purchase direct.

Telephone order trading Salespersons use the telephone to contact potential customers to try and persuade them to buy the company's products.

Sometimes the telephone canvasser will already have knowledge of the person's interest, perhaps because they have replied to an advertisement. But sometimes the canvasser will have just approached the customer by chance. The latter is sometimes referred to as *cold selling*.

The Internet Consumers can access a shopping channel through their Internet service provider. This enables them to make purchases directly from companies participating and selling through the system. The potential customer can view data related to products sellers have on offer. Having compared the offers of competing sellers, made their choice of purchases, the consumer can place their order and pay directly by credit or switch card.

Free gifts Items such as tumblers, ashtrays and pens are sometimes given away free with purchases.

Brent Cross shopping centre.
Photo courtesy of Hammerson Group Developments

Branded goods enable consumers to identify purchases quickly.

Credit facilities Many retailers offer suitable customers credit facilities, sometimes without charging interest. Some of the larger retailers have introduced their own chargecards which allow customers to buy and pay later in instalments.

Selling on credit

Selling on credit means allowing a buyer the use of goods while paying for them later, perhaps over a period of time by regular instalments. There are a variety of forms that selling on credit may take.

Trade credit

Trade credit occurs where the seller allows the buyer to have goods and pay for them after an agreed period of time. For example, a producer or wholesaler may allow the retailer to have supplies and pay for them at the end of the month. This allows the seller the opportunity to resell the goods before he has even paid for them, thus increasing the scope of his business.

Hire purchase agreement (HP)

This is a contract for hiring goods for a fixed period with an option to purchase them for a nominal sum (e.g. £1) at the end of the period.

An initial deposit is paid, which consists of a percentage of the purchase price, and a number of equal weekly or monthly instalments are repaid over a given period. Interest is charged for the credit given.

The goods purchased do not become the property of the buyer until the last instalment has been paid. The item purchased must not be sold until the last repayment has been made because the seller or finance company remains the rightful owner until the last instalment has been paid.

The seller can repossess the item if the buyer defaults on repayments.

Credit scale agreement

This is also a deposit, instalment and interest system similar to a HP agreement, but the buyer becomes the owner of the goods immediately the agreement has been made.

In the case of a credit sale agreement, if the buyer defaults on the repayment the seller or finance company does not repossess the goods but can sue for repayment of the debt.

Note: Most retailers do not finance HP and credit sales agreements themselves but use companies that specialise in this kind of finance.

Interest-free credit

The buyer is allowed to pay for purchases by regular instalments but is not charged any interest.

Credit cards

The holder of a credit card can use it to make purchases up to a set amount without paying cash. The trader claims the money due for the purchases from the company that has issued the credit card.

The cardholder is presented with an account from the issuer of the credit card. Payment of the outstanding amount can be made at once in full, or at some later time. Interest is charged on the outstanding balance.

Charge cards

Some retailers have introduced their own form of credit card for use in their stores. These allow approved customers to make purchases and charge these to their personal account which will be repaid later. The system is frequently linked to an instalment system operated by the firm, sometimes providing interest-free credit.

Mark-up and profit margin

Both of these terms refer to ways of looking at the differences between a trader's cost price and his selling price.

- *Mark-up* refers to the percentage profit which is added to the cost price by a trader to establish his selling price. For example, if an article has a cost price of 80p and it is to be sold for £1 the mark-up is:

$$\frac{20}{80} \times 100 = 25\%$$

- *Profit margin* is the percentage of the selling price which is the seller's profit. For example, on an article with a cost price of 80p which is sold for £1, the profit margin is:

$$\frac{20}{100} \times 100 = 20\%$$

Setting up a retail business

The following factors need to be taken into account when setting up a retail business.

How will the capital required be raised?

- Savings of owners.
- Borrowing from a bank or other institution.
- Contributions from partners.
- Selling shares privately or publicly.

What type of business is to be established?

- *Sole trader* – one owner running the business with or without employees to assist.
- *Partnership* – with one or more partners which enables responsibilities to be shared, but also means ownership and profits are shared.
- *Limited company* (private or public) – shareholders providing capital in return for a share of the profits and some say in the operation of the business.

Do the owners or assistants have the necessary skills?

- A thorough knowledge of the products to be sold.
- The ability to manage a business – accounts, stock records, cash flow, profit margins, wages, advertising, taxation, etc.
- The personality and temperament necessary to deal with employees and customers.

Where will the shop be sited?
Site costs vary considerably. A central or busy site may be good for trade, but will also be expensive. The entrepreneur needs to be sure that there is sufficient demand (or not too much competition) to support the shop in a chosen position.

What safeguards have to be applied?

- *Insurance* – public liability, employers' liability, fire, theft, plate glass, vehicles, fidelity bonds, bad debts, business interruption.
- *Health and safety laws* – the need to ensure that the business has complied with legal requirements to protect health, safety and welfare of employees and customers.

Activities

1. Why is the wholesaler sometimes referred to as an intermediary?
2. In what way can the wholesaler be said to 'break bulk'?
3. Why is trade credit useful to the retailer?
4. List the services that the wholesaler provides:
   (a) for the producer;
   (b) for the retailer.
5. In what way does the wholesaler help to make mass production possible?

The Home Market

6 What are the main ways in which general wholesalers and cash and carry wholesalers differ?

7 Why are retailers important to the chain of distribution?

8 Explain the difference between a pedlar and a hawker.

9 What are 'overheads'?

10 What is 'independent' about an independent shop?

11 What are chain stores and how are they generally controlled?

12 'All supermarkets are self-service stores, but not all self-service stores are supermarkets.' Explain this statement.

13 Give three examples of the economies of scale gained by operating as a multiple shop.

14 What are the main disadvantages faced by supermarkets?

15 Why is a department store sometimes called a 'shop of shops'?

16 What is a hypermarket?

17 Describe three methods of mail order selling.

18 Make a list of ten items you can think of that are sold through vending machines.

19 What is a catalogue shop?

20 Describe telephone order selling.

21 How does trade credit benefit the retailer?

22 Explain a hire purchase agreement.

23 What is the advantage to a customer of buying on interest-free credit?

24 Briefly describe the use of the credit card system in retail trade.

25 Give three examples of credit cards.

26 Explain the terms 'mark-up' and 'profit margin'.

27 Describe three factors it is necessary to take into account when setting up a retail business.

28 Why is the siting of a shop very important?

29 Describe two legal requirements that need to be observed by the shop owner.

Comprehensive Business Studies

Structured Questions

1. Look at the diagram below and answer the following questions.
   (a) What is the name given to the series of lines that many shop products have on their labels? (1)
   (b) Where would a point-of-sale terminal be found in a shop and why would it be placed in this position? (2)
   (c) How does the use of point-of-sale terminals help to reduce queues in supermarkets? (3)
   (d) How do computers help to reduce staffing levels in the retail trade? (3)
   (e) In spite of their many advantages some shoppers are not happy about the introduction of point-of-sale terminals. Why do you think that is the case? (3)

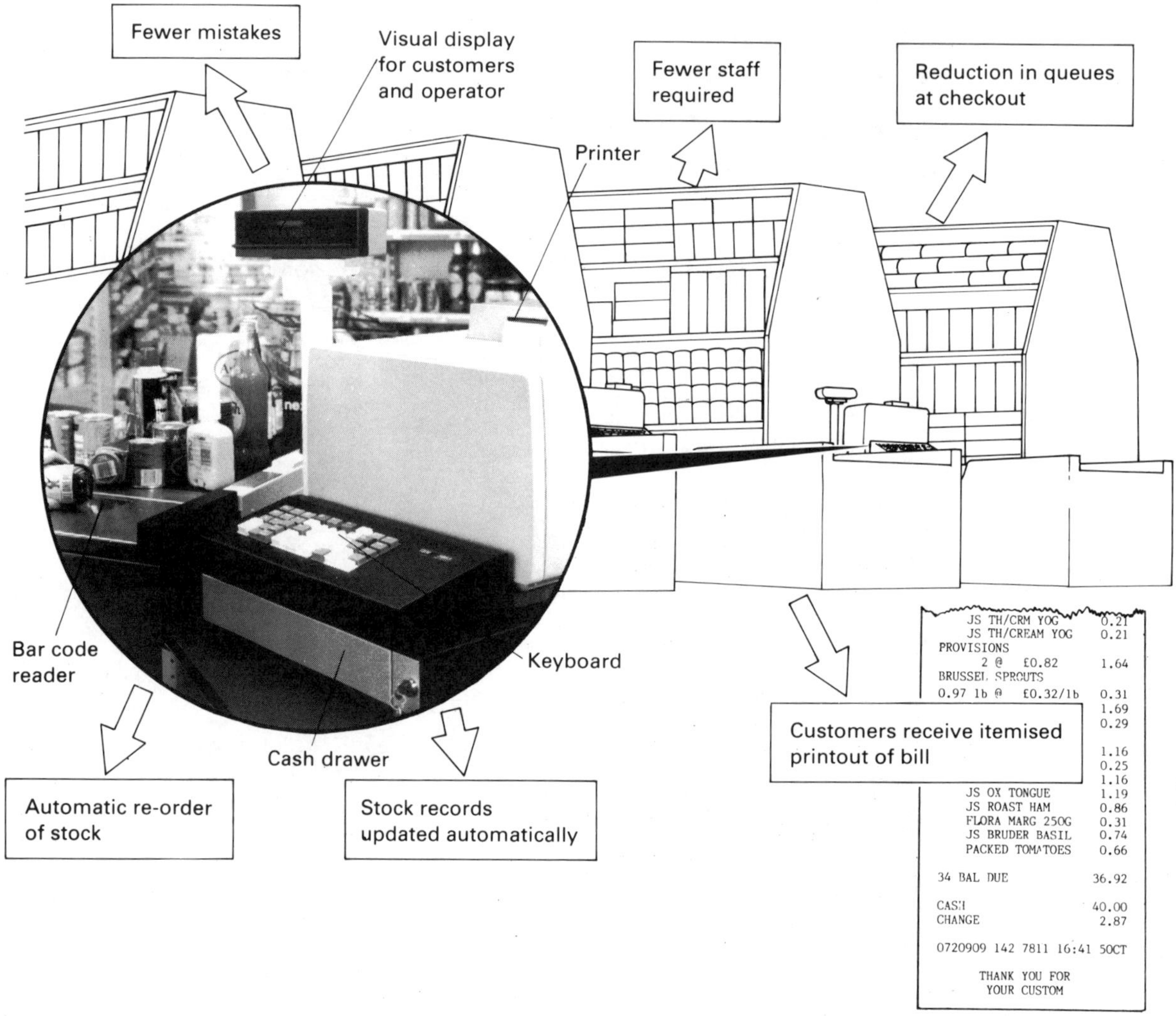

How a point-of-sale terminal improves supermarket efficiency. The illustration above shows a bar code reader being used. State one other method of reading a bar code.

(f) Explain how point-of-sale terminals help shops to improve their efficiency (4)
(g) Although computerised stock records are automatically updated, periodic manual stocktaking is also necessary. Explain why manual stocktaking has to be undertaken occasionally. (4)

2 (a) What is the name given to the computer terminal at the checkout point of a supermarket? (1)
(b) What advantages does an itemised receipt have over conventional supermarket receipts? (1)
(c) What is the purpose of a bar code? (2)
(d) Why does a computerised checkout system result in fewer mistakes? (2)
(e) Write out the following list in the correct order of sequence of supermarket operations:
- stock record updated
- itemised receipt produced
- bar code read by reader device
- products taken off shelf by customer. (2)

(f) The above illustration shows a bar code reader being used to read a bar code. State one other method of reading a bar code. (2)
(g) Although point-of-sale terminals increase the efficiency of shops many do not have this facility. Give two possible reasons why some shops do not have them. 2)
(h) Briefly describe two jobs that supermarket personnel do not have to do if computers are used in the store. (4)
(i) Details of purchases can be input to the computer by keyboard or a bar code reader. Briefly compare the two methods. (4)

3 Read the article on page 204 and answer the questions which follow.

(a) Name the site of Argyll's latest distribution centre. (1)
(b) Draw a flow diagram to show the chain of distribution used by Presto's to get most of their grocery stock. (2)
(c) What are 'short life' products? Give examples. (2)
(d) What effect will the new distribution centres have on employment in the distribution sector of the economy in general? (3)
(e) Explain the advantages that having its own distribution centre has for:
- Presto's
- Presto's customers. (6)
(f) In the light of this type of distribution expansion what is the prospect of independent grocery retailers surviving? (6)

4 (a) What is 'interest-free credit' and why do some retailers offer this facility? (3)
(b) State three essential features of a hire purchase agreement. (3)
(c) Give examples of types of goods which are (i) often and (ii) rarely purchased from a retailer on long-term credit and say why this is so. (6)

GIANT DEPOT NO 3 MAKES ITS DEBUT

JUST after *Argyll Express* went to press this month, Argyll's third new distribution centre opened, at Welwyn Garden City, Herts. Last year, depots at Bristol and Wakefield were completed and the new chain of three giant purpose-built distribution centres now forms a vital link with Argyll's existing centres at Felling, Abbotsinch and Portrack. The total depot network offers 1½ million square feet.

By March 1987, the new national network will be supplying 60 per cent of all Presto's grocery stock. The aim, by March, 1988, is to supply more than 70 per cent; eventually, 100 per cent of groceries, together with short-life products, will be delivered to the door by the company's own ordering and supply service.

The key advantage of an Argyll own-distribution system is control – over what needs to be delivered and when – to keep all the supermarkets well-stocked every day of the trading week.

Presto has had numerous food manufacturers supplying direct to its stores, a confusing and often 'clogged' system. Says Laurence Christensen, distribution director: "Presto stores' hectic 300 deliveries a week should fall to around 25."

Double

While delivery numbers plummet, jobs opportunities rise. With between 300 and 400 new vacancies created in the three new centres, the employee figure for the whole division will double. Argyll has given backing of £21 million to distribution development, a hefty and determined commitment.

Wakefield, Bristol, Welwyn and a dedicated third party depot at Bathgate, due to come on-stream next January, will together provide 842,000 sq ft of space. Wakefield centre, which opened in July last year, houses 4,000 different product lines and can deliver a phenomenal 300,000 cases of goods every week. That's typical of the performance the company can expect from its modern, computerised network.

The system is already proving its worth. It is reliable and efficient, easing the pressures on store staff and pleasing customers, who will always return to shop again in a well-stocked and well-run store.

Source: *Argyll Express*, 1987.

(d) Explain how a credit sale agreement differs from a hire purchase agreement. Which do you feel is more beneficial for a retailer to offer their customers? (8)

5 Rudge Wholesale Foods Ltd supplies a range of groceries to retailers over a 25 mile radius of their warehouse. Today their sales representative has been given the list on page 205 of 'special offers' for this week.

(a) Who pays the cost of delivering items ordered from Rudge Wholesale Foods Ltd? (1)

(b) What sort of service might a sales representative offer a customer other than selling them goods? (2)

(c) Why are several items (e.g. mixed vegetables) listed more than once and at varying prices? (2)

Rudge Wholesale Foods Ltd		Price list (canned products)		
		Price per case		
Description	Item No	1–50 Cases	51–100 Cases	101+ Cases
Carrots	18004	£5.00	£4.50	£4.00
Carrots	18017	£10.00	£9.50	£8.00
Peas	18107	£5.50	£5.00	£4.50
Peas	18108	£11.00	£10.00	£9.00
Baked Beans	18300	£4.80	£4.30	£3.80
Baked Beans	18302	£9.60	£8.60	£7.60
Mixed Vegetables	18614	£3.60	£3.20	£2.70
Mixed Vegetables	18615	£3.80	£3.40	£3.00
Mixed Vegetables	18616	£7.60	£6.80	£6.00
Raspberries	18701	£12.00	£11.00	£10.00
Sliced Peaches	18902	£11.00	£10.00	£9.00
Peach Halves	19001	£10.00	£9.00	£8.00

Trade Discount 25% Terms: 5% 7 days
Carriage paid $2\frac{1}{2}$ % 28 days
Special offer – one week only

    (d) Explain the meaning of 'Trade Discount 25%'. (3)
    (e) What is trade credit and how is it indicated on the price list? (4)
    (f) How much would a retailer pay for the following order, assuming that they pay for the goods immediately they are delivered? Show all calculations.
        59 cases peach halves
        12 cases raspberries
        15 cases sliced peaches (8)

6 (a) Why does a small retailer tend to deal with a wholesaler instead of dealing direct with producers? (2)
    (b) Give two examples of items that a consumer might buy direct from a producer. (2)
    (c) State ways in which a wholesaler might contact potential customers. (4)
    (d) Give a brief comparison of the methods of the wholesaler and retailer in the purchase and selling of goods. (4)
    (e) Explain the difference between the following types of wholesaler: general, cash and carry. (8)

7 The following questions are all related to the things that an entrepreneur would need to take into account when setting up a retail business.
    (a) What is a retail business? (1)
    (b) What is an entrepreneur? (1)
    (c) Name the type of business organisation that would be appropriate for two people setting up a small corner shop. (1)
    (d) Sate two possible ways that the necessary capital could be raised. (2)

(e) Give three examples of the knowledge or skills the owner or manager
of a shop must have. (3)
(f) What considerations would be taken into account when choosing a
site for a shop? (6)
(g) Describe three safeguards that the owners of a shop must observe
in the interests of the staff and customers. (6)

Research Assignments

1 Discuss the view that wholesalers should be eliminated because they cause an increase in the cost of goods.

2 Take any local retail business with which you are familiar and explain the sort of factors that the owner would have needed to take into account in setting it up.

3 To what extent would you say that there is genuine competition between retail outlets in your town?

4 Make a survey of the types of retail outlet in your town. Show the results of your survey in a colour-coded box diagram. What observations can you make about your findings?

5 Conduct a survey of local high street consumers that clearly identifies which retail outlets are visited most frequently. What reasons can you suggest for your findings?

6 To what extent have small retailers been affected by larger organisations in your locality? Provide evidence to support your views.

11 The International Market

11.1 The importance of international trade

The reasons countries trade

The overseas market is important to businesses and to countries as a whole. It is important to businesses because it provides potential additional income from the sale of goods and services. It is important to countries because it is by selling overseas that the home country can earn money to buy things from other countries. By doing this the quality of life of all the countries involved can be improved.

Because the trading referred to here takes place in an overseas market it is often called 'foreign trade'. Foreign trade is the buying and selling of goods and services between different countries of the world.

- *Imports* are bought from other countries and result in an outflow of funds.
- *Exports* are sold to other countries and result in an inflow of funds.
- *Visible trade* refers to the import and export of goods (e.g. food, machinery, vehicles).
- *Invisible trade* is the importing and exporting of services (e.g. tourism, transport, insurance and banking).

Countries are in many ways like a big family or a household. Both have to earn money to spend on things they need (e.g. food, shelter, clothing) and things they want (luxuries). Countries earn money by selling their products and services overseas (exporting) and they spend their money buying from other countries (importing). The result of this can be a better way of life for the population.

UK major trade in goods

	Exports £m	Imports £m
Foodstuffs	7,746.6	12,325.4
Crude materials	1,919.7	4,678.3
Fuels & oils	7,169.0	7,510.7
Manufactured goods	86,137.2	92,159.4

What general trend can you observe in the UK trading figures during the period covered by this data?

If people in a household – or countries – earn more than they spend, they can build up a surplus, become wealthy, and generally have a better standard of living. If people or countries spend more than they earn, they get into debt, and generally this leads to a poorer standard of living.

Differences between countries in the form of climate or natural resources mean that they have to trade in order to obtain goods which they cannot produce themselves, or do not find it economic to produce. One country may have natural deposits of oil or gas while another may have metal deposits not found in many other countries. By each country concentrating on the production of those goods for which it has a comparative advantage, greater output is achieved more cheaply, which is in the best interests of all people. This is an extension of specialisation or division of labour that economists refer to as following the *principle of comparative costs*.

The principle of comparative cost advantage, simply put, states that when a country is able to produce a variety of products, it will concentrate on those for which the comparative costs of production are lowest. Take Table 1 below as an example:

The table uses a hypothetical situation in which the two countries involved trade only in two goods, computers and sugar. Country A is more efficient at producing sugar than Country B, because it can produce it more cheaply. Country A is therefore said to have an absolute advantage in sugar; similarly Country B has an absolute advantage in computers. If the two countries trade freely with each other, Country A will specialise in the production of sugar and export it, while Country B will specialist in the production and export of computers. This is to the mutual advantage of both countries.

It can also be mutually advantageous to trade even if a country does not have an absolute advantage in any commodity. Table 2 below helps to clarify this:

In this second table it can been seen that Country B has an absolute advantage in the production of both computers and sugar. However, Country B has a comparative advantage only in the production of sugar: a unit of sugar in Country B costs one fifth of a computer, so sugar is relatively cheaper in Country B. Country A, on the other hand, has a comparative advantage in the production of computers.

In what ways does Britain's trade with other countries contribute to the food we eat?

Table 1

	Costs per unit	
	Computers	Sugar
Country A	600	80
Country B	500	100

Table 2

	Costs per unit	
	Computers	Sugar
Country A	600	200
Country B	500	100

The principle of comparative costs.

The International Market

From this it can be seen that it is to the mutual advantage of countries to specialise in producing and exporting commodities for which they have a comparative advantage and to import commodities from other countries where production is comparatively cheaper.

Sometimes the comparative advantage one country has over another is not the result of natural resources but is one that has been developed. For example, a country may have developed the expertise to produce a particular commodity that other countries require, for example micro-electronic components. Countries will participate in international trade in order to obtain the specialisms of others, and so gain access to a wider variety of goods. Thus by participating in foreign trade each country enhances the way of life of its people.

The UK needs to import because:

- We are not self-sufficient in foods.
- We do not have a climate suitable for producing all our needs.
- We need raw materials, some of which are only found overseas.
- We enjoy the benefits to be gained from international specialisation.

The UK needs to export (mainly manufactured goods) in order to obtain the foreign currencies required to pay for imports, and also to satisfy our desire for foreign produce. Imagine how boring our diet would be without tea, coffee, oranges and the many other products the UK buys from other countries.

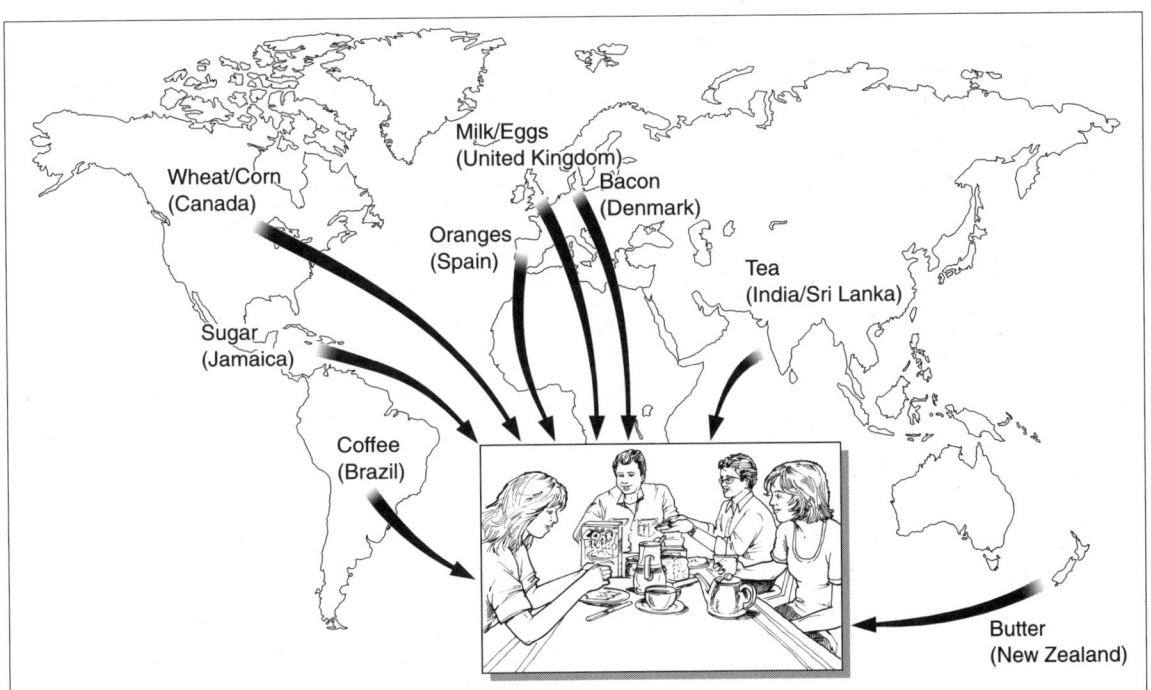

Look at the things that different countries contribute to a typical British breakfast.

11.2 Balance of trade

In the same way that every family has to budget to ensure it spends only what it can afford, so every country must also keep its spending within the limits of its income.

The family may keep a record of its income and expenditure, and countries will also record the difference in value between its imports and exports. The difference between the value of goods a country imports and exports is recorded in the *balance of trade*. Because goods can be seen they are collectively called 'visibles'.

When exports exceed imports the balance is said to be *favourable* because a *surplus* has been created which has resulted in a net flow of funds into the country.

When imports exceed exports the balance, or *trade gap*, is said to be *adverse* (unfavourable). A *deficit* (loss) has been created which has resulted in a net outflow of funds. The UK frequently has an adverse balance of trade.

Balance of trade figures (£ million)

1 Visible exports   + 48 440
   Visible imports   − 47 322
   Balance of trade   + 1 118   surplus

2 Visible exports   + 47 322
   Visible imports   − 48 440
   Balance of trade   − 1 118   deficit

11.3 Balance of payments

In our trade with other countries the UK buys and sells a number of services. Because these services cannot be seen in the same way as goods they are collectively called *invisibles*. More than one-third of the money the UK earns abroad comes from 'invisible' trade, and this is frequently sufficient to make up for the balance-of-trade deficit mentioned in the previous section.

The balance of payments is a statement of the difference in total value of all payments made to other countries and the total payment received from them. This balance includes both visible and invisible trade, and it shows whether the country is making a profit or a loss in its dealings with other countries.

- A *favourable* balance of payments is when there is net inflow of capital. The country has earned more than it has spent.
- An *adverse* balance is when there is a net currency outflow. The country has spent more than it has earned.

The balance of payments comprises the current account and the capital account. The *current account* records trade in goods and services. The *capital account* records flows for investment and savings purposes.

Balance of payments figures (£ million)

1.
Visible exports	+ 48 440		
Visible imports	− 47 322		
Balance of trade		+ 1 118	surplus
Invisible exports	+ 25 650		
Invisible imports	− 23 120		
		+ 2 530	surplus
Balance of payments on current account		+ 3 648	surplus

2.
Visible exports	+ 47 322		
Visible imports	− 48 440		
Balance of trade		− 1 118	deficit
Invisible exports	+ 25 650		
Invisible imports	− 23 120		
		+ 2 530	surplus
Balance of payments on current account		+ 1 412	surplus

3.
Visible exports	+ 48 440		
Visible imports	− 47 322		
Balance of trade		+ 1 118	surplus
Invisible exports	+ 23 120		
Invisible imports	− 25 650		
		− 2 530	deficit
Balance of payments on current account		− 1 412	deficit

Correcting a balance of trade deficit

A recurring balance of payments deficit situation is worrying for any country because it means that there is a sustained outflow of funds – the country is spending more than it earns.

A current account deficit can only be tolerated in the short term. A persistent current account deficit must be dealt with eventually because other countries will not tolerate continually having effectively to lend to the deficit country.

The following are *temporary measures* that a country can take to correct an adverse balance-of-payments problem, but these are not satisfactory in the long term because often they only delay tackling a more deep-seated problem:

- borrowing from the International Monetary Fund (IMF);
- obtaining loans from abroad;
- drawing on gold and currency reserves;
- selling off foreign assets.

The best way to solve a deficit problem is to increase exports. Governments can help to achieve this by offering incentives to firms involved in exporting goods. These incentives may take the form of tax relief and extended or special credit facilities, or *subsidies* on home-produced goods to make them cheaper.

There are a variety of other strategies that a country may use in an attempt to combat a persistent balance-of-payments deficit. These include devaluation, deflation, exchange control and import control.

Devaluation

Devaluation means lowering the value of a currency in relation to other currencies. This makes imported goods more expensive and exports cheaper. For example, if Britain's currency is devalued by 10 per cent overseas buyers will now only have to pay 90 pence for items that previously cost them £1. Conversely, you will have to pay £1.10 for imported goods which prior to devaluation cost £1.

Deflation

If people's income, or its spending power, is reduced this can lead to a reduction in imports because people will buy fewer goods, including imports. Deflation can be achieved by wage rise controls, restricting credit and hire purchase, increasing interest rates, and increasing taxes.

Exchange control

The central bank may take direct action to reduce outward flows of currency by placing limits on the amounts of foreign currency that can be bought. By refusing requests for foreign currency the central bank reduces the supply of domestic currency on the market, thus raising the price of the currency.

Import control

The two main methods of restricting imports are by the use of tariffs and quotas. A *tariff* is a duty or tax imposed on imports to increase their cost and discourage purchase. A *quota* is a numerical limit put on the numbers of a commodity which can be imported. Both of these methods are dealt with later in this chapter.

11.4 Methods of selling abroad

The channels for selling abroad can be grouped into two broad categories: (a) selling from the UK, and (b) selling from an overseas base.

Selling from the UK

There are several ways in which an exporter can sell abroad without going overseas. Advertising in foreign journals or circulating catalogues, brochures and other sales literature can be effective, although some items are not easy to describe and more direct contact is necessary. This can be achieved through contact with the agents of overseas buyers visiting the UK.

Where a firm is not large enough to operate its own export department it may use an *export house* which is a firm that specialises in securing orders from abroad. The export house may act as a merchant or an agent:

- *Merchant* – the export house actually buys the goods from the producer and then markets the goods overseas, accepting the risk of loss.
- *Agent* – the export house may market the goods on behalf of the seller from whom it receives a commission.

The International Market

Selling from an overseas base

The firm may send its own representatives overseas to make direct contact with potential customers. Alternatively, the exporter might employ an agent already based overseas and willing to seek contracts for sales in return for a commission.

Whichever of the foregoing approaches is employed, the representative or agent will be helped by trade fairs and exhibitions which provide a useful meeting place for buyers and sellers involved in international trade.

11.5 Difficulties faced by exporters

We have already recognised that it is important for a country to export in order to pay for its imports, but companies that engage in foreign trade face a number of difficulties. Some of these are also experienced in home trade, others are particularly evident in overseas trade. The main problems can be summarised as follows:

- *Language* – the exporter needs to be conversant with the language of the country to which he intends to export.
- *Differences in measurements*, weights and sizes also have to be taken into account by the exporter.
- *Suitability* of products, regulations, safety standards, etc., may differ in some foreign countries.
- *Import regulations* – the exporter must observe and be familiar with the import regulations of other countries.
- *Damage* to goods during their long journey to the customer.
- *Packaging* may need to be stronger than that used for home trade.
- *Transport* will be more difficult to organise than for home trade and the method chosen must be efficient and economic.
- *Documentation* and payment arrangements can be complicated in overseas trading.
- *Agent* – it may be necessary to find a suitable agent to act on behalf of the exporter to make contracts for the sale of goods.
- *Payment defaults* by overseas customers are more difficult to sort out than those in home trade.

Exchange rate fluctuations

Exchange rates are the prices at which one country's currency is bought and sold (exchanged) for another. Exchange rates are changing daily, and even during the day. These changes affect the buying power of currency. In the case of the pound sterling:

- A *rise* in the value of the pound results in a fall in the cost of imports, and a rise in the price of exports.
- A *fall* in the value of the pound results in a fall in the cost of exports and a rise in the price of imports.

213

From the foregoing you will have realised that exchange rates can affect business costs. For businesses that need to buy or sell foreign currency in order to operate, the daily movement in exchange rates makes it difficult to control their costs. There are ways to offset currency fluctuations (e.g. by 'forward buying' – buying currency at a fixed rate for sometime ahead). Unfortunately, all the options available have their disadvantages.

The elimination of exchange rate movements between the currencies of member countries is one of the objectives of the *euro*, the single currency of the European Union. The euro was introduced on 1 January 1999 and since that date the rate of exchange between, for example, French Francs and German Marks has remained unchanged.

11.6 Aids to exporters

Department of Trade

This is a branch of the Department of Trade and Industry. It operates a number of divisions and sub-departments and publishes journals aimed at information, helping and encouraging exporters. Help given includes:

- assessment of potential overseas markets for products;
- provision of details of current import regulations abroad (e.g. tariffs and quotas, etc.);
- advice on financial standing of potential overseas customers;
- introductions to prospective customers;
- issue of UK export licences when necessary;
- organisation of and/or assistance with international trade exhibitions or fairs;
- ECGD (*see* below).

Export Credits Guarantee Department (ECGD)

This part of the Department of Trade plays an important part in helping exporters by providing the following on a non-profit basis:

1 *Insurance* against non-payment of debts by foreign importers due to:
   (a) importer being unable to pay
   (b) export restrictions by UK government
   (c) political restraints (e.g. war or diplomatic relations) on payment.
2 *Grants* or low-interest loans to assist exporters in meeting initial expense of exporting.

Consular officials

UK government officials who are based overseas collect information useful to exporters, and give local help to traders while they are abroad. Foreign officials based in the UK are also a source of advice and information.

The International Market

Banks

The banks provide help for exporters with:

- short and long-term loans;
- financial advice;
- arranging documentary credit.

11.7 Free trade restrictions

If every country specialised in the things it does best, and then its products were freely traded anywhere in the world, all countries would gain maximum benefit. In fact, free trade between countries is difficult to organise. Countries sometimes use a variety of techniques in order to restrict free trade between countries. The following are the methods most frequently used.

Subsidies

A government may give finance towards the cost of the home-produced product to enable it to be sold at a lower price abroad.

Tariffs

These are a tax or custom duty imposed on imported goods to raise the price of foreign goods to the home consumer and thus protect the home market. There are two methods of imposing tariffs, which are collected by HM Customs and Excise Department:

- *Specific duties* are a set price for each item imported.
- *Ad valorem duties* are calculated as a percentage of the value of the imports.

Note: The importer can place goods in a *bonded warehouse* under Customs supervision until they are able to pay the duty due, or until the goods are re-exported.

Quotas

A quota is a limit on the quantity of a product allowed to enter the country during a year. An import licence must be obtained before goods subject to quota restrictions can be imported.

Exchange controls

Sometimes a country will restrict the availability of foreign currency to importers, thus restricting their ability to pay for imports.

Embargo

This is a straightforward government ban on trading between one country and another.

11.8 Reasons for trade restrictions

There are four main reasons why a country may decide to impose trade restrictions.

(a) *To protect home producers*. Infant (newly formed) industries may need protection until they have become sufficiently established to be able to compete fairly. Other industries may require protection because they are important to future national security.
(b) *To resist 'dumping'*. 'Dumping' means selling goods at a loss abroad. Some countries will dump goods abroad either to reduce supplies at home or to increase their share of the market overseas. This kind of action can be very damaging to some industries in the country where the goods are being dumped.
(c) *To safeguard jobs*. Even when goods are brought into a country fairly and competitively it may threaten a particular industry. Under such circumstances the importing country may feel it necessary to introduce trade restrictions.
(d) *To correct a balance of payments deficit*. A continuous balance of payments deficit cannot be ignored. One way in which a deficit can be rectified is by reducing imports by imposition of import control.

11.9 Free trade

Free trade exists when no tariffs, quotas or other restrictions to trade exist between countries. Free trade is important because it encourages countries to specialise in producing the goods and services they are best at supplying, and where they have a 'comparative advantage'. Specialisation between countries, each exporting the goods and services in which it has a comparative advantage, raises the standard of living in every country. The result of this is that all countries simultaneously benefit.

The World Trade Organisation

The World Trade Organisation (WTO) came into being in 1995 and is the successor to the General Agreement on Tariffs and Trade (GATT) established in the wake of the Second World War. The WTO is the only international organisation dealing with global rules of trade between nations. Its main function is to ensure that trade flows as smoothly and freely as possible. It does this by:

- Administering trade agreements
- Acting as a forum for trade negotiations
- Settling trade disputes
- Reviewing national trade policies
- Assisting developing countries in trade policy issues, through technical assistance and training programmes
- Cooperating with other international organisations

By lowering trade barriers, the WTO's system also breaks down other barriers between peoples and nations. The result is a more prosperous, peaceful and accountable economic world.

The WTO has more than 130 members, accounting for over 90% of world trade. Decisions are made by the entire membership. The WTO's rules - the agreements - are the result of negotiations between the members. The outcome of the 1986-94 Uruguay Round negotiations included a major revision of the original General Agreement on Tariffs and Trade (GATT). The updated GATT has become the WTO's umbrella agreement for trade in goods.

Services, for example, banks, insurance firms, telecommunications companies and tour operators, looking to do business abroad, can now enjoy the same principles of freer and fairer trade that originally only applied to trade in goods. These principles appear in the new General Agreement on Trade in Services (GATS).

Over three-quarters of WTO members are developing or least-developed countries. Special provisions for these members are included in the WTO agreements. These special provisions include:

- longer time periods for implementing agreements and commitments.
- measures to increase trading opportunities for these countries.
- provisions requiring all WTO members to safeguard the trade interests of developing countries.
- support to help developing countries build the infrastructure for WTO work, handle disputes and implement technical standards.

MINISTERIAL CONFERENCE

WTO'S top level decision-making body
Meets least once every two years

GENERAL COUNCIL

Normally ambassadors and heads of delegation in Geneva, but sometimes officials sent from members' capitals
Meets several times a year in Geneva

GOODS COUNCIL, SERVICES COUNCIL AND INTELLECTUAL PROPERTY COUNCIL

Report to the General Council

SPECIALIZED COMMITTEES AND WORKING GROUPS

Deal with the individual agreements and other areas such as development, the environment, membership applications and regional trade agreements

THE EUROPEAN UNION

Total population	– 373 million
Total Gross Domestic Product	– £4,585 billion
Total Exports from EU	– £1,236 million
Total Imports to EU	– £1,184 million

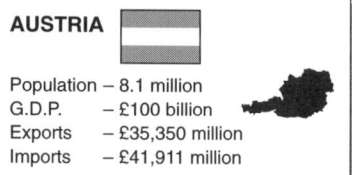

AUSTRIA
- Population – 8.1 million
- G.D.P. – £100 billion
- Exports – £35,350 million
- Imports – £41,911 million

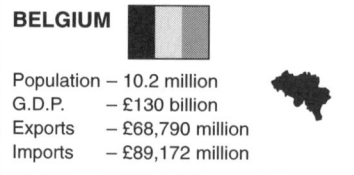

BELGIUM
- Population – 10.2 million
- G.D.P. – £130 billion
- Exports – £68,790 million
- Imports – £89,172 million

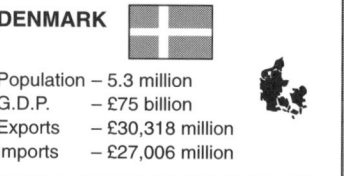

DENMARK
- Population – 5.3 million
- G.D.P. – £75 billion
- Exports – £30,318 million
- Imports – £27,006 million

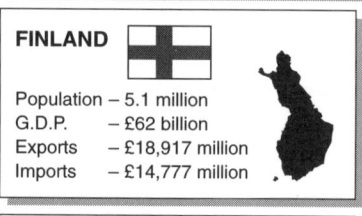

FINLAND
- Population – 5.1 million
- G.D.P. – £62 billion
- Exports – £18,917 million
- Imports – £14,777 million

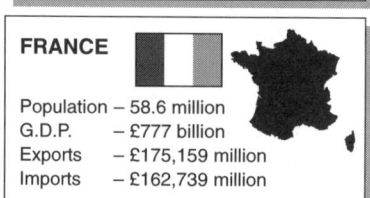

FRANCE
- Population – 58.6 million
- G.D.P. – £777 billion
- Exports – £175,159 million
- Imports – £162,739 million

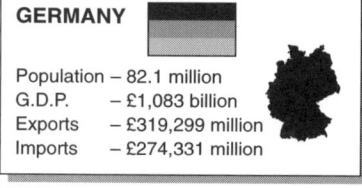

GERMANY
- Population – 82.1 million
- G.D.P. – £1,083 billion
- Exports – £319,299 million
- Imports – £274,331 million

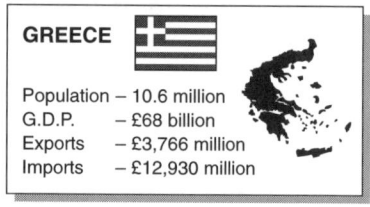

GREECE
- Population – 10.6 million
- G.D.P. – £68 billion
- Exports – £3,766 million
- Imports – £12,930 million

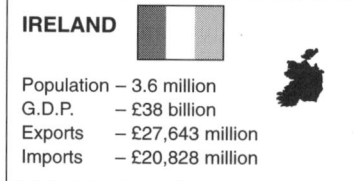

IRELAND
- Population – 3.6 million
- G.D.P. – £38 billion
- Exports – £27,643 million
- Imports – £20,828 million

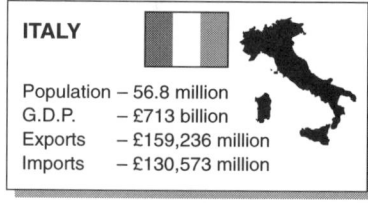

ITALY
- Population – 56.8 million
- G.D.P. – £713 billion
- Exports – £159,236 million
- Imports – £130,573 million

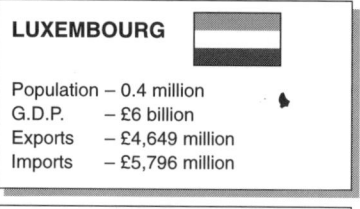

LUXEMBOURG
- Population – 0.4 million
- G.D.P. – £6 billion
- Exports – £4,649 million
- Imports – £5,796 million

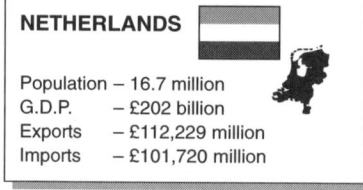

NETHERLANDS
- Population – 16.7 million
- G.D.P. – £202 billion
- Exports – £112,229 million
- Imports – £101,720 million

PORTUGAL
- Population – 9.9 million
- G.D.P. – £78 billion
- Exports – £16,433 million
- Imports – £21,783 million

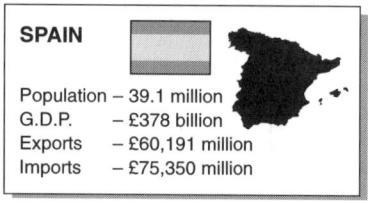

SPAIN
- Population – 39.1 million
- G.D.P. – £378 billion
- Exports – £60,191 million
- Imports – £75,350 million

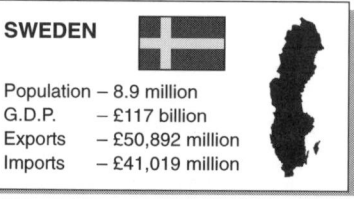

SWEDEN
- Population – 8.9 million
- G.D.P. – £117 billion
- Exports – £50,892 million
- Imports – £41,019 million

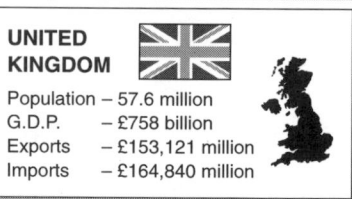

UNITED KINGDOM
- Population – 57.6 million
- G.D.P. – £758 billion
- Exports – £153,121 million
- Imports – £164,840 million

The EU gives member countries privileged access to a very large market.

The European Union

The European Union (EU) consists of a group of countries in Europe which have decided to join forces for their mutual benefit. The EU has developed from the European Economic Community - the EEC - known first as the Common Market and then later the EC, which was formed by the Treaty of Rome in 1957. The United Kingdom is a Member State of the European Union. The UK joined the founding group of six countries (Belgium, France, Germany, Italy, Luxembourg and the Netherlands) in 1973, at the same time as Denmark and Ireland. In 1981 Greece joined and it was followed by Portugal and Spain in 1986 and Austria, Finland and Sweden in 1995; this brings total current membership of the European Union to fifteen countries, and more countries are expected to become members in the future.

The main aim of the European Union is to bring about lasting peace and prosperity for all its citizens. The lifting of trade restrictions between Member States has enabled them to trade freely with each other. This means that each country has the right to move goods, services, capital and people from one Member State to another without restriction, thus strengthening economic, political and cultural links.

Aims of the EU

Although the EU is a customs union its aims are far wider-reaching than just trade agreements.

- To raise the living standards of people in member countries.
- To promote freedom of movement of labour, capital and services between merber countries.
- To encourage close co-operation between member in matters of commerce, farming, finance, social services and legal systems.
- Reduction of trade restrictions between members, and establishment of a common common traiff policy to non-members.

In February 1992, the Member States signed **The Maastricht Treaty**. That treaty provided for future cooperation and a review of the EU's political, economic and cultural links. A significant outcome of The Maastricht Treaty was the introduction on 1 January 1999 of the euro as the single currency of the EU. The Maastricht Treaty also allowed the United Kingdom to opt out of membership of the euro at its launch date and to decide at a later stage whether it wants to join or not. At the time of writing, Greece, Denmark and Sweden were also not participating in the euro.

The introduction of the euro was also accompanied by the creation of the European Central Bank (ECB), with full responsibility for monetary policy in the 11 participating countries (known as *euro-land*). The ECB is responsible for keeping inflation under control which it does through its control of interest rates within euroland.

The ECB is also responsible for the issue of euro notes and coins which will be in use from 1 January 2002. The new currency may be used by consumers, retailers, companies and public authorities for settling transactions in non-cash form ahead of the implementation date.

In June 1997 the EU governments met in Amsterdam, resulting in the signing on 2 October that year of the **Treaty of Amsterdam**. This new treaty provided for Member States to carry out further reviews of the workings of the EU in preparation for the extension of the EU to new countries.

The Treaty has four main objectives:

- to place employment and citizens' rights at the heart of the Union
- to sweep away the last remaining obstacles to freedom of movement and to strengthen security
- to give Europe a stronger voice in world affairs
- to make the Union's institutional structure more efficient with a view to enlarging the Union, with new Member States joining.

The following table summarises EU recent developments:

January 1995	Austria, Finland and Sweden officially joined the EU (EU now has 15 members and 626 MEPs)
July 1997	'Agenda 2000' report on enlargement and agricultural reform
October 1997	Treaty of Amsterdam signed
March 1998	Accession negotiations began with Cyprus, Czech Republic, Estonia, Hungary, Poland and Slovenia
January 1999	Single currency (the Euro) adopted in Austria, Belgium, Finland, France, Germany, Ireland, Italy, Luxembourg, the Netherlands, Portugal and Spain
May 1999	The Treaty of Amsterdam came into force

The EU affects British firms in many ways. For example, it issues directives that British businesses must comply with, eg those concerned with working conditions and other rules related to the social welfare of employees such as health and safety at work. These restrictions have cost implications for British companies. However, many of these directives are designed to ensure a single market within the EU so that all EU businesses compete on an equal basis. This means that British businesses have the opportunity to sell their products and services to meet different trading terms and conditions in each of the 15 member countries.

Trade and cooperation agreements

In 1994, 59% of the EU countries' trade was with each other: 52% of the UK's trade was with its European partners.

The Lome Convention helps 70 countries in Africa, the Caribbean and the Pacific develop their economic activities through the European Development Fund. In Central and Eastern European countries, technical assistance is provided to help them develop their economies into market economies. The EU has special links with Latin America, The Mediterranean and Asia.

In international agreements it is very important that the EU acts as one powerful body rather than the small individual countries trying to negotiate on their own, with big trading partners such as Japan or the USA. The EU is now able to influence strongly international negotiations such as at the WTO.

Organisation of the EU

(a) *The Commission* - made up of Commissioners appointed by the national governments of each Member State. The Commission proposes new laws, manages common EU policies and acts as guardian of the treaties setting up the Union, by making sure that the Member States carry out their decisions effectively. The Commission is based in Brussels (Belgium) and deals with all policy areas from agriculture to overseas development.

(b) *The European Parliament* - has 626 members (MEPs) who are directly elected by the citizens of each member country every five years. They meet every week in Strasbourg where the Parliament has its seat, although committee meetings are held in Brussels. Each member country has seats in proportion to its population size.

(c) *Council of Ministers* - based in Brussels, the council is the ultimate decision-making body. The Council, consisting of one minister from each member country, discusses the proposals put forward by the European Commission and ensures national interests are represented.

(d) *European Court of Justice* - safeguards the principles and laws of the community. Considers complaints and cases from member countries, private and public industries and individuals. The Court sits in Luxembourg, and there is one judge from each Member State.

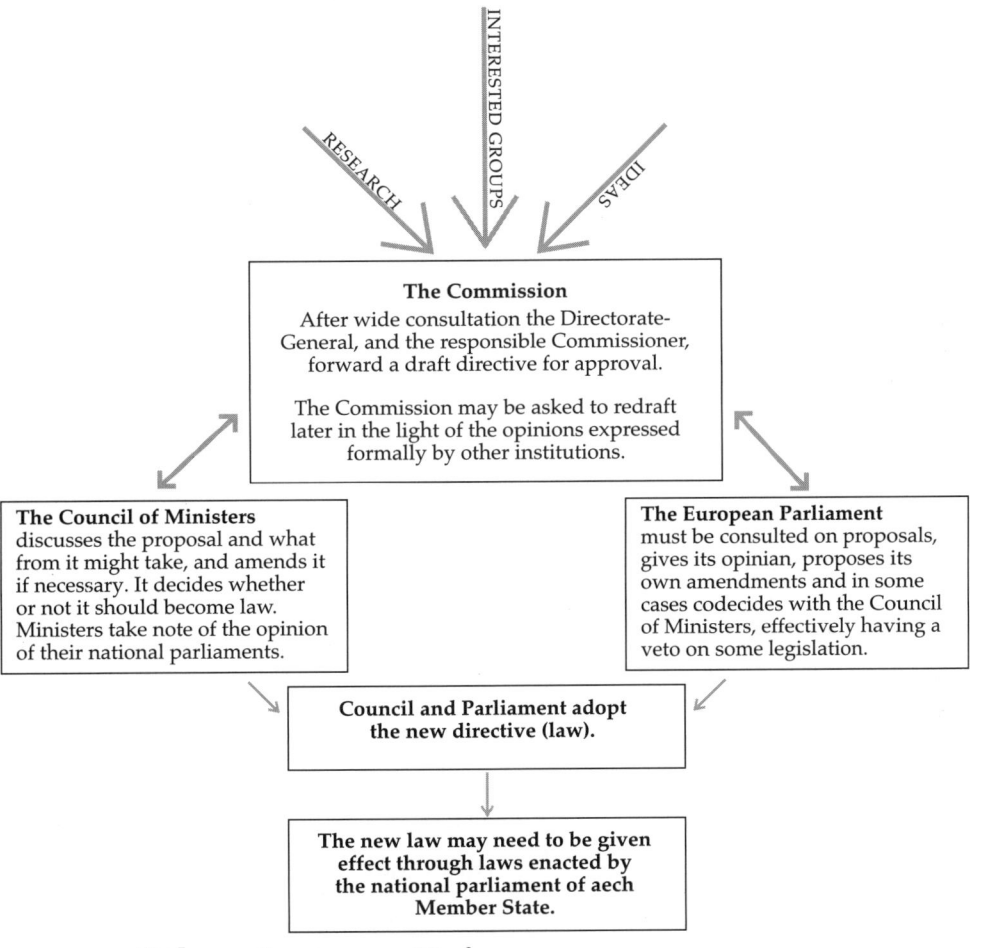

Other Customs Union

Around the world there are many other examples of customs unions. For example, in the Caribbean there is *CARICOM*. CARICOM means the Caribbean Community and it is comprised of many member countries in the Caribbean region, and 'associate countries', which can be a step on the way to becoming full members. A major focus of CARICOM is the Caribbean Common Market (CCM). The CCM has trading aims that are similar to those of the EU – a common duty-free internal tariff with no quota restrictions and common agreement between member states on the rate at which duty should be charged on goods imported from countries outside the Community.

Activities

1. Define the terms 'imports' and 'exports'.
2. Explain the term 'principle of comparative costs'.
3. Give one result of following the above principle.
4. Give two examples why international trade is important to all countries.
5. Why does Britain in particular need to impor?
6. Define 'balance of trade'.
7. Why are 'visibles'? Give three examples.
8. Explain each of the following terms:

    (a) trade gap
    (b) surplus
    (a) deficit.

9. What are invisibles'? Give three examples.
10. Explain the following statement. 'Balance of trade is related to visible trade, but balabce of payments includes both visible and invisible trade.'
11. Why is it important to have a favourable balance of payment?
12. Briefly describe ways in which an exporter can sell abroad without going overseas.
13. Explain the difference between the work of merchants and agents.
14. List eight problems, other than fluctuation in exchange rates, that are faced by exporters. Describe four of these problems in detail.
15. Clearty explain how fluctuation in exchange rates can affect the price of both imports and exports.
16. List the aid given by the Department of Trade to exporters.
17. How does the ECGD help exporters?
18. List the main ways in which banks assist exporters.
19. What are tariffs? Describe the two ways that tariffs are collected.
20. What is the function of a bonded warehouse?
21. What is a quota?
22. Why might a government subsidise home produced goods?
23. What is an embargo?
24. Describe the four main reasons countries impose trade restrictions.
25. How does the WTO help international trade to flow more smoothly?
26. What special provisions does the WTO make for developing countries?
27. What is the EU?
28. What are the main aims of the EU?

The International Market

Structured Questions

1 Study the following data and answer the questions on page 223 related to it:

> **THE BENEFITS OF FOREIGN TRADE**
>
> All countries gain advantages from trade with other countries. These advantages benefit both industry and consumers.
>
> Businesses can benefit from the opportunities they gain for increased specialisation and greater economies of scale. Another advantage of foreign trade is that the increased competition that comes from abroad encourages home-based producers to become more efficient.
>
> However, a major benefit for consumers is that they are able to choose from a wider range of goods and services.

(a) Give two examples of specialisation that are in evidence in international trade. (2)

(b) In what way can international trade provide opportunities for greater economies of scale? (2)

(c) How does competition from abroad encourage home-based producers to become more efficient? (3)

(d) List three items which consumers in your country could not buy without foreign trade. (3)

(e) Why is it more difficult for businesses to trade overseas than at home? (4)

(f) Suggest three ways that your country could encourage more overseas tourists to visit it. (6)

2 On page 224 is an imaginary advertisement placed in a trade journal by a company specialising in providing support services for businesses interested in trading in overseas markets by exporting or importing. The company is particularly active in promoting export trade.

(a) Briefly explain the difference between importers and exporters. (1)

(b) How would Easy Exports Ltd earn a living? (2)

(c) What do you think a 'profile' is likely to be in the way that the term is used in this advertisement? (2)

(d) What kind of 'trade statistics' might Easy Exports provide its customers? (2)

(e) What do you think are 'non-tariff barriers'? Give two specific examples. (3)

223

(f) Why might a business not involved in foreign trade be interested in obtaining 'profiles' of exporters, importers, manufacturers and producers?

(g) Describe the sort of 'market research data' that a firm interested in breaking into overseas trade would find useful.

NEED TRADE INFORMATION?

OUR TRADE INFORMATION NETWORK CAN PROVIDE THE FOLLOWING SERVICES

- PROFILES OF EXPORTERS/IMPORTERS/MANUFACTURERS/PRODUCERS
- TRADE OPPORTUNITIES
- MARKET RESEARCH DATA, INCLUDING IMPORT/EXPORT REGULATIONS, NON-TARIFF BARRIERS
- TRADE STATISTICS

CONTACT OUR HEAD OFFICE IN LIVERPOOL

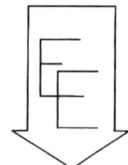

EASY EXPORTS Ltd
2 Narcot Road Liverpool L29

Research Assignments

1 It is possible for a country to have an adverse balance of trade but a favourable balance of payments. Discuss this statement using imaginary data to illustrate your answer.

2 'Overseas trade is important to every member of our country.' Discuss this statement using specific examples of businesses in your locality to justify your answer.

3 'Imports threaten home producers and can ruin national prosperity.' Discuss this statement, using evidence from personal research to support your discussion.

4 You are employed by a manufacturer of electrical goods. Explain the process by which you could go about obtaining orders for your company. Describe some of the ways in which the government agencies might assist you.

5 Visit a business convenient to you that is involved in foreign trade and investigate what marketing strategies it uses that are in your opinion different from those used in home trade. Write a report of your findings.

6 Make an investigative study of the EU and its influence on business. Use desk researched data to argue that the Union is good for businesses.

12 Business Documents

12.1 Purpose of business documents

The complete process of supplying goods and services from ordering to payment is called a *transaction*. A variety of documents are raised at various stages in the process and most of these pass between the buyer and the seller. Most of these documents are trading documents, i.e. those that are directly involved in the change of ownership. Others are sometimes used supplementary to trading documents in order to assist the trading process. These supplementary documents are particularly evident in foreign trade.

Business need documents to:

- ensure that there is no confusion about what has taken place between the buyer and seller;
- provide a record or proof of that acitivity at a later date.

12.2 Trading documents

Enquiry

The enquiry may be a letter or a standard form that is sent by the buyer to one or several firms seeking information about products or services available. Alternatively, the buyer may invite any number of suppliers to *tender*, or make an offer to supply. Based on the information received in response to the enquiry the buyer will decide who to purchase from.

Quotation

The quotation may take the form of a standard printed form, a catalogue or price list. It is an offer by the seller to supply at a *quoted* price. The quotation may also contain:

Delivery period
How long before delivery (or despatch) can be executed.

Discount offered

- *Cash discount* ('terms') – offered by seller to encourage prompt payment by buyer.

Comprehensive Business Studies

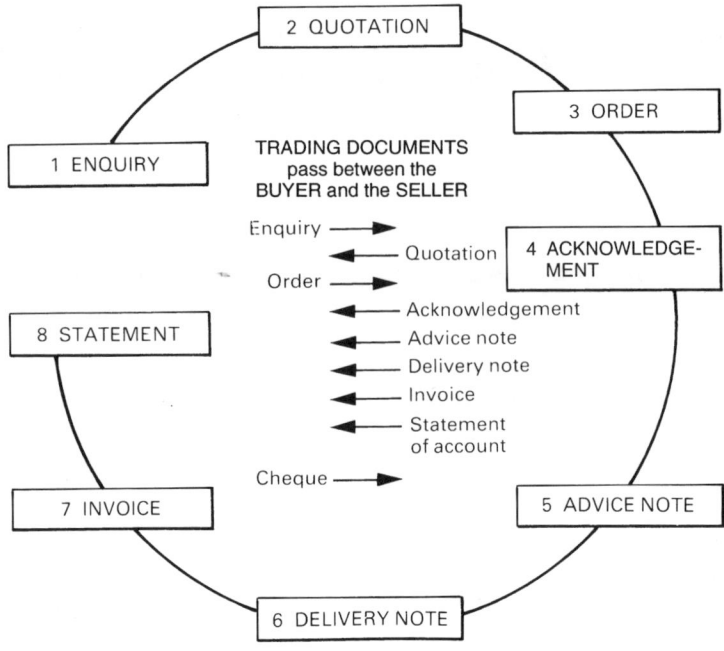

- *Trade discount* – given to people in the same trade as the seller to enable them to make a profit in resale of goods purchased.

Carriage arrangements

- *Carriage paid* – price includes transport costs.
- *Carriage forward/ex-works* – price does not include transport costs.
- *Promotional material* – catalogue, price list, samples, etc.
- *Estimated cost* – where it is not possible to give a precise price, the seller may give an estimated or expected cost.

 ## 12.3 Purchasing

Order

If the prospective customer finds the quotation of interest he will send the seller an official order. This may take the form of a letter, but more often it will be a standard form. The order will convey four pieces of information in particular:

1. number and description of items required;
2. price the buyer is expecting to pay;
3. when delivery is to be executed by;
4. delivery address, which may be different from the address from where the order has originated.

Acknowledgement

When the seller receives the order he will acknowledge receipt and confirm that it has been received safely, that the goods can be supplied by the date they are required, and that the prices stated on the order are acceptable.

12.4 Despatch

Advice note

The advice note is sent separate from the goods and its purpose is to advise the buyer that the goods ordered have been despatched, and to specify the method of transport used. If the goods do not arrive within a reasonable period of time the buyer should advise the seller.

Delivery note

This is sent with the goods when the seller uses his own vehicles. The lorry driver obtains a signature on delivery.

Consignment note

This is a document provided by the transporter of goods. The consignor (sender) fills in the form with details of the consignment, e.g. number of packages, details of consignee, etc. The consignment note accompanies the goods during transit and the consignee signs it to acknowledge receipt when it arrives at its destination.

12.5 Charging

Invoice

This important document is sent by the seller to the buyer immediately the goods have been despatched advising:

- details of goods despatched
- cost per item
- total cost, including VAT where applicable
- discounts offered, for example, trade or cash discount.

Many trading documents, and particularly those concerned with charging for goods or services supplied, show the letters E & OE somewhere. These letters stand for 'errors and omissions excepted'. The seller puts this on documents to advise the buyer that if a mistake has been made, the right to correct the error at a later date has been reserved.

Comprehensive Business Studies

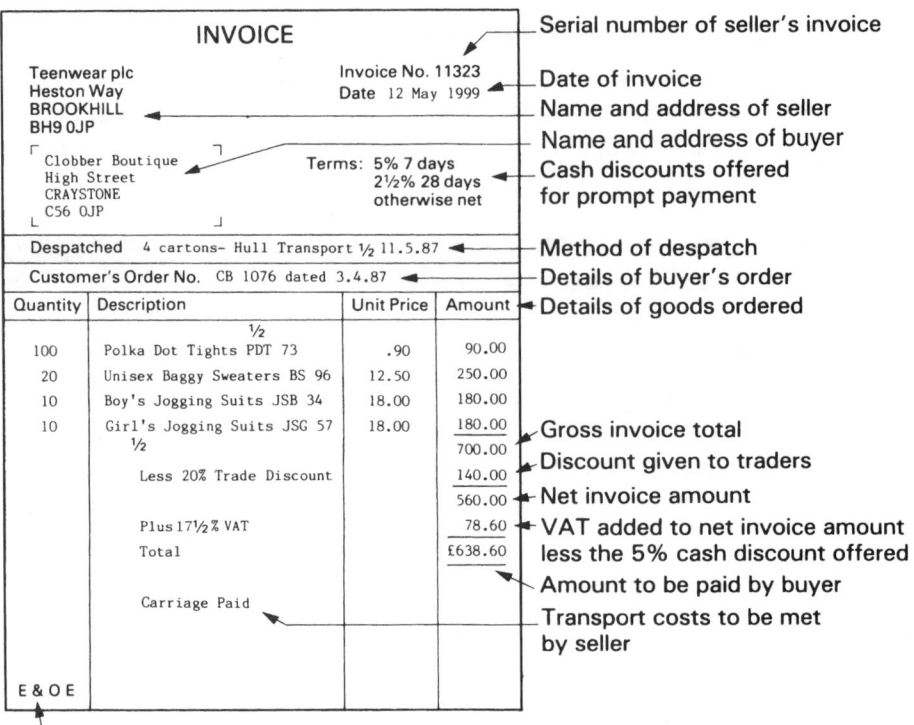

Pro-forma invoice

The pro-forma invoice is frequently used by the seller to charge a customer for goods in advance of despatch, but it can also be used when goods are sent on 'approval' or on a 'sale-or-return' basis.

Statement of account

The statement of account is sent by the seller to the buyer at the end of each month to summarise the trading position since the previous statement was issued, and to request payment of the outstanding balance. It shows all the following:

- the amount outstanding from the previous month's statement;
- the date, value and document number of each subsequent transaction;
- the cumulative balance;
- payments received since the last statement was issued;
- current balance outstanding;
- discounts offered for prompt payment.

STATEMENT OF ACCOUNT

Teenwear p/c

Heston Way
BROOKHILL
BH9 0JP

Date 1st June 1999

Clobber Boutique
High Street
CRAYSTONE
CS6 LLT

Terms: 5% 7 days

2½% 28 days

Date	Details	Debits	Credits	Amount
1st May	To account rendered April			890.36
9th May	To invoice 10109	180.10		1070.46
12th May	To invoice 11323	639.80		1710.26
20th May	To invoice 13488	83.14		1793.40
22nd May	By credit note 103		46.00	1747.40
28th May	To invoice 1446	360.80		2108.20
29th May	To debit note 112	10.60		2118.80
30th May	To invoice 1555	223.00		2341.80
31st May	By cheque payment		1000.00	1341.80

Amount outstanding £1341.80

E & OE

— Amount outstanding from previous statement.

— All amounts which increase the buyer's debt are entered in the debits column and added to the cumulative total. All amounts which reduce the customer's debt are listed in the credits column and taken away from the cumulative total.

— Amount outstanding to be carried forward to next account.

Payment for goods and services

There are a variety of arrangements that may be made between the seller and the buyer for payment of goods or services supplied, and these will be influenced by how well the seller knows the buyer. The buyer may pay:

- *In advance:*
  (a) cash with order (CWO); or
  (b) in response to a pro-forma invoice.
- *Cash on delivery (COD)*
  The carrier will be expected to collect payment before handing the goods over.
- *On receipt of invoice*
  To gain the benefit of cash discounts offered for prompt payment.
- *Against statement of account*
  Payment delayed until the end of the month to take full benefit of trade credit allowed.

The most common method of payment of debts today is by *cheque* which is used to pay for all or part of the balance of a statement. Where the buyer sends a cheque covering only some of the invoices listed on the statement a *remittance advice note* may also be sent listing the invoices which the cheque is intended to pay.

Correcting mistakes

Two documents are used to effect changes in invoice values, the credit note (usually printed in red) and the debit note (printed in black).

Credit note

This is sent by the seller to the buyer to correct an overcharge or to give a refund. It has the effect of reducing the charge made.

Reasons for issue include:

- an invoicing error has resulted in the customer being overcharged;
- some of the goods have been returned as faulty;
- too few goods were delivered;
- refund on returned packing material.

Debit note

Sent by the seller to the buyer to correct an undercharge. The debit note has the effect of increasing the charge made.

Reasons for issue include:

- an invoicing error has resulted in the customer being undercharged;
- too many goods were sent and the buyer has agreed to keep them.

Value added tax (VAT)

This is a tax levied on some goods and services. It is collected by traders by adding an amount to the purchase price and this addition is passed to the government. VAT is levied as percentage added to the purchase price after deduction of discounts.

12.6 Foreign trade documents

We have seen in the previous chapter the important part foreign trade plays in providing a country with many of the wants and needs that it cannot economically product. As with other forms of trading examined in earlier chapters, documentation is raised at various stages in the marketing and distribution of products. The following are the main documents used in foreign trade.

Bill of lading

The bill of lading is used in the shipping of goods and it represents the title to ownership of goods. On it are shown details of the goods, their destination and the terms under which the shipping company agrees to carry the goods. Three copies of the bill of lading are raised.

- One is retained by the exporter.
- One is given to the ship's captain.
- One is given to the importer who has to produce his copy to take possession of the goods on arrival.

Freight note

The bill or charge for shipping goods, the freight note is sent to the exporter by the shipping company.

Certificate of origin

This is a document certifying the country of origin of goods. This document is sometimes required by the importing country if it has been agreed that the goods of a particular country will be allowed to enter the country at a more favourable tariff rate.

Air waybill

This is used in connection with air transport and it serves as a receipt for goods by an aircraft captain to the sender of a consignment. The air waybill shows details of goods, departure and destination points, and consignor and consignee.

Manifest

A summary of all the bills of lading and cargo a ship is carrying.

Import licence

Issued by the importing government giving permission to bring certain commodities into the country. It can be used to enforce quotas.

Export licence

An export licence is sometimes needed before certain goods are allowed to leave a country (e.g. firearms, works of art, etc.).

Bill of exchange

The bill of exchange is widely used in the settlement of international debt. It is a document made out by the seller of goods (exporter – creditor) requiring the

Comprehensive Business Studies

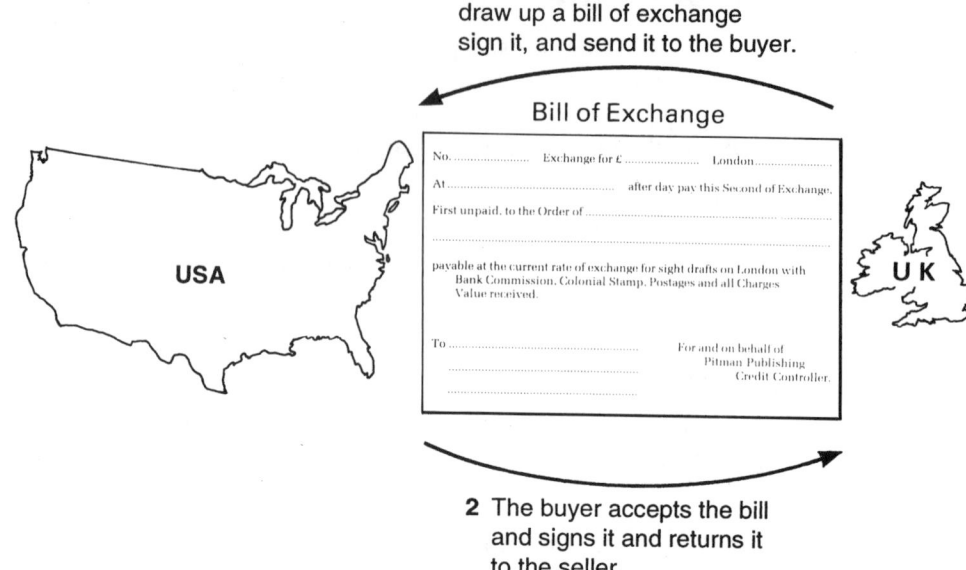

1 A seller in the UK will draw up a bill of exchange sign it, and send it to the buyer.

2 The buyer accepts the bill and signs it and returns it to the seller.

buyer (importer – debtor) to pay a named sum of money on demand, or on an agreed future date (usually three months).

The bill is signed first by the seller, and then by the buyer and returned to the seller. When the buyer has signed the bill it is said to have been 'accepted'.

The use of a bill of exchange enables the importer to obtain credit for a period of time. It also helps the seller because instead of waiting for payment he can:

- sell the bill at *discount*; or
- negotiate it by using it to pay off his own debts, or use it as collateral against a bank loan.

Note: A bill of exchange is drawn up by the seller (creditor) whereas a cheque is drawn up by the buyer (debtor).

12.7 Activities

1 What is a transaction?
2 Name the main parties involved in a transaction.
3 Why do businessess need documents?
4 What is the purpose of an enquiry?
5 State three forms a quotation may take.

6. What is an estimate?
7. Explain the difference between a trade discount and a cash discount.
8. Give three examples of promotional material.
9. Explain the difference between carriage paid and carriage forward.
10. State four types of information likely to be found on an order.
11. What is the function of an advice note?
12. Explain the difference between a delivery note and a consignment note.
13. State four items of information found on an invoice.
14. What is the purpose of putting the letters E & OE on a trading document?
15. Give two possible reasons for the issue of a pro-forma invoice.
16. What do the letters CWO and COD stand for?
17. Name the most common method of payment of debts.
18. What is the purpose of a remittance advice note?
19. Explain the difference in function between a credit note and a debit note.
20. What is value added tax?
21. A trader buys goods valued at £400. He is entitled to 25 per cent trade discount. How much will he actually pay for the goods?
22. An invoice value £200 is subject to an addition of $17\frac{1}{2}$ per cent VAT. How much will the buyer actually pay?
23. What is the purpose of a bill of lading?
24. How are the three main copies of a bill of lading distributed?
25. State one way in which an air waybill differs from a bill of lading.
26. Name the document that states where imported goods were made.
27. Explain the difference between an import licence and an export licence.
28. Give a detailed explanation of the function of a bill of exchange.
29. Explain the difference between a 'discounted' and a 'negotiated' bill of exchange.

Comprehensive Business Studies

Structured Questions

1 Look back at the flow diagram on page 226 which shows the documents that pass between the buyer and seller and answer the following questions.

   (a) What is the name given to this complete chain of events which make up a deal between a buyer and a seller? (1)
   (b) Which document would be likely to be accompanied by promotional material? (1)
   (c) At what point in this chain would be customer be asked to pay their outstanding account, and which document would request the payment? (2)
   (d) State three items of information likely to be contained in a quotation. (3)
   (e) Under what circumstances would this diagram show the words 'consignment note' and where would the words appear in the diagram? (3)
   (f) Where in the chain shown would a credit note be most likely to appear? Give three reasons why a credit note might be issued. (4)
   (g) Briefly describe the function of each of the following trading documents: order, acknowledgement, advice note. (6)

2 Look back at the invoice shown on page 228 and answer these questions.

   (a) Name the seller and the buyer involved in this transaction. (1)
   (b) What is the significance of the numbers and letters at the end of each of the addresses shown? (1)
   (c) This invoice has a number (11323). What is the purpose of including this number at the top of the document? (1)
   (d) Explain the meaning of the words 'carriage paid' on this invoice. (1)
   (e) Explain the purpose of the 'unit price' and 'amount' columns. (2)
   (f) Why are there three different dates shown on this document? (3)
   (g) How does the function of an invoice differ from that a statement of account? (3)
   (h) Explain the method of applying VAT to an invoice using simple figures (but not those shown in the example) to illustrate your answer. (4)
   (i) What would be the net value of this invoice if there was no VAT applicable and the trade discount read 25 per cent instead of 20 per cent? (4)

3 The following questions are all related to the statement of account shown on page 229.

   (a) Clearly identify the buyer and the seller on this document. (1)
   (b) How frequently are statements of this sort usually sent out? (1)
   (c) What purpose does this document serve? (1)
   (d) What was the total amount spent by the customer during the period covered by the statement? (1)
   (e) What is the implication of the letters E & OE in the left-hand corner of the document? (2)

Business Documents

    (f) Why does this document show three months, April, May and June? (3)
    (g) What is the meaning of the words 'to account rendered' and what will be the amount shown for the month following this statement? (3)
    (h) Give four possible reasons for the entry dated 22nd May. (4)
    (i) The figure in the amount column is sometimes called a 'cumulative balance'. Why is it referred to in this way, and how are these figure calculated? (4)

4 The UK company Pitman Publishing Ltd have received an order with a value of £100 000 from an Australian company, Down Under Pty. Pitman need some assurance that Down Under Pty are going to make the payment in due course. They would also like to receive the value of the order prior to supplying the goods. The diagram below shows how they have used a bill of exchange to achieve what they want. Study it and then answer the questions on page 236.

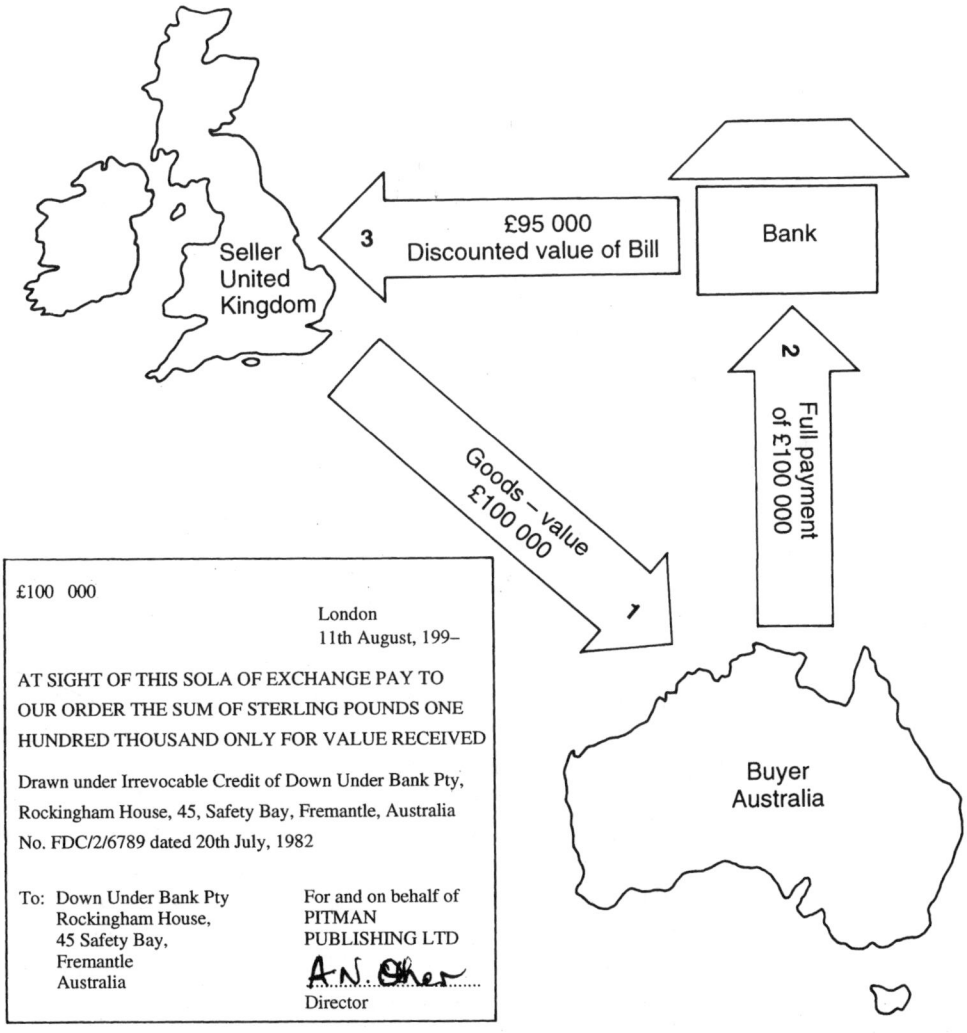

(a) A cheque is usually drawn up by the debtor. Who draws up a bill of exchange? (1)
(b) When is a bill of exchange said to have been 'accepted'? (1)
(c) Briefly describe the function of a bill of exchange as a promissory note used in overseas trade. (2)
(d) Name the *creditor* and the *debtor* of the bill of exchange shown in the diagram (2)
(e) How are Pitman Publishing assured in this case that they will receive payment for the goods they are supplying? (2)
(f) What sort of difficulties could be caused to Pitman Publishing in their transaction with Down Under Pty by fluctuating currency exchange rates? (3)
(g) How could the use of a bill of exchange help Pitman to avoid the problem of fluctuating currency exchange rates? (3)
(h) 'The person who is the beneficiary of a bill of exchange can sell it at a *discount* or *negotiate* it.' Explain this statement using information contained in the diagram to illustrate your answer. (6)

5 Refer to the following data and the information in this chapter related to bills of exchange and answer the questions that follow.

> Daly Designs have received an order for £500 000 of the products that they manufacture. The order has come from the Koh Trading Company in India, whom Daly Designs have never traded with before.
> Daly Designs estimate that they will make £200 000 profit on the deal. It will take them four months to produce and deliver the goods, and they will give their usual '28 days to pay terms'. Consequently, Daly Designs cannot hope to obtain the £500 000 payment in less than five months from the receipt of the order. They cannot afford to operate on this basis.

(a) Clearly identify the buyer and the seller involved in the case referred to here. (1)
(b) How much are Daly Designs expecting that it is going to cost them to produce and deliver the order referred to here? (1)
(c) Briefly describe two difficulties Daly Designs face in trading with a firm in another country that they would not encounter in home trade. (4)
(d) Although the prospect of an order valued at £500 000 will obviously be attractive to Daly Designs, accepting it is clearly going to cause the company a cashflow problem. Explain this statement using information from the data given to illustrate your answer. (6)

(e) One way to overcome the cashflow problem would be for Daly Designs to raise a bill of exchange. Explain how this could solve the problem, including mention of the possibility of 'discounting' or 'negotiating' the bill. (8)

Research Assignments

1. You are the managing director of a medium-sized manufacturing company engaged in the production and sale of small items of farm equipment. Design five trading documents you are likely to use in your business. Together with your designs, give a clear explanation of the function of each one, including explanations of how each form should be filled in.

2. You work for a manufacturing company that is currently only engaged in home trade, but is considering developing in foreign trade. Write a detailed report for your managing director explaining some of the ways in which documentation can support this development.

3. Visit local firms and collect samples of the documents used in *local trade* as well as *foreign trade*. Put the documents in a scrapbook under the headings:

    (a) Documents used in local trade
    (b) Documents used in foreign trade.

    Label your sample to highlight the purpose or significance of particular aspects of the documents
    or
    Display the documents you have collected on the bulletin board in your classroom or on a chart. Use appropriate headings and attach labels for a similar purpose to that above.

13 Transport

13.1 The importance of transport

Transport is a form of communication, a means of making contact between two distant points. it provides services that enable workers to go to and from work, raw materials to reach the producer, and finished products to be distributed. An efficient transport system reduces the amount of capital needed to be tied up in stocks, because new supplies can be obtained quickly. It also makes international trade possible, which is one of the important aspects of marketing and distribution discussed in Chapter 11.

Transport plays an important part in the marketing of goods because without transport raw materials would not reach the producer, and the finished articles would not be distributed.

For marketing to be effectively carried out there is a need for a sophisticated transport system which enables goods to reach the right place, at the right time, and in the right condition.

The importance of transport can easily be understood if we examine the distribution of a single product. Consider the transportation involved in the movement of bananas from the Caribbean region to the UK. The fruit must be taken from the plantation to the port where it is loaded onto a special ship with a cooling system to preserve the bananas during the long sea voyage. Upon arrival in the UK the cargo is transhipped onto road or rail transport for the journey to the wholesale produce markets. Subsequently many further journeys are then carried out by wholesalers and retailers before the fruit reaches the consumer. Timing is important at every stage of the journey to ensure that the bananas, which are harvested in a green condition, reach the consumer before the ripening process is complete. Transport is a crucial element in this timing.

In relation to transport, the *consignor* is the person sending cargo and the *consignee* is the person to whom it is being sent. The firm transporting the cargo is often called the *carrier* and cargo is sometimes referred to as *freight*.

13.2 Choice of transport

Each type of transport has its special uses. Some are more suitable for a particular task than others. Consequently, choosing an appropriate method of transport for particular circumstances is one of the skills essential for business success. Transport users will take the following factors into account when choosing the form of transport to use.

Transport

Increase in transport costs

[Graph showing Road, Rail, and Water transport cost curves with points X, Y, Z marked, and distance points A, B, C, D on x-axis]

This graph shows the costs of various means of transport.
(a) List the cheapest method of transport at each of the points shown as A, B, C and D.
(b) Which of the points X, Y or Z would you consider to be related to air transport? Give a brief explanation of your choice.

- the nature of the goods;
- how urgently the consignment is needed;
- the value of each item;
- cost of the transport;
- distance the consignment must be transported;
- the size and weight of the load;
- convenient position of terminals, e.g. station, docks and airport;
- possibility of combining loads to reduce costs;
- the reputation of the carrier.

Methods of transport

Road transport

Road transport carries 60 per cent of inland freight and 92 per cent of passenger traffic. There has been a steady growth in road traffic and this has called for the development of elaborate motorway systems to reduce congestion and maintain traffic flow.

All vehicles in Britain must be insured and those over three years old must pass a Ministry of Transport (MOT) test to show that they are fit for use on public roads.

Estimated traffic on all roads in Great Britain *Billion vehicle kilometres*

	1990	1991	1992	1993	1994	1995	1996	1997	1998
All motor vehicles	410.8	411.6	412.1	412.2	422.6	430.9	442.5	452.5	459.4
Cars and taxis[1]	335.9	335.2	338.0	338.5	345.7	353.2	362.4	370.9	375.9
Two-wheeled motor vehicles	5.6	5.4	4.5	4.1	4.1	4.1	4.2	4.1	4.0
Buses and coaches	4.6	4.8	4.6	4.6	4.7	4.7	4.8	4.9	5.0
Light vans[2]	35.7	37.2	36.7	36.5	38.3	39.1	40.4	40.8	42.5
Other goods vehicles	29.1	29.0	28.3	28.5	29.6	29.8	30.7	31.9	32.1
Total goods vehicles	64.8	66.2	65.0	64.9	68.0	68.9	71.1	72.7	74.6
Pedal cycles	5.3	5.2	4.7	4.5	4.5	4.5	4.3	4.1	4.0

1 This category includes three-wheeled cars; excludes all vans whether licensed for private or for commercial use.
2 Not exceeding 3,500 Kgs gross vehicle weight.

Source: Department of the Environment, Transport and the Regions

What general trends can you observe in the data about traffic in Britain?

Advantages of road transport

- Door-to-door service provides maximum flexibility.
- Fast over short distances of less than 200 miles.
- Risk of damage reduced by lack of need for transhipment.
- Can reach places inaccessible to other forms of transport.
- Motorway network speeds up movement and reduces congestion.
- Less tied to a rigid timetable than railways.
- Suitable for speedy direct delivery of perishable goods.
- Other forms of transport rely on road transport to connect with terminals such as airports, stations, docks.

Disadvantages of road transport

- Expensive to operate in large congested cities.
- Subject to mechanical breakdowns.
- Affected by adverse weather conditions.
- Loads are limited in size and weight.
- Some roads unsuitable for very large vehicles.
- Slower than railways over long distances.

- Wastes resources if lorry returns empty.
- Tax on vehicles and fuel must be incorporated into costs.

When planning the transport of their goods, firms have two broad choices. They can use the facilities provided by other firms, or they can form their own. In the case of air, sea and rail transport, the latter option is not realistic. However, many businesses have their own road transport fleet of vehicles.

When a firm decides to form its own fleet of vehicles, it has a number of choices, it can:

- *buy* them outright for cash. But this can have an adverse effect on the firm's cash flow situation by tying up capital that could be more profitably used in the business in other ways.
- buy them through *hire-purchase*. With this method the *hirer* pays regular instalments over a set period until the full purchase price is paid, plus a charge of *interest*. During the period of the repayments, ownership of the vehicle remains with the company providing the finance, although maintenance costs have to be met by the hirer. Ownership of the vehicle transfers to the hirer once the debt has been fully repaid.
- *lease* the vehicles for a fixed period of time. The owner of the vehicle is known as the *lessor*, the person or company leasing the vehicles from the lessor is called the *lessee*, and the contract for the arrangement is known as the *lease*. During the period of the lease the lessee pays regular amounts in hire charges to the lessor. During the lease period, maintenance costs generally have to be met by the lessee, although there are exceptions to this. At the end of the lease period the lessee may be offered the opportunity to purchase the vehicle at a favourable price.
- *rent* the vehicles. This is generally an expensive arrangement, but it may be necessary for a short period of time when there is a sudden demand for extra vehicles.

Rail transport

The railways were nationalised (taken into state ownership) in 1947 and placed under the control of the British Railways Board. Control is delegated through five regions: Eastern, Southern, Midland, Western and Scottish. British Rail also operates some ferry services. At the time of writing, ownership of the railways is in the process of being *privatised*, i.e., being sold back into private ownership.

Freightliner service

This is British Rails's high-speed container service which links up with special road and sea terminals.

Standard sizes (ISO) of containers are loaded direct from lorries on to special train bogies, and at their rail destination they are unloaded in a similar manner.

This simplified handling results in:

- improved speed and handling economies;
- simplified and more effective timetabling;

- reduced losses from damage or theft;
- direct links between terminals such as ports.

Freightliner service movements are carried out mainly at night when the lines are clear from other traffic.

Advantages of rail transport
- Easier for passenger travel than road transport.
- Faster than road over distances in excess of 200 miles.
- Less labour intensive than road transport.
- Especially suited for container traffic.
- More economical in fuel use than road transport.

Disadvantages of rail transport
- Routes determined by railway lines and stations.
- Equipment costs are very high.
- Relies on road transport for transhipment.
- Less economic than road movement for journeys of less than 200 miles.

Inland waterways (canals and rivers)

Despite the glorious past of the great canal era this form of transport has largely been replaced by road and rail transport. Its few advantages today are the smoothness of movement and the fact that it is the cheapest form of transport. But these advantages are generally outweighed by the main disadvantage which is slowness. However, there has been a drive to increase the use of canals and rivers by leisure and holiday business.

Sea transport

Shipping is particularly important to Britain as an island because it provides our main link to overseas markets. Transport is also one of Britain's invisible earners, contributing to the balance of payments (*see* Chapter 14).

There are four basic classes of ships: passenger liners, cargo liners, tramps and special freighters.

Passenger liners
Passenger liners are built primarily for passenger (particularly cruising) travel. They carry some cargo and, as they follow fixed routes and keep to a regular timetable, delivery dates can be guaranteed. However, high freight costs limit freight use to high value cargoes.

Cargo liners
This type of ship sometimes carries a few passengers, although their main purpose is to deliver cargo. They operate on fixed routes and to a regular timetable. The vessel will sail from a port on time, even if some of the scheduled cargo has not arrived.

Tramp ships

Tramps are cargo carrying ships that have no timetable or set route. They will carry any type of cargo to any port in the world. The vessels are chartered through a charter party agreement (*see* later).

The Baltic Exchange is a central meeting place in London for owners of tramp ships and merchants needing to transport goods to different parts of the world. Information about the activities of tramp ships is provided at this exchange.

Special freighters

For special cargoes there are a variety of purpose-built ships:

- *container ships* – cellular design vessels for fast load/unload;
- *bulk carriers* – ore and grain;
- *tankers* – oil and other bulk liquids;
- *ferries* – roll-on/roll-off; hovercraft have proved particularly successful.
- customs and immigration facilities;
- good links with road and rail network;
- buildings for offices and commercial services such as banks, restaurants.

Air transport

This is the youngest but most highly technical form of transport. It is constantly expanding in the volume of both passenger and freight it handles. The major British airports are controlled by the British Airports Authority (BAA).

Advantages of air transport

- It is the fastest form of transport.
- Operates to timetables, mostly on direct routes.
- Reduces risk of damage or pilferage.
- Shorter transit time reduces insurance costs.
- Packaging costs reduced.
- Particularly effective over long distances.
- Containers are now being used to speed up cargo loading and unloading facilities.

Disadvantages of air transport

- High operational costs result in high freight rates.
- Weight and size of cargo is limited.
- Sometimes affected by adverse weather conditions.
- Relies on other forms of transport to and from airport.
- Not suitable for short distances.
- Causes noise and pollution.
- Economic use is limited to certain cargoes, for example light weight, high value, urgently required commodities such as drugs, mail or perishable goods.

Pipelines

Pipelines allow the transport of commodities without using a vehicle. Examples are pipelines for gas, oil and water.

13.4 Containerisation

A container is a large pressed steel box available in two International Standards Organisation (ISO) sizes (20–40 ft × 8 ft × 8 ft or 6.1/12.2 m × 2.4 m × 2.4 m) capable of carrying twenty or thirty tonnes of cargo. The container is packed at the factory or inland pooling depot and delivered to the container terminal by rail (freightliner) or road and deposited in the container packing area in the dock container terminal.

The containers are moved around the terminal by straddle carriers. The container is loaded precisely into position in the ship's hold by special gantry cranes.

Advantages of containerisation
- Reduced staffing requirements lowers transport costs.
- Damage and pilferage is reduced.
- Packaging and insurance costs are reduced.
- Ship 'turn round' is speeded up considerably.

13.5 Transport terminology

- *Air waybill* – used in air transport as a receipt given to the consignor by the aircraft captain.
- *Bill of lading* – a document used in shipping representing:
  (a) a description of the cargo and its destination;
  (b) title of ownership of goods in transit;
  (c) a receipt for goods aboard ship.
- *Charter party* – a contract made between a shipowner and a consignor for the transport of cargo.
- *Consignment note* – accompanies goods being transported by land and is signed by consignee on delivery.
- *Delivery terms:*
  (a) *Carriage forward* – cost of transport to be paid by consignee.
  (b) *Carriage paid* – cost of transport is paid by consignor.
  (c) *Cost insurance, freight* (CIF) – cost of goods includes freight and transit insurance.
  (d) *Franco* – price of goods includes delivery to buyer.
  (e) *Free alongside ship* (FAS) – cost of goods includes delivery to side of ship.
  (f) *Free on board* (FOB) – cost includes freight as far as loading on to ship.
  (g) *Free on rail* (FOR) – transport costs are paid by the seller as far as railway.

- *Freightliner* – a container-carrying train.
- *Freight note* – a bill presented to the consignor by the shipping company for shipping goods.
- *Lloyd's List* – a daily newspaper published by Lloyd's of London listing ship movements.
- *Manifest* – a summary of all the bills of lading and cargo a ship is carrying.
- *Shipping agent* (freight forwarding agent) – companies specialising in deciding the best form of transport and arranging necessary documentation.

Activities

Make a note of it

1. Why can transport be looked on as a means of communication?
2. State one reason why transport is important to all countries.
3. List the factors that a business would take into account when deciding which form of transport to use.
4. Why are all vehicles over three years old required to pass an MOT test?
5. Give three advantages and three disadvantages of using road transport as part of the system of distribution of manufactured goods.
6. State one example where road transport would be preferable to rail transport for delivering goods.
7. Why is road transport important to both air and rail transport?
8. Describe the choices a firm has when deciding to form its own fleet of vehicles.
9. 'British Railways has been both "nationalised" and "privatised".' Explain this statement.
10. What is the freightliner service?
11. List the advantages and disadvantages of the railways as a means of carrying freight.
12. State one circumstance where rail transport would be preferable to road transport for movement of freight.
13. What is the main disadvantage of canal transport?
14. Why is sea transport particularly important to Britain?
15. Briefly describe the four basic classes of ships including mention of the circumstances or cargo for which each is particularly suited.

Comprehensive Business Studies

> 16 List the advantages and disadvantages of air transport as a means of carrying freight.
>
> 17 List three examples of cargo for which you think air transport is particularly suited.
>
> 18 Name the method of transport that does not use a vehicle.
>
> 19 What is containerisation and what are the advantages of this system for freight handling?
>
> 20 Explain the purpose of an air waybill and a bill of lading.
>
> 21 What is a charter party?
>
> 22 Explain the difference between carriage forward and carriage paid.
>
> 23 What do the following letters stand for: CIF, FAS, FOB and FOR?

Structured Question

1 Juicyfruit Ltd is a major producer and distributor of fresh fruit and vegetables. Juicyfruit sells through its own supermarket chain and also to wholesalers who trade with independent retailers. Juicyfruit's own fleet of delivery vehicles play an important part in distributing its products throughout the UK. The diagram on page 247 shows how Juicyfruit can quickly distribute its products to the UK to reach the final consumer within 24 hours.

   (a) Explain the difference between an *imported product* and a *home grown product*. (2)

   (b) Why is it important for Juicyfruit to distribute its products within 24 hours? (2)

   (c) Why do Juicyfruit's own fleet of delivery vehicles play an important part in distributing its products? (3)

   (d) Why would a supermarket chain be able to sell Juicyfruit's products at a lower price than an independent retailer? What contribution are transport costs likely to make to the price difference? (3)

   (e) Describe the way that transport arrangements might differ in Juicyfruit's distribution?
      (i) for imported goods when compared with home-produced products, and
      (ii) when products are distributed through independent retailers as compared to distribution through their own supermarket chain? (4)

   (f) Juicyfruit have decided to add fresh flowers to their product range. These will be purchased from other home producers in the UK during the summer and imported from Spain, particularly in the winter months. How will the transport arrangements for flowers be likely to differ:
      (i) between home-produced flowers and those from abroad, and

Transport

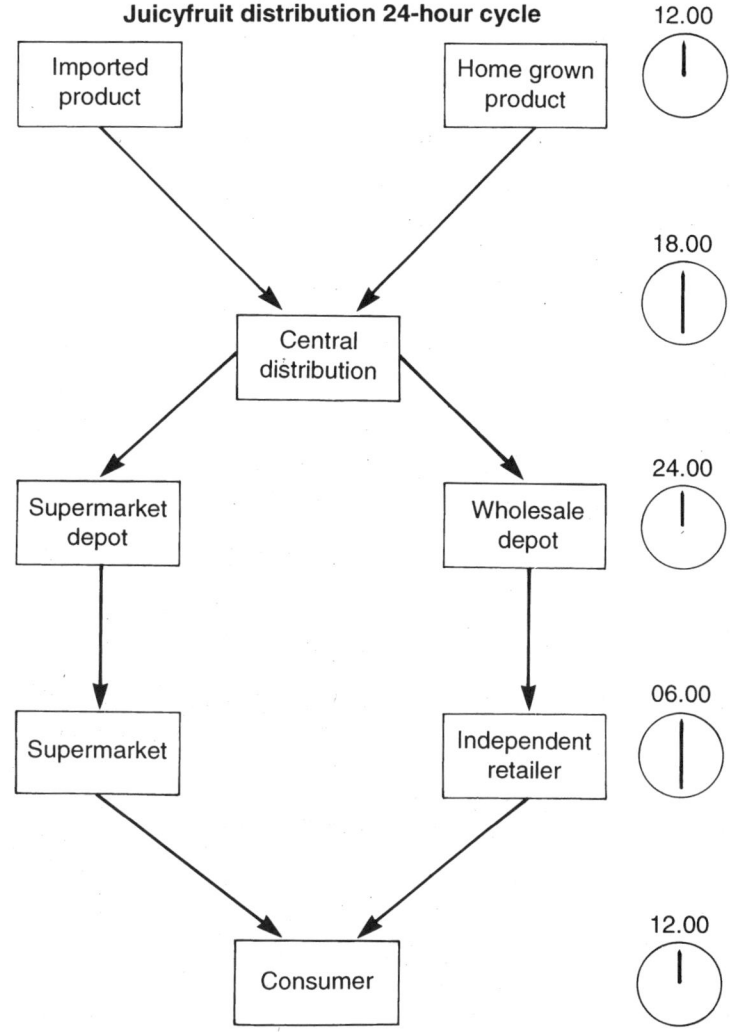

(ii) between flowers and bananas which they import from the Caribbean? (6)

2 The following graph shows the cost per mile of transporting bulky and heavy loads for various journeys up to 350 miles.

(a) (i) Which is the cheapest method of transport for a journey of 100 miles? (1)
(ii) Which is the cheapest method for journeys exceeding 300 miles? (1)
(iii) At what distance does it cost the same to transport goods by road as it does by rail? (1)

(b) Complete the table on page 248 which aims to show the difference in total cost between road and rail transport for various journeys. (3)

(c) Why does road transport have an advantage over rail transport for shorter journeys, but is at a disadvantage for journeys exceeding 230 miles? (4)

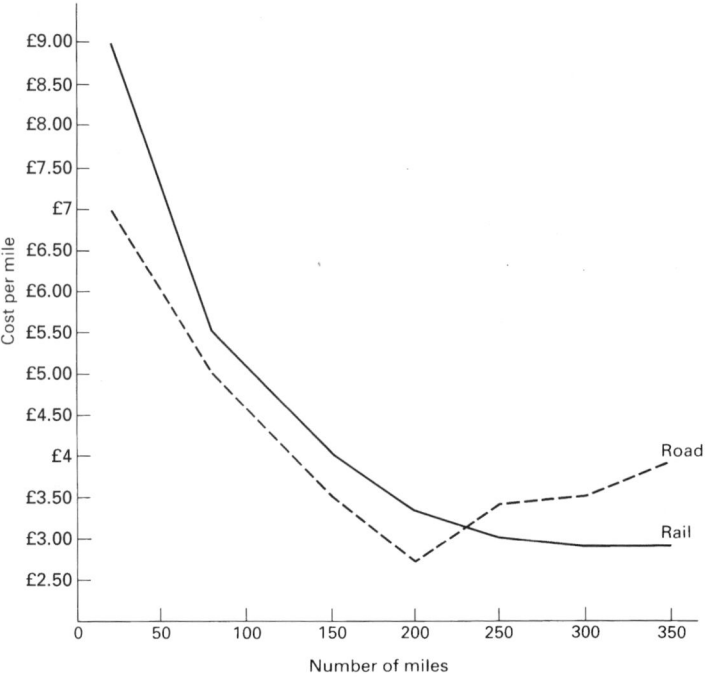

(d) Why does rail transport depend heavily on road transport? (4)

Miles	Road	Rail
125		
200		
300		

(e) Other than distance, what other factors will influence a business's choice between road and rail transport for delivering goods? (6)

3 Read the article on page 249 about transport and its importance to the market process and answer the questions below:

(a) What is meant by 'transit time'? (1)
(b) Why would transit time be more important for some goods than others? (2)
(c) Why is the marketing process so dependent upon transportation? (3)
(d) Why is 'double handling' unavoidable with some forms of transport? (4)
(e) One of the activities that firms carry out to support the physical distribution of goods is packaging. What factors would a firm take into account when designing its packaging that will help physical distribution? (4)
(f) What are the main factors likely to be considered by a business when

Transport

REACHING THE MARKET ON TIME

The marketing process cannot work unless products can be delivered when needed in an efficient manner. The marketing function that makes physical distribution possible is transportation.

Transportation is the movement of goods from where they are produced or stored to where they are sold. For transport to be effective it must be capable of delivering goods at the right times and at reasonable costs.

Transit time is the total time that it takes from pickup to delivery of the freight. Transit time is affected by *double handling* which occurs when moving goods from one form of transport to another. Wherever possible a consignor will try to avoid this happening, but with some forms of transport it is unavoidable.

choosing the method of transport to be used for the distribution of their goods? (6)

Research Assignments

1. Consider the pattern of transport communication in your town. Comment on its strengths and weaknesses from the point of view of both local traders and consumers.

2. Study any firm which you know sends its goods to a number of different markets. Comment on the various delivery methods the firm uses.

3. If a new factory were established in your locality producing household utensils for sale throughout the UK and overseas, what transport facilities would it be likely to use? Present evidence to support your research.

4. Carry out a minor research project to show how a change in some aspect of transport (e.g. road bypass, new bridge, Channel Tunnel, etc.) can create advantages for business but also perhaps disadvantages for other groups of people.

5. Complete a survey of all the businesses in a clearly defined area in your locality and identify the legal structure (legal identity) of each. Present the information collected in some appropriate diagrammatic form (with a key if necessary). To what extent are the firms investigated reliant upon the local transport network?

 Business Communication

 14.1 The importance of business communication

What is communication?

Communication is a means of making contact. The contact may be between people, organisations or between places. It is the process by which the business passes knowledge, information and even items to others. In this respect communication may take written, oral, visual or physical form.

Physical communication through transport was examined in Chapter 13. Advertising, which is another important method of communication, was examined earlier in Chapter 9. The post and telecommunication services provide important communication services by which most external business communication is carried out, and some internal communications also. These latter aspects of communication are examined in detail in this chapter.

The need to communicate

Communication is one of the most important activities of any organisation. It is used within the firm as means of controlling its operations, co-ordinating the activities of departments and employees and motivating personnel. Commu-

The transmitter   *The message*   *The medium*   *The receiver*

Business Communication

nication also provides important external links between the firm and its suppliers and customers.

There are four basic elements of all communication:

1. *The message* – the information or item that is to be communicated.
2. *The transmitter* – the sender, person or organisation that is the source of the message.
3. *The medium* – the method used, for example memo, letter, telephone, telex, fax, vehicle, etc.
4. *The receiver* – the person or organisation where the communication terminates.

For communication to be effective all the four elements above must be clear and precise. If any of them are not clear some confusion is likely to occur. For example, imagine that a person giving some instructions to others cannot express themselves clearly, or that those receiving the instructions are not very attentive. Obviously the chances of the instructions being followed are limited. The ability to communicate well is an important aspect of 'leadership' (*see* Chapter 3).

Apart from the importance of the need for businesses to transmit messages accurately, communication is also important to businesses because it not only helps them to operate efficiently, but can play an important part in creating a good public image.

Communication can be an expensive part of a firm's operations, so it is important that the most appropriate methods are chosen, and then used efficiently and economically.

14.2 Internal methods of communication

Purpose of internal communications

Informing
The different parts of the firm must be kept informed of the activities of other sections so that they can ensure that their work fits into the overall pattern.

Organising
The various sections of the firm must be organised and co-ordinated so that they carry out the part they must play in the control and operation of the organisation's activities.

Directing
Circumstances on occasions require parts of the organisation to be directed in the specific tasks and duties they are expected to carry out in order to achieve the firm's aims.

Motivating

The various levels of management use communication to motivate departments and employees in order to gain maximum benefit from their efforts.

Negotiating

Policies have to be formulated and decisions have to be taken and communicated between members of the organisation. This may well require the resolving of conflicts of interest. This may be achieved by informal discussions and interviews, although frequently it is achieved through formal business meetings.

Methods of internal communication

Written

- *Letters* are not generally used as a means of internal communication except in the case of letters such as those related to employment, for example appointments or promotion.
- *Memoranda* (memos) are the most frequent method of internal communication between members of the same firm. They tend to be brief and to the point, without formal opening or close.
- *Minutes* are summaries of discussions that have taken place at a meeting.
- *Reports* may be received from committees, by feedback from the sales force or be in the form of information supplied by specialist employees, for example technical reports, financial reports, etc.
- *Notices* may be displayed to convey information to employees, for example jobs being advertised internally, safety regulations, social/welfare information etc.
- *Suggestion schemes* make it possible for employees to communicate ideas to the management for improvements in the firm's practices.
- *Manuals* and instruction booklets covering equipment use or detailing business procedures make employees aware of company requirements and safety measures.

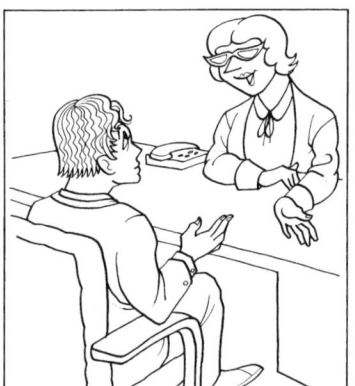 

How many methods of internal communication in this illustration can you describe?

Oral

- *Spoken* communications are the most commonly used of all means of passing information. Within the organisation this will most frequently be face-to-face contact, often in the form of instructions from superior to subordinate.
- *Telephone* and intercom usefully allow contact between sections of the organisation where face-to-face contact is not convenient.
- *Interviews* are a common means of selecting employees or considering a person for promotion, and for individual discussions.
- *Meetings* provide a convenient means of communication between several people where individual discussions are not convenient or practicable. Meetings are examined in greater detail in the next section of this chapter.

Visual

Pictures, diagrams, maps and plans, wallcharts, flowcharts, pictograms, pie charts and graphs are all ways in which visual communication is typically used within an organisation. They are used to make complicated ideas or information easier to understand. This is examined again later in this chapter, together with other applications of storage and retrieval of information.

14.3 Business meetings

Meetings are an important means of communication within organisations. They give the opportunity for exchange of ideas and collective efforts to solve problems and formulate policies. They also provide a convenient means of issuing instructions or information to many people at one time.

Principal officers

The principal officers of a meeting are the chair-person, secretary and treasurer:

- *The chair-person* is responsible for the correct conduct of the meeting.
- *The secretary* sends out notices of the meeting and a copy of the agenda, records minutes and ensures meeting decisions are carried out.
- *The treasurer* is responsible for financial matters. Sometimes the job of secretary and treasurer are combined.

Committees

- *Standing* – permanent committee elected to carry out specific regular duties such as discussion of finance, overseas policy, etc.
- *Ad hoc* (or sub) – committee elected to deal with a particular matter over a short period of time, for example the organisation of a social event or to investigate a specific short-term problem.

Types of meeting

- *General* – open to all members of the organisation, these are held monthly, quarterly or annually (annual general meeting – AGM), and used for committee members to communicate with all members of the organisation. The AGM also serves as a useful time for re-election of principal officers.
- *Extraordinary* – additional general meeting called to discuss some special business or unexpected event.
- *Committee* – only attended by committee members, these deal with a specific aspect of the organisation's function. Committees report back to a full general meeting.

Agenda

The agenda is a summary of the items of business to be discussed at a meeting. The agenda follows an accepted form of order in presentation as follows:

AGENDA

1 **Apologies** – received (usually in letter form) from those unable to be at the meeting.

2 **Minutes** – the minutes or notes made from the last meeting are read.

3 **Matters arising** (out of the minutes) – discussion and follow-up of matters or decisions taken at the last meeting.

4 **Correspondence** – discussion of important letters received since the last meeting.

5 **Reports** – may be made by people who have special information to give to the meeting, for example reporting back from the work of a committee.

6 **Special matters** – here will be discussed the purpose of the present meeting; decisions which have to be made; proposals to be discussed and voted on; action to be followed before the next meeting.

7 **Next meeting** – date, time and place of next meeting.

8 **Any other business (AOB)** – at this point members bring up matters or questions not included in the agenda.

Minutes

The minutes are a record of what was decided at a meeting and they may include a 'verbatim report', which is a word-for-word record of a report verbally presented, but more often they are a summary of what has taken place.

Voting

There are four basic ways of recording votes at a meeting.

1 *Secret ballot* – votes are marked on a slip of paper by the voters and then put into a ballot box for later counting.
2 *Show of hands* – hands are raised and counted for or against a motion.
3 *Standing* – at large meetings voters may be asked to 'stand and be counted'.
4 *Proxy* – members unable to attend meetings may vote by post or give permission for someone else to vote on their behalf.

14.4 External communications

Business correspondence

External communications are the ways in which a firm makes contact with other organisations and people with which it is involved, for example customers, suppliers and other sections of the organisation which are sited elsewhere. The effectiveness with which these communications are carried out can enhance or tarnish the firm's reputation, and help or hinder its efficiency.

The most basic way that a firm makes contact with others is through correspondence (letters). Although letters are slower than the telephone and other electronic means of communicating, they are relatively cheap. They are also in printed form which enables them to be stored in a simple filing system, and to be read without the aid of 'reading' or transmission devices.

Most business letters have a printed letterheading. This shows the name of the firm, the address, and other information that is important to people the firm corresponds with. The letterheading also reflects the individuality of the firm, perhaps in the form of a logo, trade mark or special form of lettering.

There is a basic format that most business letters tend to follow. Quite apart from the style or structure of the letter the wording is important. This needs to be clear and precise if the message it contains is to be conveyed accurately.

14.5 Information technology

Storage and retrieval of information

The use of modern technology for communication within organisations (both internally and externally) is increasingly evident today, particularly for the storage and retrieval of information. Word processors and computers are playing a major part in this important aspect of business. The following are typical business applications of this technology.

- *Company registers* – of shareholders are constantly changing as company shares are bought and sold. A company can speedily update these records.

Comprehensive Business Studies

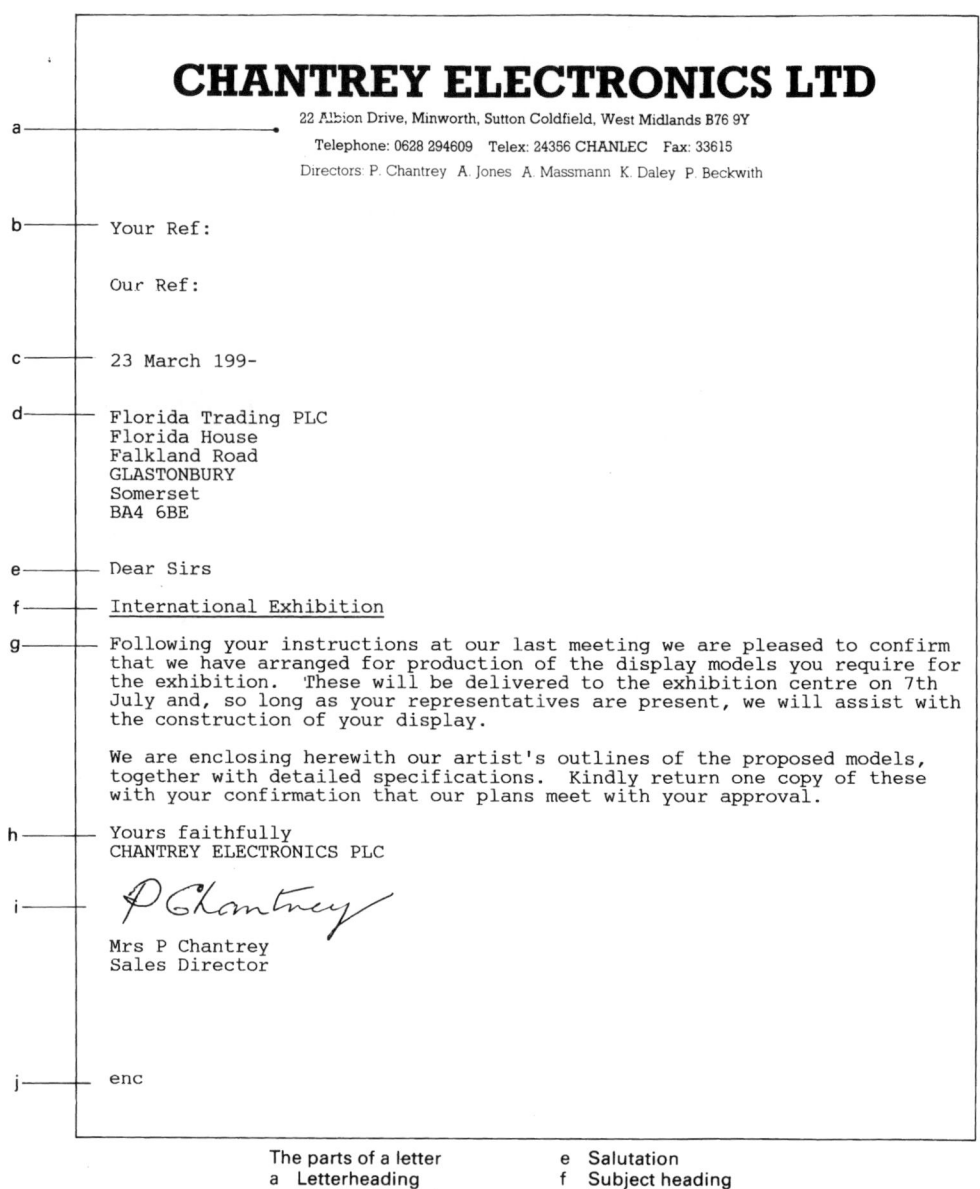

The parts of a letter
a Letterheading
b Reference number
c Date of letter
d Name and address of addressee
e Salutation
f Subject heading
g Body of letter
h Complimentary close
i Signature
j Enclosures

- *Stock records* – automatic updating of records as stocks are removed or added to store. Warnings are automatically given when stock levels fall too low, and immediate stock valuation is available.
- *Payroll* (wages system) – maintenance of payroll and personal records for employees. Automatic calculation of wages, income tax, national insurance and issue of P60s, etc.
- *Word processing* – copies of letters, invoices and statements of account can be typed into a computer and stored on disc or tape for later retrieval for review

Business Communication

Today computers are playing a major part in communication and they can present data in a variety of stimulating and meaningful screen displays.

on a visual display unit (VDU) or hard copy. Word processors are playing a major part in this kind of computer application. Standard letters can be stored on 'memory' for future recall and updating for reproduction, thus allowing much of the repetitive typing to be reduced.

- *Accounts* – issue of invoices, statements of account and maintaining records of customers' accounts.
- *Display* – of data in graphic form is particularly effective with a VDU. Graphs and charts can be displayed in a variety of forms and colours to give a simple representation of complicated data, making it easier to understand. For example, a comparison of the performance of different members of a sales team becomes immediately clear when displayed in the form of a bar chart or graph.

Comprehensive Business Studies

Spreadsheets and databases

Spreadsheets and databases are two important ways of using computers for the storage and display of information.

Spreadsheets

A spreadsheet is a computer software package that allows the computer operator to enter and store data in columns and rows of figures, called *cells*, to be spread out on a VDU screen in 'grid' format. This data can be printed out as a whole or in part.

Spreadsheets are used particularly for financial planning, and the preparation of management reports. They are also used to carry out 'experimental' work. For example, a spreadsheet can be used to assess what would happen to a set of figures if a particular factor were changed.

Databases

A database is a form of electronic filing. It is an organised collection of data. The information is held in such a way that it can be recalled and updated as required.

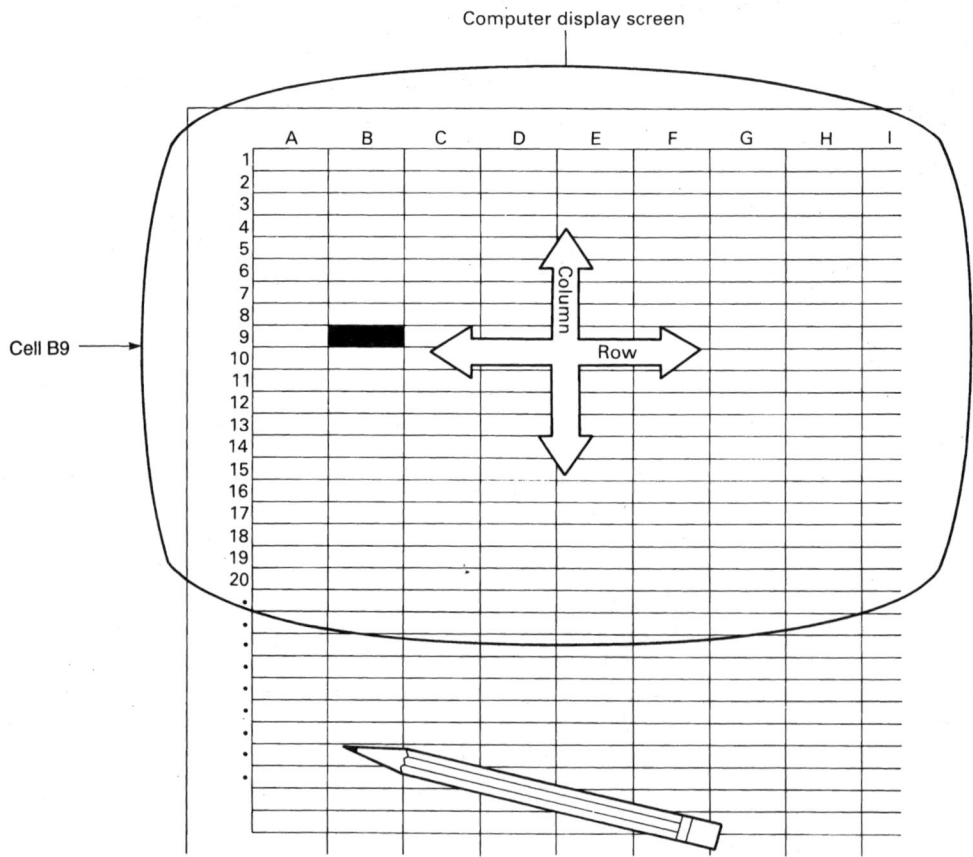

Spreadsheet worksheet.

It is simple to search and sort the information held in a database. For example, the data base can be interrogated to locate a particular item of information, or instructions can be given to sort the database records into a certain order.

Once the database has been searched, sorted and updated records can all be printed or in part.

The Internet

The *Internet* is a network of computers interconnected around the world. Subscribers to the service can link to other subscribers through an *Internet service provider*, who is located relatively near the user.

To become an *Internet user* it is necessary to pay a fee to the service provider, plus the cost of a telephone call while connected to the Internet. The cost of the call is related to the distance to the (local) Internet service provider, even though the connection may be to a computer in a foreign country.

The Internet can be used for searching for information, sending electronic mail (E-mail), downloading computer files, and has many other uses.

14.6 Postal communications

Businesses need to be able to communicate with each other in order to exchange the correspondence and documentation necessary for transactions to take place. The variety of postal services available enable businesses to send and receive letters, parcels and payments. The existence of these services makes a considerable contribution to the effective operation of industry and commerce.

Letter services

In the UK we say that we have a two-tier postal service. *First-class mail* is faster and costs more than *second-class mail*.

Today, in a move towards greater mechanisation of mail handling, the Post Office has identified standard sizes of envelopes (Post Office preferred–POP) which help the mechanised handling of mail movement. In addition, postcodes help to sort mail automatically.

- Every street has a separate postcode.
- The postcode is shown as letters and numbers at the end of an address.
- Using the postcode speeds up mail movement.

Business reply service

The trader provides potential customers with specially printed envelopes displaying a licence number and the class of postage. The trader pays postage on letters received, thus encouraging custom.

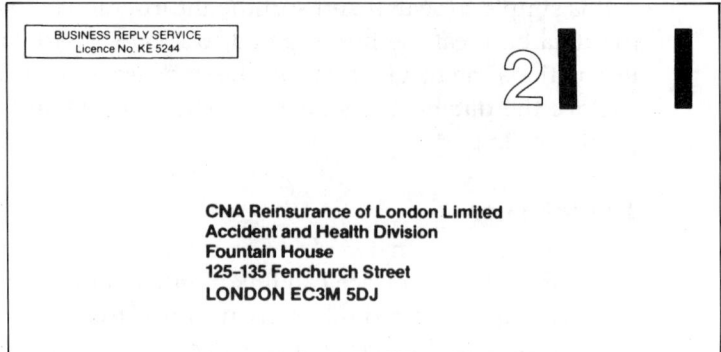

Business reply service envelope.

Freepost

This service also allows people to write to traders in reply to advertisements without paying postage, as long as the envelope is addressed in a special way.

- The address must include the word FREEPOST.
- Only second-class service is available.
- The trader is saved the expense of providing envelopes.

Registered post

This service provides compensation to the sender for a lost postal packet. The compensation paid for a loss is proportionate to the value of the packet and the registration fee paid on posting. The letter or packet to be posted in this way must have a large blue cross on it. A certificate of posting is issued as proof of posting, and a signature is obtained on delivery. All valuable items should be sent using this service.

Recorded delivery

The recorded delivery service is cheaper than registered post, but in the case of a loss only a nominal compensation is paid. The service provides proof of posting and delivery and is suitable for important documents (e.g. a final demand for payment of a debt) but is not suitable for posting valuables.

Selectapost

This service arranges for an addressee's mail to be subdivided (e.g. into departments) prior to delivery so long as some indication of the division required is shown in the address.

Poste restante

Packets may be sent to a post office in a particular town 'to be called for'. The destination Post Office keeps the packet for up to two weeks and only releases it upon proof of identity. The service is particularly useful to sales representatives who are unsure where they will be residing during their sales tour.

Business Communication

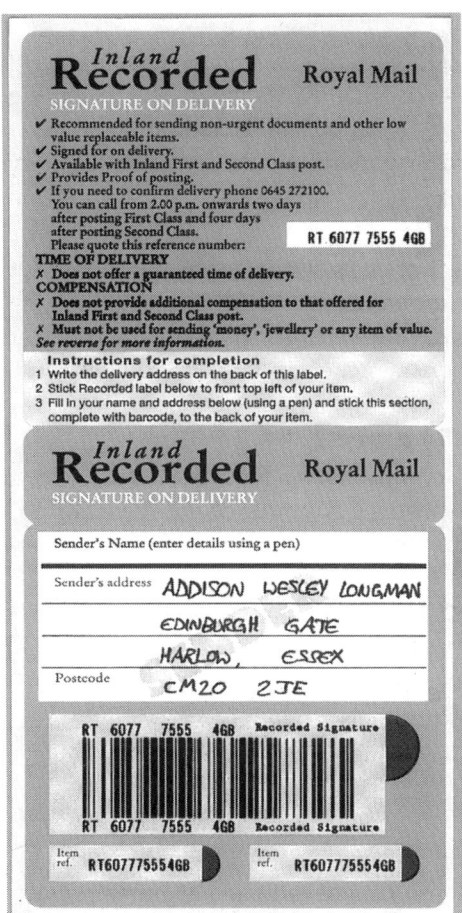 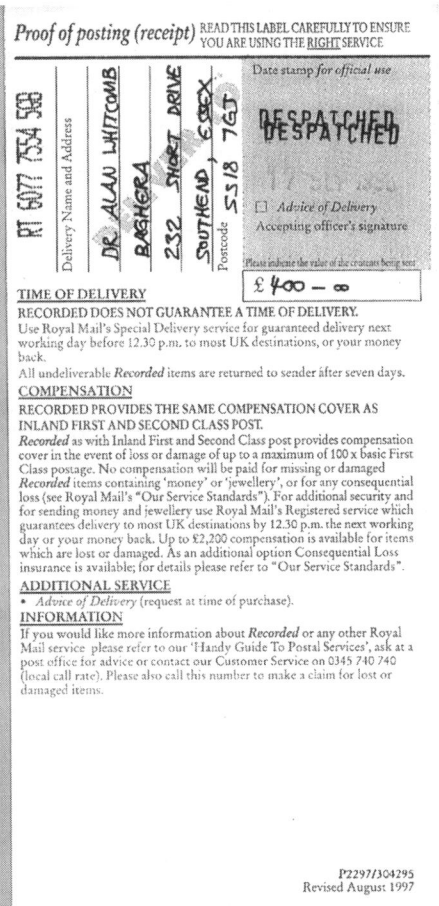

Certificate of posting

- The Post Office gives a receipt to confirm a package has been handed over the counter.
- No charge is made for this receipt.
- Useful in establishing date of posting when there is a possibility of dispute.

Parcels and special services

Parcel post

Used for packages too large for letter post, and up to size and specified weight limits. A 'postage forward' (postal charges to be paid by receiver) service is available using special labels and a licence allowing use of the service.

Swiftair

This service is available for all letters to Europe and for airmail letters to countries outside Europe. Items are handed over a post office counter and an additional fee is paid. The packet receives accelerated treatment within this country, and within the country of destination.

Express post

Letters and parcels up to a certain size and weight are accepted for delivery by special messenger. The word EXPRESS must be written clearly in the top left-hand corner of the package. Charges are based on distance as well as weight and, therefore, the service is only generally used for relatively short distances.

Special delivery

Available as part of the first-class service only, special delivery is carried out by messenger after the packet has arrived at the destination post office. It is suitable for use as a complementary service to the delivery of letters, parcels, recorded delivery and registered post. Packets must be marked 'special delivery'.

Compensation fee (CF) parcels

The Post Office will pay compensation for any parcel lost or damaged in the post if CF has been paid on posting. Amount of compensation is related to fee paid and a nominal maximum amount. Not suitable for very valuable items.

Cash on Delivery (COD)

For a small charge the Post Office will collect a specified amount (not exceeding £100) before parting with a package and pass it to the person who sent the parcel. The money collected is known as a *trade charge*. All letters and packets sent COD must be registered.

Datapost

- Provides door-to-door overnight delivery service.
- Packets are collected and can be returned at times pre-arranged with the Post Office.
- Particularly suitable for exchange of data such as computer material.
- International service also available.

Franking machines

- Machines are bought or hired from firms licensed by the Post Office.
- Hirer pays for units of postage value.
- Machine is used to stamp letters and parcels with postage paid amount.
- A logo can be printed at the same time as postage paid to advertise company's products.

A postal franking by machine with a slogan.

14.7 Telecommunications

Telecommunications and technological change

Although the postal services described in the previous sections are varied and effective, they have one major limitation. Even the speediest of the postal services cannot compare with the instant delivery of messages possible through most telecommunications services.

The essence of speed has become an increasingly important aspect of business communication. Stockbrokers and other organisations in the financial markets need to know minute by minute changes in market prices; companies want to be able to contact their representatives in their cars at any time; contracts, plans, specifications and other important documents need to be transmitted around the world in seconds; access to a wide range of information from databanks must be at fingertip control. All of these facilities, and many more, are available through an ever increasing number of telecommunications services which have not been slow to exploit new advances in technology.

Telephone

Telephone services

Advice of duration and charge (ADC)

Call connected and timed by operator. Caller is advised cost of call by operator when call is terminated.

Alarm call

Subscriber arranges for exchange to ring a specified telephone number at a particular time.

Transferred charge call (reversed charge call)

Operator connected call when the receiver of the call accepts the charge.

Personal call (person-to-person)

Telephone operator connects caller with a particular person. Charge does not begin until the requested person is obtained.

Telephone credit card

Allows holder to make operator connected calls and charge costs to their normal telephone bill.

Comprehensive Business Studies

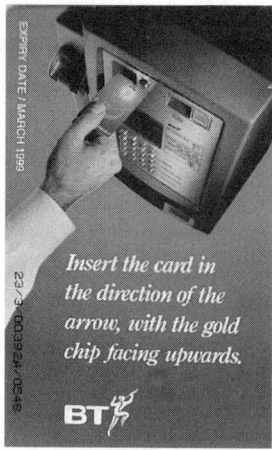 

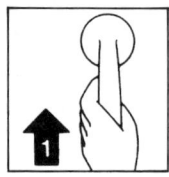 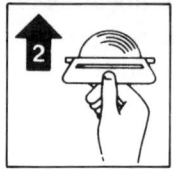  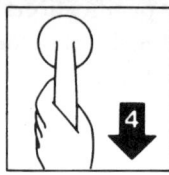 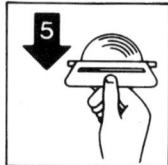

Freefone

Operator connected calls on a transferred charge basis. Used by businesses that wish to allow their customers or agents to make telephone calls to them without payment, thus encouraging custom.

Call card

Call cards can be bought in the Post Office and some newsagents and used in special public call boxes. They are a useful alternative to coins.

Telephone directories

Issued free to subscribers together with dialing code booklets. Subscribers are listed alphabetically. Those who choose not to be listed are known as 'ex-directory'.

- *Classified Trades Directories* (Yellow Pages)
  Lists local businesses alphabetically by trade.

Correspondence facilities

Electronic mail (E-mail)

Electronic mail refers to a variety of facilities which allow businesses to exchange printed communications rapidly using telecommunication links. The most common method is to send a message in standard format from one computer to another. This may be done through telephone links to a network. A *network* is a group of computers linked together. The most extensive network of computers is the *Internet*, which was examined earlier.

Facsimile transmission services (FAX)

This service provides facilities for transmission of black and white documents, letters, photos, etc, via telephone links.

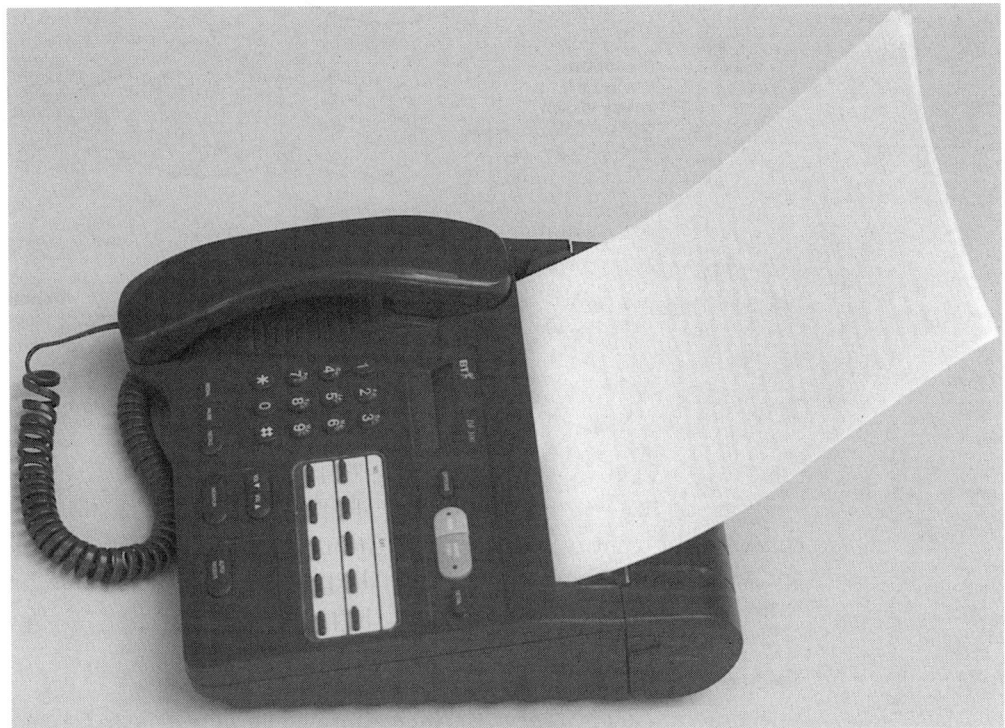

A modern fax machine is rather like a desk-top photocopier, and can actually be used to make photocopies.

The prepared A4 size document is fed into a machine and a copy of it is immediately transmitted to another machine sited elsewhere at home or abroad. The facilities can be used as an electronic mailing service, reducing the need to use conventional postal services. Fax messages can be prepared on a personal computer and transmitted direct in a single operation.

Conference facilities

Video conferencing

Attending conferences and meetings between executives is time-consuming and expensive. Those attending have to:

- travel many miles to get to the meeting place;
- face the hazards and delays likely to occur;
- arrange overnight accommodation.

Video conferencing allows people to hold face-to-face discussions, but without the inconvenience of everyone travelling to the same meeting place. Video

Modes of presentation

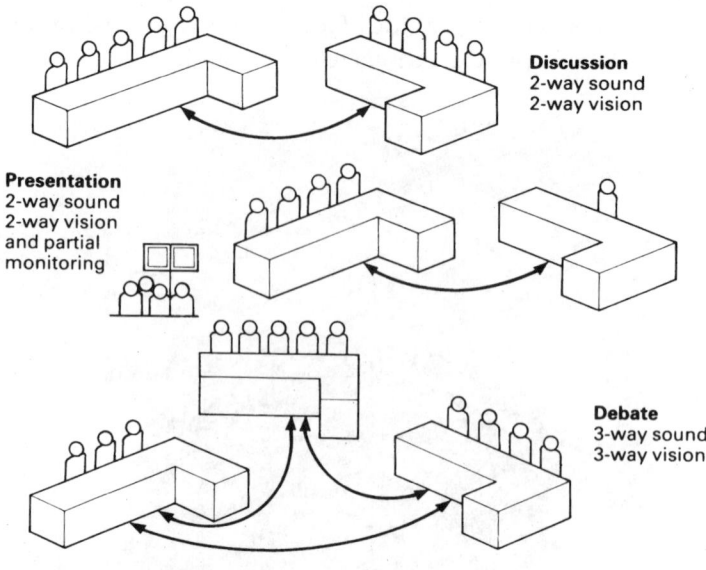

Video conferencing

conferencing centres exist in cities throughout the UK, which link up by sound and vision, so that discussions can take place as if all those attending the meeting were present in the same room.

Teleconferencing

Teleconferencing is a service which allows several people to be connected by telephone at the same time, allowing an audio conference to take place.

Data links

Datel

A telecommunications system which allows a computer in a firm to communicate with computers on sites in other parts of the country, and in many overseas countries.

Prestel

Prestel is a two-way computerised information service. The service can be used by anyone who has a specially adapted television set and a telephone. The telephone connection is used to obtain up-to-the-minute news and information from an extensive databank for display on the television screen. The Prestel service can respond to questions presented to it. For example, the databank can be asked about road or weather conditions, availability of air or theatre tickets, and bookings can be placed and accepted through the system.

Business Communication

Teletext

The CEEFAX and ORACLE services are provided by the broadcasting authorities whereby people with suitable televisions can call on a wide variety of information and news items from a central databank. These are sometimes referred to as viewdata systems because the information is viewed, but they do not respond to inputs in the ways that the Prestel system does.

Internal telecommunications

- *Intercom* – used for verbal communication between offices, departments or boss and secretary. Message relayed through small loud-speaker.
- *Telephone answering machine* – apparatus connected to telephone to record message when telephone is unattended.

Ceefax.

Combined telephone answering machine.

Office switchboard system.

- *Private manual branch exchange* (PMBX) – switchboard requiring telephone operator to connect all calls incoming, outgoing and between extension.
- *Private automatic branch exchange* (PABX) – switchboard providing automatic transfer of internal calls and connection to outside line by dialling a special number (9).
- *Paging* – lightweight receiver carried on person which 'bleeps' when signal sent out to tell holder to telephone some central point.

14.8 Activities

1. Why is communication important to a firm?
2. Name the four basic elements of communication.
3. What is the purpose of the internal communications of a firm?
4. List the main methods of internal communication available.
5. Give an example of the way in which graphs and charts may be used as a means of communication.
6. Name the two principal officers of a meeting.
7. What is the function of the chairman of a meeting?
8. Describe the purpose of three types of meeting.
9. What do the letters AGM stand for?
10. List in correct order six items shown on an agenda.
11. What do the letters AOB stand for?
12. Explain the difference between the minutes and a 'verbatim' report.
13. Describe four methods of voting at meetings.
14. What is the purpose of the external communications of a firm?
15. List the four main forms of external communication.
16. Briefly describe three different ways that a business might use information technology.
17. Explain the terms 'spreadsheet' and 'database'.
18. Why do you think the Internet is becoming increasingly important to businesses?
19. Why are postal services important to businesses?
20. Why do we say we have a two-tier postal service in the UK?

21 What are POP envelopes?

22 What is the correct name for the letters and numbers at the end of an address?

23 Compare the business reply service with Freepost.

24 Describe the registered post and recorded delivery services giving appropriate examples when each would be used in preference to the other.

25 Name the postal service where mail is subdivided prior to delivery. Give an example of how use of this service would help the firm that is receiving the letters.

26 Briefly describe the poste restante service and give an example of how it might be employed by a company engaged in sales.

27 What is the purpose of a certificate of posting?

28 Who would pay the postal charges for a package that is sent 'postage forward'?

29 The Swiftair and Express service provide 'special' handling of packets. Explain what is special about this service.

30 What is the basis of the charge to send a package by express post?

31 Briefly describe the special delivery service.

32 What do the letters CF stand for?

33 What do the letters COD stand for? Why is this service of particular use to a mail order company?

34 Briefly describe the Datapost service and give one example of how it might be used by a firm.

35 What is a franking machine? How can the use of such a machine help to increase efficiency in dealing with outgoing mail?

36 What is the main advantage that telecommunication has over postal communications?

37 Give three examples of circumstances in which businesses particularly need telecommunications facilities.

38 What is an ADC telephone call? What type of business might use this service?

39 Who pays the cost of a transferred charge call?

40 Give an example of a situation where a business might decide to make a personal call.

41 What is the purpose of a telephone credit card? Give one example of how a firm might use this service.

42 Who pays the cost of freefone telephone calls? How might a company use this facility?

43 What kind of information is to be found in Classified Trades Directories?

44 Briefly describe a fascimile transmission service.

45 What is video conferencing and how can this save time and expense for businesses?

46 'Although Prestel and Teletex have some similarities, Prestel has a far wider application.' Explain this statement.

47 What is an intercom?

48 With a telephone answering machine you can be in when you are out. How could this machine be particularly useful to a small business person?

49 What is paging?

Structured Questions

1 The following questions are all related to the business reply service and you should consult *The Post Office Guide* for relevant information.

(a) Refer to *The Post Office Guide* and find out the following information related to the Business Reply Service:
- How much in addition to the first or second class postage is payable by the addressee for each item received? (1)
- The additional fee charged is subject to various discounts depending on the number of items received by the addressee per year. What would be the percentage discount for 100 000 items received during one year? (1)

(b) How does the business reply service encourage potential customers to write to advertisers? (2)

(c) Briefly explain the purpose of the 'licence' necessary for a business to operate the business reply service. (2)

(d) Summarise the regulations for the use of pre-paid stationery for this service. (4)

(e) Compare the Business Reply Service and Freepost including examples of circumstances where a business might decide that one is preferable to another. (10)

2 Look at the advertisement on page 272 and answer the following questions.

(a) What is a credit reference agency? (2)
(b) What sort of information will a credit reference agency hold on a databank? (2)
(c) Jenny Fox applied for a loan from a finance company. She was refused the loan because her name is included in a credit agency 'black list'.
- What is a 'black list'? (2)
- Assuming that the information held on computer file is incorrect, what action can Jenny take? (3)

(d) Where do credit reference agencies obtain the information contained in their computerised references? (3)
(e) How might a business legally use a credit reference agency to its advantage? (4)
(f) Examples of 'wise' use of personal computer data include the police and doctors. Briefly describe three other 'wise' examples and one 'unwise' example. (4)

3 Consider the information below and answer the questions here and on page 273.

(a) What do the letters MD stand for? (1)
(b) What is the function of an MD? (2)
(c) In what ways can Dorothy's firm's problem be seen to be one of communication? (3)
(d) Imagine that you are Dorothy's personal assistant. Compose a brief memo to all senior staff requesting that they attend a meeting next

A question of communication

Dorothy Whitehead is the Managing Director (MD) of a medium-sized company in the North East. Her firm manufactures a range of cardboard boxes. In the years since the firm was established in 1980, Dorothy's company has steadily increased its sales until about six months ago. Then Dorothy noticed a distinct fall in orders received, even though the firm's prices still compared favourably with those of competitors.

One of the regular customers who had ceased to place orders was AJ Products of Redditch. Dorothy arranged to visit Mr Jones the MD of AJ Products, in an attempt to find out why his company had not placed an order with her firm for some time.

'Your sales staff could do with a bit of a shake up', said Mr Jones, 'Whenever my people 'phone your firm the person they want to speak to is never there, and it seems that the people in the office never know where they are or when they are likely to return. We have requested that someone 'phones us back, but this doesn't happen. And another thing, the people you have answering the 'phone are not particularly helpful, in fact some of them could be said to be downright rude. Quite frankly, until your staff learn to be a bit more helpful and efficient I can't see any immediate prospect of further trade between our companies.'

Comprehensive Business Studies

Who's checking on the computers when the computers are checking on you?

Where would you expect to find the biggest list of people's names in the country? Perhaps your first thought would be the telephone directory.

If so, you would be wrong. Certainly there are over 23 million telephone subscribers in the UK and the gas and electricity boards and some government departments have similar sized information or data banks.

But even these do not match, for example, the 40 million separate records kept by the nation's leading credit reference agencies. And the Department of Health and Social Security has records on virtually everybody in the country.

The increasing use of computer technology allows such information to be compiled quickly and referred to almost instantaneously from anywhere in the country.

So why should this concern you? Well, as someone who will have to face the challenge of leaving school and establishing a career, you may well find that you, yourself, are soon placed upon such a list – if you are not on one already!

In most cases, these lists, and the information they contain, are used wisely, as part of everyday life. For instance assisting police in their enquiries, government departments in deciding upon benefit entitlements, and many Doctors in providing health care.

These activities are sensible enough, assisting rather than hindering the normal processes of society. However, there can be problems, for if the information on the lists is incorrect, or if your details are mixed up with someone else's then things may go wrong. You may find your claim for benefit payment or credit being turned down, the mortgage for a house you want to buy refused, or even the police arresting you, all because of a simple mistake in the records.

Happily, this doesn't happen too often. But when it does, you will want to know how to identify – and to correct – that mistake.

The Data Protection Act is now here to help, giving us all new rights. Rights which enable us to inspect the information held about us on computer records, and to correct it if it is wrong. As importantly, the Act also allows us to claim compensation if we are damaged by any misuse of this information.

The Act is supervised by the Data Protection Registrar. He can follow up any complaints about the misuse of computer records, no matter how large or small the organisation concerned.

For more information on the Data Protection Act, please contact:-

Information Services (BTA), Office of the Data Protection Registrar, Springfield House, Water Lane, Wilmslow, Cheshire SK9 5AX Telephone: 0625 535777.

Wednesday at 5.00 pm to discuss the problem. Include an indication of what the meeting will be about. (4)

(e) Dorothy has asked you to open the meeting by giving a brief summary of the reasons why the firm has been losing orders. Write out notes for this introduction to the meeting.

(f) Assuming that you were given sole charge of improving the company's image, explain the steps you would take in an attempt to solve the current problem. (6)

4 Look at the article below and then answer the following questions.

(a) How does a 'laptop' differ from a portable computer? (2)

(b) In what way can a laptop computer reduce time wastage for a busy executive? (2)

(c) State four items that a business person would be likely to produce using a laptop computer and while travelling. (Questions (d) and (e) over the page.) (2)

Computing on the move

CAR

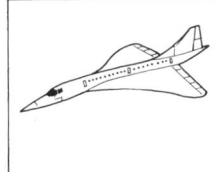
PLANE

TRAIN

Laptop computers provide tremendous benefits for those who need computing power while on the move. And when used in conjunction with the telephone network, laptops become the business traveller's lifeline for essential and complicated messages to and from base.

The computer industry differentiates between what it calls a portable and a laptop. Portables are full-sized mains-driven desktop micros that can be carried, e.g. to a car boot and then, set up at home.

Laptops are light, slim machines that can literally sit on your lap while you are in a car, train or aircraft seat. They are often battery-powered, and to minimise power loss the screens are usually liquid crystal displays (LCDs) – the same technology used in calculator screens. Depending on the machine's power, memory size and storage capacity, laptops can be used for all the jobs that are normally done on desktop micros, i.e. wordprocessing, communicating with electronic mail services, data storage, production of spreadsheets, keeping diaries, calculating figures, etc.

Both types are useful because they enable constructive use to be made of time often wasted while travelling or in hotel rooms. Memos, telexes, letters and reports can be written on the move and either printed on an office or portable printer, or sent to another computer over the telephone. Up-to-date price lists and quotations can be printed on demand for customers.

(d) What sort of information would a business executive be likely to want to receive from their base while travelling? (4)

(e) Why is the use of a laptop computer limited by its power, memory store and storage capacity? (6)

Research assignments

1 Considering the speed of telecommunications why do postal services continue to play an important part in business operation? Support your study with data obtained through local research, e.g. a firm you are familiar with.

2 Take one large and one small business in your area. Compare the communication methods they use and comment on any differences found.

3 Choose any firm in your area. Explain why telecommunications is an important aspect of the firm's operations.

4 Investigate any firm in your community and describe the forms of internal communication it employs.

5 Produce evidence to show why businesses are becoming increasingly reliant on information technology.

6 'Information technology has now become economically viable for even the small business.' Discuss this statement using evidence from personal research of small businesses to support your discussion.

15 Banking

15.1 Central banks

Most major countries today have a single central bank which plays a major role in controlling the monetary system. Our central bank, the Bank of England (the Bank), is the heart of the British banking system, exerting a considerable influence on other parts of the banking sector.

The functions of the central bank

It is the government's bank

This is the major function of the Bank. In this respect it manages the government's banking accounts, for example for the Exchequer and other government departments.

The Bank advises the government on formulation of monetary policy and assists the government in carrying out that policy.

The Bank also handles the arrangements for government borrowing:

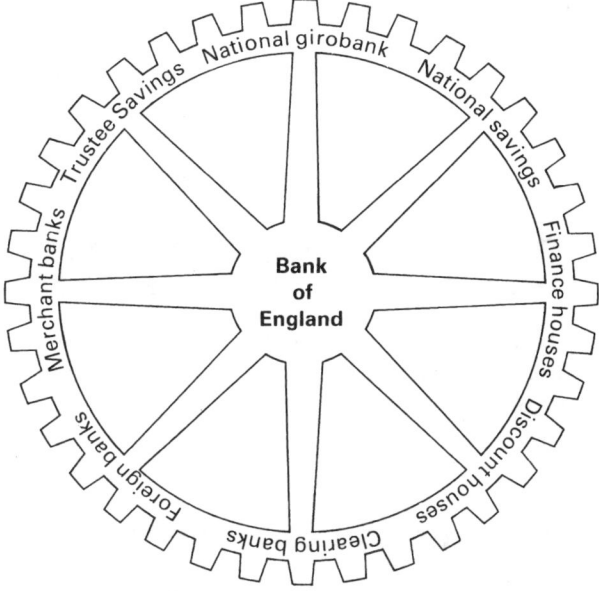

The bank of England is at the centre of the British banking system.

- short-term – principally through the sale of Treasury bills;
- long-term – management of government stocks which form the bulk of the national debt.

Management of the exchange equalisation account is also carried out by the Bank and it is through this that the Bank can influence the value of sterling by selling or buying pounds to affect the foreign exchange market prices.

It controls the note issue
The Bank has the sole responsibility for the issue of banknotes in England and Wales.

It is the bankers' bank
Each of the clearing banks has an account with the Bank, and during the process of cheque clearing (see later) debits and credits are made to theses accounts as a means of interbank settlement.

The clearing banks keep about a half of their liquid reserves (short call money) deposited at the Bank and use these for settling debts among themselves (e.g. in cheque clearing activities).

The commercial banks rely on the Bank if they run short of money or require loans.

It has international responsibilities
The Bank provides services for other central banks and some of the world's major financial organisations such as the International Monetary Fund (IMF).

It is the 'lender of last resort'
If the commercial banks run short of cash they recall deposits they have in the money market. This leaves the discount houses short of funds. The Bank of England 'lends as a last resort' to the discount houses, but at a higher rate of interest than that obtainable elsewhere in the City.

15.2 Central banks and monetary control

The Bank of England (like other central banks) is responsible for carrying out the monetary policy of the government. This particularly involves the Bank in exercising control of the money supply and the lending activities of the banks. It does this in a number of ways.

Open market operations

The Bank seeks to keep interest rates within an unpublished band through its bill dealing with the discount houses. By buying and selling bills from and to discount houses the Bank influences the amount of funds available to the banking system as a whole.

Basically, this action influences short-term interest rates, but leaves the influence of long-term rates to market forces.

Minimum lending rate (MLR)

The use of MLR has currently been suspended by the Bank, although it can be reintroduced at some future date, maybe temporarily. When in operations, MLR is the minimum rate of interest at which the Bank will normally lend to the discount houses. All other interest rates tend to follow MLR movement when used in this way.

Cash at the Bank

The Bank requires all institutions in the monetary sector with eligible liabilities of £10 million or more to keep $\frac{1}{2}$ per cent of their eligible liabilities in non-interest earning balances at the Bank of England. Eligible liabilities are the liabilities of the bank *less*:

(a) funds lent by one institution in the monetary sector to any other;
(b) money at call (can be withdrawn on demand) placed with money brokers and jobbers in the Stock Exchange, and secured on gilt-edged stocks, Treasury bills, local authority bills and eligible bank bills (e.g. bill of exchange).

Money at call

Each bank whose bills are recognised as eligible is required to maintain:

(a) 6 per cent of its eligible liabilities with members of the London Discount Market Association (LDMA) and/or with money brokers and gilt-edged jobbers;
(b) the proportion held with members of the LDMA must not fall below 4 per cent on any one day.

Special deposits

Banks and deposit-taking institutions with eligible liabilities of £10 million or more can be called on to deposit a percentage (decided by the Bank) of their liabilities with the Bank, which earns interest at a rate close to Treasury bill rate. This process can be used as a means of withdrawing cash from the money market.

Lender of last resort

(See also the earlier section on the functions of the Bank). If the commercial banks run short of cash they recall their loans made to the discount market. Consequently, the members of the discount market are forced to borrow funds from the Bank which charges a rate of interest higher than that charged anywhere else in the City.

15.3 Special financial institutions

Merchant Banks

These are not banks in the commonly understood sense but private firms that offer highly specialised services almost exclusively for business customers. The main activities of merchant banks can be divided into acceptance house activities, issuing house activities and capital market activities.

Acceptance house activities

The traditional activity of merchant banks is 'accepting' (i.e. lending their name to) a bill of exchange issued by less well-known traders, so that it becomes more acceptable because of the bank's good reputation in the financial world. By endorsing the bill, the accepting house guarantees payment of the bill should the drawer default. (See Chapter 11 for application of bills of exchange in finance of international trade.)

Issuing house activities

Merchant banks play a major role in assisting in raising company finance by sponsoring first issues of company shares on behalf of their clients, or acting as intermediaries between companies seeking capital and those willing to provide it. It should be noted that not all issuing houses are merchant banks (see Chapter 17 for notes on share issue).

Capital market activities

In addition to raising capital for companies by their issuing house activities, merchant banks are also involved in a wide range of other capital market operations some of which are as follows:

- they operate some current account services for customers;
- they accept larger (e.g. over £25 000) deposits, generally for one year or more;
- they offer consultancy services to businesses wishing to become limited liability companies;
- they advise on company problems such as capital reorganisations, dividend policy, mergers and takeover bids;
- they provide finance for hire-purchase, local government and industry;
- they operate unit trusts (see also Chapter 17);
- they assist in the investment of trustee funds for large institutions;
- they act as agents to companies establishing branches overseas;
- they deal in the precious metals market.

Discount houses

The London Discount Market Association (LDMA) consists of twelve companies basically concerned with borrowing and investing money on a short-term basis. The majority of the dealing is carried out by telephone and personal contact.

The main functions of the discount houses can be summarised as follows:

- accepting very short-term deposits from businesses, particularly banks, in return for a low rate of interest;
- using funds raised in this way to purchase a variety of assets, for example Treasury bills, bills of exchange and gilt-edged securities;
- providing immediate finance for companies by discounting reliable bills of exchange, that is buying them for less than their face value and holding them until they mature to obtain the full value, or reselling them and charging a higher rate of discount to achieve a profit.

Foreign banks

There are now about 400 foreign banks (particularly from European countries) in London existing to give service and credit to companies from their own countries operating in Britain. A number of these banks have expanded their activities and they now make substantial sterling loans to British borrowers.

Finance houses

The Finance Houses Association (FHA) consists of forty-three member companies who control 80 per cent of the instalment credit business in the UK.

15.4 The clearing banks

'Clearing' banks are so-called because they handle the exchange and settlement of cheques through the clearing house system which is dealt with later in this chapter.

The functions of the clearing banks can be summarised as follows:

- acceptance of deposits of money;
- provision of a system of payments mechanism;
- supply of finance;
- provision of a wide range of services.

15.5 Bank accounts

There are three basic types of bank account: budget account, deposit account and current account.

The budget account

This type of account helps to even out the payment of annual household expenses. Upon payment of an agreed weekly or monthly amount the bank gives the account holder permission to draw cheques, standing orders or direct debits up to a given credit limit. The limit is calculated proportionate to the regular in-payment. While the account is in credit, the money earns interest, and interest is charged when the account is overdrawn. There is also a charge for each cheque or other withdrawal.

The bank budget account is particularly useful for someone who finds it difficult to organise and stick to their own personal budget plan.

The deposit account

The bank deposit account is used by individuals and businesses for the safe-keeping of funds not needed for immediate use. Credit slips are used to pay money, cheques, postal orders, etc. into the account.

No cheque book is issued with this account and, therefore, transfer of sums of money from the deposit account is normally in the form of cash. The bank can request seven days' notice of withdrawal of money from the account, although this rule is usually waived, especially for relatively small amounts.

Depositors are paid interest on money left in the account, and the bank then lends the money to borrowers who are charged a higher rate of interest. A statement of account is issued periodically to the account holder. The account cannot be overdrawn (see later).

The current account (cheque account)

This type of account is used by individuals and businesses for the safekeeping of funds needed for current use, in other words funds which are required to be immediately available.

The current account can be opened with a small deposit, a specimen signature, and a reference from someone acceptable to the bank.

Credit slips are used to pay deposits into the account and cheques are used to draw cash or transfer funds to others. Funds can also be withdrawn from the account twenty-four hours of the day through a cash dispenser.

Interest is not always paid on this type of account although some banks have experimented with paying interest on the maintenance of a minimum balance. Bank charges may be incurred if a minimum balance is not maintained.

A statement of account is issued to the account holder periodically or on request, and a current balance figure can also be obtained twenty-four hours a day through a cash dispenser.

With the permission of the bank the current account may be 'overdrawn', that is the account holder will be allowed to draw on more money than is in the account. This is examined in more detail later.

A 'joint' account may be shared by two or more persons. In the case of a joint account or a business account, the account holders can make a variety of arrangements for signing cheques, for example signed by any one, or any two of a number of authorised signatories.

15.6 The cheque system

Cheques

A cheque is a written instruction to the bank (the *drawee*) to pay money to the account holder (the *drawer*) or to another person (the *payee*). Most cheques are *order* cheques, which means they must be signed (*endorsed*) on the reverse by the named payee if they wish to pass it on to someone else.

Although today we recognise cheques as special slips of printed paper, these are only issued by banks for both the convenience of their account system, as well as to help account holders. However, there is no reason why the instruction to the bank cannot take the form of a letter, or even a less formal message. There have been occasions when, for a variety of reasons, these instructions have been written on such widely diverse items as a door, a paving slab, various items of clothing and even a fish.

Things written on a cheque

- The date from which the value of the cheque is payable (a post-dated cheque is one dated for sometime in the future).

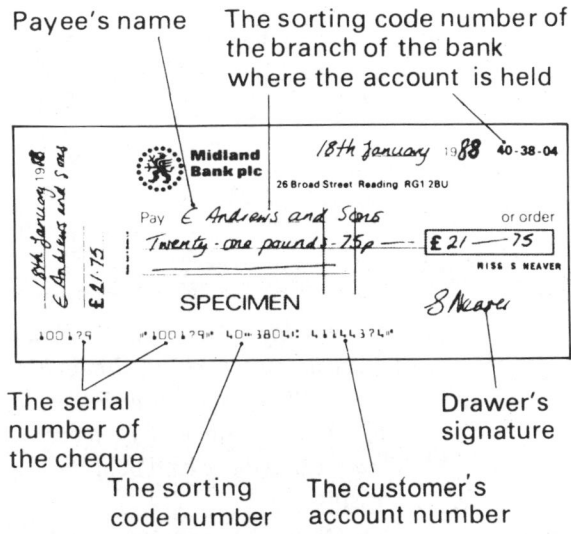

The bank will ensure that the cheque:
- *has been written out correctly*
- *has not been altered*
- *has a valid date*
- *has a signature which compares with the specimen held.*

- Name of payee (person cheque is to pay).
- Amount to be paid in words.
- Amount to be paid in figures.
- Signature of drawer (person from whose account funds are to be withdrawn).

Open cheque (uncrossed)

The open cheque does not have two parallel lines drawn across it. It is 'uncrossed'. The payee of an open cheque can:

- pay the cheque into his own account;
- pass it to someone else by endorsing it;
- exchange it for cash at the bank on which it is drawn.

The open cheque can be paid out to whoever presents it at the bank, and, therefore, it is not very safe. Banks prefer their customers to use crossed cheques and open cheques are used far less frequently than crossed cheques.

Crossed cheque

A crossed cheque has two parallel lines drawn vertically across it. This type of cheque must be paid into a bank account and cannot be exchanged for cash except by the drawer at his own bank, or at another bank with the use of a cheque card. These rules help to eliminate fraud in the use of cheques.

If you look at the cheque shown on page 281 you will see that it has a 'general' crossing; there is nothing written between the lines of the crossing. This means

1 This crossing ensures that the cheque can only be paid into the account of the payee, although they can pay it into their account through any branch they wish.
2 This means the same as the above crossing except that the cheque can only be paid in at the branch stated in the crossing.
3 When written as a cheque crossing this warns anyone other than the payee accepting the cheque that they do so with some degree of risk. The risk they face is that if the cheque has been stolen or fraudulently used, then the person accepting it is liable to refund the rightful owner with the amount shown on the cheque.

that the cheque must pass through a bank account and cannot be exchanged for cash. However, a cheque with this sort of crossing can still be endorsed and passed to someone else, and such a cheque is still open to fraudulent use, although less so than the open cheque.

There is a variety of wordings that can be written between the lines of a cheque crossing to give more specific instructions on how the cheque may be used, and to make it safer. The three most frequently used 'special' cheque crossings are shown on page 282.

Dishonoured cheques

Cheques which are not passed for payment by the drawer's bank are said to have 'bounced' or to have been dishonoured. When a cheque is refused for payment the drawer's bank will write 'refer to drawer' or R/D on the cheque and return it to the payee who must find out from the drawer why the cheque has not been honoured.

Reasons why a cheque might 'bounce'

- Cheque contains an error or is unsigned.
- Cheque is 'stale' (more than six months old).
- Signature differs from specimen held at bank.
- Drawer does not have sufficient funds in account.
- Cheque has been altered.
- Cheque is post-dated.
- Cheque has been 'stopped' by the drawer (drawer has instructed bank not to make payment).

Bank statement of account

The bank statement of account is issued to the account holder periodically or on request. The account holder can also obtain a figure to show the current balance in the account from the bank cash dispenser which will provide information and cash twenty-four hours of the day. The statement sums up all the transactions which have taken place since the last statement was issued and shows the current balance held in the account.

Amounts which reduce the balance (e.g. cheques issued) in the account are shown in the payments column, and amounts which increase the balance in the account are shown in the receipts column. As each payment or receipt is recorded a new balance figure is shown in a third column.

Cheque clearing

The reader's attention is directed again to the point made earlier that a cheque is an instruction to their bank by the drawer of the cheque. Consequently, when a payee deposits a cheque into their account it does not mean the transfer of funds has taken place. The instruction is to the drawer's bank, and transfer cannot be

		DEBIT	CREDIT	BALANCE
MIDLAND BANK PLC COVENT GARDEN BRANCH 16 KING STREET LONDON WC2E 8JF				
MISS A. N. OTHER				
Statement of Account				
1999 Sheet 42 Account No. 51149903				Credit C Debit D
AUG 5	BALANCE BROUGHT FORWARD			62.08 C
AUG 8	AUTOBK COVENT GDN2	10.00		52.08 C
AUG 9	100142	35.00		17.08 C
AUG 10	100146	10.30		
AUG 10	100147	8.15		
AUG 10	AUTOBK NATW 601533	10.00		11.37 D
AUG 15	100148	10.00		21.37 D
AUG 16	100144	5.00		26.37 D
AUG 19	100149	10.00		
AUG 19	PITMAN PUBLISHING		506.33	469.96 C
AUG 22	AUTOBK NOTT HILL GT	15.00		
AUG 22	SUNDRIES		65.00	519.96 C
AUG 23	100473	41.00		
AUG 23	AUTOBK NATW 503021	60.00		418.96 C
AUG 24	100150	80.00		
AUG 24	100474	160.00		
AUG 24	AUTOBK NATW 503021	10.00		168.96 C
AUG 30	AUTOBK COVENT GDN2	10.00		158.96 C
AUG 31	100476	38.40		
AUG 31	AUTOBK COVENT GDN	20.00		
AUG 31	AUTOBK NATW 503021	45.00		55.56 C
SEP 2	AUTOBK NATW 503021	10.00		45.56 C
SEP 6	AUTOBK NATW 503021	10.00		35.56 C
SEP 6	BALANCE CARRIED FORWARD			35.56 C

A bank statement.

carried out until the drawer's bank has received the instruction. In the meantime the payee cannot draw on the amount stated on the cheque. The process by which cheques are passed for payment is known as the *clearing system*.

A cheque can only be 'cleared' for payment at the bank on which it is drawn. If the drawer and payee use the same branch bank then, so long as the drawer has sufficient funds, a simple paper transfer is carried out within the branch bank. If the drawer and payee use the same bank but different branches the system of clearing the cheque for payment is still relatively simply carried out through the headquarters of the bank.

If the drawer and payee have accounts with different banks the cheques are cleared through the *Bankers' Clearing House* where representatives of all the clearing banks meet daily to exchange cheques they have received belonging to other banks.

At the Clearing House the representative from the headquarters of each clearing bank meets the representatives of the other banks and gives them cheques drawn on their banks and accepts cheques drawn on his bank. During this process an account is kept of the value of the cheques changing hands. The difference between the value of the cheques received and handed over shows how much each of the banks owes the other. This information is used daily to credit or debit the balances of the clearing banks which are kept at the Bank of England.

The cheque passes through a complete cycle, from the time the drawer writes out the cheque until the drawer's bank has released the payment to the payee, in just three days.

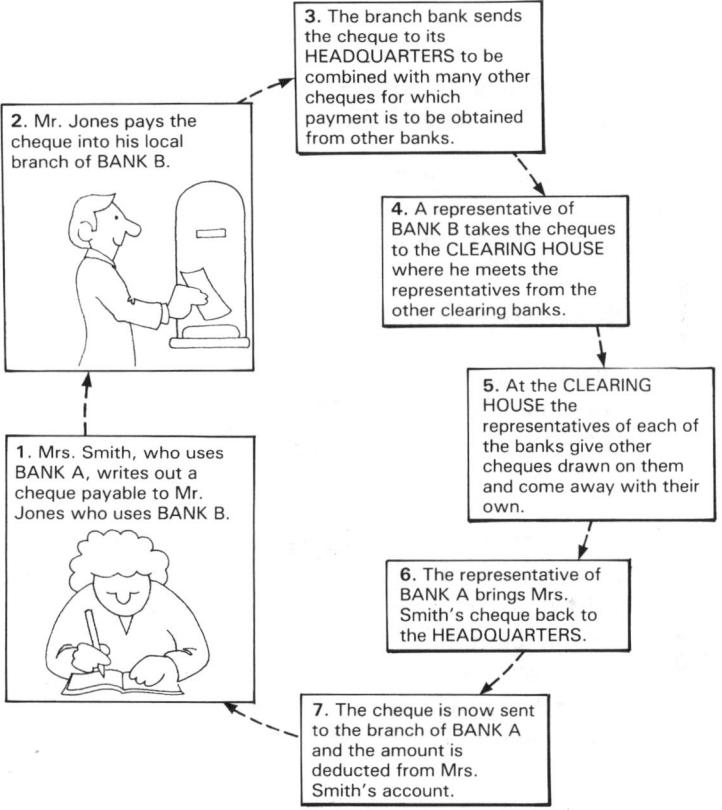

The lifecycle of a cheque.

15.7 EFTPOS

A payment system called EFTPOS is an important development of the banking system. This title stands for 'Electronic Funds Transfer at Point of Sale'. EFTPOS is a method of paying for goods or services in shops, garages, etc., using electronics instead of paper.

To operate the system the account holder has a plastic card (such as a credit card or cash card) and a means of identification (e.g. a Personal Identification Number or PIN). When the customer gets to the shop till and is required to pay for their purchases they give their card to the cashier who runs it through a computer terminal. The amount to be paid is displayed at the top of a small key-pad on which the shopper keys in their secret PIN number. The computer checks that the card and the PIN number match up, and that there is enough money in the account. If all is in order, the money is taken out of the customer's bank account (if a cash card is being used) and transferred directly into the shop's account. With credit cards the statement comes later in the usual way.

In due course EFTPOS will be increasingly used in the many places where payments need to be made by consumers to traders.

15.8 Bank services

There are a wide range of services that are provided by the commercial banks, National Girobank, and increasingly by the building societies. These assist businesses and individual consumers by making it easier to make payments.

Standing order

Imagine that a company has purchased an item of equipment on hire purchase. This could mean that every month someone in the firm has to remember to write out a cheque and covering letter, and address an envelope and post it to the hire-purchase company.

This is not only time-consuming and inconvenient. but there is the danger that the payment could be overlooked, perhaps damaging the firm's reputation for paying debts promptly. The bank standing order service solves this problem, for individuals or organisations, by making regular payments of a set sum from one bank account to another on behalf of the customer.

This service is available to current account holders and it saves the bank customer the need to remember, and to post off, payments. The service is only useful if the amount to be transferred does not change.

Direct debit

This is a variation of the standing order service. Instead of instructing the bank to make regular payments on their behalf, customers fill in and sign a form which gives permission for a payee a withdraw regular amounts from their account. The amount may be varied by the payee and notified to the account holder at some later time. This service is suitable for repayments of forms of credit where the repayment amount may vary due to changes in interest rates.

The standing order and the direct debit have dual roles in respect of business application. They not only make it easy for the business to make regular payments, but they also enable businesses to receive regular payments from their customers.

STANDING ORDER MANDATE

TO **Lloyds** Bank PLC
ADDRESS **16, Waterend Rd, Kendal, Cumbria**

	BANK	BRANCH TITLE (Not address)	SORTING CODE NUMBER
Please pay	Midland	Bridge Rd	40 — 15 — 20

	BENEFICIARY'S NAME	ACCOUNT NUMBER
for the credit of	Sally Carstairs	1 0 0 9 2 3 4 1

	AMOUNT IN FIGURES	AMOUNT IN WORDS
†the sum of	£	

	DATE AND AMOUNT OF FIRST PAYMENT		DUE DATE AND FREQUENCY
commencing	*NOW	£ 100	and thereafter every	month

	DATE AND AMOUNT OF LAST PAYMENT		
*until	—	£ —	*until you receive further notice from me/~~us in writing~~
quoting the reference	—		and debit my/~~our~~ account accordingly.

*Delete if not applicable
†If the amount of the periodic payments vary they should be incorporated in a schedule overleaf

THIS INSTRUCTION CANCELS ANY PREVIOUS ORDER IN FAVOUR OF THE BENEFICIARY NAMED ABOVE, UNDER THIS REFERENCE.

SPECIAL INSTRUCTIONS —

ACCOUNT TO BE DEBITED	ACCOUNT NUMBER
current account	7 1 2 4 6 0 8 1

SIGNATURE(S) **J. C. Carstairs**   DATE **6.4.1999**

NOTE: The Bank will not undertake to (i) make any reference to Value Added Tax or other indeterminate element
(ii) advise payer's address to beneficiary
(iii) advise beneficiary of inability to pay
(iv) request beneficiary's banker to advise beneficiary of receipt

Standing order form.

Bank giro

The bank giro is a method of transfer (credit transfer) of funds directly into the account of someone else, who may hold his account at another branch or even a different bank to the person making the payment. The person making the payment does not have to hold a bank account as in-payment can be made with cash or cheque. There are two basic methods of credit transfer that are generally used, the single transfer and the multiple transfer.

Single transfer

A bank giro form similar to that on page 288 is filled in to make a single payment directly to a stated bank account. The major suppliers of domestic facilities, such as gas, electricity and water, help their customers to use the system by printing bank giro credit forms at the bottom of their bills.

Single transfer bank giro form.

Multiple transfer

Using this method the drawer only writes out a single cheque to pay several bills or a number of different people.

A list or schedule is passed to the bank showing details of a number of different accounts to be credited by direct transfer. The account holder writes out a single cheque in favour of the bank itself and the bank credits each payee, saving the account holder the necessity of writing out many cheques.

The system can be used to pay the bills of several traders but it is particularly useful in paying the wages of many employees.

Bank cards

It is sometimes said that we have become a largely 'cashless' society. This not only refers to the cheque and giro systems of money transfer already examined, but also to the function of some of the bank cards that are now being used, often reducing the need for cash transactions. Three of the main bank cards are now examined, but it should be remembered that there are card systems apart from those issued by the banks (e.g. retailers' charge cards, telephone credit card and others discussed in other chapters) which also contribute to the conception of a 'cashless' society.

Cheque card

Cheque cards are issued by banks to reliable, well-established customers. The card is used to guarantee payment of a cheque up to a maximum amount which is stated on the card. The card shows an identification number and a specimen signature, and payment of a cheque cannot be stopped if a cheque card has been used to guarantee it.

Credit card

Credit cards are a financial service run by the commercial banks. The card shows the identification number and specimen signature of the rightful owner who can use it for purchasing without using cash or cheque.

Banking

The card-holder signs for goods or services and presents the card to the trader. The bank pays the trader and the customer later pays the money to the bank. The system is used by account holders for shopping, travel, garages, restaurants, etc.

- A monthly statement is sent to the account holder.
- No interest is charged if the account is paid immediately.
- Interest is charged on balances left outstanding.

Cash dispenser card

The bank customer is issued with a card and a secret personal identity number (PIN) known only to them and the bank. The cash dispenser card also has its own separate identity code incorporated into it.

A cash dispensing machine is set into the wall outside the bank and is connected to the bank computer. The card-holder feeds his card into the machine and 'keys in' the PIN.

If the card data and the keyed in PIN match up with the record the bank computer holds, the dispenser issues the money requested up to a daily individual limit. The customer's account is immediately automatically debited with the amount withdrawn.

The machine operates twenty-four hours a day and it will also provide information such as current account balance.

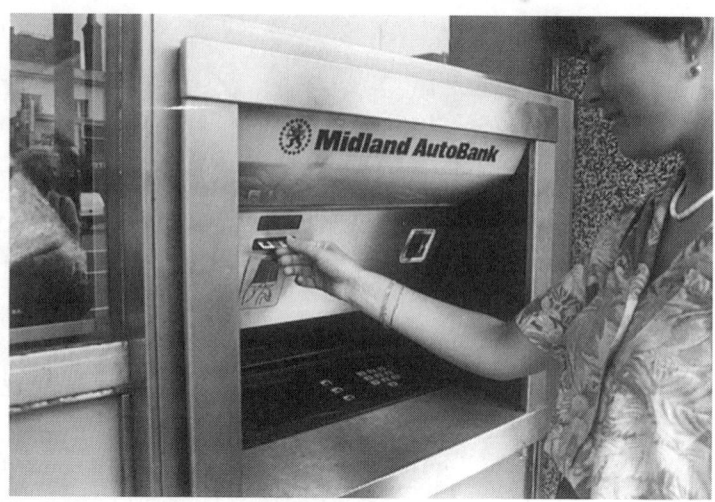

Miscellaneous bank services

Night safe
This facility is provided by banks to enable customers to deposit money when the bank is closed. Cash for depositing is placed in a special cash wallet together with a credit or paying-in slip. The wallet is dropped into the bank through a trap in the wall, and the amount enclosed is credited to the customer's account on the morning of the next bank working day. This service is particularly used by traders wishing to make deposits at the end of a day's trading.

Safe deposit box
This is a secure box kept in the bank's vault for the customers for the safe-keeping of valuables, important documents, etc.

Traveller's cheques
These are special cheques charged against a bank and, therefore, guaranteed by the bank. This makes them acceptable throughout the world and useful to the business person or the individual when travelling. They can be purchased at the local bank for use abroad to obtain foreign currency. The cheques are 'safe' because if they are lost or stolen abroad they can immediately be cancelled and the bank will replace them. A further safeguard requires those encashing the cheques to sign in front of those cashing them, having first produced proof of identity (e.g. passport).

Bill of exchange

A method of payment whereby the seller draws up a document and the buyer signs it (the opposite of the normal cheque transaction) agreeing to pay at some future date. The bill of exchange can be kept until payment is made, sold to someone else at a discount (*discounted*), or used as collateral against a loan (*negotiated*). These bills are particularly evident in international trade where exporters use them to guarantee payment for goods prior to despatch.

Bank draft

This is a cheque drawn on a bank instead of a person's account. A bank draft is guaranteed by the bank (which makes it as good as cash) because the customer pays the value of the draft in advance.

Banks also render a wide variety of services too numerous to deal with fully here, these include:

- investment advice;
- wills and trustee advice;
- sale of foreign currency;
- taxation guidance.

Borrowing from a bank

There are three main methods of borrowing from a bank: overdraft, loan and bridging loan. Banks often require some form of security (called 'collateral') to safeguard against possible non-repayment of the amount loaned. Collateral might take the form of property deeds, stocks and shares, or other items of value that can be sold by the bank in the event of default by the borrower.

The bank manager takes the following information into account before agreeing to allow a customer to borrow from the bank:

- income of the individual or organisation;
- debts and commitments of the borrower;
- assets owned by the borrower;
- past banking record of the borrower.

Note: Interest is the 'price' of borrowing money or the 'reward' for leaving money in the bank.

Overdraft

With permission of the bank the current account holder may write out cheques for more money than there is in the account. When this happens the account is said to be overdrawn or 'in the red'. The actual amount the account is overdrawn by is known as the *overdraft*.

Irrespective of what overdraft facility is granted, the customer is only charged interest (calculated daily) on the actual amount overdrawn. Any deposits made to the account while it is overdrawn have the effect of reducing the overdraft, while any cheques paid out increase it.

The overdraft tends to be used for temporary or short-term borrowing when the borrower is not sure exactly how much is needed, or for how long it is needed.

Loan

In the case of a bank loan, the total amount requested is transferred to the customer's account and, therefore, the customer is required to pay interest on the total amount borrowed, even if all the money is not used immediately.

The loan is repaid in regular fixed amounts, including interest, over a specific period of time agreed between the bank and the customer.

The bank loan tends to be used for a particular purpose when the amount required and length of repayment time is known, because the annual rate of interest on a loan is likely to be less than that of an overdraft.

Bridging loan

A bridging loan is provided by a bank as a temporary measure for a very short period (a few days or weeks) until other expected funds become available.

15.10 Activities

Make a note of it

1 Name the institutions which make up the British banking sector.
2 What do we mean when we say that the Bank of England is a central bank?
3 State one way in which the Bank of England influences the value of sterling.
4 Briefly describe the functions of the Bank of England and say how they differ from the functions of the commercial banks.
5 What is the purpose of the Bank of England's open market operations?
6 What do the letters MLR stand for? What is the purpose of MLR?
7 Briefly describe what is meant by 'money at call'.

8. What are 'special deposits'?
9. In what way does the Bank of England act as 'lender of last resort'?
10. Why are merchant banks sometimes referred to as acceptance houses?
11. In what way does a merchant bank help in raising capital for businesses?
12. List six other services which are provided by merchant banks for businesses.
13. What is the London discount market?
14. What are the main functions of discount houses?
15. Name the form of business that controls the majority of the UK instalment credit business.
16. In what way does National Girobank differ from other banks?
17. Why are commercial banks often referred to as 'clearing' banks'?
18. What are the four main functions of the clearing banks?
19. Compare a bank budget account with a personal budget.
20. Give a brief description of the deposit account.
21. How does the function of a current account differ from that of a deposit account?
22. What is a cheque? List the five things written on a cheque by the drawer.
23. Who is the drawer, the payee and the drawee of a cheque?
24. How is a cheque endorsed? What is the purpose of doing this?
25. In what way will a bank examine a cheque before passing it for payment?
26. Explain the difference between an open cheque and a crossed cheque.
27. Use simple diagrams to help you to explain the special ways a cheque may be crossed to make it safer.
28. What is a dishonoured cheque? Why might a cheque be dishonoured?
29. What is the function of a bank statement of account?
30. Explain clearly how the bankers' clearing system works.
31. What is EFTPOS and how does the system benefit both the trader and the shopper?
32. Compare the standing order and direct debit services.
33. Give a description of the bank giro service.

34 Briefly say why it is sometimes said that we have become a largely 'cashless' society.

35 Clearly explain the difference between a cheque card and a credit card.

36 What is the purpose of a cash dispenser card? What safeguards are there to prevent dishonest use of this service?

37 Explain the difference between a bank loan and a bank overdraft.

38 What factors does a bank manager take into account before agreeing to allow a customer to borrow from the bank?

39 How does a bridging loan differ from other forms of bank loan?

40 Why is the bank night safe service of particular use to retail traders?

41 What is the purpose of traveller's cheques? What makes them readily acceptable as well as 'safe'?

42 Why are bills of exchange particularly evident in international trade? Explain the difference between discounting and negotiating a bill of exchange.

43 Why would a bank draft be more acceptable than a cheque for making a large payment?

Structured Questions

1 This question is related to the bank cash dispenser system information on page 295.
   (a) Why is the machine referred to here called a 'cash dispenser'? (1)
   (b) What do the letters PIN stand for? (1)
   (c) Explain the words 'permitted daily amount' included in this explanation. (2)
   (d) The first question the bank will ask a customer who reports their cash dispenser card as stolen is usually, 'Has the PIN been revealed?' Why do you think this question is asked? (3)
   (e) Why do you think that different parts of the bank are involved in the issue of a cash card and PIN? (3)
   (f) In what way does the cash dispenser system make it difficult for someone to fraudulently obtain cash? (4)
   (g) State two checks that the bank computer carries out before issuing cash. (6)

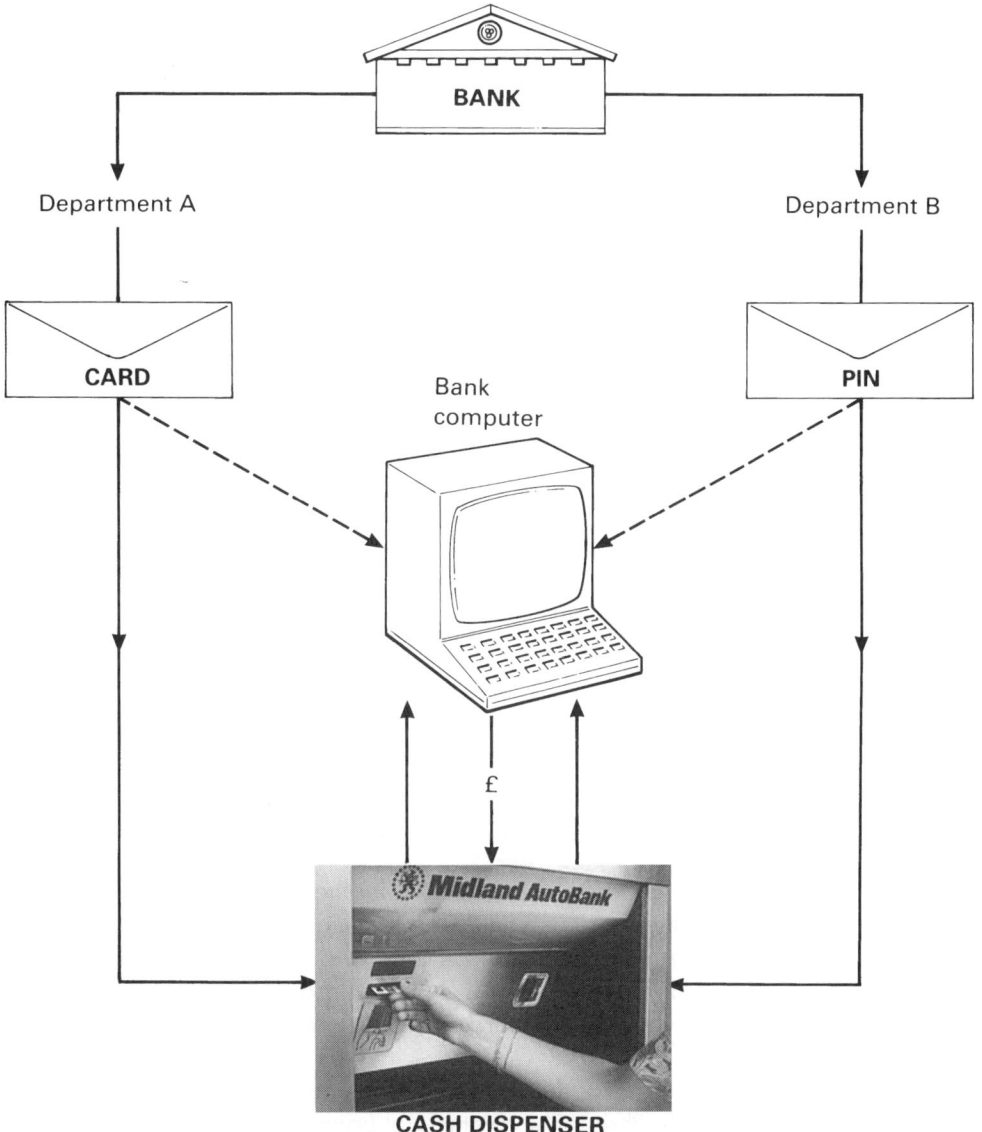

The cash dispenser system. Different departments of the bank are involved in the issue of a cash card. One department sends out the card which shows a number that can be 'read' by a cash dispenser. Another part of the bank issues a personal identification number (PIN) to the account holder. Both of these are filed in the bank computer. The account holder puts the cash card into the cash dispenser and keys in their PIN. Both numbers are relayed to the bank computer, and if they pair up correctly the machine will issue cash up to the permitted daily amount, so long as enough funds are available. The customer's account is debited immediately. Should some unauthorised person try to use the card, after the person has made a few unsuccessful attempts at obtaining money by guessing the PIN, the machine will confiscate the card.

2 Refer to the life assurance schedule below.

LIFE POLICY SCHEDULE

TYPE OF ASSURANCE
Certain "TYPES OF ASSURANCE" appearing in the schedule are defined below.

WHOLE LIFE
The benefit is payable on the death of the life assured.

ENDOWMENT
The benefit is payable on the termination date or previous death of the life assured.

TEMPORARY
The benefit is payable on the death of the life assured on or before the termination date.

FAMILY INCOME
The benefit is payable only if the life assured dies on or before the termination date and consists of annual instalments of a capital sum commencing on the date of death with subsequent instalments on each anniversary of that date. The last instalment shall fall due on the anniversary prior to the termination date and shall be proportionate to the remaining period.

THE ASSURED
DAVID H. LETCHFORD AND CHRISTINE A. MOODY

POLICY NUMBER
CR 2931812

COMMENCING
16. 6.1978

THE LIFE ASSURED	DATE OF BIRTH
DAVID H. LETCHFORD	12. 4.1954
CHRISTINE A. MOODY	10. 3.1954

TYPE OF ASSURANCE	BENEFIT	TERMINATION DATE
MORTGAGE ENDOWMENT	£11,000 DECREASING AS IN SCALE BELOW WITH PROFITS ON £1,100 PLUS	16. 6.2003
FAMILY INCOME	£1,100 PER ANNUM WITHOUT PROFITS	16. 6.2003

PREMIUM (ceasing on death of the life assured)	FIRST PAYMENT DUE	FREQUENCY	LAST PAYMENT DUE
£8.51	16. 6.1978	MONTHLY	16. 5.2003

WHERE PAYABLE	SURRENDER VALUE
LIVERPOOL	AFTER FOUR YEARS' PREMIUMS PAID

ADDITIONAL INFORMATION
REFERENCES TO THE DEATH OF THE LIFE ASSURED SHALL MEAN THE FIRST OF THE LIVES ASSURED TO DIE.

THE POLICY SHALL BE SUBJECT TO THE SPECIAL OPTIONS ATTACHED HERETO.
IF DEATH OCCURS WITHIN 3 YEARS PRIOR TO THE TERMINATION DATE THREE ANNUAL INSTALMENTS OF FAMILY INCOME SHALL BE PAYABLE.

ADDITIONAL INFORMATION
THE MORTGAGE ENDOWMENT BENEFIT AS IN SCALE BELOW IS PAYABLE ON DEATH IN YEAR ENDING ON DATE SHOWN OR £1,100 PAYABLE ON SURVIVAL TO THE TERMINATION DATE, WITH PROFITS IN EITHER EVENT ON £1,100

16.6.79	£11,000	16.6.88	£9,911	16.6.97	£6,644
16.6.80	£10,934	16.6.89	£9,702	16.6.98	£6,006
16.6.81	£10,857	16.6.90	£9,460	16.6.99	£5,280
16.6.82	£10,769	16.6.91	£9,196	16.6.00	£4,466
16.6.83	£10,659	16.6.92	£8,888	16.6.01	£3,553
16.6.84	£10,549	16.6.93	£8,536	16.6.02	£2,508
16.6.85	£10,417	16.6.94	£8,151	16.6.03	£1,331
16.6.86	£10,274	16.6.95	£7,711		
16.6.87	£10,109	16.6.96	£7,205		

(a) What is the premium payable under the policy shown? (1)

(b) What is the maximum time the premium is payable for? (1)

(c) Calculate the amount that C Moody would receive from the family income part of the policy if D H Letchford died on 2.4.2002.

(d) Explain why D H Letchford and C Moody may have taken out this policy. (3)

(e) The premiums for this policy could be paid by standing order or direct debit through a commercial bank. Explain how each of these facilities operate and say, with a reason, which you feel would be most appropriate in this case. (5)

(f) Compare an endowment policy to any Savings scheme as a method of saving. (8)

3 Look at the bill on page 297.

(a) With which bank do the Essex Water Company hold their account? (1)

(b) (i) Calculate the total standing charge on this bill. (1)
    (ii) Why are standing charges levied? (2)

(c) If Mr Leicester paid this bill by cheque through the post, on the cheque who would be:
    (i) the payee;

Banking

ESSEX WATER COMPANY

Principal Office: Hall Street, Chelmsford, Essex CM2 0HH
Revenue Office: P.O. Box 700, Chelmsford, Essex CM2 0DP

If you have a query about this bill please telephone
CHELMSFORD (0245) 491011

WATER SERVICES BILL

For all other queries please telephone Chelmsford (0245) 491234

Customer Reference Number	Owner No.	Supply size in millimetres Water / Sewerage	Year Commencing
433 852 00301 6		15	1ST APR 1999

MR W LEICESTER
42 GREEN LANE
CHELMSFORD
CM23 9HQ

433 S T A T E M E N T
852 - - - - - - - - - -
00301 FOR INFORMATION ONLY

RE:

Rateable Value £	Yearly Rate p in £	Rate Based Charge £	Standing Charge £	Amount £	Total £
WATER SUPPLY CHARGES FOR ESSEX WATER COMPANY					
302	12.000	36.24	14.00	50.24	50.24
SEWERAGE-ENVIRONMENTAL CHARGE FOR ANGLIAN W.A.					
302	28.490	86.04	23.40	109.44	109.44

YOU MAY SETTLE THIS ACCOUNT BY A SINGLE PAYMENT OF XXXXXXXX REACHING THE COMPANY

ANNUAL AMOUNT DUE £ 159.68

PAYMENT WILL BE AUTOMATICALLY DEDUCTED FROM YOUR ACCOUNT - SEE DETAILS BELOW

ALTERNATIVE INSTALMENTS AND VARIOUS WAYS TO PAY ARE EXPLAINED ON THE BACK OF THIS BILL

Girobank National Trans cash Bootle Merseyside GIR 0AA | **PAYMENT SLIP** | **Bank Giro Credit**

	Customer reference number	Credit account number	Amount due	By transfer from Girobank a/c No
135 205	433 852 00301 6	357 0959	£	

Cashier's Stamp   ITEMS
Signature ....   Date ....
FEE   57-09-59   National Westminster H.O. Collection Account Essex Water Company

Total Cash
Cheques etc.
£

Name of Customer: MR
Year Commencing: 1ST APR 99

Please do not write or mark below this line

IN ACCORDANCE WITH YOUR SIGNED MANDATE YOUR VISA CARD ACCOUNT WILL BE DEBITED FOR £79.84 ON 28/04/88 AND FOR £79.84 ON 28/10/88

V7003570959 91   X

(ii) the drawer;
(iii) the drawee? (3)
(d) In the interest of security such a cheque should be crossed. What could Mr Leicester write between the lines of the crossing to make the cheque safer? (1)
(e) How is this particular bill going to be paid? (2)
(f) State two advantages of using this method of payment from the point of view of:
(i) Mr Leicester;
(ii) The Essex Water Company. (4)
(g) Describe two ways in which this bill could be paid with the aid of National Girobank. (6)

Buying on credit

Most people need to buy on credit at some time in their life, particularly when purchasing consumer durables which become increasingly important once we set up a home of our own.

There are times when we need to purchase something essential, such as a cooker, which is beyond our immediate means. But advertisements frequently tell us that 'credit facilities are available'.

If you want to purchase a modern cooker, you may well have to pay £400. Often you will be required to pay a deposit calculated as a percentage of the cash price. The balance would be required to be repaid in regular instalments over a period of time.

If you are under 18 years of age you will be unable to undertake a formal purchase on credit due to a law that prevents this. However, your parents could act as guarantor on a credit purchase made by you.

Source: CSO, *Financial Statistics*

Banking

4 Consider the data on page 298 and answer the questions which follow.

(a) What does the term 'credit' means? (1)

(b) How does a parent acting as 'guarantor' make it possible for someone under 18 years of age to enter into a credit agreement? (2)

(c) What is meant by the 'cash price' in relation to a credit purchase? (2)

(d) Why do 'consumer durables' become increasingly important once we set up a home of our own? (3)

(e) Explain how the bank standing order service assists someone making repayments against a credit agreement. (3)

(f) Complete the following table of data related to the purchase of a cooker on credit:

Cash price	£400
Minus 10% deposit	?
Plus interest	£120
Balance	?
12 payments of	?

(3)

(g) How does a credit sale agreement differ from a hire purchase agreement? (6)

Research Assignments

1 What evidence is there that we are now largely a cashless society?

2 Make a comparison between a commercial bank and another financial institution as a means of money transfer from the point of view of a large business organisation.

3 Choose any large firm selling consumer durables and describe the various methods of payment it allows customers to use. State which methods you would personally prefer, giving reasons for your choice.

4 A business has a project that is expected to earn a 10 per cent rate of return each year. How will interest rates influence the decision of the business on whether to proceed or not? To what extent will this be likely to be related to the government's monetary policy?

5 Explain the differences between central banks, merchant banks, commercial banks and building societies. Refer to the *Yellow Pages* for your area and count the number of each in your area. Comment on your findings.

6 How do interest rates affect the demand for money? Does it matter?

16 Business Finance

16.1 Sources of finance

Finance is a business's most important resource because it is through finance that a business obtains all its other resources. Money itself is less important to a business than the assets that are bought with it and are used in the business to create wealth for the firm. Money (and the things bought with it) used in a business is known as *capital*.

A business needs sufficient capital to get started, and once it is established, it needs further finance to keep trading or to meet the cost of expansion. Finance is needed to meet expenses, such as wages and raw materials, or to buy machinery or premises. Money is not as important to a business as the ability to use it to create *revenue* (or *income*) for the business.

Start-up finance

Money has to be provided to start up a business. The entrepreneur can use their own money or someone else's. It is often the case that the initial capital will come from both these sources. The problem with using someone else's money is that it must be repaid at some time, and *interest* will have to be paid while the *loan* is in effect. The interest paid has the effect of reducing the profit the business achieves. For this reason, borrowing from others tends to be a short-term option for business finance.

Government grants and loans

Governments want to encourage businessess to form and prosper because this provides employment for the population and creates national wealth. The help provided by governments frequently changes but can include grants and loans, taxation concessions, buildings at special low rents, relocation grants, etc.

Longer-term finance

All businesses need longer-term finance as they grow in order to sustain their growth and prosperity. This longer-term finance can come from internal and external sources.

Internal sources of finance refers to the capital the business generates itself:

- *retained profits:* profit created by the business and not taken out by the owners.

- *the sale of assets:* a business may sell assets (e.g. some of its shops) to raise finance to expand another division of the business. The business would need to take care to ensure it was not selling assets that are vital to the future prosperity of the firm.

External sources of finance are funds that the business raises from sources outside its operations:

- *bank overdrafts:* these are a flexible form of borrowing since there are no fixed repayment schedules and interest is only charged on amounts outstanding.
- *factoring:* this involves a business passing its debts to a specialist financial institution known as a *factoring company*. The factoring company pays the business the value of the debts owed to it – less its own charges (which can be high). The factoring company then assumes full responsibility for collecting the amounts owed.
- *hire purchase:* a business may purchase equipment and pay for it by regular, predetermined instalments over a specific period of time. Interest is usually payable for such arrangements. However, sometimes an *interest-free* facility is given.
- *leasing:* this is an arrangement whereby a business (the *lessee*) pays for the use of equipment over a period of time. The equipment remains the property of the owner (the *lessor*). At the end of the lease period the lessee might have the option of purchasing the equipment at a favourable price.
- *longer-term bank loans:* this form of finance is usually used for specific development plans such as purchase of additional premises or machinery. Such loans usually carry a fixed rate of interest, and repayments have to be made within an agreed schedule.
- *additional owners:* by taking in a new *partner* or selling *shares* new capital is created for the business. However, in doing this, control of the business by the original owners is diluted.

16.2 Financial projections

Deciding a price

The primary aim of a business is to make a profit for its owners or shareholders. How successful the business is in achieving this aim depends upon how efficiently its capital is employed. You will see later that it is possible to get an idea of a business's success by examining the financial facts and figures set out in its accounts and balance sheet. But how does a business set about making a profit?

One of the most tricky questions for a firm to answer is what price should it charge for its goods or services. At first glance, this looks a simple question to answer. Surely all that needs to be done is to add up all the costs incurred in producing the goods or service and then add on a bit extra as profit, making sure that the eventual selling price remains in line with competitors.

However, firms incur two different types of costs, namely *fixed* and *variable*. Fixed costs (e.g. rent and business rates) are relatively constant up to the point where a business decides to change significantly the scale of its operations. These are costs that have to be met even if a firm's output is just one item. One the other hand, variable costs (e.g. materials and wages) change in accordance with a firm's level of output; thus, as output goes up so do total variable costs. However, it is not practicable to add up these two costs until a decision has been made about how much a firm plans to sell.

Example

A firm sells only one product and has only two relatively fixed costs, ie rent and business rates. Its variable costs are £20 per article produced.

Rent and business rates	£10,000
Cost of producting 1,000 units	£20,000
Total costs	£30,000

The cost of producing each article is £30 (ie £30,000 divided by 1,000).

So to make a profit, the firm must sell each article for more than £30. If the goods are priced at £35 each and all 1,000 items are sold, there will be a profit of £5,000 (£35 × 1,000 *less* £30,000 costs).

But what happens if the firm decides to produce 2,000 units? Fixed costs remain at £10,000 while production costs double to £40,000. However, the cost per article reduces to £25 because the fixed costs are spread over a greater number of articles. And if all 2,000 items are sold at £35 each, profits increase fourfold to £20,000 (ie £70,000 revenue *less* £50,000 costs).

On the other hand, if the firm produced 1,000 articles but only sold 500, its revenue would drop to £17,500 and there will be a loss of £12,500.

There are many other ways of deciding a price when marketing goods and services, and these variety of approaches are dealt with in Chapter 8.

Breaking even

You can see from the above that there is a need to keep several factors in focus at the same time, e.g. costs, sales, volume, selling price and profit margin. The manner of doing this lies in a sales volume/price equation applied over a given period of time. This equation is shown in graphical form on page 303.

In the graph, the vertical axis shows the value of sales and costs in £000s and the horizontal axis shows units of sales volume in thousands. In this case the volume is 60 000 units.

The lower horizontal line represents the fixed costs. These do not change as the volume of sales increase. The graph shows an example of fixed costs of £3000. The next horizontal line shows the firm's profit objective (what it is aiming to achieve). In this case it is £2000. To obtain this profit, sales of 60 000 units for a total of £8000 will have to be reached.

The top angled line represents the variable costs. There costs vary directly with

Business Finance

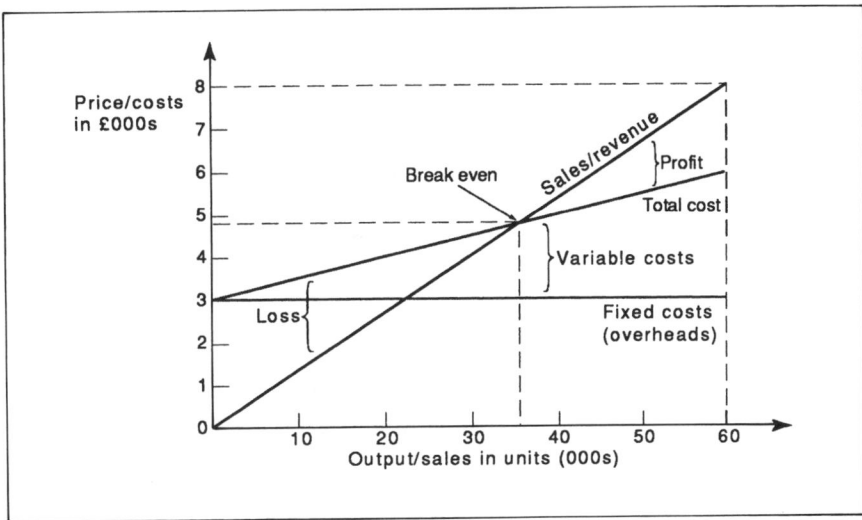

output and include items such as raw materials; every extra unit produced adds to variable costs.

The lower angled line shows how much sales revenue is needed to cover fixed costs and variable costs (to *break even*). In this hypothetical case it is necessary to sell 36 000 units to break even.

From this illustration it can be seen that 'break even' is the point where income from sales equals costs. In other words, it is the point which sales must exceed in order for a profit to be achieved. Conversely, if sales do not reach break-even point the business will make a loss.

16.3 Cash flow

Even though a business may be in a profitable position, it may find on a day-to-day basis that its income is less than its costs. The relationship between money coming into a business and money going out is known as *cash flow*. From the diagram, you will see that unless receipts from sales equal the level of expenses, the firm will have a cash flow problem.

A business can try to asses its cash flow position by drawing up a *cash flow statement*, showing how much money is expected to come into the business over a period of time, and how much it is expecting to have to pay out.

Example

The Florida Trading Company produces ornamental pots. Of whatever it sells, 50 per cent of its income goes in expenses. Most customers take at least four weeks to pay for the goods supplied. Today, in the fourteenth week of this year's trading, Florida has received an order of £5000 worth of pots. Should it accept the order? At first sight the answer to this might seem to be obviously 'yes'. But look at the simple cash flow forecast on page 304 and then see what you think.

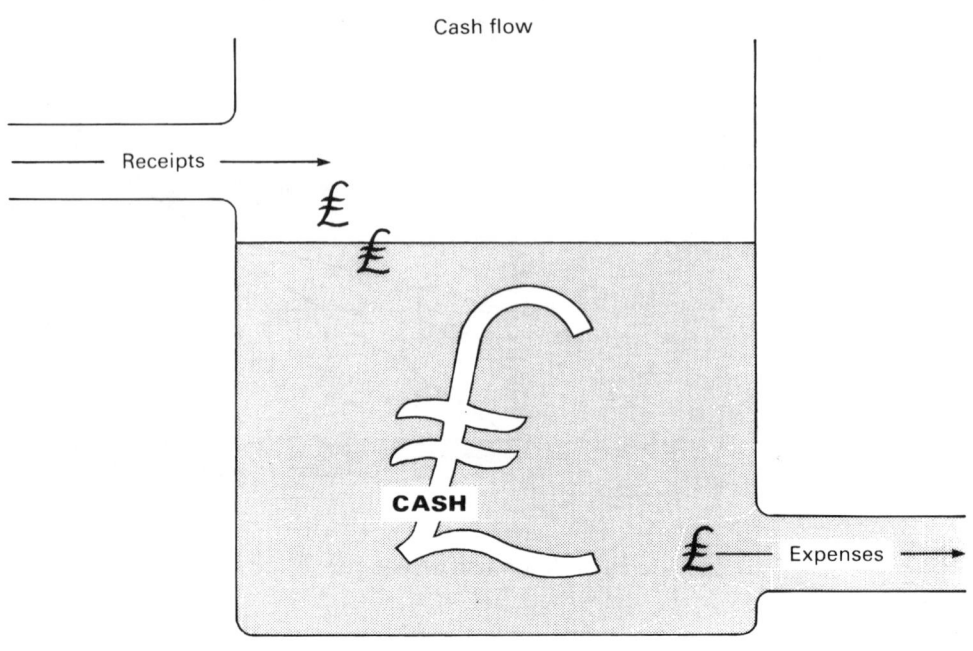

Cash flow forecast **Florida Trading Company Ltd**					
Week	11	12	13	14	15
Cash at bank	£5000	£3500	£3000	£1500	?
Order received	£5000	£5000	£5000	£5000	?
Cost of production	£2500	£2500	£2500	£2500	?
Cash receipt	£1000	£2000	£1000	Nil	?

From the cash flow forecast you can see that at the start of week 11 of this year's trading Florida had £5000 at the bank. It then received an order worth £5000 which will cost £2500 to produce. In that same week one of its customers paid Florida £1000. On this basis Florida started week 12 with a cash balance of £3500 (£5000 minus £2500 plus £1000 = £3500). Now follow this process through to weeks 14 and 15 – you will see that Florida has a cash flow problem. This is sometimes called a 'liquidity problem'.

The difficulty described here does not mean that Florida should not accept the new order, but it does mean that they have to decide how they will finance the cost of production if they do accept it. Should they borrow from the bank – which will take some of their profit? Should they pressurise some of their customers to pay outstanding debts – which may cause them to lose customers?

To achieve even cash flow is far from simple. It is important to recognise that payment for goods or services supplied will often not be received until some future date. This means that the business must budget with this possibility in mind.

Business Finance

A firm's cash flow position might be improved by obtaining *trade credit* from suppliers by getting them to wait for payment for a mutually agreed period for goods or services supplied. Another way of solving a cashflow problem is by using a 'factor'. A firm that is owed money can 'sell' its debts to a type of business called a 'factor'. The factor collects all the payment due and pays the firm the amount owed, less the charges for the factoring service. A greater percentage of the payments due may even be paid by the factor before they have been collected. The charges for the factoring service can be very high but can solve a cash flow problem and can also save a business the cost of employing its own staff for debt collection. However, factoring also eats into profits.

16.4 Costs and revenues

A business can be looked on as a simple system: it buy things (*inputs*), it does something (a *process*) to the inputs and then sells the results of that process (*outputs*). The outputs could be goods or services (the enterprise's *product*). The product(s) could be made by the business, or they could be items bought for resale.

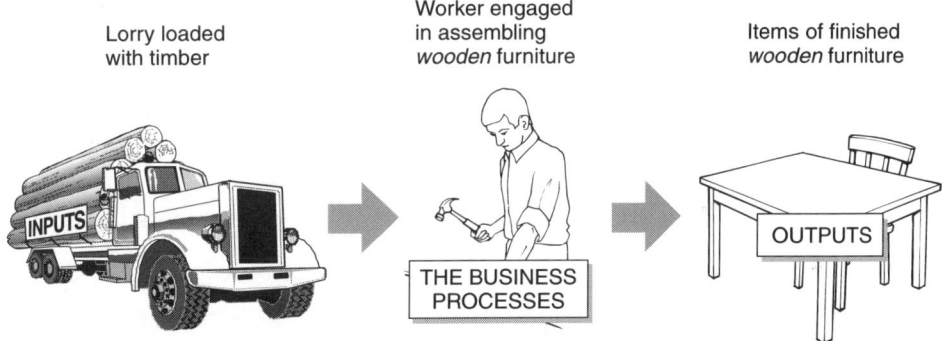

A business can be seen as a simple process

The money that a business uses to pay for its inputs is called its *costs*. These costs can be devided into *fixed costs* and *variable costs*.

Fixed costs are those that have to be paid and do not alter (hence term *fixed*), irrespective of what the level of output is. Examples are; rent on premises, insurance premiums, business rates, office salaries and interest on loans.

Variable costs are related to output, and vary (go up and down) in line with the level of output, e.g. the amount of business done. Examples are raw materials and other stocks used, wages and electricity related to producing or selling, and transport.

It is useful to bear in mind that even fixed costs can change in the long term because, if output increases sufficiently, these may have to increase. For example, increased shop, office, or factory space may be needed. By adding together fixed costs and variable costs, we arrive at the *total costs* of the business. The enterprise must cover these costs in order to make a profit. It is important that a business keeps control over its costs in order to *maximise* its profits (achieve the best possible). For example, a producer will want to ensure it keeps raw materials wastage as low as possible, and a retailer will want to deter shoplifting.

The money a business receives from selling its products or services is its income or *revenue*. The revenue of a business is linked to the price and volume of its outputs. The greater the volume, the greater will be the revenue (but not necessarily a greater profitability). A business will want to sell each unit of output at a price greater than the total cost of the unit. This additional sum is called the *profit element* or *mark-up*. (See also Chapter 8.)

16.5 A firm's accounts

As you read earlier, it is possible to find out information about the 'healthiness' of a business from its accounts. All businesses are required to prepare accounts at the end of their financial year for tax purposes, but only public companies are required to publish their accounts.

The main accounts are the *Trading Account* and the *Profit and Loss Account*. The Trading Account compares the cost of stock sold against income from sales in order to determine the *gross profit* or *loss* for the period in question (usually a year).

Turnover

This refers to the gross income or sales of an organisation over the previous year. Turnover can indicate how 'active' the firm has been in a given period. Generally speaking, the greater the turnover the more business the firm is doing, although this is not always the case.

Net turnover

This is calculated by taking the total sales of the business minus the value of goods returned or credit notes issued.

Rate of turnover/rate of stock turn

Rate of turnover is the number of times the average stock of business has been sold in the year. There are two methods of calculating the rate of stock turnover depending whether the stock is looked at in terms of cost price or selling price:

$$(1) \text{ Rate of turnover} = \frac{\text{Cost of stock sold}}{\text{Average stock at cost price}}$$

$$(2) \text{ Rate of turnover} = \frac{\text{Net turnover}}{\text{Average stock at selling price}}$$

Average stock is worked out by taking the stock value at the beginning and at the end of the trading period, adding them, and dividing by two.

Example

		£
Jan 1	Stock	4 000
Dec 31	Stock	6 000 +
		£10 000

$$\text{Average stock} \quad \frac{£10\,000}{2} = £5\,000$$

Applicatiom

Daly Designs plc has a net turnover of £50 000 and average stock at cost price is £5 000

$$\frac{50\,000}{5\,000} = 10 = \text{Rate of stock turnover}$$

Importance of rate turnover

Rate of turnover is important because it indicates how 'busy' the firm is. The figure can be used to make comparisons with the previous years of trading or with the rate of other firms engaged in the same type of business.

An increasing rate of turnover indicates that the firm is doing more business in real terms, assuming all other things remain unchanged. It is selling more products, so profits should also be increasing.

Firms involved in different forms of business will have varying rates of turnover. For example, a grocery store will have a far higher rate of turnover than a jewellers.

16.6 Profit

Profit is the reward the business person receives for taking the risk involved in business and for being able to combine all the factors required to produce and sell goods or services.

The profitability of a business can be looked at from the point of view of gross profit or net profit.

Gross profit

The gross profit of a firm is the net sales minus the cost of the goods sold. Gross profit can be expressed as a percentage of the cost or selling price.

Comprehensive Business Studies

Example

	£
Selling price	1.00
Cost price	0.75
Gross profit	0.25

$$\text{Mark-up (on cost price)} = \frac{25}{75} \times 100 = 33\frac{1}{3}\%$$

$$\text{Profit margin (on selling price)} = \frac{25}{100} \times 100 = 25\%$$

Gross profit takes no account of the overheads the business has to pay, for example wages, advertising, heating, etc.

As a percentage figure gross profit can be used for comparison with previous trading periods, and with the gross profit of other firms. The method for calculating the gross profit percentage is as follows:

$$\text{Gross profit percentage} = \frac{\text{Gross profit}}{\text{Turnover}} \times 100$$

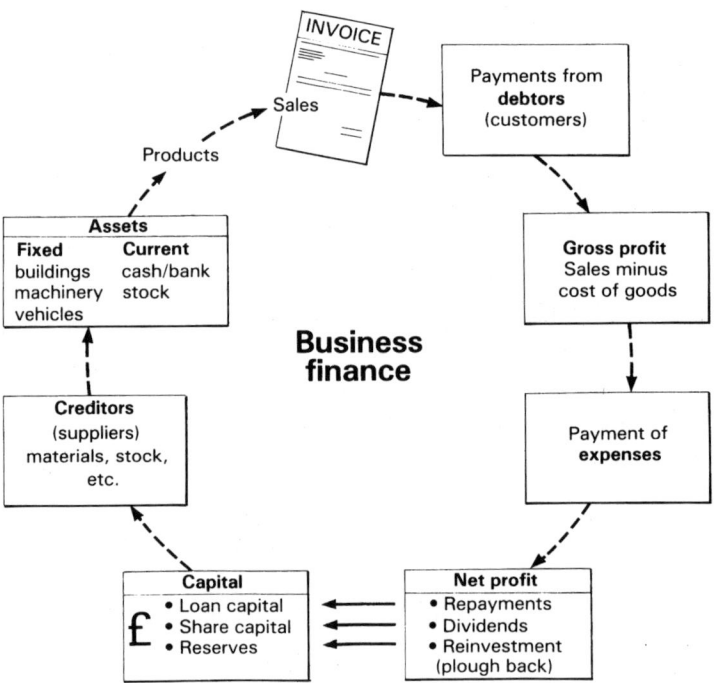

Example

	£
Turnover	80 000
Cost of goods	60 000
Gross profit	£20 000

As a percentage $\dfrac{20\,000}{80\,000} \times 100 = 25\%$

Falling gross profit

Most businesses require a gross profit of between 20 per cent and 40 per cent to ensure they are covering their overheads (expenses) easily. Over the years, gross profit percentage should stay relatively stable. If it starts to drop there is cause for concern. If it drops too much the business may fail to cover its overheads, and start to make an overall loss. There are a number of reasons for falling gross profit percentage including:

- staff stealing stock or takings;
- stock being damaged or allowed to perish;
- rising cost of stock not being passed on to customers.

Net profits

This is the residue of gross profit after allowing for expenses incurred in carrying on the business such as wages, rent, rates, advertising and bills of all kinds.

Net profit = Gross profit − Expenses

If expressed as a percentage, net profit can be used to make comparisons.

Method

$$\text{net profit percentage} = \dfrac{\text{Net profit}}{\text{Turnover}} \times 100$$

16.7 Balance sheets

A *balance sheet* shows the financial position of a business at a particular point in time: it is a 'snapshot' of the business's financial status. The balance sheet shows what the business owns (its assets) and what it owes (its liabilities).

Balance Sheet **Daly Designs plc** as at 31 Decmber 19—

Liabilities	£	Assets	£
Capital owned	100 000	Fixed assets	
Long-term liabilities		Land & Buildings	80 000
Mortgage	44 000	Equipment/Fittings	20 000
		Vehicles	10 000
Current liabilities		Current assets	
Tax to be paid	2 400	Stock*	32 000
Bank overdraft	5 600	Debtors	12 000
Creditors	8 000	Bank balance	5 400
		Cash float	600
	£160 000		£160 000

*at cost price

The items in a balance sheet are usually analysed under the following headings:

Fixed capital/assets
Durable (long-term) assets of a business which are used over a long period of time and are tied up in permanent use. Examples: land, buildings, machinery, furniture, vehicles, etc.

Circulating capital/ current assets (working capital)
Capital which is continually changing in quantity, total value or nature. Examples: stocks, cash, bank balance, and the amount of money owed to a firm by its customers (debtors).

Employed capital
This is the total value of long term capital employed in the firm and includes issued share capital plus reserves plus long term loans.

Current liabilities
Debts which will have to be repaid in the near future. Examples: bank overdraft, debts owed to suppliers (creditors), taxes payable to the government, etc.

Capital owned
Net value of the assets owned by a business. In other words, it is total assets minus current liabilities.

Liquid capital
That part of the current assets which are cash or are easily changeable into cash without delay, for example bank balance, cash in tills and debts owed by others (debtors).

Business Finance

Net working capital

Current assets minus the current liabilities. Net working capital is particularly important because it takes into account the possibility of all the creditors to the business calling for payment. Therefore, it is important for a business to have sufficient working capital to exist as far as possible without borrowing from a bank.

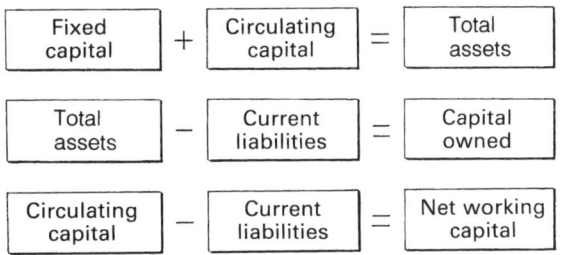

Daly Designs plc

	£		£		£	£		£
1 Fixed capital	80 000	+	?	+	10 000		=	110 000
2 Circulating capital	?	+	12 000	+	?	+ 600	=	?
3 Employed capital	100 000	+	?				=	?
4 Current liabilities	?		?		?		=	16 000
5 Capital owned	?	−	?				=	144 000
6 Liquid capital	12 000	+	?	+	?		=	18 000
7 New working capital	?	−	16 000				=	?

Refer to the balance sheet on p. 310 and complete the above analysis of the trading figures of Daly Designs plc.

An important analysis of a firm's balance sheet is its *liquid capital ratio*, frequently referred to as the *acid test*. The purpose of this test is to establish whether the business can meet its short term debts without having to sell any of the stocks it holds, which might take some time to convert into cash. The acid test ratio is the value of the current assets less stock as a proportion of the value of the sum total of current liabilities.

For the owners of the business, another important analysis is the *return on capital invested*, which shows how much profit has been made as a percentage of the capital originally put into the business. The return on investment must be sufficient to make it worthwhile for the owners of the business to face the risks of business. If the return on the investment is not sufficient the owner(s) may be tempted to place their money in other less risky forms of investment.

$$\text{Return on capital invested} = \frac{\text{Net profit}}{\text{Capital at start of year}} \times 100$$

16.8 Activities

1. Why is finance so important to businesses?
2. What is 'start-up finance'?
3. How would you say that the term 'capital' is broader than the word 'money'?
4. Why do you think it is useful to divide sources of business finance into 'internal' and 'external' sources?
5. Briefly describe two internal sources of business finance and external sources.
6. What is the main aim of a business?
7. Describe the difference between fixed and variable costs and explain why the unit cost per article decreases when output increases.
8. What do you understand by the term 'breaking even'?
9. What steps must a firm take in order to avoid creating a cash flow problem?
10. Give three examples each of 'fixed' and 'variable' costs.
11. Why is it important for a firm to control its costs?
12. How do we establish the 'total cost' of a good or service?
13. Why does increased revenue not necessarily result in increased profit?
14. Define 'turnover'. Explain the difference between gross turnover and net turnover.
15. What is 'rate of turnover' and why is this important to a firm?
16. The following figure relate to Akela Ltd:

    Jan 1   Stock   £ 6 000
    Dec 31   Stock   £ 9 000
    Net turnover   £60 000

    Calculate the rate of stock turnover and estimate whether the rate would be good for a butcher's shop. Give reasons for your answers.
17. Explain the relevance of 'high', 'low' and 'increasing' rates of turnover to the business person.

18. Define 'profit' and explain the difference between gross profit and net profit.

19 Give three examples of 'overheads'.

20 State at least four reasons that might account for a falling gross profit.

21 What is the purpose of a balance sheet? What kind of information is contained in a balance sheet?

22 Explain the main difference between 'assets' and 'liabilities'.

23 A firm has fixed capital of £60 000, circulating capital of £6 000 and £7 000 current liabilities. What is its capital owned and its net working capital?

24 What is the 'acid test' and why is it an important measure of a firm's balance sheet?

25 Why is the 'return on capital invested' an important figure to the owners of a business?

Structured Questions

1 Sources of capital funds (£m) for industrial and commercial companies 1992–1997

	1992	1993	1994	1995	1996	1997
Retained profit	24 328	18 618	20 569	18 236	26 771	33 019
Bank borrowing	3 981	6 340	5 847	6 568	1 552	7 967
Ordinary shares	879	900	1 660	1 033	1 872	1127
Debentures and preference shares	−22	523	738	245	608	249
Other	3 167	2 590	3 069	3 175	3 733	1 350
Total	32 333	28 971	32 621	29 257	34 536	43 712

(a) How much capital was raised by the sale of ordinary shares in 1997? (1)

(b) Calculate the percentage of the total capital (to the nearest 5%) that the most popular source represented in 1997. (2)

(c) What explanations can you suggest for the low investment through bank borrowing in 1990? (2)

(d) State three factors that a bank would take into account before granting a business a loan. (3)

(e) If you own a large number of shares in a company which needed £$\frac{1}{4}$ million to finance expansion, would you prefer the capital to come from (i) retained profits (ii) the issue of new shares or (iii) through a bank loan? Give reasons for your choice. (4)

(f) What role is played by (i) merchant banks and (ii) the Stock Exchange in the raising of new capital for industry? (8)

Comprehensive Business Studies

2 Refer to the data about wealth creation and the figure below, and answer the questions:

(a) How much money has the firm put back into the business this year? (1)

(b) If the firm spent £229.6m on raw materials, etc., and achieved sales of £308.8m., why is it not possible to say that the firm made £79.2m profit? (2)

Wealth: its creation and distribution by a company

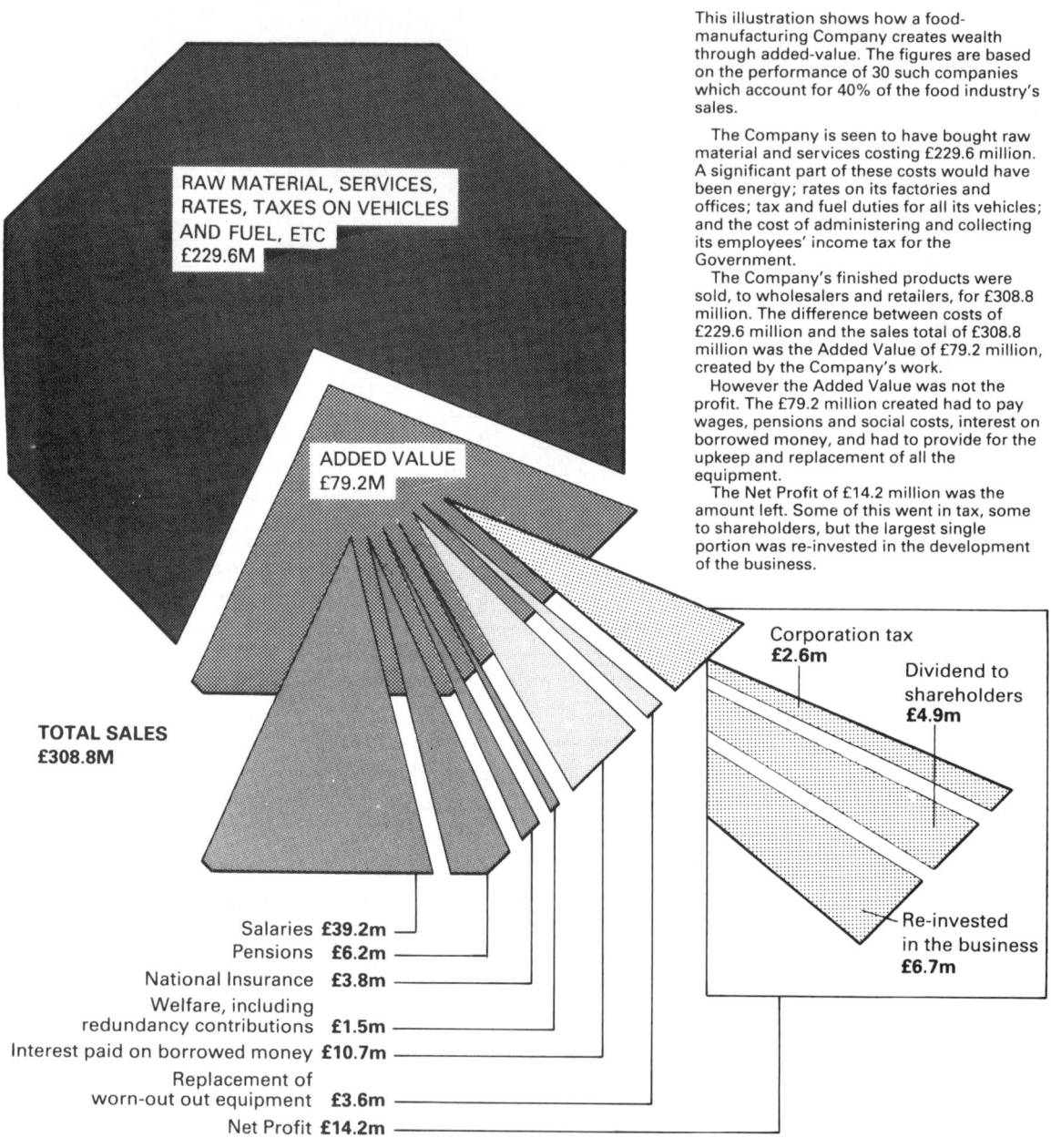

This illustration shows how a food-manufacturing Company creates wealth through added-value. The figures are based on the performance of 30 such companies which account for 40% of the food industry's sales.

The Company is seen to have bought raw material and services costing £229.6 million. A significant part of these costs would have been energy; rates on its factories and offices; tax and fuel duties for all its vehicles; and the cost of administering and collecting its employees' income tax for the Government.

The Company's finished products were sold, to wholesalers and retailers, for £308.8 million. The difference between costs of £229.6 million and the sales total of £308.8 million was the Added Value of £79.2 million, created by the Company's work.

However the Added Value was not the profit. The £79.2 million created had to pay wages, pensions and social costs, interest on borrowed money, and had to provide for the upkeep and replacement of all the equipment.

The Net Profit of £14.2 million was the amount left. Some of this went in tax, some to shareholders, but the largest single portion was re-invested in the development of the business.

(c) Part of the added value was used to pay 'social costs'. Give two examples of social costs included in the data. (2)
(d) Define the term 'overheads' and give two examples of overheads this firm has to meet. (2)
(e) How does net profit differ from gross profit and how much gross profit did this company make? (3)
(f) Explain the words corporation tax and dividend used in the data. (4)
(g) In what ways does the data shown demonstrate that this firm is generating wealth as well as profit for its owners. (6)

3 Read the following data and the extract below from the quotation that Akela Ltd has received for the purchase or lease of a 16 workstation computer system with a file server.

IT: RENT OR LEASE?

Many companies fail to recognise the true cost of buying their own information technology equipment, or how much it costs to maintain it.

It is a fact that companies also frequently fail to include depreciation allowances in their costings. Consequently, it is not unusual to find that when the time comes to renew equipment some firms find themselves hard pushed to finance replacement. Sometimes the answer can lie in leasing.

Leasing refers to annual renting of equipment as opposed to outright purchase. It is usual for such arrangements to be linked to specific time contracts, e.g. three-year or five-year lease. Often the difference in cost between purchase and lease over, say, a five year period is minimal, but leasing can be attractive as a means of solving a cash flow problem.

Purchase price
£30 066
  +£793 annual maintenance

Lease (per year)
£11 590 3 year contract
£7 562 5 year contract

(a) What do the letters IT stand for? (1)
(b) Briefly explain the difference between leasing and purchase. (2)
(c) How can leasing help to solve a cash flow problem? (2)
(d) What is 'depreciation' and why is it important that a firm includes allowances for this in their costings? (3)
(e) Assuming Akela Ltd purchased outright, what would be its total cost, including maintenance:
   (i) over a three year period?
   (ii) over a five year period?
   Clearly show all workings and give one advantage of outright purchase over a leasing arrangement. (3)
(f) What would be the cost in total for Akela to lease the equipment:

(i) for a three year contract?
(ii) for a five year contract?
    Show your calculations and say why there would be no
    maintenance costs involved. (3)
(g) Using data supplied in the quotation to Akela Ltd, write a report to
the Finance Director summarising the alternative courses of action
that could be taken regarding purchase or leasing, and making your
own recommendation. Give reasons for your choice. (6)

4 Refer to the balance sheet for Daly Designs plc on page 310 and answer these questions.

(a) What type of business organisation is Daly Designs? (1)
(b) Which date of each year would Daly Designs consider to be the start
of their financial year? (1)
(c) What is the purpose of a balance sheet? (2)
(d) Other than the shareholders of the company, state two groups of
people who would be particularly interested in reading the accounts
of Daly Designs. (2)
(e) Give two examples of current liabilities that could be owed by Daly
Designs and say why it is important that these should not grow too
high. (3)
(f) Who are likely to be Daly Designs' 'debtors' and how has their debt
likely to have been created? (3)
(g) Name four items that could be included in the fixed assets figure of
'equipment and fittings'. (4)
(h) Write down one example of each of the following and distinguish
between each of them:
(i) fixed assets and current assets;
(ii) liabilities and assets. (4)

5 Refer to the illustration on page 308. The following questions are all related to
the circular flow diagram shown.

(a) What is the purpose of an invoice? (1)
(b) Define the term 'fixed assets'. (1)
(c) One of the examples of current assets shown listed in the diagram is
stock. Give two reasons why it is important that a firm does not hold
too much stock? (2)
(d) How is the gross profit figure obtained? (2)
(e) What are 'dividends' in relation to business finance? (2)
(f) Explain the meaning of the term 'reinvestment' used in the diagram. (2)
(g) Distinguish between the following forms of capital – loan capital,
share capital and reserves. (3)
(h) Explain the differences between gross profit and net profit. What are
the implications for a firm if its expenses exceed its gross profit? (3)
(i) Name four expenses that are likely to be involved in the difference
between gross profit and net profit. (4)

Business Finance

Research Assignments

1. Make a comparison between the final accounts of two firms of similar size and comment upon the differences between them.

2. Ivor is the director of a small but successful landscape gardening business in a town about 20 miles from where you live. He wanted to raise £100 000 to expand his business and set up a new site in your locality.

   (a) Examine the ways in which he might raise the £100 000 he needs.
   (b) Present a report recommending a local site for consideration by Ivor.

3. Discuss why it is important for a company to maintain proper financial records both from the point of view of its owners as well as for taxation purposes. Obtain examples of documents used by companies in this way and present them as a collection to support your discussion paper.

4. Why is cash flow forecasting important to all types of business? Use simple data to illustrate your answer using a small manufacturing company as an example.

5. Explain the various ways that a business might raise capital (a) for short-term and (b) for long-term use. Why does a firm need to make the distinction between sources of capital?

6. 'Break-even charts do not give a precise picture of when a business will begin to make a profit, but they do provide a useful guide.' Explain this statement including a simple but clearly labelled break-even chart to illustrate your answer.

7. Write to a major public company in your region and ask for a copy of its most recent annual report and accounts. From the accounts explain in your own words the following:
   (a) How the net profit (or loss) figure is arrived at.
   (b) What percentage of the company's profit is paid to the shareholders and what percentage is retained.
   (c) Give your personal view of the prospects you see for the business and shareholders in the year ahead.
   (d) Describe how a limited company may increase its capital employed:
      (i) temporarily;
      (ii) permanently.

8. What is meant by a company's capital? How is it that a business might only have £1000 in petty cash and at the bank, and yet have capital of £50 000? Use specimen figures to illustrate your answer.

9. A large public company needs further capital for expansion. Describe three

different ways in which it might try to raise this money, including your views on what factors will be likely to influence the method chosen.

10 The following is the balance sheet of a retailer:

	£		£
Owner's savings	850	Fixed assets	8225
Mortgage	8000	Current assets	625
	8850		8850

(a) What is meant by each of the following:
   (i) mortgage?
   (ii) fixed assets?
   (iii) current assets?
(b) Why distinguish between these different aspects of a balance sheet?

11 (a) Ask a local retail trader to allow you to produce a specimen balance sheet which shows the value of his 'fixed' and his 'working' capital.
(b) Explain what is meant by 'fixed' and 'working' capital, using data from your balance sheet to clarify your explanation.

17 Company Shares

17.1 Selling new shares

If a company wishes to raise capital it has two basic choices. It may either raise the capital privately, or invite the public to buy shares in the company. The second alternative, selling shares, is an attractive option because the money raised in this way does not have to be repaid.

A new issue of shares may be made by:

- a new company forming
- a private company changing into a public company
- an existing company wishing to raise more capital.

New shares may be offered to the public in three main ways:

1. *The company may issue a prospectus* as part of the process of managing the sale of its shares. This is a leaflet or advertisement giving details of:

   - the history of the company
   - its plans for the future
   - the amount of capital it needs to raise
   - an invitation to the public to buy shares.

   A closing date for applications is set, and after that date the shares are allotted to those who have applied to buy.

   If the issue is *over-subscribed*, in other words, people wish to buy more shares than are available, the applicants receive a percentage of the shares they requested. If the issue is *under-subscribed* the company could end up not raising all the capital it needs. This is where it is an advantage to use an *issuing house* to sell the shares on behalf of the company because the issuing house will often underwrite the complete issue. This means that if all the shares are not sold, the issuing house undertakes to buy all the remaining shares, thus guaranteeing the company will raise the total capital it requires.

2. *The company may offer the shares for sale*: In this case the company will sell the shares outright to an issuing house who then dispose of them as best as they can, ensuring the company will receive all the capital it needs.

3. *The company may 'place' the shares* with Stock Exchange dealers, who offer them to their clients, and to other dealers.

Contract note

BOUGHT	BY ORDER OF	BARGAIN NUMBER 23(W)	BARGAIN DATE & TAX PT 24th Nov. 19x2		A. N. BROKER & CO 99 THROGMORTON STREET – LONDON EC2X ABC	
	Miss A. BUYER 38 High Street ANYTOWN AN6 5QT			LONDON – CHICAGO – SYDNEY – HONG KONG TELEPHONE: 01–588 2355 (20 lines)	TELEX: 44259 PARTNERS	V.A.T. REGISTRATION NUMBER: 242 0024
	A Public Company Ltd. £1 Ordinary Shares			T. H. WOOD		S. G. CORK
AMOUNT	PRICE		CONSIDERATION	A. B. JONES		S. H. THUMB
				C. D. SMITH		A. K. WOOD
				K. A. WIER		B. G. OAK
500	£1.28		£6 0.00	T. D. CHILD		R. N. SWEEPER
				CONSULTANT T. C. BOOTH		
		TRANSFER STAMP	13.00 N	A. N. BROKER & CO.		
	1.65% on £640.00	CONTRACT STAMP COMMISSION V.A.T. 17½%	0.30 N 10.50 T 1.84	CONTRACT STAMP £0.30		
				MEMBERS OF THE STOCK EXCHANGE Subject to the rules and regulations including temporary regulations of The Stock Exchange. For Capital Gains and V.A.T. purposes this contract note should be retained. An asterisk means commission is shared with		
E & O E	FOR SETTLEMENT 6TH December 19x2 TOTAL £		665.44	yourselves a member of the staff or an agent V.A.T. Symbols; T = Taxable; E = Exempt; N = Outside the scope		

The contract note is a document that provides evidence that an investor is in the process of transfer of ownership of shares. It tells the investor:

- the number of shares bought or sold;
- the unit price;
- the commission to be paid by the investor to their agent;
- government taxes – contract stamp, VAT and transfer duty;
- total payment due to the agent;
- settlement date.

17.2 Selling second-hand shares

When a company invites the public to invest in it the managers then put the money invested to permanent use. They will buy the buildings, machinery, stock and other assets that the business needs to operate. The money cannot be returned to the investor because it has been used. The only way that the shareholders can get their money back is by selling their shares to someone else. The Stock Exchange provides a market place where they can do this.

The Stock Exchange is a market place for the buyers and sellers of all kinds of existing securities. It is a 'free' market, that is one where the prices of securities are allowed to fluctuate in response to supply and demand. The market price of shares is particularly influenced by the past performance and profitability of a company. General market trends can provide an indicator or barometer of the future outlook for industry and the economy as a whole.

The fact that the Stock Exchange enables people to dispose quickly of any listed shares they hold is particularly useful for individuals but also for institutional investors (those who collect and invest the savings of many others) such as insurance companies, pension and union funds and investment and unit trusts. These organisations need to obtain a good return on the capital invested for their members, but at the same time the securities must be easily turned into cash.

The Stock Exchange is often referred to as if there were only one exchange, the London exchange. However, there are in fact a number of other Stock Exchange trading floors in important provincial centres in the UK. They all work closely together following the same rules and standards. The stock market business is worldwide, and there are exchanges situated in many other countries.

The Stock Exchange is controlled by the Stock Exchange Council which is elected by the members of the Stock Exchange. The Council has the following functions:

- it controls the admission of new Members;
- it disciplines Members who are guilty of misconduct;
- it formulates the Stock Exchange rules;
- it settles disputes between Members;
- it provides settlement and information services to Members.

Types of company security traded

Companies do not only raise money by selling shares. Sometimes they sell other forms of investments. 'Security' is the collective name given to the various categories of investments they offer to investors.

Debentures

Debentures are in effect a loan to a company and are often referred to as 'stocks'. They receive a fixed rate of interest which must be paid even if the company does not make a profit. Debenture holders have no involvement in the management of the company.

Debentures may be secured against specific assets or by a general charge on all the assets of the company, and are backed by an agreement similar to a mortgage. They may be bought and sold on the Stock Exchange and are redeemable at a fixed date or before.

Preference shares

Ordinary preference shares

Preference shareholders have a priority call on the profits of the company after debenture holders. Preference shares pay a fixed rate of dividend, but only if sufficient profits are available to make a payment. Usually preference shares carry no voting rights.

Cumulative preference shares

If cumulative preference shareholders do not receive their full dividend in one year, the balance is carried forward and must be met from profits earned in subsequent years, and until these have been paid no payment can be made to ordinary shareholders.

Comprehensive Business Studies

Participating preference shares

Because of the relatively safe nature of preference shares, and the fact that they pay a fixed rate of dividend, the preference shareholder does not reap any additional reward when the company does well and makes good profits.

Sometimes companies will create participating preference shares in which preference shareholders can take dividends at a fixed rate and, if there is still any profit left after payment of other dividends, the participating preference shareholder may receive a further dividend additional to the fixed rate already paid.

Ordinary shares (equities)

Ordinary shares or 'equities' represent a share in the ownership of a company. Each share is entitled to an equal proportion (dividend) of the company's profits. The amount of dividend to be paid is decided by the directors of the company

Share prices.
(a) (i) Which three shares have the highest price shown?
    (ii) Which three shares have the highest yield?
(b) Why is the yield figure important when deciding whether to buy a particular share?
(c) Why do you think there is such a wide variation in share prices?

322

and is dependent upon the profitability of the firm and, therefore, ordinary shares are somewhat speculative.

In return for accepting the speculative risk involved, the ordinary shareholder usually stands to receive a relatively high return on the investment. The shareholder may gain not only through his share of the company's profits, but also from an improvement in the current market price of the shares. In addition, the ordinary shareholder has some power (through voting rights) in the running of the company.

Ordinary shareholders are generally the last in line for distribution of profits, and, therefore, they are the most risky form of shareholding. However, they can give the highest rate of return when the company is successful.

The money paid for a share when it is first issued is used by the company and cannot be returned to the investor. However, ownership of ordinary shares can be bought or sold second-hand on the Stock Exchange. Ordinary shares with the highest status as investment are known as 'blue chips'.

The share certificate provides proof of ownership of shares.

 ## The return on shares

A dividend is a payment from a company's profits to its shareholders. It is the 'reward' paid to the investor. The dividend is usually calculated as a percentage of the nominal or par value of the share, for example as a percentage of the issue price or the price the share was originally sold for (normally 25p or £1). If the dividend is declared to be 9p, then investors will receive 9p for each share they hold e.g. in the case of shares with a par value of £1 = 9%.

However, the owner of the shares may well have bought them at a price above (or below) their par value. In this case the investor is interested in the 'real' return of his investment, taking into account the current market price. This is called the yield.

The yield on a share is calculated as follows:

$$\frac{\text{Dividend}}{\text{Market value}} = \text{yield}$$

The 'market value' refers to the price paid for a share on the Stock Exchange. If a shareholder had paid £2 for a share with a par value of £1 and a dividend of 9p is declared, the yield would be 4.5%

$$\frac{9p}{£2} = 4.5\% \text{ yield}$$

17.5 Factors affecting share prices

Obviously, if speculators could accurately predict share price movement they could guarantee that they would make a fortune several times in one week. However, investment in shares remains speculative because there are numerous factors that influence a rise or fall in share prices.

Some of these factors can be summarised as follows:

- supply and demand for the shares;
- recent performance of the company: good or poor profits;
- political changes affecting the company, for example change of government;
- changes in interest rates or taxation;
- popularity or otherwise of the company's products;
- changes in market trends;
- takeover or merger being considered;
- general national prosperity;
- industrial disputes, or settlements.

17.6 Activities

1. Briefly describe the main methods involved in selling new shares.
2. Why is the return on debentures invariably poorer than the return on equities?
3. How do preference shares differ from ordinary shares?

Company Shares

  4 'Ordinary shares are the most risky form of investment, but they can also be the most rewarding.' Discuss this statement.

  5 What is meant by the 'par value' of a share?

6 Explain the difference between the dividend and the yield of a share.

7 How is share yield calculated?

8 List at least six factors that influence the market value of shares.

Structured Questions

A NEW DEAL FOR SMALL SAVERS

A new era in savings has been introduced by the Government with the new Individual Savings Account or ISA.

ISAs are intended to appeal to the millions of Britons who currently do not have any private savings. ISAs are low contribution, easy access accounts for investing in cash (some National Savings products and building society accounts), shares, National Savings and life insurance.

A major benefit of ISAs, from the point of view of the saver, is that the savings grow and gains received are free of both income tax and capital gains tax. In addition to this, any UK shares invested get the extra advantage of a ten per cent tax credit on their dividends for the first five years of ISAs.

Anyone over the age of 18 can have an ISA, but they must be a UK resident for tax purposes. Each ISA holder can invest up to £52,000, spread over a ten year period.

The Government wants ISAs to give savers instant access to their money. But ISAs can also have savings plans in them whereby the saver agrees to leave their money for a certain period, or give a set period of notice before taking the money out, for higher returns.

1 Read the data shown here regarding ISAs and answer these questions.

  (a) What do the letters ISA stand for? (1)
  (b) Who can have an ISA? (1)
  (c) How much can an investor save in an ISA? (1)
  (d) Briefly describe what an ISA is. (2)
  (e) Who are the main target audience for the ISA? (2)
  (f) What do you understand by the statement, 'ISAs are low contribution, easy access accounts'? (2)
  (g) In what ways can ISA holders obtain a higher return on their investment? (2)
  (h) Give three reasons why the ISAs are likely to appeal to the small investor. (3)

325

(i) In what ways would you say that the development of ISAs will help business? (3)
(j) Why would the Government want to encourage investment in business enterprises? (3)

2 Refer to the illustration of the record of a share transaction shown on page 320.

(a) Name the company that issued this document. (1)
(b) Who now owns the shares shown on the record illustrated? (1)
(c) When these shares were first issued they cost £1 per share. What was the original total purchase price for the same quantity of shares, and what gross total gain in value has been achieved since first issued? (2)
(d) Give three possible different reasons why these shares have risen in value. (3)
(e) How can the new owner of these shares be confident that they have obtained them at a fair price? (3)
(f) How is a new owner of shares 'registered' and what do they receive to prove their shareholding? (4)
(g) What would be likely to happen to the total value of these shares in the following circumstances. Give a reason for each of your answers.
   (i) A Public Company Ltd has received a large overseas order for its products.
   (ii) A Public Company Ltd has one major competitor, Tokyo Traders plc. This competitor has had a disaster and its plant has been destroyed by fire.
   (iii) All of the employees at A Public Company Ltd belong to one union. The union has instructed its members to begin industrial action. (6)

3 These questions are all related to the illustration of an extract of share prices typically shown in a financial newspaper given on page 322.

(a) If you refer to the last entry in the data (P&O) you will see it records −4. A little higher in the display you will see the Clarkson entry shows +2. Explain these plus and minus figures. (1)
(b) What is meant by the 'yield' of a share and why is this particularly important? (2)
(c) List three shares in the data which show a high yield. What would be the advantage of buying these shares? (3)
(d) List three shares with a low yield. Why could there be some benefit in buying low yield shares such as these? (3)
(e) What is an investment trust? How does investing money in these differ from placing money in ordinary shares? (3)
(f) You want to buy 1000 shares in Globe (Investment Trusts), and you ask a broker to purchase them at a limit of 143p per share (that is,

Company Shares

no higher than 143p, and lower if possible). By referring to the information on page 322 answer these questions:
  (i) What price would your broker buy at?
  (ii) What is the highest and lowest price Globe shares have been in the past year?
  (iii) How much in total would you be required to pay for the 1000 shares?
  (iv) Your broker will charge commission. What is commission in this respect? (4)

(g) Suggest some factors which are likely to affect the general rise and fall in share prices. Why is your purchase in investment trusts less likely to be affected by these fluctuations? (4)

Research Assignments

1 Choose ten different shares and monitor the movement of their market price over a period of six months. Present your record in diagrammatic form and explain the reason for the changes you observe.

2 Choose three contrasting methods of saving and investment and record their profitability over a six-month period. Give reasons for any differences in the rate of return you identify.

3 Congratulations! You have inherited £60 000. Invest this money in three contrasting ways and record the progress of each £20 000 over a six-month period. Give reasons for any differences in the return achieved.

4 Discuss the view that although the Stock Exchange does not provide new capital for firms, it has an important role in encouraging people to invest in the first issues of shares.

5 Take any five companies of your choice that are listed on the Stock Exchange. Invest an imaginary £5000, approximately £1000 in each company. Record the weekly change in value of each of your holdings over a twelve-week period. At the end of twelve weeks compare the total current value of your five shares with the original amount invested.
  Write a report that summarises your results and offer reasons for the changes that have taken place.

6 Why is it possible for £1000 invested in government bonds to become worth, say, £1500 in five years, whereas the same amount invested in a portfolio of ordinary shares could realise a market value of twice the original investment in just one year? Use examples from the press to support your answer.

18 Insurance for Business

18.1 The purpose of insurance

All individuals and businesses face a wide variety of risks, but only some of them suffer a loss during the course of a year. Insurance provides a system of providing compensation to those who do suffer such a loss. Simply put, insurance is an agreement between an insurance company (the *insurer*) and a business or individual (the *insured*) who wants financial protection that compensation (*indemnity*) will be paid if a particular loss occurs.

Insurance companies are businesses and, therefore, they charge for their services. The charge the insurers make is called a *premium* and the contract drawn up between the insurer and the insured is known as the *policy*. The purpose of insurance is to uphold the principle of indemnity, that is, to put someone who has suffered a loss back into the position they would have been in had the loss not been suffered. Insurance companies are able to compensate people and organisations in return for a relatively small charge. This is because insurance 'pools risks'.

Pooling of risks

To offset the possible effect of a loss, all those at risk can contribute a relatively small sum of money (the premium) to a fund (a 'pool') operated by an insurance company. The many small sums people pay in premiums help to form a large pool of money. When a contributor to the pool suffers a loss there is enough money in the pool to compensate (indemnify) them. The result of cooperating with others in this way is that risks are 'spread' or 'shared' between many people and organisations that have contributed to the insurance pool. For this reason insurance is sometimes said to be the 'pooling of risks'.

British insurance is the country's largest single source of 'invisible earnings' (*see* Chapter 14). British insurance companies insure the industries, buildings, ships, etc. of other countries. In addition, insurance companies of other countries seek to be insured by British insurance companies, thus spreading the risk of cover they have offered in their own countries. This process is known as 'reinsurance', that is accepting an insurance risk and then transferring it (or part of it) elsewhere.

When Britain receives payment from other countries for insurance, the effect is of bringing foreign money into the country, thereby assisting our balance of payment figures.

Insurance for Business

18.2 Uninsurable risks

Not all risks can be insured.

The success of insurance is based on statistical analysis. Underwriters have to judge correctly how much they should charge to cover a particular risk if they are to have sufficient money in the pool to pay out against claims, and also meet running costs. From statistical records of claims underwriters can calculate the probability of a loss occurring, and fix the appropriate premium. Generally, insurance companies are willing to consider giving cover on all types of risks where they can calculate the probability of loss involved. But it is not possible to insure against happenings that are inevitable. The following are typical examples of uninsurable risks:

- when the probability of loss is inevitable (an exception is life assurance);
- where there is insufficient past experience to assess the premium;
- if the proposer does not have an insurable interest;
- against fair wear and tear such as rust and corrosion;
- that a business enterprise will be successful.

18.3 Principles of insurance

Insurance is successful and trusted because the parties honour certain basic principles:

Insurable interest

(a) Only the person who stands to suffer financial loss or liability can insure against a particular risk.
(b) To have insurable interest the insured must own, or be responsible for, the article to be insured.

Utmost good faith

(a) This insurance principle requires the parties to an insurance contract to be truthful.
- The insured must disclose all relevant facts to the insurer.
- The insurers must honour all the promises in their policy.

(b) Intentional withholding of information invalidates the contract.

Indemnity

(a) This is the insurance principle by which a policyholder is compensated for the loss incurred.
(b) The insured should not profit if the event insured takes place.
(c) If the insured overinsures an item (more than the true value), in the event of a loss s/he will only be compensated for the true value.
(d) If a loss occurs where the item is underinsured, the policyholder will only receive a proportion of the loss.

    e.g. House value   £100,000
         Insured for   £ 80,000
         Damaged by fire   £ 20,000 (i.e. one-fifth)
         Compensation
         (one-fifth)   £ 16,000

(e) *Contribution.* This aspect of indemnity applies when more than one insurer is liable for a loss. In this case, each contributes a proportionate amount to the compensation. For example, a camera lost on holiday could be the subject of both a house contents policy and also holiday insurance.
(f) *Subrogation.* This word means 'to take the place of'. Having received compensation from the insurer the insured has no further rights over the item insured. The right of ownership (e.g. for scrap value) passes to the insurer after the insured has accepted claim compensation. The compensation has taken the place of the item insured.
(g) *Proximate cause.* The insurer is *not* only liable for a loss caused directly by a risk insured against. An insurance claim would be valid not only for damage caused by fire, but also for repairs to doors damaged by firemen breaking in to tackle the blaze. This damage is not caused by the fire, but it is directly related to it.

Insurance for Business

18.4 Types of insurance

There are four broad categories of insurance: fire, life, accident and marine. These categories can be remembered by memorising FLAM which is a combination of the initial letter of each word.

Fire

Fire insurance, as the name suggests, primarily covers fire risk. But many policies combine cover with other risks such as theft, storm, flood and lightning, etc.

This form of insurance can include cover for loss of earnings (e.g. by businesses) or rental of alternative property while a building damaged by fire is being repaired.

Fire policies exclude certain special conditions such as fire resulting from earthquake or riots. In addition, items of high value (e.g. paintings, jewellery, antiques, etc.) must be insured separately.

Life assurance

This type of cover is referred to as 'assurance' rather than insurance. In the case of insurance, cover is given against a risk that *may* happen. Life assurance covers an event that *will* happen – death. There are two main types of life assurance, whole life and endowment.

1 *Whole life* policies provide for a payment after the death of the insured with the idea of providing for the dependents of the deceased.
2 *Endowment* policies provide for the payment of a basic sum at a certain age or on death of the insured, whichever occurs first. This provides not only for dependents, but a useful sum of money for the insured if he survives the period. A variation of this type of policy is one 'with profits' which, for a higher premium, entitles the insured to a share in the company's profits.

Accident

This type of insurance covers a wide range of policies. The following are the main examples.

Motor

Any vehicle taken on public roads is required to have a certain minimum level (third party) of insurance to ensure that drivers can meet their liability for injury to others. The two commonest types of motor insurance are:

1 *Third party, fire and theft* – the motorist insures the liability for damage to other people and their property, plus the loss or damage to his own car through fire or theft.
2 *Comprehensive* – policies not only give the above third party cover but also provide compensation for accidental damage to the vehicle of the insured.

Personal accident and sickness

These are policies which can be taken out against death or disability in special circumstances, for example holidays, flights, etc.

Liability

This type of policy covers the risk of liability for the injury or death of someone else. There are two main forms:

1 *Employer's liability* – covers the employer's legal liability for the safety of each employee.
2 *Public liability* – covers the liability of individuals and businesses for members of the public visiting their premises.

Property

Covers a wide variety of items from goods in transit or in store to buildings or contents. Applies to both the business person and the private householder.

Credit

Covers against losses resulting from bad debts, for example the failure of customers to pay for goods obtained on credit.

What insurance risks can you see in this illustration? Which ones do you think an insurance policy would not cover?

Fidelity

Used particularly by businesses to protect against loss by fraud and stealing by employees.

Insurance for business

- Employer's liability
- Public liability
- Damage to premises
- Stock damage
- Consequential loss (earnings)
- Theft, burglary
- Motor fleet
- Bad debts
- Product liability

Business interruption (or consequential loss)

Loss from fire in business premises may not only result in physical damage. Business may have to be suspended for a time resulting in loss of earnings for both the owners of the firm and the employees. Insurance cover is available for such losses and the cover can include loss of wages, rent and the cost of temporary alternative accommodation.

Marine

Marine insurance in Britain mainly centres around Lloyd's of London, which plays a major role in this worldwide market. This insurance is applied to ships and their cargoes. There are four broad categories of marine insurance.

1 *Hull insurance* – covers damage to the vessel itself and all its machinery and fixtures.
2 *Cargo insurance* – covers the cargo this ship is carrying.
3 *Freight insurance* – it is customary for an insurance policy to be taken out to cover the possibility that for some reason the shipper does not pay the transport (freight) charges to the shipowner.
4 *Shipowner's liability* – the owner of a vessel has to insure himself against a wide variety of events, for example collision with other vessels or dock, injury to crew members or passengers, pollution of beaches, etc.

18.5 The insurance contract

Insurance is provided by insurance companies, friendly societies, Lloyd's underwriters and the government (national insurance). Non-government insurance may be taken out through agents working for a particular company or brokers selling insurance for a number of companies. Whichever approach is used a basic procedure is followed.

Proposal

This form is provided by the insurer to be completed by the person seeking insurance cover (the proposer). The form consists of a number of questions which the proposer must answer truthfully (in 'utmost good faith'). When completed and signed by the proposer it represents a proposition from the proposer to the insurer.

Premium

If the insurer is willing to provide cover on the terms of the proposal he will quote a premium, which is the amount the proposer must pay into the pool to effect cover.

Policy

Once the contract is completed the insurer issues a policy which states the details of the contract between the insured and the insurer. The following documents may also be issued in association with the insurance policy.

- *Certificate of insurance* – for employer's liability and motor insurance, the law requires evidence of cover to be provided by this certificate.
- *Cover note* – this is a temporary document provided whilst the certificate of insurance is being prepared.
- *Endorsement* – a notice of an amendment to a policy, usually by the insurer. The endorsement is attached to the policy and thereafter becomes part of the contract.
- *Renewal notice* – issued by the insurer prior to expiry date, invites the insured to renew the cover and advises the renewal premium and the date on which it is due.

Claim

If the risk insured against takes place the insured completes a claim form and submits this to the insurer for consideration. *Loss adjusters* are frequently engaged by insurers to ensure that claims are settled fairly from the point of view of both the insured and the insurer.

18.6 The insurance market

Insurance companies

Insurance companies have branches spread throughout the country to issue policies and deal with claims. 'Friendly' societies specialise in life and sickness assurance. Those wishing to take out insurance cover can approach insurance companies directly or through insurance agents or insurance brokers.

Insurance for Business

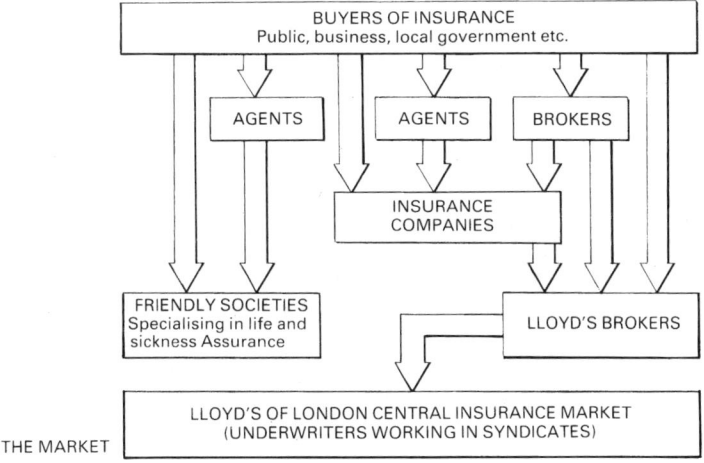

The insurance market.

Insurance *agents* work for an insurance company or a friendly society selling only the policies of that company.

Insurance *brokers* work independently of insurance companies and, therefore, are able to give unbiased advice as to which is the best policy to buy.

Whether it is decided to buy insurance direct from the insurance company, their agents, or brokers, the cost of the insurance cover is the same because the agent or broker is paid by the company which actually provides the insurance policy.

Lloyd's of London

Lloyd's of London is a corporation that provides market facilities for members engaged in selling insurance. There are two classes of membership of Lloyd's – Llyod's brokers and underwriters.

Underwriters are the only people allowed to accept insurance at Lloyd's. Underwriters are backed by their own personal wealth and have unlimited liability to indemnify insurance claims made against them. Underwriters frequently form into groups called *syndicates* who work together to accept larger shares of risk than a single individual could manage.

Llyod's brokers are the source of contact with Lloyd's insurance market. The function of Lloyd's brokers is to get the best deal they can for their clients, who may be insurance companies or large organisations such as businesses and local government.

The Lloyd's broker approaches underwriters who specialise in the risk to be covered. The premiums offered by several underwriters are compared, and the best offer is accepted. Sometimes the risk may be divided between several underwriters. Should a claim occur under the latter circumstances, each of the underwriters contributes to the compensation in proportion to the amount of the risk they have accepted.

18.7 Activities

1. How does insurance spread risks?
2. Why are some risks uninsurable? Give four examples.
3. In what way would you say that insurance could be said to have a statistical basis?
4. Explain, giving an example, the meaning of insurable interest.
5. Describe the insurance principle which requires the parties to an insurance contract to be truthful.
6. Insurance is said to be a contract of indemnity. What does this mean?
7. What do the terms contribution and subrogation mean in relation to insurance?
8. Give an example, and explain the insurance term proximate cause.
9. Name the four main types of insurance.
10. Explain the difference between insurance and assurance.
11. In relation to life assurance, explain the terms whole life, endowment, with profits.
12. Briefly explain the differences between third party, third party fire and theft and comprehensive motor insurance.
13. Why would a shop owner be likely to take out both employer's liability and public liability insurance?
14. Describe the process of putting an insurance contract into effect including mention of the documents and payment involved.
15. Why is the certificate of insurance particularly important to both employers and motor vehicle drivers?
16. Explain the purpose of a renewal notice.
17. What is the function of a loss adjuster?
18. Briefly describe the difference between an insurance agent and an insurance broker.
19. What is Lloyd's of London?

Insurance for Business

Structured Questions

1. Look at this article taken from the business section of a newspaper and answer the questions below.

   (a) What is the purpose of insurance? (2)
   (b) What is meant by underinsurance? (2)

Business News
The Danger of Being Underinsured

In a recent case two workmen of a firm were removing a large boiler from a cheese processing plant. The workmen secured a rope round one of the pillars supporting the factory. As a result the building collapsed causing £500 000 of damage, and the manufacturer had to close down the plant for several weeks.

The company presented a claim to its insurers for the repairs to the plant, and for the cost of the loss of business. But the insurers would only meet 80% of the value of the claim because the firm was underinsured. Although the firm took a variety of measures to find the shortfall, they could not make up the balance from their resources. And financial institutions were unwilling to loan money to a business that was in fact standing idle.

Within three months the firm was forced into bankruptcy, and what had been a thriving business employing 15 workers ceased to exist.

   (c) Why is insurance unable of fulfil its main purpose in the example shown in this article? (3)
   (d) State at least three different categories of insurance that a business will generally need that a private individual will not require. (3)
   (e) Briefly describe how the insurance company will have decided that it can only meet 80 per cent of the cost of the claim of the dairy producer? Why not 85 per cent? (4)
   (f) What led to the failure of the firm? How could this have been avoided? (6)

2. Refer to the diagram of the 'insurance pool' system on page 338.

   (a) Explain what is meant by saying that insurance is based on 'the pooling of risks'. (2)
   (b) Not all of the money in an insurance pool comes from the policyholders' premiums. So where else does the money come from? (2)
   (c) The majority of the money in the insurance pool is used to pay compensation to policyholders. Where else does the money from the pool go? (2)

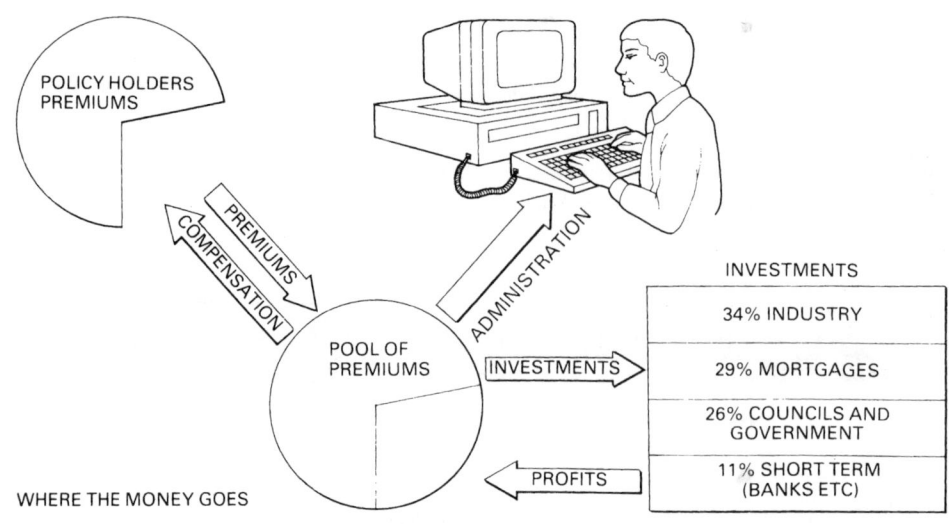

The insurance pool.

(d) Explain each of the following words contained in the diagram:
(i) policyholders; (ii) premium; (iii) compensation. (3)
(e) Describe some of the administration costs an insurance company is likely to have. (3)
(f) For an insurance pool to work effectively and fairly, certain principles have to apply to all insurance contracts. Name four of these principles and explain fully what they mean for a person seeking insurance. Give an example in each case to show how these principles work. (8)

3 These questions are all related to the diagram of the insurance market shown on page 335.

(a) Briefly describe examples of the special insurance-related work that friendly societies do. (2)
(b) How do insurance companies make a living? (2)
(c) Explain the difference between the work of insurance agents and high street brokers. Which is a business likely to use? (4)
(d) How does the function of a Lloyd's broker differ from that of a high street broker? (4)
(e) Explain the function of 'underwriters' and 'syndicates' in the insurance market. (8)

4 (a) In relation to insurance briefly describe the meaning of the following terms:
(i) indemnity (2)
(ii) utmost good faith (2)
(iii) insurable interest (2)
(iv) subrogation. (2)

Insurance for Business

(b) State one type of insurance which you would particularly recommend for each of the following. Give a different example in each case and explain the reason for your choice.
    (i) A factory engaged in manufacturing a highly inflammable product. (3)
    (ii) A firm employing six sales representatives each of whom drives a company car. (3)
    (iii) A shop employing people handling large amounts of cash. (3)
    (iv) A partner in a firm of solicitors. (3)

5 The questions below are all related to the flow diagram shown below.
  (a) What is the difference between the insurer and the insured? (1)
  (b) At what stage in the process of taking out insurance does the 'proposer' become the 'insured'? (1)
  (c) Why is a business less likely to consult an insurance agent than an insurance broker? (2)
  (d) What advantage could there be in a firm taking out insurance through a broker rather than going straight to an insurance company? (2)
  (e) State two factors that the insurance company will take into account when calculating the premium it will charge the firm taking out insurance. (2)
  (f) Explain each of the following terms used in the flow diagram:
    (i) proposal; (ii) premium; (iii) policy. (3)
  (g) Give three examples of advice that an insurance company might give to a firm interested in taking out insurance cover. (3)

STEPS IN TAKING OUT BUSINESS INSURANCE

1. The business considers the many risks that it faces.
2. The firm decides what type of policies will cover the risks and the amount of cover required.
3. The business can seek advice from an insurance company or an insurance broker.
4. The company fills out a proposal form giving details of the cover required.
5. The insurer accepts the proposal and calculates the premium required from the insured.
6. The insured pays the first premium and the insurer issues the policy.

(h) The following are typical types of insurance cover required by a business: (i) employer's liability; (ii) public liability; (iii) consequential loss. Briefly describe each of these giving appropriate examples of situations when each would apply in business operations. (6)

Research Assignments

1 On the news today the weather forecasters stated that recently installed computerised equipment will enable them to give 24 hours advance notice of weather conditions. In what way could this help to reduce insurance claims? What evidence can you provide to support your answer?

2 'Insurance is important to individuals, organisations of all kinds and the economy as a whole'. Discuss this statement and provide examples from magazines and newspapers to support your answer.

3 'Insurance is based on statistics.' Explain this statement giving specific examples of the kind of information insurance companies use in calculating premiums. What is the significance of this to business?

4 Give a detailed description of the insurance market, including particular reference to the operation of Lloyd's of London. To what extent can we say that there is business activity at all levels of insurance operations from individual transactions to the central market?

5 Take any local business with which you are familiar and describe any four risks the company should insure against, and explain three circumstances against which the firm cannot obtain cover.

6 Collect examples of insurance proposal forms for different types of risk, e.g. private car, life, public liability, premises. Compare contrasting questions asked on the forms and comment on the differences between the forms.

19 ▶ National Accounts

19.1 The standard of living

What is the standard of living?

The term *standard of living* refers to the quality of life that the people of a country have – for example, the type of houses they live in, the quality of food they eat and the clothes they wear. Obviously, this is dependent upon the work people do and the wages they receive. Even the methods that workers use to travel are seen as contributory to the standard of living, as are methods of communication used and entertainment that they have ready access to. The level of education the population receives is also seen as important.

The standard of living is often reflected in the average lifespan of the people of the country. It is likely that people who live where there is a high standard of living will generally live longer than those who have a poor standard of living.

Look at the following table containing data relating to the average life expectancy of people in a number of well known countries. What reasons can you give to explain the differences that exist between countries and between the sexes?

Country	Male	Female
Afghanistan	43	42
Barbados	73	77
Great Britain	72	78
Grenada	69	74
Jamaica	75	78
Libya	64	69
Madagascar	50	53
Nigeria	47	49

It is generally the case that countries with a poor standard of living are located in the tropics whilst countries which have higher living standards are found in the colder areas. This does not imply that the standard of living is a result of temperature or climate; rather it is very much to do with the stage of development that the country has reached, and the resources it has available. And, of course, the way that these resources are developed affects the standard of living.

Cost of living

As you can imagine, measuring the standard of living is a formidable task because there are so many factors involved, and some of these are difficult to quantify. Some of the main methods of measuring national prosperity will be examined shortly, but the *cost of living* gives some indication of the quality of life of people, and how it is changing from one year to another.

The 'cost of living' refers to how much can be bought with a person's net income (after deduction of income tax). Measuring the cost of living is important because it is continually changing and, therefore, it shows whether 'real' income is changing – in other words, are people better or worse off taking into consideration rising costs and income increases? Measurement of the cost of living is achieved by constructing a *price index*. There is more than one type of price index, but the most popular and more generally well known index is the Retail Price Index (RPI).

The RPI is made up from the prices of goods and services purchased by consumers. It is often used in the UK and other parts of the world as a basis for negotiation of wage increases. The objective of doing this is to ensure that workers' wages maintain a constant value in 'real' terms.

A *cost of living index* is constructed by taking the total value of a collection of items purchased by consumers in a particular year, which is referred to as the *base year*. We say that the index figure for that year, say 1993, is 100. The same items are subsequently valued periodically (usually annually) and general price movements can be plotted for a group similar to the one shown here.

Depending upon whether each new plotted position is above or below the base line it is possible not only to know if prices have generally risen or fallen, but also to establish an approximation of the percentage of change. The change can then be equated with wage rises in order to establish if workers end up better off in real terms.

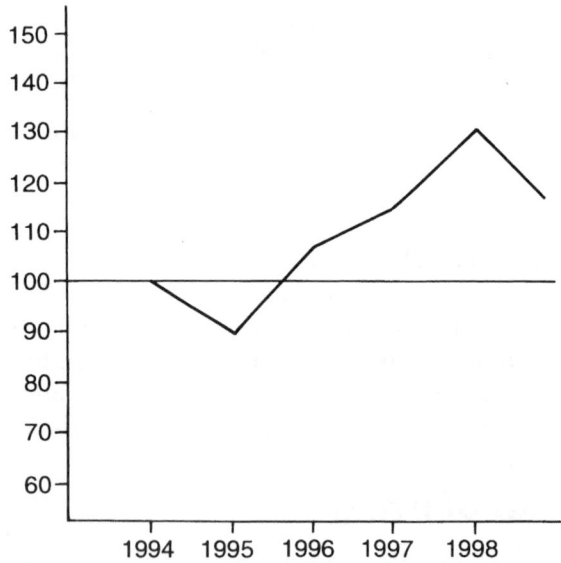

A *cost of living index*.

National Accounts

Useful though it is, a cost of living index gives only a limited indication of the state of the economy of a country. Statistics included in the national accounts are a more revealing indication of the state of the economy.

19.2 National income

Economic growth refers to an increase in the output of all things we consume, use, invest in or otherwise produce. Economic growth is important because it usually means that the country is increasing its wealth, and probably improving its living standards. One way to assess economic growth is through measurement of the national income.

What is national income?

Imagine you were asked to calculate the total income of your family for the year, how would you go about doing so? You would probably add together the total yearly income of each member of the household, including any return received from savings or investments. But there are other ways of reaching the same figure. For example, it can also be obtained by adding together the total amount spent, and the total amount saved by each member of the family in the year. You should understand that both methods reach the same answer because both look at the same amount of money, but in a different way. The national income of a country can also be assessed in a similar way.

If you were asked to assess your income you would refer to wages and other returns which add to your wealth. You would not count money you invested in the building society last year, but you would include the interest you received

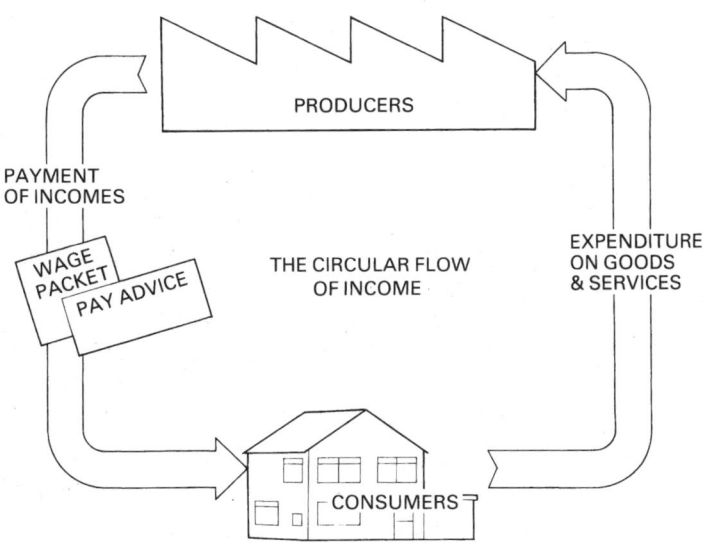

Circular flow of income.

this year. Income is a *flow*, and not a stock of money or equipment. National income is concerned with new additions to the wealth of the country.

There are three approaches that can be used to measure the national income, and all the methods should reach the same answer because in a way they are all measuring the same thing.

1 *Income method* – the aggregate value of all forms of income, including personal incomes, profits of firms, rents, etc.
2 *Output method* – the total net output of every form of production taking care not to count any output twice. 'Net' in this case means including an allowance for capital consumption (depreciation – fall in value due to wear and tear) on all buildings and machinery.
3 *Expenditure method* – the total value of all expenditure by consumers, firms and the government.

Measurement of all the foregoing three ways of looking at national income are made annually by the British government and are published in the Blue Book on national income and expenditure.

National income accounting problems

Quite apart form the obvious difficulty of data collection there are a variety of problems associated with the foregoing methods of national income measurement. The following are some of these problems.

Money terms

It is not possible to add together things such as tons of fish, bottles of wine and thousands of tractors. To evaluate items such as these we have to express them in money terms. But the value of money is constantly changing, and this can result in inflation causing it incorrectly to appear that national income is increasing. What is important is the *real* increase in national income and to establish this requires allowances to be made for the changing value of money. The government Blue Book on national income and expenditure contains tables of consumers' expenditure taking into account changes in the value of money.

Double-counting

Double-counting can occur when output is considered. If timber is included in output measurement, should furniture made from timber also be included? The answer to this difficulty is that each firm should only count the value added to products by its activities. Theoretically this avoids counting output more than once, but in effect the result is still not a very precise measurement.

The 'black' economy

Babysitting, bartending, taxi driving and car repairs are typical examples of jobs that are sometimes being done 'on the side', that is without the Inland Revenue knowing about them because the income is not declared for tax purposes. The work is usually done for cash rather than cheque payment, and for a charge lower

National Accounts

than for 'official' work. Activities such as these are sometimes called the 'hidden' economy, but most commonly they are referred to as part of the 'black' economy.

Probably every developed country has its own 'black' economy, and in some countries it is so substantial that it props up the official economy. It has been estimated that the 'black' economy adds almost a third to the gross national product.

The 'black' economy is to be condemned because tax evasion by some in this way increases the tax burden of others. However, more important here is the fact that the 'black' economy creates a problem for recording domestic statistics. The main source of information for the income method is the Inland Revenue, but we have seen that the 'black' economy shows that a large proportion of income is not recorded.

Uses of national income statistics

The final national income figure is only an estimate because of the foregoing and other accounting difficulties which result in discrepancies. However, in spite of all the difficulties of measuring national income the figure has several uses.

1 *Changes in living standards* – most governments use national income statistics to indicate changes in living standards.
2 *Comparisons with other countries* – it enables comparisons to be made between one country and another.
3 *Economic growth* – a comparison can be made between one year and another in respect of economic growth.
4 *Instrument of economic planning* – it provides the government with information which can be used to assess the effectiveness or otherwise of its past policies. This information can then be used in the planning of the economy, and implementation or redistribution of wealth.

National income and standard of living

While national income is of vital importance in determining our standard of living, a high national income does not necessarily mean a high standard of living exists generally.

To illustrate this point, let us imagine that there is a Middle East country called Hullabahoo, and that country had made dramatic economic growth because of the discovery of vast deposits of oil five years ago. If Sheik Shinpad, ruler of the state of Hullabahoo, receives the vast majority of the national income, the country may be earning more, but its people will see little improvement in their living standards. Therefore, the way that the wealth is distributed is just as important to the population as the national income.

Gross national product (GNP)

When we looked at the output method of measuring national income earlier we said that an allowance was made for 'capital consumption' or loss in value (depreciation) of buildings and machinery. In other words, in the case of national income measurement we only know the total production output after taking away that allowance. But in national accounting it is useful to be able to measure the total value of all things actually produced in a country, that is a figure which does not include a reduction for capital consumption.

In Britain, the principal measure of the total output of the country is called gross national product (GNP). The word 'gross' indicates that no deduction has been made for capital consumption.

The word 'national' in this instance does not imply that GNP is the total output produced within the borders of the UK. The GNP measure includes some output taking place and produced by resources owned by people from other countries. Clearly, this outflow cannot be counted as part of our national income. At the same time, some sources of output are situated in other countries but owned by UK citizens. Therefore, the GNP can be defined as the total output of all the resources owned by residents of this country, wherever the resources themselves are situated.

Measure of the total output actually produced within the borders of the UK is called the gross domestic product (GDP). In this respect GDP can be defined as the output of all resources located within the UK, wherever the owners of the resources happen to live. In a similar manner to GNP, the GDP becomes net domestic product when an allowance for depreciation is deducted from it. In many ways GDP is the more important measure.

National Income of Noland

Simple imaginary analysis by expenditure method

	£ billions
Consumer expenditure	168.2
Public authorities expenditure	60.1
Gross domestic fixed capital investment	43.5
Value of physical increase in stocks	2.1
Exports of goods and services	73.3
Total final expenditure	347.2
less imports of goods and services	− 67.1
less taxes	− 38.3
plus subsidies	+ 4.1
Gross domestic product	245.9
Net property income from abroad	+ 2.2
Gross national product	248.1
less capital consumption	− 36.9
National income	211.2

The national cake

The amount of wealth or gross national product the country is generating each year is sometimes referred to as the 'national cake'. The UK national wealth 'cake' is made up of contributions from various parts of the economy and commercial activities such as services, distributive trades and transport make the largest con-

National Accounts

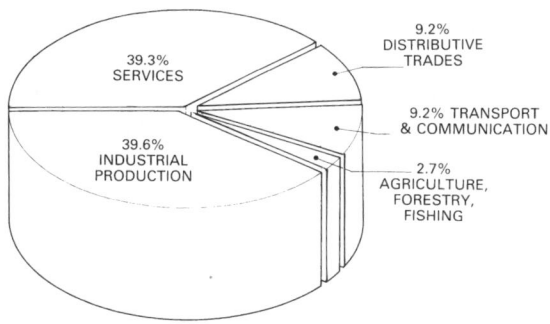

Where the national wealth comes from.

tribution, followed by a smaller contribution by industrial production and a yet smaller contribution by agriculture, forestry and fishing. This illustrates the importance of commercial activities to the economy.

Wealth in this sense is more than a stock of money and possessions. Wealth is the total of what the economy produces each year in the form of goods such as clothing and food, or services such as those of doctors or teachers. We normally find it convenient to measure wealth in money terms, but this can create problems because not all wealth can be counted in money terms. For example, how do we put a precise value on the quality of education, medical care or environment? And yet sometimes the effect of things such as these can be greater and more important than the production of goods to which we normally attribute wealth.

The well-known saying 'you cannot have your cake and eat it' is undoubtedly true, and yet many people want to do just this. As a country we cannot have what we have not earned; we cannot eat more cake than we have. Consequently, the bigger slice of the cake one person or group takes, the less there is left to distribute to others. Clearly, we must make a bigger cake before we can distribute bigger slices from it. This is often the source of a continual wrangle between governments, employers and workers over demands for wage increases.

National expenditure

While the gross national product tells us what was produced in a country, national expenditure tells us who bought what was produced. In this respect we can say that national expenditure is the sum of:

1 *Private expenditure* – this includes every kind of consumption spending by the population, from food and clothing to cars and entertainment (but excluding the purchase of homes).
2 *Public expenditure* – central and local government spending on goods and services, for example salaries of teachers and soldiers, provision of pensions and family benefits, etc. (but excluding capital expenditure on durable assets such as buildings).

3 *Gross domestic capital formation (GDCF)* – this refers to the total investment by business firms, public enterprises and public authorities in new fixed capital such as new plant and equipment, buildings, ships and other durable means of production. The purchase of new dwelling houses is also included in GDCF.

4 *Overseas trading* – the effect of the net difference between the value of UK exports and imports of goods and services (balance of payments).

From the foregoing it can be seen that national expenditure is necessarily identical in value with the national product because it is merely another way of classifying the same information.

Public expenditure

This term refers to government spending. In the UK there are two types of government, central and local government. Central government governs the whole country, whereas local government is concerned with management of a smaller part of the country. Central government is the most important single spender in the UK, and local government is responsible for a considerably smaller proportion of public expenditure.

Central government expenditure

- *EC Budget* – Member States contribute to the EU Budget.
- *Defence* – maintenance of defence systems, army, navy and airforce.
- *National Health Service* – provision of hospitals, doctors, dentists, pharmacists, etc.
- *Social security and personal social services* – which includes benefits for the elderly, disabled and sick, unemployed, family (child benefit, etc.), widows and social security payments.

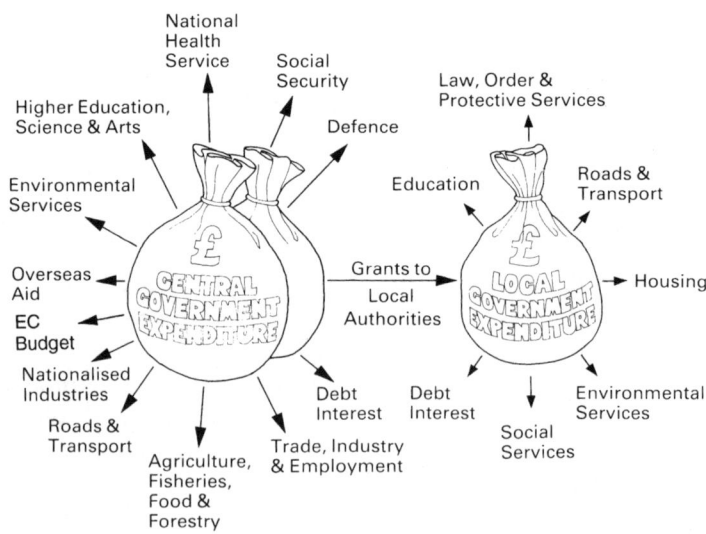

National Accounts

- *Higher education, science and arts* – grants to universities, subsidies for scientific research, subsidies for the arts.
- *Grants to local authorities* – mainly in the form of the rate support grant – particularly used to pay employees such as teachers, dustmen, social workers, clerks and other council employees.
- *Trade, industry and employment* – operation of job centres, skill centres and the Training Agency, and grants to encourage firms to move into development areas.
- *Overseas aid* – money lent to poorer countries.
- *Agriculture, fisheries, food and forestry* – grants for research, land reclamation and subsidies to farmers, etc.
- *Roads* – money for trunk roads and motorways, and subsidies for various forms of state-run transport such as railways.
- *Debt interest* – when the government spends more than it obtains in revenue it has to borrow. The total amount owed is known as the national debt. The government has to pay interest on this debt.

Local government expenditure

- *Education* – the provision of nursery, primary, secondary and further education is the single most important item of local authority expenditure.
- *Law, order and protective services* – the police and fire services are the major items of this aspect of local government expenditure.
- *Roads and transport* – local authorities are responsible for minor local roads. They may also subsidise some aspects of local transport.
- *Housing* – provision of council houses and sheltered accommodation.
- *Environmental services* – refuse collection, parks and cemeteries, etc.
- *Social services* – old people's welfare, and facilities for other people who need help, for example 'battered' wives and children or poor families. Also libraries, museums, sports facilities, magistrates, ambulances and probation services.
- *Debt interest* – like central government, local councils also borrow money and have to pay interest on it.

19.5 National debt

If you spend more than you earn you will end up in debt. There are two ways you can put the matter right. You can earn more or you can borrow to pay off the debt. In the latter case you are creating another debt, but delaying ultimate payment. The government faces a similar problem.

Each year the Chancellor of the Exchequer prepares the Budget in which he plans the next year's government revenue and expenditure. If expenditure equals revenue the budget is in *balance*. When income exceeds expenditure a *surplus* has been created, and a *deficit* results when expenditure exceeds income.

The public sector borrowing requirement (PSBR) indicates the extent to which the public sector borrows from other sectors of the economy and overseas to balance its deficit on the expenditure and revenue accounts. The public sector includes central government, local authorities and public corporations. PSBR is an important indicator of how the government's policies are affecting the economy.

The national debt is the total amount owed by central government to people both in Britain and abroad. The national debt has accumulated over many years and today the total is so huge it is no longer possible for it to be repaid, although it is still important to restrict growth of the debt as far as possible. Wherever there is a budget deficit, PSBR bridges the gap and results in an increase in the national debt. Most of the national debt is owed to British residents who hold government stocks or money invested in the various forms of national savings.

19.6 Growth and development

Growth refers to an all round expansion of the economy. It is concerned with the *quantitative* increases in the country's output. It is concerned with the *rate* of economic change, e.g. increases in tourism, increases in production, increased construction of roads, the building of more schools and hospitals, etc.

Growth can be measured by changes in GNP, which reflects general increases in total net output. *Negative growth* means that the country is doing less well than the previous year; *zero growth* indicates that there has been no change when compared with previous years. Obviously, all governments are keen to see their countries achieve growth because it generally results in an improved standard of living and greater economic and political stability.

Development is not the same as growth. It is a qualitative concept and is more concerned with the *pattern* of economic change. Development refers to the provision of facilities that enable growth to take place, e.g. availability of resources such as machinery and a workforce with appropriate education and skills. Often development will take place in just some sectors of the economy but provide thrust for other sectors. In order to have development, there must be growth. However, there may be growth but no development. Highly developed countries are better able to exploit their natural resources than underdeveloped countries, consequently more advanced economies have a better standard of living.

An underdeveloped country tends to have the following features:

- poor economic performance
- high rate of population growth
- low standard of living
- relatively short life expectancy
- high unemployment
- considerable dependency upon agricultural employment
- poor educational opportunities.

Many (but not all) European countries, the United States, Japan and Australia are examples of highly developed economies. By contrast, most underdeveloped countries are situated in Asia and Africa. The Caribbean countries are at the stage part way between the two extremes. They are sometimes referred to as *developing countries*. Many other countries are also in this category.

Economic growth

Whist economic growth is the desire of all governments it is affected by the following factors.

Investment

Capital accumulation and the use of this to create further wealth through the provision of capital or equipment is essential to economic growth. For this reason the government will be keen to encourage saving and investment and will also allocate a large share of its resources towards development.

Technical progress

Economic growth is promoted by exploitation of technical development so that increased productivity can be achieved with the same resources. For this to take place the workforce must have the skills to take full advantage of new technology. Consequently, there must be adequate investment in education as well as technology.

Balance of payments

A persistent adverse balance of payments will hinder growth and development. A continued unfavourable balance will 'bleed' the country of capital that it needs to direct towards development and growth. It will also have the effect of discouraging capital inflow from overseas investors who will be more interested in investing in more stable economies with healthy balance of payments positions.

Government expenditure

Government spending is so extensive that its has the power to stimulate particular sectors of the economy when carefully directed. Public expenditure should be used, at least in part, to stimulate those sectors of the economy that will assist future output.

Activities

Make a note of it

1. 'The cost of living is just one aspect of the standard of living.' Explain this statement.
2. What is the retail price index?
3. How is the retail price index constructed?

4. Define national income.

5. What do we mean when we say that income is a 'flow' and not a 'stock' of wealth?

6. Describe the three methods of measuring national income.

7. What are the problems of measuring national income?

8. What useful purpose is there for measuring national income?

9. Define the term 'per capita' income.

10. 'Rising national income does not necessarily imply a rising standard of living.' Discuss this statement.

11. List the factors that influence national income.

12. Define gross national product and say how this figure differs from national income.

13. The gross national product is sometimes referred to as the national 'cake'. What makes up the national cake? Why is it true to say that we cannot 'have our cake and eat it'?

14. What is 'national expenditure'?

15. What is the national debt and why does it exist? To whom is the debt owed?

16. In what way is growth different from development?

17. How does 'zero' growth differ from 'negative' growth?

18. Give simple definitions to show the difference between an underdeveloped country, a developing country, and a highly developed country.

19. Why are all governments keen to see economic growth?

20. Simply state the main factors that affect economic growth.

Structured Questions

1. (a) What is meant by the 'standard of living' of a country? (2)
   (b) Why do some countries have a higher standard of living than others? (3)
   (c) Describe four factors that influence the standard of living. (4)
   (d) What is 'per capita income'? To what extent would you say that this can be seen as an indication of the standard of living of a country? (5)
   (e) In what way could we measure the standard of living of any country? (6)

National Accounts

2 (a) What is the purpose of a government's budget? (2)
(b) Explain the difference between a budget surplus and a budget deficit (2)
(c) State three services that governments provide which private enterprise would be unwilling to supply at an economic price. (3)
(d) List three methods governments use to influence business activities. (3)
(e) To what extent would you argue that governments interfere too much in business activities? (4)
(f) One type of business that all governments try to influence is importing and exporting.
  (i) Why is this of such importance?
  (ii) How do governments try to influence this aspect of business? (6)

3 The following questions are all related to national income.

(a) One way to calculate national income is by aggregate expenditure. State another method. What problems are encountered using this method? (3)
(b) Explain the difference between GNP and national income. Why is the distinction between them important? (4)
(c) Outline four measures of national income and output of an economy. (4)
(d) Give four reasons why national income is an imperfect measure of the well-being of our country? (4)
(e) Briefly outline five ways that the real national income of our country may be increased. (5)

4 The following table shows a variety of comparative data related to a number of countries. Answer the questions that follow.

(a) Which country has the highest GNP and which has the lowest? (1)
(b) Why is the GNP measured in US Dollars for all countries in the table? (2)

	Country	GNP $US	Birthrate per 1000	% urban dwellers	Life expectancy	Calories per day	% in agriculture
Market (capitalist) economies	Sweden	14 881	11	83	75	2 849	6
	USA	11 363	16	76	74	3 580	4
	Japan	9 352	16	76	76	2 552	10
	UK	8 873	12	76	73	3 340	3
Centrally planned (socialist) economies	China	2 086	18	65	70	3 460	17
	Poland	1 876	21	62	70	2 880	44
High income (oil producing) countries	Kuwait	18 086	36	58	69	2 728	17
	Libya	7 289	50	41	56	2 690	21
Middle income (developing) countries	Costa Rica	1 860	31	43	70	2 329	38
	Bolivia	757	47	33	51	1 970	65
	Philippines	733	40	36	59	2 241	69
Low income (developing) countries	Uganda	222	46	17	54	2 146	68
	Bangladesh	145	40	11	47	2 113	71
	Ethiopia	97	49	13	40	1 826	76

(c) State four differences between countries with a high GNP and those with a low GNP. (2)
(d) GNP is used in the table as a measurement of a country's national income. An alternative measure could have been GDP.
  (i) What do the letters GNP and GDP stand for? (2)
  (ii) Why do you think GNP was used in this table (3)
(e) Compare the data for GNP and that for birth-rate and comment on any relationships you can identify. (4)
(f) Explain why it is that there is such a large difference between GNP of countries in the table. (6)

Research assignments

1 Find out the amounts your government spends on each of the main components of its expenditure. Present the data researched in some appropriate graphical form. Write a summary report which includes explanation of the ways your government raises the revenue it needs.

2 (a) Give a detailed description of *five* contrasting services provided by the government of your country.
  (b) In what ways would you say that there is a need for your government to improve the social services it provides? Give reasons for your answer.

3 Why is it difficult to use national income statistics to compare the standard of living in different countries? What other statistics might you consider using in order to make a realistic comparison?

4 Using real data, explain the way that your government attempts to redistribute incomes. Quote the source of your data.

5 A major priority of all governments is the provision of welfare for its citizens. To what extent would you say that this is dependent upon growth and development?

6 By examination of your household or a local firm, show that national income can be measured in terms of output, income or expenditure.

20 Taxation and Inflation

20.1 Principles of taxation

Everyone pays tax in some form, either directly or indirectly. The government does not just take money from us without reason. The money taken is used to control and direct the economy as well as to fund government expenditure.

A tax is a compulsory money payment by individuals and businesses levied on income, property and the use of goods and services which has to be paid to the state. Government decisions about taxes and public spending are referred to as 'fiscal policy'.

The following four 'rules' of taxation were stated by Adam Smith over 200 years ago, but they are still sound guides that apply today.

1 *Equality* – taxes should be based on the ability to pay. Those with higher incomes should pay a higher proportion of their income in tax than those with low incomes. Thus, people bear an equal burden rather than all paying the same amount.
2 *Economic* – taxes should be collected as economically as possible because there is little to be gained if the cost of collection is more than the money received.
3 *Certainty* – the easier it is to understand a tax system the less incentive there is to evade paying the amount levied. The form and manner of payment, and the quantity to be paid should be clear and unambiguous to the contributor and everyone else. In other words, the tax system should be clear enough so that those liable know what is expected of them.
4 *Convenience* – a tax should be convenient to collect. The Pay As You Earn (PAYE) method of collecting income tax is convenient because it is collected by the employer before the employees receive their pay. PAYE is also a convenient system because it fits in with the normal activity of regular payment of wages.

20.2 Functions of taxation

There are five functions of taxation.

To raise revenue

The main function of taxation is to raise *revenue* to pay for things provided by the state which private enterprise would be unable or unwilling to provide at prices the majority of the population are generally able to pay. Police, medical care, education and roads are examples where provision is largely met through taxation.

To maintain economic stability

Governments use taxation to exercise overall control of the economy in a manner that attempts to level out the 'highs' and 'lows' in economic activity, to promote economic growth and to try to achieve full employment. A major factor involved here is the control of inflation.

To influence expenditure

Taxation can be used to influence the level of total expenditure. The higher the level of taxation the lower the level of real expenditure is likely to be and vice versa. This principle can be used to deflate or reflate the economy. Inflation is examined later in this chapter.

To redistribute income

Taxation can be used to effectively redistribute income and capital ownership in the community, by taxing some members of the community higher than others, e.g. redistribution in favour of poorer members of the community. Redistribution of income will, in the long term, influence the distribution of wealth.

To satisfy specific objectives

Taxation can be used to achieve specific objectives such as:

- to discourage habits like smoking, drinking and gambling;
- to encourage activities such as healthy eating and safe driving;
- to stimulate production, exporting and improvement of balance of payments;
- to encourage movement of industry into depressed areas;
- to promote mobility of labour.

Methods of taxation

Progressive, proportional and regressive taxes

These ways of looking at the different forms of taxes compare the amount of tax paid to the income of a person.

- *Progressive tax*. The proportion taken in tax rises as income rises; it takes a larger proportion of income from higher income groups. Income tax is a progressive tax.
- *Proportional tax*. A change in a person's income does not on average affect the

proportion of their income that they pay in tax. National insurance is an example of a proportional tax.
- *Regressive tax*. The proportion of income taken in tax falls as income rises. Value added tax (VAT) is regressive because it is charged at a uniform rate irrespective of the purchaser's income.

Direct taxation

A direct tax is one which is paid directly to the tax authority by the person against whom the tax is levied. Income tax, corporation tax, capital gains tax, capital transfer tax and North Sea oil tax are examples of direct taxes.

Income tax

Income tax is both a direct tax and a progressive tax. It is a tax on personal earned income. Wage earners are allowed a certain amount in tax-free allowances and the rest of their income is taxed. The proportion of tax paid increases as taxable income increases.

Corporation tax

Corporation tax is a tax on the profits of companies. Similar to individuals and income tax, companies are allowed to deduct certain expenditure as tax-free allowances from their gross profit. The remaining net profit is liable for tax.

Capital gains tax

When individuals sell assets such as shares, land, property and works of art, any profit or gain above a certain 'threshold' is liable for capital gains tax. Certain personal assets such as a person's home are exempt from this tax.

Inheritance tax

Inheritance tax is a tax on gifts or gratuitous transfers of personal wealth from one person to another, whether they take place during a person's lifetime, or on their death. The rate of tax varies according to the sum transferred. There are various exemptions available to certain forms of enterprise such as farming and small businesses, and transfers to and from a husband or wife. There is also a 'threshold' below which transfers are tax free.

Indirect taxation

An indirect tax is paid by the taxpayer indirectly to the tax authority, i.e. levied on one person but is collected and ultimately paid by someone else such as a retailer, for example value added tax.

Value added tax (VAT)

VAT is the most important indirect tax in Britain, because it is the main general expenditure tax levied by central government. It is a tax imposed on the value added to goods and services at every stage of production.

When several traders are involved in the movement of goods from the producer to the consumer, each will charge VAT to the person to whom they sell. Each trader, however, only pays to Customs and Excise the amount of VAT they have charged their customers less the amount of tax paid to their suppliers. In this way we can see that each trader pays VAT on the difference between what he has sold the product for and what he paid for it. This difference is called 'value added'. Therefore, tax is paid on the value that has been added to the product, and this is how this tax gets its name.

The rate of VAT to be charged is announced by the Chancellor of the Exchequer in the Budget, and the rate is varied from time to time. Some goods and services are not liable for VAT because they are zero rated or exempt.

Where VAT is applicable, it is charged on the net value of the goods or services, in other words, the value of the invoice after taking into account trade or cash discounts (even if the buyer does not take advantage of them).

Example 1

	£
Gross invoice value	10 000
less 20% trade discount	2 000
	8 000
plus $17\frac{1}{2}$% VAT	1 400
Invoice total	£9 400

Example 2

	£
Gross invoice value	40 000
less 25% quantity discount	10 000
	30 000
plus $17\frac{1}{2}$% VAT	5 250
Invoice total	35 250

Protective (customs) and excise duties

These taxes are collected by HM Customs and Excise Department and are charged in addition to VAT on a variety of important goods such as alcohol and tobacco products.

All revenue duties are termed as excise, which is payable on both imported and home-produced goods. Protective duties refer to customs duties on non-EU goods, used to put into effect the common external tariff policy of EU member countries which was examined earlier in Chapter 11. The purpose of protective duties is to raise the final market price of cheaper foreign products to a level with which home producers can compete.

Other forms of taxation

National Insurance (NI)

NI is a form of direct taxation where contributions are made by both employers and employees. The money raised by this tax is used specifically for the National Insurance Fund, the National Health Service, and the Redundancy Fund.

Employers have to pay contributions for every person they employ. Not surprisingly this tax has been called a 'tax on jobs', because every new person employed is an additional financial burden for the employer.

Motor vehicle duty

Sometimes referred to as 'road tax' or 'car tax'. The owners of motor vehicles must pay a tax for each vehicle used on public highways.

Local authority tax

Local authorities, such as Country Councils, receive money in the form of grants from central government, this is supplemented from local taxation. Unlike most other taxes, local taxes are not levied by the Inland Revenue but are raised by local authorities. In the UK the main local taxation is that paid by businesses and local residents.

20.4 Economic effects of taxation

Effective taxation should achieve the functions stated earlier but at the same time meet the longstanding principles of taxation (equality, certainty, convenience, economic). No single tax can meet all of these requirements and raise all the revenue governments need, consequently governments use a variety of methods of taxation which tends to even out some of the inadequacies of some of the taxes. A key source of debate is whether direct or indirect taxation is more appropriate.

The main advantage of direct taxes is that the rate charged can easily be changed or varied for different circumstances. For example, the overall rate of income tax can be simply changed centrally by the government, and it is possible to have varied rates, i.e. it is generally charged at a progressively higher rate to the rich and, conversely, at a lower rate to the poor. The PAYE system ensures that income tax is not only relatively easily collected (employers do much of the work) but it also allows the taxpayer to make contributions in small regular payments.

The main disadvantage of direct taxes is that they are expensive to administer and collect; many civil servants are involved and complicated rules and paperwork persists. Direct taxation often results in disputes between taxpayers and tax officials over the amount of tax due. In addition, those who do not pay their income tax by the PAYE method can fall into the trap of not saving sufficient money to pay one or two large payments a year.

Indirect taxes have the advantage in that they are relatively easy and cheap to collect, the amount to be paid is generally clear and unambiguous, and it is difficult to evade paying them. In addition, indirect taxation collects money from foreigners (e.g. tourists) whereas they do not pay direct taxes.

The main disadvantage of indirect taxes is that they are regressive in that poorer people tend to pay a higher proportion of their income in tax than those on higher incomes. For example, payment of a purchase tax or VAT is at the same rate whether one is a high earner, a low earner, or even a non-earner.

20.5 Inflation

Earlier in this chapter we saw that one of the functions of taxation is to maintain economic stability. One of the main threats to this stability is inflation, and governments throughout the world are continually striving to offset the effects of it.

Inflation describes a situation when prices are persistently rising and the real value of money is declining, which means that the cost of living has increased. If people's incomes do not improve, then their income purchases less. Under such circumstances we say that real income has fallen, and this leads to a fall in the standard of living unless some factor changes.

Inflation in the UK is usually measured by the *Retail Price Index (RPI)*. This involves measuring the collective prices of a selection of goods and services which a typical household would purchase over a period of a month. Around 600 items are included in the RPI and each month researchers compare 130 000 prices of the 600 items in a variety of retail outlets to measure changes that have taken place.

If the average of all the prices is 1 per cent higher than the previous month, this indicates that inflation is approximately 12 per cent per year.

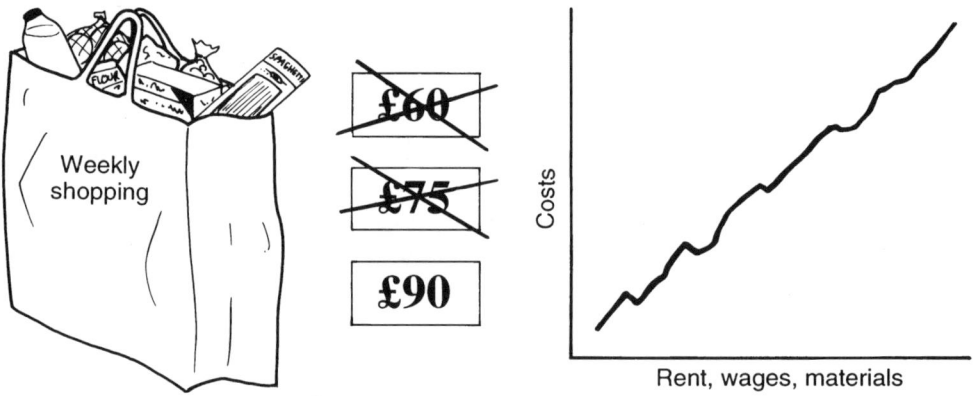

Rising costs push inflation up.

Types of inflation

Inflation is the result of many factors but two broad types of inflation can be distinguished: 'cost-push' inflation and 'demand-pull' inflation.

Cost-push inflation

This form of inflation is caused by rises in the cost of factors of production such as raw materials or labour, for example oil prices or wages. For instance, wage increases may not be matched by increased productivity. When such increased costs are passed on to the consumer in the form of increased prices this results in cost-push inflation. The resultant increase in the cost of living encourages workers to press for further wage increases causing a continuing inflationary spiral with rising wages chased by rising prices, or vice versa.

Demand-pull inflation

This type of inflation involves 'too much money chasing too few goods', that is an excessive supply of money relative to the goods and services available for purchase. Upward movement of wages can be an explanation of this, but 'too much money' usually refers to excessive credit expansion, for example easier bank loans and hire purchase, etc., which encourages people to spend money that they do not immediately have available.

The effects of inflation

Inflation has the effect of making us all worse off. If your country has more inflation than other countries this will mean that your prices will rise faster.

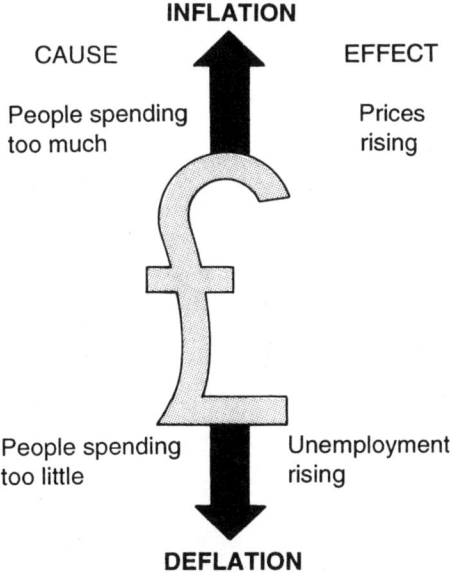

Consumer spending has an important effect on inflation.

Consequently, your exporters will find it harder to sell their products. Consumers both in your country and abroad will be less inclined to buy the more expensive home-produced goods, preferring the less expensive foreign products. This will lead to reduced output at home and job losses, further adding to the rate of inflation. The following summarises the main effects of inflation:

- Prices are persistently rising, resulting in a decline in the standard of living, especially for those on fixed incomes.
- Saving is discouraged because people recognise that money saved will buy less in the future.
- Exports become more expensive because of increased production costs. Consequently, there is a tendency to import more goods since they are relatively cheaper than domestic production.

- People who owe money to others (*debtors*) gain from inflation, whereas those who are owed money (*creditors*) lose.

Controlling inflation

If a government believes that demand-pull is the cause of inflation it can put a number of measures into effect. The government can:

- reduce its own demand for goods and services;
- encourage increased productivity;
- try to reduce demand by consumers and producers;
- make credit more expensive and more difficult to obtain;
- take more in taxes than the government spends;
- introduce controls, e.g. of wages, prices, imports.

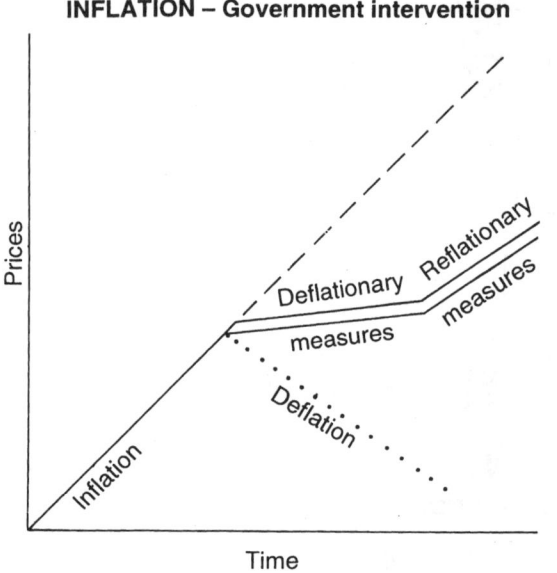

INFLATION – Government intervention

Summary

Inflation – persistent rise in the general level of prices of consumer goods and services.

Cost-push inflation – inflation caused by increases in costs to producers (e.g. higher wages or material costs).

Demand-pull inflation – inflation caused by more demand in the whole economy than can be supplied at existing prices.

Deflation – where the value of money is rising while prices are falling.

Deflationary measures – strategies used by the government in an attempt to reduce spending in the economy (usually through monetary or fiscal policies).

Reflationary measures – strategies used by the government to increase demand and encourage growth.

Hyperinflation – when prices are rising so fast that generally people prefer to spend their money rather than hold on to it.

The inflation line shows what the trend would be if inflation remained unchecked. The double line shows the possible effects of deflationary or reflationary measures.

Where cost-push inflation is thought to be the cause the remedies are more complex, and often open to political argument. For example, the prices of imported goods and raw materials are outside the control of the government. However, some control can be exercised over wage increases and the cost of home-produced goods through a firm prices and incomes policy, although the desirability of this is subject to political debate and there is no clear evidence that such a policy works.

Taxation and Inflation

20.6 Activities

1. Describe the principles upon which taxation should be based.
2. Explain the five functions of taxation.
3. Explain the differences between the proportional, progressive and regressive forms of taxation.
4. Distinguish carefully between direct and indirect taxation. Include a description of at least two of each forms of taxation to illustrate your answer.
5. How does the tax VAT get its name? Calculate the missing figures in the following table.

	(a)	(b)	(c)	(d)
Gross invoice value	240	1200	800	?
less 20% trade discount	?	?	?	100
Total goods	?	?	?	400
plus $17\frac{1}{2}$% VAT	?	?	?	?
	£?	£?	£?	£?

6. Explain the difference between protective duties and excise duties.
7. What is National Insurance and why is it sometimes referred to as a 'tax on jobs'?
8. To what extent does the current council tax meet the four principles stated by Adam Smith?
9. Define direct taxation and describe the forms it can take.
10. How does indirect taxation differ from direct taxation?
11. Describe the forms of indirect taxation commonly used.
12. Do you feel direct or indirect taxation the more appropriate? Give reasons for your answer.
13. What is inflation? How does 'cost-push' inflation differ from 'demand-pull' inflation?
14. What are the effects of inflation?
15. What steps might a government take in order to control inflation?

Comprehensive Business Studies

Structured Questions

1. Look at the notice of coding (Form P2) below and answer the following questions.

```
┌─────────────────────────────────────────────────────────────────┐
│  ☐   [crown]   Inland Revenue          Issued by                │
│                PAYE-Notice of Coding   H.M. Inspector of Taxes  │
│                Please keep this notice CODSALL                  │
│                for future reference    QUEENS RD                │
│                and let me know of any  CODSALL                  │
│                change in your address. SHROPSHIRE               │
│                Form P3(T) enclosed                              │
│                (or previously sent)              TF3 3CC        │
│                explains the entries.                            │
│                                                                 │
│      125                                                        │
│                                        Please use both lines    │
│      ┌──────────────────────┐          of this reference if you │
│      │ MR K PEARSON         │          write or call - it will  │
│      │ 21 HIGH STREET       │          help to avoid delay.     │
│      │ NEWTOWN              │          125/D701                 │
│      │                      │          TN  11  06  60  A        │
│      │           ZT1 1AB    │                                   │
│      └──────────────────────┘          Date  10.05.98           │
│                                                                 │
│  This notice cancels any previous notice of coding for the year │
│  shown below. It shows the allowances which make up your code.  │
│  Your employer or paying officer will use this code to deduct   │
│  or refund the right amount of tax under PAYE during the year   │
│  shown below.                                                   │
│  Please check this notice. If you think it is wrong please      │
│  return it to me and give your reasons. If we cannot agree you  │
│  have the right of appeal.                                      │
│  Please let me know at once about any change in your personal   │
│  circumstances which may alter your allowances and coding.      │
│  By law you are required to tell me of any income that is not   │
│  fully taxed, even if you are not sent a Tax Return.            │
│                                                                 │
│  See │ Allowances      │  £   │ See │ Less Deductions │   £    │
│  Note│                 │      │ Note│                 │        │
│  ────┼─────────────────┼──────┼─────┼─────────────────┼────────│
│   17 │ PERSONAL        │ 3295 │     │                 │        │
│      │ ALLOWANCE       │      │     │                 │        │
│      │                 │      │     │                 │        │
│      │                 │      │     │ Less total      │        │
│      │                 │      │     │ deductions      │        │
│      │ Total allowances│ 3295 │     │ Allowances set  │  3295  │
│      │                 │      │     │ against pay etc.│        │
│                                                                 │
│       Your code for the year to 5 April 1999 is  329L          │
│                                          Please see Part B      │
│                                          overleaf               │
│  P2 (T)                                                         │
└─────────────────────────────────────────────────────────────────┘
```

(a) What do the letters PAYE stand for? (1)
(b) What is the purpose of sending the notice of coding to the taxpayer? (1)
(c) What should the person receiving this notice do if they do not agree with any of the information shown on it? (2)
(d) Briefly explain how the tax code is calculated. (3)
(e) Why is income tax said to be both a direct tax and a progressive tax? (3)
(f) To what extent do you feel that the PAYE system meets Adam Smith's 'rules' of taxation? (10)

2 Study the following and answer the questions below.

A budget for the poor?

Tax rates and allowances

Before the budget

Taxable income (£)	Rate (%)	Cumulative tax (£)
0-4300	20 (the lower rate)	860
4,301-27,000	23 (the basic rate)	6,104
Over 27,000	40 (the higher rate)	

After the budget

Taxable income (£)	Rate (%)	Cumulative tax (£)
0-1,500	10 (the starting rate)	150
1,501-28,000	22 (the basic rate)	5,980
Over 28,000	40 (the higher rate)	

Personal allowances	Old	New
Basic amount	£4,335	£4,385
Age 65-74	£5,410	£5,720
Age 75 and over	£5,600	£5,980
Married allowances		
both under 65	£1,900	£Nil
Husband or wife aged 65-74	£4,965	£5,125
Husband or wife aged 75 or over	£5,025	£5,195
65 or over - Income limit	£16,200 a year	£16,800 a year

(a) What was the highest rate of income tax:
 (i) before the Budget (1)
 (ii) after the Budget? (1)
(b) Calculate the increase in the sing;le person's allowance given in the Budget. (1)
(c) State two possible reasons why the government was able to reduce income tax rates (2)
(d) Calculate the new tax bill of a married man aged under 65 earning £17,500 a year (3)
(e) Did the Budget make the income tax more or less progressive? Explain your answer fully. (6)
(f) How might the changes affect:
 (i) workers
 (ii) unemployment
 (iii) overall spending in the economy? (6)

3 (a) What is the current basic rate of income tax in the UK? (1)
 (b) Express the higher rate of income tax in the UK in terms of pence in the £. (1)
 (c) What is the meaning of 'fiscal policy'? (2)
 (d) What indicates that a tax is 'regressive'? (2)
 (e) Briefly describe two methods of taxation that can be used generally to promote economic activity. (4)
 (f) Identify two social problems and two economic problems which exist in the UK today. (4)
 (g) Choose two social problems and two economic problems and show how each might be solved using taxation. (6)

4 (a) What is inflation? (1)
 (b) State two categories of people who would benefit during a period of high inflation. (2)
 (c) Give two ways in which the process of inflation may begin. (2)
 (d) Give three reasons why prices are more likely to rise as employment approaches the full level. (3)
 (e) What do the letters RPI stand for? How does the RPI indicate the level of inflation. (4)
 (f) Explain the difference between cost-push inflation and demand-pull inflation. (4)
 (g) Briefly describe policies a government could follow in an attempt to check:
  (i) cost-push inflation;
  (ii) demand-pull inflation. (4)

Research Assignments

1 Why does any government need to redistribute income? To what extent do you feel taxation achieves this aim? Give specific examples to illustrate your answer.

2 Using data quoted from any reliable source, describe the effect of inflation on your country and explain how the government is attempting to control it.

3 Describe four taxes levied on individuals by the government. How far do you consider them to be either progressive or regressive?

Taxation and Inflation

4 Explain the difference between direct and indirect taxation. How, if at all, do they affect the rate of inflation as measured by the Retail Price Index? Use official data to support your observations.

5 Use a collection of newspaper articles and headlines, together with our own explanations, to show the difference between demand-pull and cost-push inflation. What policies might a government adopt to reduce inflation?

6 Investigate the following question over a six-month period. To what extent is your family's personal rate of inflation the same as the official government rate?

7 Discuss the suggestion that the British taxation system is progressive. Provide evidence to support your views.

8 Should the government levy a 'health tax' on alcoholic drink to partly fund the National Health Service? Include a survey of local views.

9 Identify a varied selection of 30 goods and monitor price changes over a three-month period. Make a personal record of the rate of inflation. Write a detailed report of your findings, including appropriate charts and graphs.

21 Population

21.1 Importance of population

Consider making a list of every single item that you have consumed during the last three days. Assuming that you can remember every item, the list that you will end up with will be surprisingly long. But you will no doubt be well aware that there are people throughout the world who are suffering from malnutrition. In fact, two thirds of the world's population is in this position. The source of this problem can be found in our inability to grow enough food to feed an increasing world population. The shortage of resources required by the world population is not restricted to food alone; many other material shortages also exist such as housing, education, medical care, etc.

Obviously many of the existing shortages would be easier to resolve if there were fewer people in the world, yet some countries are actually trying to persuade their inhabitants to have more children to increase the size of their population. But serious consideration of the problem will lead you to realise that it is not just the size of population, but also the structure of it that is important. For this reason *demographic* (population) studies are important to economic planning. It must also be remembered that population not only provides the labour to produce goods and services, but it is also a source of demand for the goods and services which the labour produces. Population studies are also important because changes that occur require changes in planning strategies to ensure that resources are used efficiently. For example, a straightforward increase in population will require increased resources devoted to education, welfare services and medical care.

21.2 Factors influencing population size

Before 1801, when the first *official census* (official counting of the inhabitants of a country) was held, there was little information on the size of Britain's population although it has been estimated to have been about $5\frac{1}{2}$ million in 1688. In 1801, and periodically ever since, the government ordered the first official census of the UK.

The census does more than just count the total population. It breaks the data into a variety of categories, e.g. men, women, single, married, widowed, divorced, number of children, teenagers, working people, retired people, etc. The census counts people in relation to the types of houses they live in, the kind of job they do, how they travel to and from work, and their country of origin.

Population

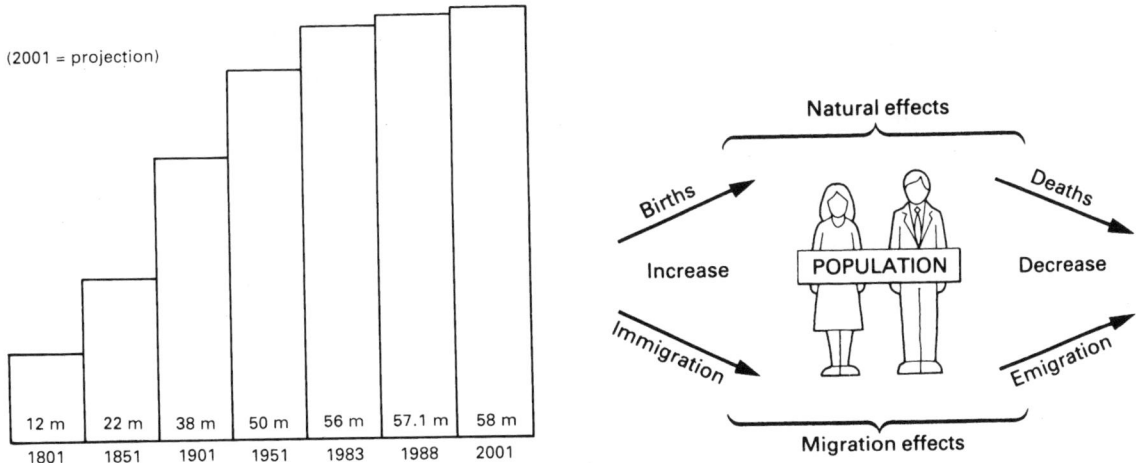

UK population growth (millions).

The data obtained from a census is used, particularly by the government, to decide what revenue it needs and how it should be used. For example, it is used to work out how much is needed for pensions, health care, etc. The census also shows how the workforce is changing and moving to other areas. This information is used when planning building programmes, e.g. factories, housing, etc.

You can see from the diagram below that the population of the United Kingdom has steadily increased since 1801, with some levelling off in recent times.

There are three factors which influence the size of population – migration, births and deaths.

Migration

Migration refers to the movement of people from one country to another to live. More people may come into a country to live (immigration), and people may leave their home country to go and live abroad (emigration). Depending whether immigration exceeds emigration, or vice versa, the population increases or decreases.

Migration into and out of UK		
1981	Inflow	153,000
	Outflow	233,000
1986	Inflow	250,000
	Outflow	213,000
1991	Inflow	267,000
	Outflow	239,000

What general trend can you observe in this data showing migration into and out of the UK between 1981 and 1991?

Migration is influenced by economic conditions and official policies and controls. Poor economic conditions in one country and brighter prospects in another country encourage migration. But some countries may enforce controls which limit immigration or emigration, and this can influence population size.

Birth rate

The birth rate can be expressed as a percentage or as a figure representing the number of births per thousand of the population. From the diagram below it can be seen that the trend in the UK is one of a steadily decreasing birth rate since 1801. The birth rate is affected by a number of factors:

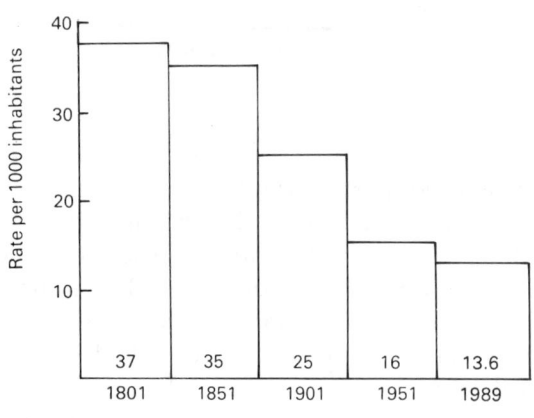

UK birth rate from 1801.

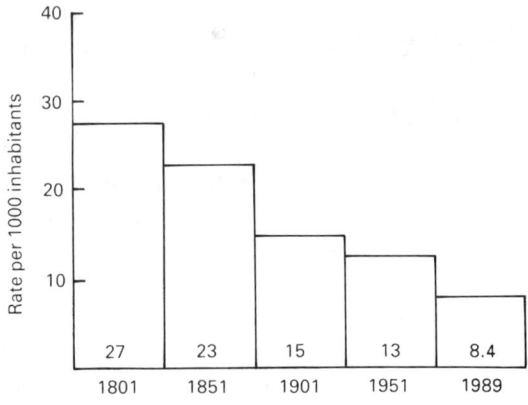

UK death rate from 1801.

- *Standard of living* – where a standard of living is high, the birth rate tends to be low. When the standard of living is low, the birth rate tends to be high.
- *Attitudes, customs and beliefs* – religious beliefs (e.g. Catholicism) and attitudes to contraception influence the birth rate. A reduction in prejudice to women working, coupled with a desire for a better standard of living that can be achieved by both partners of a marriage working, affects the willingness of women to have children.
- *Women of child-bearing age* – assuming that the average number of children born to women remains unchanged, then the greater the proportion of women of child-bearing age, the higher will be the birth rate.
- *Government policies* – the birth rate is influenced by the level of welfare benefits, child benefit and rate of taxation, all of which are directly controlled by the government. The government also influences the provision of facilities which provide advice on contraception and family planning (e.g. through the education system), which also affects the birth rate as do laws and attitudes to abortion.

Death rate

The death rate is the number of deaths per thousand of population per year. It can also be expressed as a percentage figure. Obviously, if people begin to live longer this contributes to an increase in the size of the population. This is the case in the UK. It can be seen from the diagram above that there has been an almost continuous decline in the death rate since 1801, although the trend has evened out in recent times. The reasons for the fall in death rate are clearer than those influencing the fall in the birth rate.

- *Standard of living* – improved living standards such as better housing, clothing and diet contribute to better health and reduce mortality.
- *Medical knowledge* – advances in medical knowledge, new discoveries, drugs and inventions have all contributed to a significant reduction in the death rate.
- *Public health measures* – many basic services provided by local authorities have improved considerably and have contributed to a reduction in illness and disease. For example, improvements in services such as refuse collection, water purification and sewage disposal have contributed to a reduction in death from infectious disease.

21.3 Optimum population size

Overpopulation

This creates many problems, whether it occurs in a single country or worldwide. Poverty, food shortages and a low rate of investment are all features of overpopulation. It is a familiar feature of an agriculture-based society which experiences difficulty in accumulating sufficient capital necessary to industrialise the economy. The difficulty in accumulating capital for industrial development occurs because a large percentage of all available resources is needed to keep the population alive.

Declining population

This also creates problems. A falling population implies that the average age of the population is increasing. This reduces the mobility and the quality of the labour force. It also makes demands for higher welfare benefits and a higher taxation on the younger sections of the working population. There is a greater need for hospitals, old people's homes and related services. On the other hand, there could be a reduced need for schools and teachers.

If the population is declining, a smaller domestic market exists – there are fewer customers for the goods and services produced. This can reduce the opportunities for large-scale production and the economies of scale associated with it. It may also result in reduced enthusiasm and initiative in the workforce.

Optimum population

The optimum, or most beneficial, population is one which makes maximum effective use of the resources (land, labour and capital) available. Optimum population is that which gives the highest output per head of population.

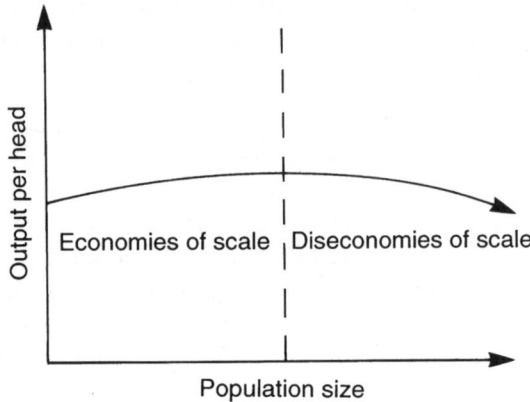

Optimum population.

- If the average output per head is rising as population increases, then the country is underpopulated.
- If the average output falls as population increases then the country is overpopulated.

21.4 Distribution of population

Age distribution

Age distribution refers to the numbers of the population in the different age groups. Age distribution is important because it is directly related to the proportion of producers to consumers. It is influenced by both past and present birth and death rates.

When looking at the age distribution of the population it is usual to classify the population into three groups.

1 Those below school leaving age.
2 Those of working age.
3 Those above retirement age.

Obviously, those of working age are required to support people within the other two categories.

Working population

All these people are at work or available for work. The size of the workforce will be influenced by:

- total population size
- school leaving age
- retirement age
- percentage of non-workers in the working age group
- people working who are beyond retirement age
- age distribution of population
- sex distribution of population.

In the UK we say that the population has 'aged' during the twentieth century. In other words, there has been a tendency for an increase in the proportion of those above retirement age; those leaving the workforce to retire are exceeding those entering employment. This trend has its origins in past and present birth and death rates, but it has also been influenced by an increasing number of young people entering full-time education and other 'non-employment' schemes beyond school leaving age, and a tendency for people to retire earlier than they used to.

Dependency ratio

The dependency ratio is the proportion of the working population to the non-working (dependent) population:

$$\frac{\text{Number of workers}}{\text{Number of dependents}} = \text{Dependency ratio}$$

Economic effects of an ageing population

1. *Changes in spending patterns* – as the population ages spending patterns change; there is an increased demand for goods related to the older population, and reduced demand for goods for the young.
2. *Increased dependence on working population* – as the proportion of non-working population increases there is an increase in the number of those dependent on the output of the current working population (increased dependency ratio).

Years of age	Further expectation of life	
NOW	MALE	FEMALE
20	54.6	58.3
25	49.9	53.6
30	44.9	48.8
35	40.1	44.0
40	35.3	39.1
45	30.6	34.3
50	26.1	29.7
55	21.9	25.3

Expectation of life table.

3 *Less adaptive workforce* – there is a reduced mobility and adaptability of the labour force because an older population tend to be less energetic and enterprising than a younger population. Alternatively, we could say that there is a need for the younger proportion of the population to be more mobile, adaptive, energetic and enterprising.

Sex distribution

As long as the proportion of males to females is similar, sex distribution is of less significance to population than age distribution.

In the UK more males are born than females and men outnumber women of all age groups up to 44 years of age. But in the older age groups there are a greater number of women than men. Whilst this may at first sight seem a contradiction, the reason for the differences is quite simple; more women survive beyond the age of 45. Three factors explain this:

1 *Work pressure* – physical and mental pressure of work affects men more than women.
2 *Emigration* – more men leave the UK than women.
3 *Wars* – affect the male population more than the female population.

Geographical distribution

Geographical distribution refers to the distribution of the population in different regions at various dates. We can usually see a direct relationship between location or relocation of industry and geographical distribution of the population.

In the UK we have seen that as the location of industries has changed, so has the geographical distribution of the population. Prior to the Industrial Revolution, the population was located mainly in rural areas, and concentrated in areas where the farming land is good (particularly in the south-east). Following the Industrial Revolution there was a movement from the countryside into towns, and particularly into the northern parts of Britain where the major impact of the development of coal, steel, cotton and shipbuilding was taking effect. As these industries declined between the wars and after 1945, newer industries in light engineering located in the Midlands and the south attracted labour away from the north.

Occupational distribution

Occupational distribution statistics show the numbers of people employed in various occupations. Job distribution depends on a country's stage of development. Underdeveloped countries tend to have a large proportion (75 per cent) of their workforce employed in the agricultural sector, while developed countries have 10 per cent or less in this section of the economy.

By examining such statistics over a period of time we can see changes that have taken place. For example, prior to the Industrial Revolution Britain's workforce was largely involved in agriculture. The Industrial Revolution necessitated

Population

movement from agriculture into manufacturing and construction industries. This trend has continued and it has also contributed to increased employment in the tertiary sector. The table opposite shows the movement away from the primary industries such as farming, forestry, fishing and mining. However, the percentage of the total workforce employed in manufacturing has changed little.

	1841		1901		1981		1991	
	'000s	%	'000s	%	'000s	%	'000s	%
Agriculture, forestry, fishing	1 639	22.3	2 243	11.8	360	1.7	268	1.2
Mining, quarrying	225	3.2	944	5.0	337	1.6	154	0.7
Manufacturing	2 452	35.5	7 000	36.9	6 038	28.1	5 437	24.4
Construction	377	5.5	1 336	7.0	1 132	5.3	1 038	4.7
Transport/ communications	200	2.9	1 497	7.9	1 429	6.6	1 354	6.0
Others	2 014	30.6	5 954	31.4	12 229	56.7	14 021	63.0
Total	6 097	100.0	18 974	100.0	21.525	100.0	22 272	100.0

21.5 Mobility of labour

Mobility in this respect is the movement between occupations. The efficient working of any economy depends not only on the size and structure of the workforce but also how mobile it is, so that maximum use is made of it. Mobility of labour can be viewed in two ways.

1 *Geographic (lateral) mobility* – the ability to move from one area to another.
2 *Occupational (vertical) mobility* – the ability to change one's job, profession or industry.

Obstacles to mobility of labour

Look at the following list of factors that inhibit labour mobility. Which ones can you identify that can be clearly associated with geographic mobility and which are related only to occupational mobility?

- *Inertia* – the desire to remain in one place.
- *Family and friendship ties* have to be broken.
- *Education* of children may be disrupted.
- *Re-housing* involves costs and inconvenience.
- *Prejudice* – people may dislike particular jobs or areas.
- *Knowledge* of alternative jobs is not always readily available.
- *Wages* of alternative occupation may be unattractive.
- *Retraining* costs may be too high.
- *Skills* to do alternative employment may be lacking.
- *Trade unions* may resist occupation movement.

Comprehensive Business Studies

21.6 Activities

1. What do you understand by the word demography?
2. Give four reasons why population studies are important.
3. What is a 'census'?
4. What has been happening to the size of the UK population since 1801?
5. Explain the meaning of the word 'migration' and show its relevance to population.
6. Define birth rate and list the factors which affects its growth or decline.
7. What trend can be seen in the UK birth rate over the last 150 years?
8. What factors influence the death rate and why is this figure important to population?
9. Why are overpopulation and declining population problems?
10. What do you understand by optimum population?
11. 'The age distribution of the UK population has increased during the twentieth century.' Explain this statement.
12. What is the dependency ratio?
13. Explain the term 'sex distribution of population.'
14. Give a brief description of the geographical distribution of the UK population since the Industrial Revolution.
15. What does examination of statistics related to UK occupational distribution show us?
16. What is mobility of labour and what factors influence it?

Structured Questions

1. Consider the following diagram on page 377 and answer the following questions.
   (a) What was the population of the UK in 1951? (1)
   (b) What has happened to the percentage of the 0–14 year-olds in the population since 1901? (2)

Population

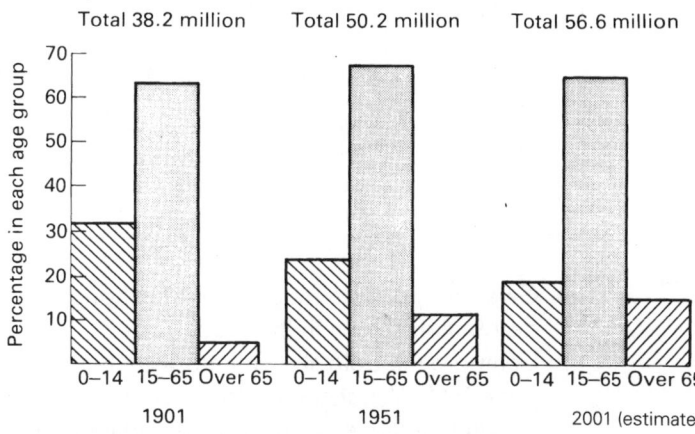

Source: *Adapted from Annual Abstract of Statistics*, HMSO.

(c) Calculate the number of 0–14 year-olds in the UK for 1984. (3)
(d) Why is the age distribution of the UK often shown using the categories that have been used in the data? (2)
(e) (i) What evidence is there in the data that the UK has an ageing population? (2)
  (ii) What factors have contributed to the ageing of the UK population? (4)
  (iii) What are the economic implications for a country of having an ageing population? (6)

2 The following table shows the changes in occupational distribution in Anytown, 1978–98.

Employment in Anytown, 1978–98

% of employment in:	1978	1988	1998
Primary sector	6	3	1
Secondary sector	70	40	30
Tertiary sector	20	52	58
Unemployed	4	5	11
Working population (000s)	500	520	540

(a) What do you understand by 'occupational distribution? (1)
(b) Give two examples of jobs in each of the primary, secondary and tertiary sectors. (3)

(c) Summarise the main trends that can be observed in this data. (3)
(d) Complete the following table, showing all your calculations.

Anytown – actual numbers employed

No. of people employed	1998
Primary sector	?
Secondary sector	?
Tertiary sector	?

(3)

(e) Give four possible reasons for the changes in Anytown occupational distribution shown in the data. (4)
(f) Compare the data shown here with that contained in the table on page 375. What comparison can you make between the trend shown here for Anytown and the national data shown on page 375? (6)

3 (a) 'The census does more than count the population.' Explain this statement. (2)
(b) Define the term 'optimum population'. (2)
(c) 'If the size of the population is too small the country may not be able to fully use its productive potential'. Why is this statement true? (3)
(d) 'Beyond the optimum population size diseconomies occur'. Explain this statement. (3)
(e) Give two examples of factors that influence the birth rate and two that influence the death rate. (4)
(f) Refer to the data on page 375 showing changes in occupational distribution of the UK population. Explain the reasons for at least three of the changes contained in the data. (6)

Research Assignments

1 There has been a considerable increase in the number of people employed in the tertiary sector in the UK. Use locally researched data to show whether this is also the case in the area where you live. Write a report to summarise your findings.

2 What effect has the national fall in the birth rate had in your local area?

3 To what extent is your local population economically mobile?

22 The Role of Governments

22.1 The responsibilities of governments

In all countries the government plays a crucial role because it has such a wide-reaching effect on the community. The level of government involvement in the economy or the life of the country will be influenced by the type of economic system that the country has – free, planned or controlled, or mixed (*see* Chapter 1). The UK economy is largely a 'mixed' system, that is a mixture of the free and controlled economic systems. In other words, there is some government involvement in the economy and the life of the country. The extent of this involvement can be dependent upon political influences (refer also to Chapter 7).

The responsibilities of governments can be categorised into four major areas:

1 Promotion of law and order and defence

The government is the protector of the people. The general aim is to ensure that all persons in the community receive 'just treatment'. Law and order is important in society because it promotes economic stability. For example, tourists are not likely to want to visit a country where there is unrest and instability. Similarly, investors will be less likely to put their money into a country where law and order is not evident.

In order to meet this responsibility the government must promote appropriate legislation and provide police and courts of justice to administer law and order in the country. The government also has to make provision for defence (e.g. armed forces) against external dangers, and to provide diplomatic representation abroad.

2 Strategic planning

The government will develop plans for particular sectors of the economy. It may want to promote development in particular industries, or in specific locations. To support such a plan the government may provide grants, subsidies or 'soft' loans, advisory services and other agencies to industries or people it wants to influence.

As part of their strategic planning many governments provide public utilities, such as water and telephones, whereas some governments prefer these in private ownership. Many aspects of public transport are also provided or regulated by governments.

3 Provision of social services

The government will provide services which private enterprise would be unable or unwilling to supply at a price that all people could afford to pay, e.g.

education, health, welfare, culture and sanitation. The provision of social services is examined in more detail later in this chapter.

4 Management of the economy

The government is charged with overall control of the economy. It will aim to achieve a high level of employment and to encourage economic growth through sound productivity. It will want to manage the National Debt, protect the country's balance of payments position and maintain its foreign reserves.

The Budget

In order to meet the foregoing responsibilities the government will need to raise the necessary revenue and exercise control over the economy. In Chapter 20 we have seen the part that taxation measures play, and in Chapter 15 we saw how governments can influence the financial markets. The Budget plays a key part in the government's strategies for managing the economy.

There are two main functions of the Budget:

1 *to regulate the economy* by influencing the demand for goods and services;
2 *to redistribute income and wealth* among the sections of the community.

The government makes public its Budget every year. The Budget summarises what services the government intends to provide for its citizens, how much money is needed, and how it intends to raise the necessary revenue. The Budget may also set out measures to be taken to stimulate or depress key areas of the economy and to encourage saving and investment.

The main source of government income is from taxation. Changes in taxation can affect businesses in a variety of ways. For example, if the government increased taxation on cars, people will probably buy fewer. This will lead to reduced sales and lower profits. This would, of course, result in increased unemployment, which in turn will mean that consumers have less money in order to buy cars, and so on.

22.2 Government assistance to entrepreneurs

It is in the interest of all governments to help businesses to achieve their full potential because in doing so businesses contribute to the ideal of full employment and add to national prosperity. Most governments will try to support businesses by providing the following:

- An environment that is conducive to economic growth. It will do this by setting rules for business operations, and providing utilities and other facilities which support business activities.
- Promotion and maintenance of competitive markets. Governments will prevent companies from abusing their power by taking action against monopolistic

activities. This benefits businesses that are not in a monopolistic position, as well as safeguarding the consumer.

Trade promotion

The government provides various forms of assistance to encourage trade, particularly in respect of the exporting sector. The latter is recognised as of special importance in contributing to the balance of payments (*see* Chapter 11). The following are typical examples of government assistance in promoting trade overseas and at home:

- foreign market intelligence
- Export Credits Guarantee Department
- subsidies
- regional aid.

Foreign market intelligence

The government will provide information about foreign markets and trading opportunities. For example, it will advise on the market potential for an exporter's goods and provide details of regulations and other specific local requirements in the target market. The government will also assist in the process of advertising and marketing the country's products abroad, e.g. co-ordinating participation in overseas trade fairs.

Much of foreign market intelligence operations are carried out by governments through their embassies and diplomats abroad. These officials will also register protests on behalf of their country if free trade is unduly threatened by the import controls of foreign governments.

Export Credits Guarantee Department

This government department supports exporters by providing:

- insurance against non-payment of debts by foreign importers;
- grants or low-interest loans to assist exporters in meeting the initial expense of exporting (*see* Chapter 11).

Subsidies

When a government is faced with a persistent adverse balance of trade it might tackle the situation by imposing import duties (tariffs/taxes) which would discourage imports by making them relatively more expensive. This can have an adverse effect in causing overseas governments to impose taxes on our goods in retaliation.

An alternative strategy would be to give subsidies (grants) to home producers. This would have the effect of making UK goods cheaper and enable them to compete more effectively against cheap imports.

Regional aid

Regional aid refers to grants or loans or tax relief given to firms and local authorities to create jobs or to improve the infrastructure in areas where there is high unemployment and poor living conditions. The aid aims to attract firms into areas identified by the government for special treatment (*see also* Chapter 2).

22.3 Government intervention in business

Governments throughout the world intervene in business activities for a variety of reasons and to different degrees. Sometimes they might do so in order to support enterprises, in other circumstances governments might be motivated by a need to control or regulate them.

Consumer protection

Consumer protection refers to the range of measures that exist to help consumers to make wise purchases and to protect them from exploitation. Consumer protection is dealt with in detail in Chapter 9.

Governments accept some of the responsibility for consumer protection and demonstrate this in a variety of ways, including the following:

- by contributing to consumer education and advice;
- by establishing and enforcing appropriate legislation;
- by the control of quality and weights and measures;
- by the monitoring and control of prices;
- by the promotion of fair trading practices;
- by the supervision of credit facilities.

The National Consumer Council

The Council was set up by the government in 1975 to carry out research into consumer problems. It acts as a pressure group and has strong links with other consumer organisations. As such, the Council can give businesses advice to help direct their marketing strategies, and it can also put pressure on businesses when they are acting in a manner that is not in the interests of consumers.

Monopolies, mergers and restrictive practices

A *monopoly* is a situation where a firm holds such a large proportion (25 per cent or more) of the market that it could control the supply and price. A firm in a monopolistic position could exploit the consumer by restricting output and charging high prices.

Where a monopoly exists in the public sector the government has direct access to the means of protecting consumer interests. Where the monopoly exists in the private sector it is important that the government ensures that those with a large share of the market do not exploit their strong position in a manner that is not in the interest of consumers.

A *merger* refers to the joining together of two firms into a larger unit. This can be against public interests if it results in a monopolistic position which is exploited by the firm.

A *restrictive practice* is any activity by a firm aimed at reducing competition, e.g. by price fixing and forming groups of firms (*cartels*) to control output and other factors influencing conditions of sale.

There are two main elements which support the UK government's legal framework for preventing businesses from restricting competition or engaging in activities which are unfair to the consumer.

The Monopolies and Mergers Commission

The Commission can investigate to see if a firm or firms are operating against the public interest. It also investigates mergers and takeovers to ensure that firms with a large share of the market do not exploit their position against the interest of the public.

The Commission reports its findings to the Director General of Fair Trading. Action can be taken to remedy any trading situation found to be against the public interest, and recommendations are made to the government.

The Restrictive Practices Court

The Court investigates cases where firms are engaged in activities which have the effect of fixing prices in a manner that is against the public interest. For example, a group of firms might agree to fix their prices (*a price ring*) or a firm could decide that it will only supply certain retailers (e.g. those who do not cut prices).

Costs and benefits of business activity

Any decision or action a business takes will have costs and benefits. The costs and benefits to the business are called *private costs* and *private benefits*, and these can usually be quantified in financial terms. Where business decisions or actions affect society they are called *social costs* and *social benefits*, and they are often more difficult to measure in financial terms – for example, how do you put a definite financial cost on noise and dirt? Governments have to safeguard the interests of society by ensuring that it is not unjustifiably affected by business activity.

Private costs and benefits

If a business intended to expand its factory, the *private costs* could include:

- the cost of additional land needed
- planning and building costs
- interest charges on capital being borrowed.

The *private benefits* could be:

- increased value of total assets

- greater revenue (income)
- bigger profit.

You will have probably recognised from the foregoing examples that the private costs and benefits described here would be reflected in the accounts of the business. For example, planning and building costs will be registered as debts the business has incurred, whereas the greater income achieved may well show up as increased profit in the end of year figures.

Social costs and benefits

Unlike private costs and benefits, social costs and benefits are not reflected in the accounts of the business. This is because they have effects outside the firm. Social costs and benefits often involve factors that cannot be readily measured in financial terms. The process of comparing such factors is called *cost benefit analysis*.

The *social costs* of the above factory expansion could include:

- increased noise and pollution
- greater traffic congestion
- loss of green, open areas.

The *social benefits* of such a development could be:

- increased local employment
- improved local prosperity
- direct purchasing opportunities for the community.

Where a business development is likely to cause concerns and objections from the local community a *cost benefit analysis* can help to put the arguments for and against it in perspective. It can also help to identify unfair pressures on the community and ways that it can be compensated for the problems created. It is an important role of both central and local government to protect the public and their community from unjustifiable business decisions and developments.

Import controls

Sometimes governments may feel it necessary to place controls on goods being brought into the country in order to protect industries in the home market, or to secure a favourable balance-of-payments position (*see* Chapter 11). There are two basic methods of import controls – *quotas* and *tariffs*.

- *Quotas* – are a limit on the quantity of a product that is allowed to enter the country in a given period of time. Sometimes the government may implement an *embargo* which is a complete ban on the import of certain goods (or goods of a specific country).
- *Tariffs* – are a tax on imports which has the effect of raising the cost price of the import. The tax may be *specific* or *ad valorem* (for an explanation of these terms *see* Chapter 11).

The Role of Governments

Taxation

Taxation of income, goods and property can also be used to influence and to encourage industry and commerce. For example, increasing taxation on certain products can depress demand and discourage production, and vice versa. Taxation is dealt with in depth in Chapter 20.

Nationalisation

We have seen in Chapter 4 that sometimes the state will take over the ownership of certain industries. When a business is taken into public ownership in this way it is said to have been *nationalised*. Sometimes enterprises are in state ownership but have not been nationalised, in other words, they are enterprises that have been originally established by the government. State ownership of industries is a prominent feature of controlled economies, and to a lesser extent is found in mixed economies.

State control of industries in this way allows the government to ensure that certain goods and services are made available at an economic price, and it also makes it possible to plan for particular sectors of the economy. You should refer again to Chapter 4 for wider examination of state ownership of industries, and particularly the arguments for and against state ownership.

22.4 Social services

In modern society the responsibilities of government are now seen to include the provision of social services at a national and personal level such as social security, medical and health care, education and welfare facilities including sanitation, housing, roads and some aspects of transportation.

It is generally recognised that a government has an obligation to provide its citizens with social services because without government intervention many in the community would be denied these basic material needs. In this respect the government takes a political decision to provide these services either free or at a cost subsidised by funds obtained from taxation.

Education

Education is an example of the high degree of specialisation in modern developed societies. In the UK, instead of every worker trying to provide their own needs, each specialises in doing one thing and pays others to provide everything else. This is the case with education. Parents do not have the expertise or the time to educate their children. So they pay for schools and teachers to do the educating whilst they carry on their own specialisms, which in turn help to supply schools and teachers with their needs.

The UK has a strong tradition of state-provided education. The government funds most education at the primary, secondary, tertiary and higher levels. A well-educated population is generally recognised as making an important contribution to commerce and industry. Better educated and healthier workers are more productive and less of a burden on the state than people who are not. Conversely, low educational standards generally lead to less output for the economy. Education not only helps to provide the knowledge and skills that enable workers to be useful to business, but it also helps to make the workforce more flexible and mobile. In this sense education contributes to human wealth.

Health

A healthy population is important to all countries and, therefore, promotion of healthy living and medical care is an important responsibility of government. This will include not only the provision of medical facilities such as hospitals, but also the broadcasting of information on health-related matters such as sensible diet, hygiene, contraception, etc.

Health care has become increasingly important in most developed societies. As income rises, people tend to demand more health care. For the whole UK economy, incomes have gone up fairly steadily since the 1950s and so has the demand for health care.

One of the reasons for the rising demand for health care services is due to the change in attitudes towards such care. We expect more and better health care in the UK today. In some ways this is a result of the government's efforts to raise public awareness of the need for healthy living, including dietary influences.

The UK is one of the few countries in the industrialised world to have a free health service. In effect the service is not truly free because it is funded by the National Insurance scheme (explained below). In most other countries health is looked after by private insurance schemes. In some countries every person is required to join a scheme, whereas in others it is voluntary.

National Insurance (NI)

National Insurance, which is a system contributing to health care, is operated by many countries as a social service. It should be noted that National Insurance is not only concerned with health care, although this is one of its main aims, In the UK National Insurance is compulsory for all working people and the benefits are available to all the population.

National Insurance is an example of the way that some governments ensure that medical and health care and other support services are available for all members of the community. National Insurance is a scheme which aims to raise money through premiums deducted from wages, with contributions (approximately two-thirds) from employers. The funds raised in this way are used to provide the benefits outlined in the diagram above.

National Insurance contributions are paid into the National Insurance Fund and are used only to pay for National Insurance benefits (e.g. retirement pensions, unemployment benefits) and a small part of the National Health Service. National Insurance contributions are paid by workers and their employers and are calculated as a percentage of wages.

The Role of Governments

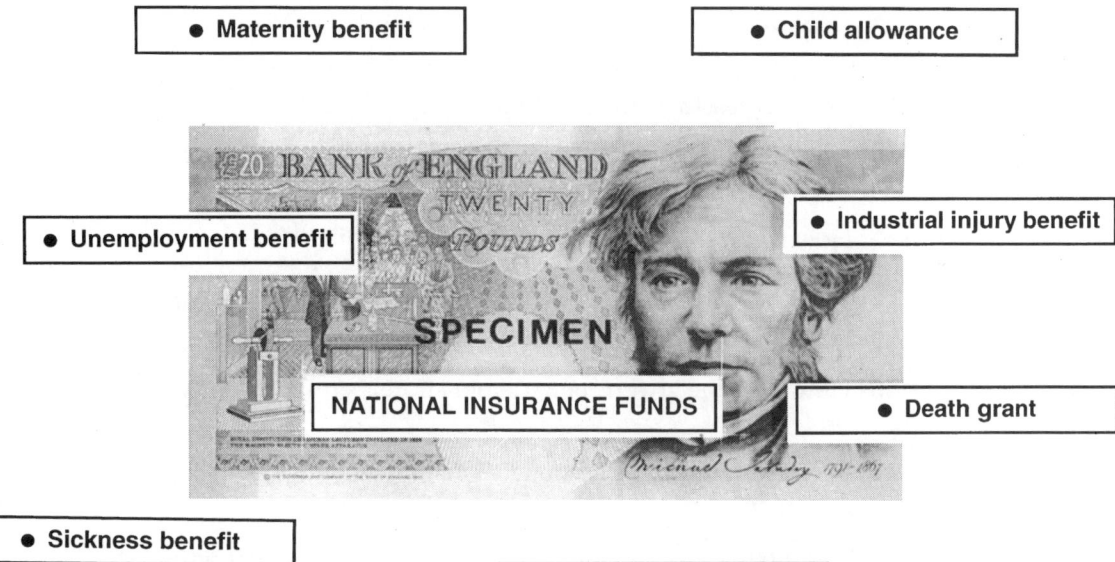

Some of the benefits of National Insurance.

Recreational facilities

Recreation also plays an important part in both the health, education and leisure of both citizens and tourists. The governments of most developed countries provide libraries, botanical gardens and recreational parks for the use of both local residents and visitors. Sport is also encouraged by the government, often with a Sports Minister as administrator. In addition, there are national galleries of art, museums and zoos, all considerably influenced by government. The foregoing are just some of the many social services that countries provide for their citizens – it would be impossible to include all of them here. However, the importance of social services is demonstrated by the fact that most governments establish separate ministries or departments with responsibilities for the various areas of social services. For example, there may be a department of education, transport, health, etc.

Activities

1. Describe the four main areas of responsibility of governments.
2. What is the purpose of the government budget?
3. Why is it in the interests of all governments to assist entrepreneurs?

4. How can a government assist the promotion of trade?
5. Why should a government be keen for a business involved in exporting to be successful? How could it help such a business?
6. How does the Export Credits Guarantee Department encourage foreign trade?
7. How could the use of subsidies help to solve a balance of trade deficit?
8. What is the purpose of regional grants?
9. Why do governments intervene in business activities?
10. How does the government demonstrate its responsibility for consumer protection?
11. In what way can the National Consumer Council help both the consumer and businesses?
12. Explain the meaning of the terms monopoly and merger.
13. What is the function of the Monopolies and Mergers Commission?
14. To what extent does the Restrictive Practices Court regulate business activities?
15. Explain the difference between private costs and benefits and social costs and benefits.
16. What is 'cost benefit analysis'?
17. How can cost benefit analysis help to protect society from unjustified business actions?
18. Why would a government impose controls on imports and what form might these controls take?
19. In what ways can the government's taxation policies affect businesses?
20. For what reason might a government want to own certain industries?
21. Why does a government have an obligation to provide its citizens with social services?
22. Why is education important to commerce and industry?
23. In what ways does the UK government try to promote a healthy population? How does it finance this?
24. How are funds raised through National Insurance used?

The Role of Governments

Structured Questions

1 Study the information below and answer the questions that follow.

> ### Working hours
>
> British trade unions have been trying for many years to reduce the working hours of employees, and governments have from time to time attempted to restrict the hours a business can operate. This has particularly been the case with regard to the times shops can open.
>
> Unions and the government do not necessarily have the same objectives in mind, and in any case it seems that there are always workers who are willing to work unsociable hours.

(a) What do you consider as 'unsociable working hours'? (1)
(b) Give two examples of ways in which the government might try to restrict the hours a business can operate. (2)
(c) State two reasons why the government might want to influence the hours a business can operate. (2)
(d) State two differences in the reasons which unions may have to try to influence working hours from those of the government. (2)
(e) Give three economic or social reasons why some workers would be more willing than others to work unsociable hours. (3)
(f) Allowing all businesses to operate unrestricted hours can affect different groups of people in varied ways. Describe the ways in which it could affect each of the following:
 (i) the employee
 (ii) the employee
 (iii) the government
 (iv) religious groups. (4)
(g) Write a report that argues against allowing businesses to operate unrestricted hours. (6)

2 Study the information on page 390 and answer the questions below.

(a) What is 'The Budget'? (1)
(b) Explain the terms *surplus* and *deficit* used here. (2)
(c) State two examples of sources of government income as a result of measures contained in the Budget. (2)
(d) List three major elements of central government expenditure. (3)
(e) If there was high inflation because consumers were spending too much money, the government could create a budget surplus by increasing taxation and lowering its own spending. What could be the effect of this on business? (3)

389

The Budget

The Chancellor of the Exchequer presents the main Budget once a year, and occasionally mini-budgets in between. Sometimes a budget *surplus* is achieved and sometimes a *deficit*. The Chancellor may prefer a deficit at a time of high unemployment but a surplus to check inflation.

(f) Describe four circumstances in which business organisations would want to influence government budgetary measures. (4)

(g) Give two examples of ways that individuals, and three examples where businesses, are affected by government fiscal policies. (5)

3 Study the information below and answer the questions which follow.

(a) Define the term 'monopoly'. (1)
(b) Why do monopolies occur? (2)
(c) Give three examples of how a monopoly can occur. (3)
(d) Explain how a monopoly can bring advantages and disadvantages for the public. (4)

Monopolies

In the UK economy there are many examples of industries that are dominated by a few very large firms. Even where there are a lot of firms the competition between them may not be particularly effective.

When the supply of a product is controlled by one or a group of firms acting together we say that a monopoly exists.

Monopolies can be granted by law. For example, if you invented something you would be given the right (by patents) to have complete control of the production and sale over a given period of time.

Sometimes the advantages of a monopoly outweigh its disadvantages and for this reason governments have sometimes not interfered, and may even encourage it. But the disadvantages of monopoly, particularly from the point of view of the consumer, have generally caused governments to exercise some control over it.

(e) In what ways might the government try to restrict mergers and monopolies? (4)
(f) What are the reasons for saying that monopolies should be the subject of state control? (6)

4 Consider the following information and answer the questions which follow.

> ## Noland needs new life
>
> Business activities in the country of Noland are slowing down. Many people are being laid off work and each week reveals substantial numbers of businesses going bankrupt. There are overpopulated areas where unemployment is abnormally high and there is insufficient industry. The government has an important part to play in reviving economic activity.

(a) State two reasons why business activities in a country might be 'slowing down'. (2)
(b) What could the government do to influence consumer behaviour, particularly in order to help increase economic activity? (2)
(c) In what ways could a government relieve the pressure of industry and population in congested areas? (3)
(d) Describe two social problems and two economic problems that could result from the situation described above if the government did not intervene. (4)
(e) What strategies could the government use to increase employment in areas in which unemployment is abnormally high? (4)
(f) Governments sometimes give tax relief and other incentives to small firms. Describe how such a policy could help to solve the situation described above. To what extent do you agree that the government is justified in interfering in business activities in this way? (5)

5 Read the two newspaper extracts related to the proposed development of a retail park in an expanding rural area on page 392 and then answer the questions that follow.

RETAIL PARK DEVELOPERS SEEK SUPPORT

Jenny Davidson, planning director of the planned new retail park, talked today of the 'wonderful opportunities that will be brought to the local community by the proposed development incorporating many retail outlets'.

Mrs Davidson highlighted the many new jobs that would be created, both during the construction period and after the stores are up and running. She emphasised the increased prosperity the development will bring to the locality and asked for the support of the local community.

RETAIL PARK – PUBLIC MEETING PLANNED

At last night's council meeting Councillor Howard brought to the attention of the members the many concerns he had received from local residents about the proposed development of a retail park on the recreation ground to the west of the town. He warned councillors that public objections to the development were growing.

The council decided that a public meeting should be called with an open invitation to all parties involved.

(a) Give one possible private cost and one private benefit of the development referred to in these two newspaper extracts. (2)

(b) On what social cost grounds might the local community object to the proposed development? (2)

(c) Why is it more difficult to measure social costs and benefits than private ones? (3)

(d) Briefly describe how you would form a group of residents with the aim of trying to stop the proposed development. (3)

(e) In what ways could the group you have formed gain publicity for their cause? (4)

(f) Outline a possible cost benefit analysis that could be put to the public meeting, fairly putting arguments for and against the proposed development. (6)

The Role of Governments

Research Assignments

1 To what extent do you agree or disagree with the view that the provision of social services is too generous and, therefore, taxation is higher than necessary? Provide examples to support your views.

2 Design a questionnaire which concisely states the social welfare services provided by the state, and then present a series of questions aimed at identifying the social services residents in your locality use most frequently. Present your findings using tables and charts and present a summary.

3 'Cigarette smoking has a private cost to the individual and a social cost to the economy.' Investigate this statement including data obtained by personal survey to establish private costs and data from government departments to identify social costs. Present your discussion of the statement in the form of a report that aims to raise awareness of the real cost of smoking to the economy.

4 What evidence can you find to support the view that there is a difference in living standards between the South East and the rest of the UK? What influence can the government have on this?

5 Make a collection of newspaper articles from your local press related to matters of local concern, and related to business activities. Divide your articles into issues that you feel could be solved by local government and those that are central government responsibility. Write a summary report, in two parts, to say how you feel the issues should be tackled:
(a) by local government;
(b) by central government.

6 Take any local development taking place in your locality involving or affecting business developments, and carry out a cost benefit analysis. Write a report of your analysis, including field research of views from a cross-section of the community – including both the business and non-business community.

Index

ACAS, 129
Accounts, 38, 75, 306–307, 257
Accounts department, 56
Acid test, 311
Acknowledgement, 226, 227
Adam Smith, 355
Administration department, 56
Ad valorem duties, 215
Advertising, 13, 15, 16, 56, 91, 92, 138, 143, 144, 166–172, 192, 250
Advertising agency, 170, 171
Advice note, 226, 227
Advisory, Conciliation and Arbitration (see ACAS)
After-sales service, 141, 144
Agenda, 254
Agent, 212
Aims (see business aims)
Air waybill, 231
Annual percentage rate, 174
Application form, 93
Applications for employment, 92–94
Appraisal, 97, 110–111
APR (see Annual percentage rate)
Aptitude test, 95, 99
Arbitration, 126
Argos, 197
Articles of association, 74, 76, 77, 78
Artwork, 170
Assets, 32, 301, 308, 309, 310
Association of British Travel Agents, 152
Automation, 25, 39, 48
Automats, 197
Automobile Association, 133

Bad debts, 152
Balance of payments, 210, 242
Balance of trade, 210
Balance sheet, 309–312
Baltic Exchange, the, 243
Bank accounts, 279–281
Bank cards, 288–289
Bank draft, 291
Bankers' Clearing House, 284–285
Bank giro, 287–288
Banking, 11, 15, 16, 38, 192, 275–299
Bank loan, 292
Bank of England, 275–276, 277
Bank overdraft, 292, 301
Bankruptcy, 72
Banks, 73
Bank services, 286–291
Bank statement of account, 283, 284
Barter, 1–2
Batch production, 24
Benefits, 383, 384 (see also Private benefits and Social benefits)
Bill of exchange, 231–232, 279, 291
Bill of lading, 231
Birth rate, 370
Black economy, 344–345
Blue chips, 323
Board of directors, 60, 62, 75, 76

Bonus, 113
Borrowing, 291–292
Boycott, 128
Brainstorming, 170
Branding, 142, 146
Brand loyalty, 159
Brand name, 142
Break-even, 302–303
British Standards Institution, 177
Budget account, 280
Budget, the, 380
Building societies, 81
Burger King, 80
Business aims, 47, 71–72
Business communication, (see Communication)
Business correspondence, (see Correspondence)
Business documents, 225–237
Business environment, 1–18
Business finance (see Finance)
Business functions, 47–49
Business growth, 81–84
Business location, (see Location of business)
Business management, 49–55
Business objectives, 47, 71–72, 83
Business organisation, 47–70
Business plan,
Business rate, 302
Business reply service, 259–260
Business, role and functions of, 47–49
Business size, 32–36, 55–57
Business, types of, 71–90
Buyers, 148, 150, 213, 225, 227, 228, 229

Capital, 15, 24, 26, 32, 48, 50, 75, 78, 79, 199, 300, 308, 310
Capital market, 278
Careers officers, 91
Caribbean Community, 221
CARICOM (see Caribbean Community)
Carriage arrangements, 226
Carrier, 238
Cartels, 151
Cash card, 289
Cash dispenser, 280, 289
Cash flow, 303–305
Cash on delivery, 229, 262
Cash with order, 229
Catalogue, 225
Catalogue shops, 197
Caveat emptor, 172
CBI, (see Confederation of British Industry)
Ceefax, 267
Census, 368
Central banks, 275–276
Centralisation, 64–65
Centralised economy, 9
Certificate of incorporation, 77
Certificate of origin, 231
Certificate of posting, 261
Chain integration, 82, 83
Chain of command, 57

394

Index

Chain of distribution, 188–189, 192
Chain stores, 192, 194
Chain of production (see production)
Chairperson, 76, 129, 252
Chambers of commerce, 152
Charge cards, 199
Charging, 227–230
Cheque, 230, 281–285
Cheque card, 288
Cheque clearing, 283–285
Chief accountant, 76
Chief buyer, 76
Choice, 6–7, 159, 191, 192
Circular organisation, 63
Citizens' advice bureaux, 176, 177
Clearing banks, 279
Closed shop, 128
Cold selling, 197
Collateral, 291
Collective bargaining, 125–127
Collective economy, 9
Commerce, 10, 11–13, 15
Commission, 112, 213
Committee, 253
Committee organisation, 62–64
Commodity departments, 195
Communication, 13, 15, 16, 50, 57, 144, 166, 250–268 (see also Postal communication and Telecommunication)
    internal to business, 252–253
    postal (see Postal communication)
    telecommunication (see Telecommunication)
    visual, 238
Companies Acts, 75, 77
Company registers, 38, 255
Company secretary, 76, 79
Company shares, (see Shares)
Comparative advantage, 208, 209, 216
Comparative costs, 208
Compensation, 100
Compensation fee (CF) parcels, 262
Competition, 9, 81, 141, 150–151
Competitions, 144
Computers, 25, 39, 37–38, 48, 160, 255, 256, 255–259
Conciliation, 125–126
Confederation of British Industry (CBI), 128–129, 131, 133
Conference facilities, 265–266
Conglomerate, 82, 83
Consignment note, 227
Consignor, 238
Construction, 10, 11, 16
Consular officials, 214
Consumer, 15, 16, 138, 139, 144, 159, 343
Consumer advice centres, 176
Consumer credit, 13
Consumer Credit Act 1974, 174–175
Consumer goods, 26
Consumer hire agreement, 175
Consumer law, 173–176
Consumer protection, 172–178, 382
Consumer Protection Act 1987, 176
Consumer Safety Act 1989, 175
Consumers' Association, 132, 177
Containers, 244, 241–244
Contract, 213
Contract note, 320
Contract of Employment, 100, 115
Control, 51, 151
Controlled economy, 8, 9
Co-operatives, 71, 80
Coordination, 51
Corporate identity, 72
Correspondence, 255

Cost, 147, 226, 242, 302, 305, 383, 384 (see also Private costs and Social costs)
Cost benefit analysis, 384
Cost-effective, 194
Costing, 138
Cost of living, 341–343, 360
    index, 342
Cost-plus pricing, 143
Cost-push inflation, 360
Costs, 48, 143, 305–306
Council tax, 143
Credit, 174–175, 191, 195, 198
Credit cards, 199, 288
Credit limit, 280
Credit note, 230
Creditors, 72, 232, 308, 362
Credit reference agencies, 174
Credit referencing, 174
Credit sale agreement, 175, 198
Credit token agreement, 175
Credit transfer, 114, 287–288
Current account, 278, 280–281
Curriculum vitae, 92–94
Customer concept, 139, 140
Customers, 141, 143, 144, 146, 159, 160, 172, 195, 197, 229, 308
Customs and Excise duties, 358
Customs regulations, 152
Customs unions, 217

Databases, 258–259
Data links, 266
Datapost, 262
Data Protection Act 1984, 118
Datel, 266
Death rate, 370, 371
Debentures, 321
Debit note, 230
Debtor, 232, 308, 362
Debts, 74, 152, 229, 230
Decentralisation, 64–65
Decision making, 83, 159, 162
Deflation, 211, 212
Delegation, 50–51, 64
Delivery note, 226, 227
Delivery period, 225, 227
Demand, 141, 147, 148–149, 151
Demand-pull inflation, 361
Demarcation dispute, 127
Department of Health, 176
Department of Prices and Consumer Protection, 176
Department stores, 195
Dependency ratio, 373
Deposit account, 280
Depressed regions, 29
Design Council, 177
Desk research, 165
Devaluation, 211, 212
Development, 350–351
Development areas, 31
Diminishing returns, 34–35
Direct debit, 280, 286
Directing, 50
Directors, 78, 79
Direct services, 10, 11, 13–14
Discount houses, 279
Discounts, 144, 225, 227, 229, 232
Diseconomies of scale, 32, 372
Dishonoured cheque, 283
Dismissal, 50, 100–101
Displays, 144, 146, 257
Distribution, 80, 138, 143, 188–189, 238
Division of labour, 4 (see also Specialisation)

395

Index

Documents, business, (see Business documents)
Door-to-door selling, 193
Drawee, 281
Drawer, 281, 282, 283
Dumping, 216
Duties, 215

E & OE, 227, 228, 229
Economic growth, 345
Economic planning, 345
Economic problem, the, 8
Economic stability, 356
Economic systems, 7–10
Economies of scale, 32–34, 75, 80, 81, 372
Economists, 150
Economy, management of, 380
Education, 26, 385–386
Efficiency, 24
EFTPOS, 285–286, 4
Electronic funds transfer, 285, 290
Email, 264
Embargo, 216
Emigration, 369
Employees, 24, 48, 72, 101–122, 123, 129, 143
Employers, 91, 94, 98, 100, 101–122, 123, 129
Employers' organisations, 128–130
Employment,
   Act 1988, 100, 115, 129–130
   agencies, 91
   hours, 115–117
   terms of, 115
Enquiry, 140, 225, 226
Enterprise zones, 31
Entrepreneurs, 24, 27, 72, 79
Environment, 30
Environmental health departments, 176
Equal Pay Act 1970, 118
Equilibrium price, 149
Equities (see Ordinary shares)
Estimate, 226
Euro, the, 214
European Commission, 220
European Community (see European Union)
European Court of Justice, 220, 221
European Free Trade Association, 217
European Monetary System, 214, 220
European Parliament, 219, 220
European Union (EU), 173, 217–221
Exchange control, 211, 212, 215
Exchange equalisation account, 276
Exchange rate, 2, 213–214
Exchange value, 149
Exhibitions, 144, 168, 169, 213
Expenditure, 356
Expenses, 308
Export Credits Guarantee Department (ECGD), 381
Exporters, 15, 213–214, 231
   aids to, 214–215
Export house, 212
Export licence, 231
Exports, 207, 218, 361
Express post, 262
Extractive industries, (see Production, primary)
Ex-works, 226

Factories Act 1961, 117
Factoring, 301
Factors of production, (see Production, factors of)
Fair Trading Act 1973, 174
Farming, 10, 12, 16
Fidelity bond, 200

Field research, 165
Finance, 13, 15, 16, 33–34, 48, 152, 300–318
Finance houses, 279
Finance Houses Association (FHA), 279
Financial projections, 301–303
Fishing, 10, 12, 16
Fixed costs, 143, 302, 305
Flexible working time, 116–117
Flow production, 24
Food and Drugs Act 1955, 173
Foreign banks, 279
Foreign exchange, 276
Foreign trade (see International market)
Foreign trade documents, 230–232
Formal organisation, 59
Franchisee, 79
Franchising, 79–80
Franchisor, 79
Franking machine, 262
Free economy, 8–9
Free gifts, 144, 151, 197
Freepost, 260
Free samples, 144, 151
Free trade, 215–221
Freight, 238, 242 (see also Transport)
Freightliner service, 241–242
Freight note, 231
Fringe benefits, 113, 115
Fuel, 30
Functional organisation, 61–62

General Agreement on Tariffs and Trade (GATT), 216–217
General National Vocational Qualifications, 98
Giffen goods, 148
Gift tokens, 144
Gilt-edged securities, 279
Goodwill, 151
Go slow, 128
Government, 131, 176, 300, 370
   assistance to entrepreneurs, 380–382
   expenditure, 348–349
   influence on location, 29, 30
   role of, 130, 130–131, 379–393
Government stocks, 276
Grants, 29–31, 214, 300
Greenpeace, 132
Grievance procedure, 101, 115
Gross domestic product, 218
Gross profit, 307–309
Gross national product (GNP), 345–347
Group dynamics, 51–52
Groups, 52–53, 159
Growth, 350–351 (see also Business growth and Economic growth)

'Halo effect', 96
Health, 25, 142, 371, 386
Health and safety, 117–118, 200
Health and Safety at Work Act 1974, 117–118
Hidden persuaders, 159, 167–168, 172
Hire purchase, 198, 241, 301
Holding companies, 71, 80
Home market (see Market, home)
Horizontal integration, 82, 83
Human Resources Department, 91–94, 95, 99 (see also Personnel Department)
Human Resources Manager, 97
Hypermarkets, 195

Immigration, 369
Imperfect competition, 150
Import control, 211, 212, 384
Importers, 15, 16, 143, 231, 232

Index

Import licence, 232
Import regulations, 213
Imports, 207, 218
Impulse buying, 194
Income, 159, 300, 305, 343, 344
Income redistribution, 356
Income Tax, 112, 342 (see also Taxation)
Indemnity, 328
Independent shops, 193
Induction, 97
Industrial action, 127, 130
Industrial disputes, 127–128
Industrial inertia, 30
Industrial relations, 123–137
Industrial tribunal, 100, 129
Industry, 15–16
Infant industries, 216
Inflation, 360–363
    controlling, 362
    effects of, 361
    types of, 360–361
Informal organisation, 64
Information technology, 255–259
Insurance, 13, 15, 16, 143, 192, 200, 214, 328–340
    accident, 331
    certificate, 334
    claim, 329, 334
    contract, 333–334
    contribution, 330
    cover note, 334
    fidelity, 333
    fire, 331
    indemnity, 330
    insurable interest, 330
    liability, 332
    life, 331
    marine, 333
    market, 334–335
    motor, 330
    policy, 334
    pooling risks, 328
    premium, 334
    principles of, 329–330
    proposal, 334
    proximate cause, 330
    renewal notice, 334
    subrogation, 330
    terminology,
    types of, 331–333
    uninsurable risks, 329
    utmost good faith, 330
Integration, 82–83
Interest, 24, 25, 241
Interest-free credit, 198
Intermediate areas, 31
International market, 207–224, 225, 238
International Monetary Fund, 211, 276
Internet, 197, 259, 264, 267
Interviews, 94–97, 162, 163, 165, 252, 253
Investor, 75
Investors in people, 98–99
Invisible trade, 207, 210, 328
Invoice, 140, 226, 227–228, 230, 256, 308
Issuing house, 278

Job description, 91, 92, 115
Job enlargement, 51, 110
Job enrichment, 110
Job evaluation, 111
Job production, 24
Job satisfaction, 50, 110
Job specification, 91, 115

Joint account, 280–281
Just in time manufacturing,

Kentucky Fried Chicken, 80

Labelling, 146
Labour, 24, 25–26, 30, 48
  quality of, 25–26
  supply, 25,   3
Laissez-faire, 8
Land, 24–25, 30, 48
Large business, 55–57, 72, 194
Lateral integration, 82, 83
Law and order, 379
Leadership, 51–53, 251
    styles of, 53
Leaflets, 168
Lease, 241
Leasing, 241, 301
Legal Department, 56
Legislation, 152
Lender of last resort, 276, 277–278
Lessee, 241
Lessor, 241
Letters, 92, 252, 256, 259–261
Liabilities, 309, 310
Limited liability, 72, 75
Limited liability company, 72, 76, 200
Line management, 57, 97
Line organisation, 59–60
Linkage industries, 30
Liquid capital ratio, 311
Living standards, (see Standard of living)
Lloyds of London, 335
Loans, 300
Local authorities, 176–177
Location of business, 29–32, 200
London Discount Market Association (LDMA), 277, 279
Loss, 80, 210
Loss leaders, 144, 194
Luncheon vouchers, 115

Mail order, 143, 195–196
Mail shot, 168
Management, 25, 33, 48–55
    communication, 54–55
    functions of, 50–51
    responsibilities of, 49–50
Managing director, 55, 58, 60, 61, 63, 75, 76
Manifest, 231
Manuals, 252
Manufacturers associations, 152–153
Manufacturing, 10, 11, 15, 16
Marginal output, 33
Market economy, 8
Market, home, 188–206
Marketing, 48, 80, 138, 165, 238
Marketing concept, 139, 159
Marketing Department, 138–158, 139–140
Marketing economies, 33
Marketing mix, 140–144
Marketing strategy, 138, 142
Market, international, 207–224
Market-orientated pricing, 143
Market pull, 30
Market research, 138, 139, 159–187
    agency, 163
    experiments, 160–162
    methods, 165
    observational, 162, 165
    procedures, 164–165
    questionnaires, 160, 161

Index

surveys, 162
team, 162–163
types of, 160–162
Market segmentation, 163
Market traders, 193
Mark-up, 199, 306, 308
Mass production, 191
Media, 144, 168–169, 178
Meetings, 252, 253–255
Memorandum, 252
Memorandum of association, 76–77, 78, 79
Mentor, 97
Merchandising, 146–147
Merchant, 212
Merchantable quality, 175
Merchant banks, 278
Mergers, 383
Migration, 369–370
Milk, 14
Minimum lending rate, 277
Mining, 10, 12, 15
Ministry of Agriculture, Fisheries and Food, 1976
Ministry of Transport, 239
Minutes, 252, 254
Misdemeanour, 100
Mixed economy, 8, 10, 84
Mobility of labour, 373–376
Monetary control, 276–278
Monetary union, 220
Money, 2–3
Money at call, 277
Monopolies and Mergers Commission, 383
Monopoly, 81, 83, 133, 150, 151, 382–383
Mortgage, 81
Motivation, 51, 53, 110–122, 172, 252
Motor vehicle duty, 359
Multinational, 83
Multiples, 194
Municipal undertakings, 84

National accounts, 341–354
National Consumer Council, 382
National debt, 276, 349–350
National expenditure, 347–349
National income, 343–345
National insurance, 112, 358–359, 386
Nationalisation, 84, 241, 385
National Vocational Qualifications, 98
Needs, 22
Negotiating, 252
Net profit, 307, 307, 309
Night safe, 290
No-strike agreements, 127
Note issue, 276
Notice, 100

Objectives (see Business objectives)
Office of Fair Trading, 174, 176
Offices, Shops and Railway Premises Act 1963, 117
Official census, (see Census)
Oligopoly, 150, 151
Open market operations, 276–277
Opportunity cost, 7
Optimal population, 371–372
Oracle, 267
Order, 226
Ordinary shares, 322–323
Organisational structure, 57–64
Organisation charts, 64
Organising, 51
Output, 147
Overdraft, (see Bank overdraft)

Overpopulation, 371
Overtime ban, 127

Packaging, 141, 143, 144, 146, 159, 175, 191, 194, 213
Paging, 268
Parcel post, 261
Parent company, 83
Partnership, 73–74, 76, 200, 301
Partnership Act, 73, 74
Pay,
    advice, 114
    deductions from, 112–113
    rates of, 112
Pay As You Earn (PAYE), 355
Payee, 281, 282
Payment defaults, 213 (see also Bad debts)
Payments for goods, 229–230
Payroll, 38, 256
Penetration price, 143
Perfect competition, 150
Personal assets, 72
Personal credit agreement, 175
Personal identity number (PIN), 285–286, 289
Personal selling, 144
Personnel, 48
    department, 56, (see also Human Resources Department)
    manager, 76
Picketing, 128
Pilot experiments, 162
Planned economy, 9
Planning, 50
Plough back, 48, 50
Point of sale, 168
Population, 218, 368–378, 386
    age, 372, 373
    declining, 371
    dependency ratio, 373
    distribution of, 372–375
    growth, 369
    importance of, 368
    mobility of, 375
    occupational distribution, 374–375
    optimum, 371–372
    size, 368–372
    working, 373
Postal communications, 13, 15, 259–263
Post dated cheque, 281
Post restante, 260
Power, 30
Preference shares, 321, 322
Premises, 146
Pressure groups, 131–133
Prestel, 266
Price, 140, 141, 142–143, 144, 146, 147, 148, 149–150, 151, 159, 225, 241, 301–302, 320, 342, 361
Price plateau, 142
Prices Acts 1974 and 1975, 174
Primary data, 164, 165
Private benefits, 383, 384
Private costs, 383, 384
Private enterprise, 71–72, 76
Private limited company, 74–75
Private ownership, 73–79
Privatisation, 84, 241
Producers, 15, 32, 138, 190, 191, 216, 343
Product, 140–142, 144, 147, 159, 160, 305
Product demonstrations, 144
Product development, 138
Product mix, 146
Product range, 141, 146
Production, 1, 3, 7, 22–46, 47–48, 80, 138, 172, 208
    aims, 22

398

batch, 24, 28
chain of, 14
department, 56
direct, 15
factors of, 24–28,
flow, 24, 28
indirect, 15
job, 24, 28
levels, 22–23
manager, 76
mass, 191
methods of, 28–29
organisation of, 22– 46
primary, 10–11, 14, 15, 16
scale of, 24
secondary, 10, 11, 14, 15, 16
tertiary, 10, 11, 14, 15, 16, 188
types of, 10–15
Productivity deals, 111, 113
Product lifecycle, 144–146
Professional associations, 177
Profit, 25, 27, 32, 47, 48, 78, 79, 80, 81, 147, 159, 302, 305, 306, 307–309
Profit and loss account, 306
Profit margin, 199, 308
Profit maximisation, 147–148, 306
Profit motive, 9
Profit sharing, 74
Pro-forma invoice, 228
Progress chasers,
Promotion, 140, 141, 144
Promotional material, 226
Promotional mix, 144
Prospectus, 77, 319
Public company, 75–79
Public corporations, 84–85
Public enterprise, 71–72, 84–85, 84–85
Public expenditure, 348
Public limited company, 72
Public relations, 151–152
  officer, 151
Purchasing Department, 56
Pyramid organisation, 57

Qualifications, 91
Quality, 24, 141
Quality control, 29
Questionnaires, 160, 161, 162, 165
Quota, 215, 231, 384
Quotation, 225, 226

Race Relations Act 1976, 94
Rail transport (see Transport)
Raw materials, 10, 11, 15, 30, 143, 238, 305
Recorded delivery, 260, 261
Recreation, 387
Recruitment, 48, 91–109
Redundancy, 101
Redundancy Payments Act, 101
References, 91, 94, 100
Regional aid, 382
Regional development grants, 29–31
Registered office, 79
Registered post, 260
Registrar of Business Names, 76
Registrar of Companies, 76, 77, 78, 79
Remittance advice note, 230
Rent, 24, 143, 241
Reports, 252, 254
Representative sample, 162
Resale Prices Act 1964, 173
Resignation, 100

Resources, 7, 24
Restrictive Practices Court, 383
Restrictive Trade Practices Act 1976, 175
Retail business, setting up, 199–200
Retailers, 143, 152, 192–200, 188, 189, 190, 192–200
Retail parks, 195
Retail price index, 342, 360
Retail trade, 11, 15, 16
  functions of, 192
  types of, 192–198
Retained profit, 300
Return on capital invested, 311
Revenue, 147, 300, 305–306, 355–356
Risk, 72, 311
Robots, 3, 38
Royal Automobile Club, 133

Safe deposit box, 290
Salaries, 99
Sale of Goods Act 1979, 175–176
Sale or return, 228
Sales concept, 139
Sales department, 56
Sales manager, 76
Sales personnel, 144
Sales promotion, 143, 144
Sales representatives, 144
Samples, 144, 151
Sampling, 160, 162, 163–164
Save-As-You-Earn, 113
Savings, 361
Scale of preference, 7
Scarcity, 6–7, 24
SEAQ (see Stock Exchange)
Secondary data, 164, 165
Selection, 48, 91–109
Selectpost, 260
Sellers, 150, 175, 213, 226, 227, 228, 229, 232
Selling abroad, 212–213
Services, 10, 11, 15, 16, 159, 210, 238
Sex Discrimination Act 1975, 94, 118
Share certificate, 323
Shareholders, 72, 74, 75, 78, 255, 323
Shares, 48, 74, 77, 78, 83, 113, 301, 319–327 (refer also to Stock Exchange)
  prices, 324
  return on, 323–324
Shift work, 116
Shipping, 230 (see also Transport, sea)
Shops, 143
Short list, 94–97
Sit-in, 128
Siting a business (see Location of business)
Sleeping partner, 74
Small business, 55–57, 71–72
Social background, 160
Social benefits, 383, 384
Social class, 163
Social costs, 383, 384
Socialist system, 9
Social services, 379–380, 385–387, 385–387
Social welfare, 220
Sole proprietor, 71, 73, 76, 200
Sole trader, (see sole proprietor)
Space buying, 170
Span of control, 57–58
Special business relationships, 79–81
Special deposits, 277
Specialisation, 3–6, 15, 216
Special offers, 144, 146
Specific duties, 215
Sponsorship, 144